EUROPE UNITED

EUROPE UNITED

One football fan
One crazy season
Fifty-five UEFA nations

Matt Walker

riverrun

First published in Great Britain in 2019 by

riverrun

An imprint of
Quercus Editions Ltd
Carmelite House
50 Victoria Embankment
London EC4Y 0DZ

An Hachette UK company

A CIP catalogue record for this book is available
from the British Library

HB ISBN 978 1 78747 612 7
TPB ISBN 978 1 78747 611 0

10 9 8 7 6 5 4 3 2 1

Typeset by CC Book Production
Printed and bound in Great Britain by Clays Ltd, Elcograf S.p.A.

Papers used by Quercus are from well-managed forests and other responsible sources.

Contents

FIFTY-FIVE FOOTBALL NATIONS

It was one of those dull Christmas days, grey light, my body awash with excess food and alcohol from the last weeks of 2015. I looked at my bookcase across the lounge. It was well organised, alphabetically by theme. There were a lot of travel guides peeling gently from years of sun exposure, Murakami novels and football books. A book about football in Liechtenstein stood out: an unread present from years before.

I wondered what could be written about football in Liechtenstein. Liechtenstein are as poor at football as you would expect a micro-state to be. I was curious and started reading. I liked the underdog and was, after all, a lifelong Fulham fan, a team that had languished in the lower divisions during my youth. It was the inspiration for my own offbeat challenge to watch football across the entirety of Europe.

'Ideas are like beards. Men don't have them until they grow up' was a quote from Voltaire that made me smile. I needed a break from my job as a statistician for the Ministry of Justice but also a focus, a structure, to my travels. I couldn't find anyone who had watched football in all fifty-five UEFA nations in one season, or at least nobody who had written a book about it. The football would vary widely in its quality but the contrasts would be fascinating. I started dreaming of stadiums, packed or sparsely populated, the colours of the fans and the teams, the heady atmosphere of watching football in summer sun, the freezing winter nights clasping a cup of something hot. These scenes appealed to a keen photographer like me, the accompanying story even more so.

I grew up in the green south of England, over forty miles away from Craven Cottage. None of my school friends watched live football. But I shared traits with my father, who follows Fulham and worked for an airline, and my mother, a lover of wildlife and Def Leppard. My father, like many of his era, used to alternate between watching Fulham and Chelsea play until the latter raised their ticket prices. My mother, meanwhile, never really got the tribalism of football. We took her to Fulham against Manchester United in our debut Premier League season in 2001, but she was most enthused by a flock of geese flying over the Thames. Yet she did at least agree that their pet spaniel could be called 'Murphy', after Danny Murphy scored an unlikely header to preserve Fulham's top-flight status fourteen minutes from the end of the 2007–08 season.

I love maps, people and places. I backpacked around the world after graduating and watched my first football match outside England in the Malaysian part of Borneo: Sabah v Terengganu in March 1999. David Rocastle, the Arsenal and England midfielder, played for Sabah that evening, one of his last games before he retired through injury and died of cancer two years later at the age of just thirty-three. Over the next few years, I watched football in countries such as Iran, Mexico and Colombia, and nearly jumped out of the stadium when a firework went off behind me in Medellín. Football and travel seemed a natural blend and an obvious focus for time away from the office.

Before settling on Europe, I considered watching league football in the other continents over one season. The compact CONMEBOL confederation of ten South American members was culturally the least varied. The CONCACAF region of North and Central America and the Caribbean had a more challenging forty-one members, perhaps too many of them holiday islands. The Asian Football Confederation consisted of a far-reaching forty-seven members, from Palestine to Australia, and would be a traveller's nirvana. But there would be plenty of political hurdles to overcome in the Middle East. I considered the immense African confederation of fifty-six countries for precisely one minute. This was easily the most expensive, I would need two passports for all the visas, and I imagine few dream of spending a year in sub-Saharan capital cities. The Oceania region of New Zealand and thirteen paradise islands in the Pacific sounded more like a retirement cruise than a football challenge.

I was content to focus on Europe, a diverse footballing landscape then encompassing fifty-four nations ranging from the big European leagues to micro-states such as Andorra and Liechtenstein. I was fascinated by the geographic quirks. UEFA includes the Faroe Islands and Gibraltar, two nations that are territories of others; countries like Kazakhstan and Turkey that straddle two continents; and Israel, who play in UEFA for political reasons and are not part of continental Europe at all. I had already visited eighty countries around the world. But there were plenty of new European countries and cities to explore. And a huge variety of exciting football.

I decided to watch top-division football, for consistency, during the

3

2017–18 season. The earliest season started in the Republic of Ireland during February 2017 and the latest in Gibraltar ended in June 2018. It was often easier to consider my challenge as watching all the leagues that led to qualification for the 2018–19 Champions League and Europa League. And, for simplicity, I shortened its scope to one year: from June 2017, when I left my office job, to May 2018.

I smashed the previous season's fixtures into a spreadsheet. It was feasible, but it was tight and I didn't have much contingency. Kosovo joined UEFA in May 2016 to become the fifty-fifth UEFA nation. I had enough time to squeeze them in. Jersey applied to join UEFA, potentially provoking an avalanche of applications from non-independent islands. Fortunately for my challenge, and for the name of my 55footballnations.com website, Jersey's bid was rejected in February 2018. Europe would remain fifty-five football nations for now.

I needed to get approval to take unpaid time off. Osama, Director of Analysis at the Ministry of Justice, reviewed career break applications from his staff, of which caring responsibilities and further studies made up the overwhelming majority. 'This is brilliant', said Osama, a big Manchester United fan, approving it instantly. I should not have been surprised. Osama was in Barcelona for the dramatic 2–1 win over Bayern Munich in the 1999 Champions League final. At the same time I was silently cheering on Manchester United from the reception in a grungy Varanasi hostel whilst its workers slept on the floor. I often found a connection between football and travel.

My challenge was alive. I was going to have to live off adrenalin and cheese sandwiches to succeed. I saved some money, started planning in earnest and got in some match practice in unfamiliar surroundings. I mainly watch Fulham play in England, an experience enhanced and clouded by passion and routine. I visited Luton Town in League Two and Woking in the National League. I spoke to Luton's supporters' club and the Dutch Cards, a pack of fans who travelled from the Netherlands to watch Woking play. I took photographs and notes until my only pen ran out.

My last few days at work were a blur. I encouraged colleagues to wear old football shirts to my leaving drinks. Steve, the Chief Statistician, wore a battered MSV Duisburg jersey. I chose Chievo Verona, the Italians who had the most unlikely of forays into the Champions League in 2006, their nickname 'the flying donkeys' being strangely apt for my lunatic challenge. I promoted my travels by organising a sweepstake. Ministry of Justice workmates each drew one UEFA nation out of a football hat. The three highest-scoring matches I watched – only the first match in each nation counted, and ties would be separated by the earliest goal – would scoop either £55 or a copy of this book. Steve drew Scotland. I shook my head. 'I don't think that's going to win, Steve.'

I learned some Russian and packed my bags for a footballing journey of a lifetime. I took a spare pen.

AN UNLIKELY FIRST

1 Georgia

My Tbilisi taxi driver played soulful folk and local rap as we sped through the dark streets. He said that traditional folk music was still more popular here. I loved finding out something new about a country in those very first moments. The following morning, I ate khinkali, delicious stuffed dumplings where the light-coloured pastry was twisted to form a doughy top (which I later found out was not supposed to be eaten). The rich voice of Nick Cave that floated around the café somehow matched the sumptuous mushroom filling. I had sampled Georgian food and music in my first few hours, before taking a 16p bus to the leafy suburb of Vake to find something out about Georgian football.

I wasn't even supposed to start my travels in Tbilisi. Georgia had moved to a summer league in 2017, joining the Nordic countries, the Republic of Ireland and other ex-Soviet states by starting their season in the spring and completing it in the autumn. I had only found out about this switch a few months previously and now needed to squeeze in a Georgian league match before my more logical easterly journey from Iceland to Kazakhstan.

The Georgian Football Federation in Vake is housed in a curious building shaped like a suspended half-crescent moon. I clambered up a stairway and was chuffed to meet Nika Jgarkava, the Federation's vice-president. 'I wish we could have this conversation in Gori', were his opening words. Dila Gori against Locomotive Tbilisi was my first match. The stadium in Gori was being renovated for the 2017 European Under-19 Championship and the match had been switched to Tbilisi. My first country, city and stadium had changed. I really hoped that this was not a sign of things to come.

Nika was enthusiastic about my mission and, as a self-confessed Georgian football geek, wanted to undertake his own: to visit every football pitch in his country. He was an ardent Dinamo Tbilisi fan and had worked for the club before joining the Football Federation. Nika explained that his club allegiance did not affect his current position. He took pleasure from being neutral and, if anything, sided with other clubs when forced to decide between them and Dinamo.

I asked about Georgia's recent move to a summer league that ran from March to November. Nika had well-honed answers. 'Georgia is not good for maintaining grass due to the difference in climate between summer and winter. For half a year the grass sleeps.' The aim was also to give clubs six months to prepare for participation in European competitions. All four Georgian clubs crashed out in their first ties in 2017, three of them hammered by teams from Azerbaijan, Slovakia and Poland. It would take time to see if the switch in season and reduction from fourteen to ten teams improved the league. The Georgian league was starting from a low base with low attendances.

Football used to be more popular when Georgia was part of the Soviet Union. Dinamo Tbilisi, who won the Soviet title in 1964 and 1978, represented national pride then, serving as an outlet against repression as large crowds watched them play the likes of Spartak Moscow and Dynamo Kiev. The Georgian top division, the Erovnuli Liga, was gradually becoming more popular amongst teenagers from outside the capital who had never watched Soviet football. Summer football might also increase attendances. 'You can go with your shorts and towel to the game in Batumi', said Nika.

I asked a few people what they thought of Georgian football. 'Total bullshit', said a local in a Real Madrid shirt who watched their 4–1 victory over Juventus in the Champions League final alongside me in the Hangar Bar. 'No one cares', said the young guy working at my hostel. Georgians wanted to win, and boxing, wrestling, rugby and basketball were more popular. It was important for Georgians to be stronger than Russia, perhaps to forge their own identity in sports less closely associated with the Soviet era.

The current weakness of the national team was not helping. Georgia produced the likes of the former Manchester City star Giorgi Kinkladze, former Rangers and Blackburn Rovers stopper Zurab Khizanishvili and classy AC Milan defender Kakha Kaladze. The latter, twice a Champions League winner, was still plastered on billboards everywhere, but more for his politics: he was running for mayor of Tbilisi. There were no Georgian poster boys playing in Europe's top leagues. And Georgia had the ignominy of being seeded in the bottom pot for the 2018 World Cup qualifying, along with Andorra, Kazakhstan, Liechtenstein, Luxembourg, Malta and San Marino.

Georgian club and mainstream football websites listed different kick-off times for Dila Gori against Locomotive Tbilisi. Nika double-checked with his president. 'It is 7.30 p.m.', he confirmed. I really didn't want to miss my first match. I was buzzing after leaving Nika, my first football contact on the opening day of my epic adventure, for the pine-scented hillsides of Vake Park. I absorbed the views in this particularly leafy part of Tbilisi and visited the beautiful old houses in the open-air ethnographic museum. I walked to a nearby restaurant and ate veal and potatoes in a rich, country-style sauce, dressed with garlic and a little too much oil. I didn't even mind when the wind blew my beer over.

I was, after all, a touch fortunate just to be here. I'm a very tall and quite active person and was shocked to be diagnosed with a crippling blood clot in my leg just four weeks before. I was prescribed blood thinners, which increased my mobility enough to limp on the plane to Georgia. My hand luggage was stuffed full of syringes, hardly the clobber I expected to be accompanying me on a football odyssey.

I was full of relief, excitement and optimism. The spring flowers dotted around Vake Park promised good weather ahead, and I glimpsed the Mikheil Meskhi Stadium through the treeline. The seemingly random squares of blue, yellow, green and white seats looked enticing from several hundred metres above. The music then started at the stadium, easily audible on the stiff breeze. My heart skipped. This was the opening theme to a year of unpredictable football and experiences.

Dila Gori, the notional home team, were responsible for leasing the stadium. The 2015 Georgian champions were obviously unconvinced about the appeal of a Friday night game in Tbilisi and had opted against printing tickets, instantly quashing my hopes of collecting a ticket from every match. A steward gave me some sunflower seeds, carefully wrapped in newspaper, as I entered. Free entrance and a free snack. I was definitely winning.

The following day I visited Gori: a town best known for being the birthplace of Joseph Stalin. The former Soviet leader's image is still revered in the strange, near celebratory, museum and in a supermarket window. I climbed the much-reconstructed fortress, which offered a panoramic view of the great mountains of the Caucasus and a lower ridge that framed Dila Gori's home. 'You get a nice view of the castle from the stadium and good view of the stadium from the castle', was Nika's accurate description. It was a pity I couldn't watch a match there.

The fading sun lit up the unfilled multicoloured seats that began to remind me of a Mondrian painting. Nika had warned me that the attendance would be low. Locomotive Tbilisi, despite being an old name with historic links to the country's railway workers, did not have a large fan base. Still, I was expecting more than 200 people at a free match in a capital city of more than a million. There were more locals scoffing burgers in the nearby Wendy's than in a stadium with more than 24,000 empty seats.

The teams greeted each other in line and their hand slaps reverberated around the desolate stadium. The match kicked off and my challenge was properly underway. The first action was a sickening crash of skulls for a high ball that made me wince. Dila Gori defender Popkhadze was stretchered off and substituted. The Dila Gori ultras – two dozen youths, one drum and a red and blue flag – arrived in the far stand. 'Dila Gori' echoed around the stadium.

Georgia was renowned for its highly technical players, and there was plenty of skill on show from the seventh- and fifth-placed teams in the Georgian league. Dila Gori's talent was partly imported: two Brazilians and a Congolese started; another Brazilian and a striker from Sierra Leone appeared as substitutes. Locomotive was a team built on academy graduates, although it was their experienced centre back Rekhviashvili who caught my eye. Long-haired and slightly rotund, Rekhviashvili looked like an ageing heavy metal drummer and, one foray aside, did not partake in any running. But he could read the game, and his encouraging shouts lingered on the evening breeze. The first goal of my travels was a penalty. Locomotive's Arveladze, who had something of Dimitar Berbatov about his languid style, bamboozled a hapless defender and was tripped; Sikharulidze converted. Locomotive scored another: a lovely reverse pass from Arveladze and Sikharulidze tapped in his second.

I walked out of the stadium at half-time. Three old ladies on rugs tried to sell me more sunflower seeds. I didn't want to break my one-pack-per-game rule. I tried to speak to the middle-aged men behind me through Google Translate and a smattering of Russian. One was the father of Mujrishvili, the Dila Gori goalkeeper. I kindly exonerated him from both goals, although the second was a touch soft. He was more hopeful than I was that Dila Gori would get back in the game. Rousing screams directed at individual players suggested that many in the crowd were supporting family members more than either team.

Dila Gori controlled second-half possession. Rekhviashvili, my heavy metal hero, made a tremendous, goal-saving block and dominated the air. Locomotive had lost their previous five league matches, and the relief at their 2–0 win was palpable. Their goalkeeper was mobbed by his wife and four children. The rest of the team politely applauded the scattered stands. I felt an air of triumph. The match had been no classic and the deadened atmosphere was redolent of an office Monday. But my travels had started.

Tbilisi was a city with a pleasing setting, surrounded by steep rocky ridges that framed the gushing Kura River. It has one of the least consistent architectural styles of any European capital. Modernist creations rub shoulders with communist edifices; ancient churches are surrounded by a dash of brutalism; a brash rococo opera house stands amid European-style uniformity. But the old town was still pleasingly ramshackle in places. My hostel was located in an area that was mafia-ridden in the early 2000s. Georgia was one of the world's safest countries now; the criminals had been flushed out to Russia.

Georgia is well known for its wine. I had sampled Georgian wine in England and not been very impressed, and recounting this story was an easy way to procure many free samples in the wine shops of central Tbilisi. WineLab, on a street off Freedom Square, was the classiest. Georgians are friendly and proud of their country. 'Is this your first time in Georgia?' the owner asked. I mentioned my football travels and his ears twitched. I could detect football in people's veins. The shop's owner was Giorgi Gogorishvili, grandson of Mikheil Meskhi, the greatest ever Georgian footballer. The stadium from my very first match was named after him. This was like bumping into Bobby Charlton's grandson in Oddbins.

Giorgi, whose own football career was prematurely wrecked by injury, was immediately hooked. He was an engaging man, still unmarried well into his thirties, his dancing eyes practised in chasing women. His grandfather, Meskhi, made thirty-five appearances for the Soviet Union and played alongside Lev Yashin at the 1962 World Cup. This was an incredible achievement for a Georgian. 'You needed to be two or three times better than a Russian player to be chosen for the USSR', said Giorgi. Meskhi was not selected for the 1966 World Cup despite being in rude form. Giorgi showed me grainy clips of his grandfather, all feints and blistering speed, on his laptop. Footage showed Meskhi on teammates' shoulders after his testimonial between Dinamo Tbilisi and the Uruguayan side Nacional. At the time a watching Argentinian had assumed this was for being man of the match and was aghast that a player so far ahead of his generation was retiring. Giorgi clearly enjoyed retelling this anecdote.

Giorgi took me to his car, parked near the flower market. 'They all know me here', he said, smiling at the flower sellers. I calculated how much more Giorgi's dark Mercedes was worth than my camera and jumped in. We drove to a restaurant where we supped on German beer, grilled meats, tomatoes and khachapuri, a rich cheese pie, in the cool green hills overlooking Tbilisi. Giorgi tasted the tomatoes suspiciously. 'Not Turkish tomatoes', he said decisively. We feasted on the sweet fruits of the fine spring after imported food had sustained Georgia through the harsh winter.

He was sanguine about the current crop of Georgian players, acknowledging their skill and also their susceptibility to success going easily to their heads. Giorgi knew another Giorgi, Giorgi Kinkladze. 'Everyone is called Giorgi in Georgia. You say "Giorgi" here and half the restaurant will turn around. Kinkladze is quite fat now', he remarked. I was not surprised, if he ate cheese pie with any sort of regularity.

Lela, Giorgi's current girlfriend, joined us, her long dark hair swept around an angelic face. Giorgi flashed his mobile in her face. 'Look, grey eyes, not a proper Georgian', he joked. Giorgi liked her lithe Russian physique and Georgian fire. There was a cosmopolitan streak to him and many other metropolitan Georgians that stemmed from living at the crossroads of Europe and Asia. Georgia is the product of an intoxicating mix of influences. It is one of the most forward-looking of the former Soviet nations, but one deeply rooted in its considerable history. I was happy that the political situation in the Caucasus dictated I would need to return three more times to Georgia to travel between its southern neighbours: Azerbaijan, Armenia and Turkey.

Locomotive and Dila Gori finished sixth and seventh. Goal-scorer Sikharulidze was top scorer in the league with twenty-five goals, earned his first Georgia cap and a move to the Czech top-division side Slovácko. Kaladze became mayor of Tbilisi in November 2017.

FOREIGN IN NORDIC LANDS

2 Iceland

Iceland is on fire. The country has become a top tourist destination and the national team are icons. On the flight to Reykjavik I watched *Inside a Volcano*, the documentary tracking Iceland's successful qualification campaign for Euro 2016. The character and togetherness of the national team came through in a way I couldn't imagine happening with England. 'Why can't we always play together in a team in some league?' questioned one player in the film. They would be a frightening prospect, like Bolton Wanderers under Sam Allardyce. I wondered if the Icelandic league also had these traits.

The tourist boom has helped slash car rental prices in Iceland. My budget extended to a Chevrolet Spark – the only time I would hire a car in my first twenty-two countries. I'm not particularly fond of driving alone and it was even more difficult to concentrate with such distracting scenery. I motored through ashen landscapes brightened by a glaring sun, the roads lined by beautiful purple lupins. I completed the Golden Circle, a dramatic collection of natural sites that were desolate when I visited as a teenager but now swarmed with other tourists. I hiked away into clouds of tiny black and white butterflies at Þingvellir, the national park that became Iceland's first in 1930, a thousand years after the country's original parliament was founded there. This isolated country certainly didn't feel like a football destination.

It's hard to find Icelandic football stadiums, set low amidst residential neighbourhoods, so I was pleased to eventually find Victor Olsen, Chief Operating Officer of Stjarnan, at their Stjörnuvöllur complex. Stjarnan means 'the star' in Icelandic. Victor was my star. He was blond and burly, and spoke flawless English with an Icelandic slant. Victor explained that Stjarnan were the most famous Icelandic club owing to their elaborate goal celebrations in 2010. 'This was a silly season, we played only offensive football, games were like 4–4. Celebrations required a lot of energy, the focus wasn't on the football. The day before each match at training there was a need to do something new. At one point coach said, "this is enough, start again after we win the league".' Stjarnan had benefited financially from the attention, though, developed the club through revenue raised from advertising and won their only title in 2014. Stjarnan still got requests. 'Could you do the fish, the toilet?'

Stjarnan played European football for the first time in 2014 and beat Bangor City, Motherwell and Lech Poznań on the way to playing Italian giants Internazionale in the play-off round of the Europa League. Stjarnan were out of their depth and lost 9–0 on aggregate. 'Even our fastest player, it was like he was walking.' Inter sold their Croatian midfielder, Mateo Kovačić, to Real Madrid shortly afterwards. The video clip of him playing against Stjarnan was, Victor joked, 'like Messi against children'.

Victor also talked more seriously about some of the challenges Stjarnan faced. A large chunk of the club's budget came from UEFA – even losing in the first qualifying round of the Europa League was worth 240,000 euros – but the strength of the Icelandic krona had reduced its value. The recent increase in visitors was also causing difficulties for the club. The upcoming Europa League draw was a nervous day for Victor as he was tasked with chartering a plane in the middle of the tourist high season. The draw was only ten days before their first qualifying round match.

I liked Victor and the atmosphere around the club. But Stjarnan were playing the following day and I had the chance to watch another league match in the greater Reykjavik area – where seven of the twelve top-division clubs were based – that evening. 'You should go', ordered Victor. There was only a friendly rivalry between clubs in Iceland.

I felt a little out of place at Breiðablik. My heart was with Stjarnan. I tried to talk to a couple of fans outside the stadium. It was hard going. Breiðablik has a big academy and there were hundreds of elf-like children clad in green, mothers in chunky knitwear and the occasional icy old-schooler. A bouncy castle, hot dogs and sodas for sale outside the Kópavogsvöllur Stadium made this feel more like a village fête than a Reykjavik derby. I was surprised to hear the galloping 'Run to the Hills' by Iron Maiden aired before such a family affair. The match against Valur attracted a large and youthful attendance. The overspill sat on picnic blankets in the drizzle.

I sat next to Gunnlaug, the father of Breiðablik's right-sided midfielder, Höskuldur Gunnlaugsson. Gunnlaug's enthusiasm for football had been curbed after watching Liverpool in their glory years when he was growing up. His wife seemed to love every minute, vividly recalling the ecstasy of past victories and the pain of defeats. She later winced as her son was clattered. The team announcement was a nightmare of Icelandic numbers and too many 'ssons'. Gunnlaug helped me out. I wanted his son to have a good game. There was a bit of the Ray Parlour about his perm, a hairstyle in stark contrast to the close shave favoured by most Icelandic players. He had a worthy second job, helping the disabled, and studied in the winter months when football was impossible.

Tokić, a journeyman Croat, exchanged passes with Eyjolfsson, Gunnlaugsson's childhood friend, and cutely fired into the roof of the net to put Breiðablik into an early lead. After the deadly silence of my match in Georgia, this kick-started some atmosphere, with shrill and youthful screams, an inoffensive mantra of 'Breiðablik, Breiðablik' and the lonesome beat of a drum. Gunnlaugsson had a sure touch; his set pieces, such an important part of the Icelandic game, were decent, but he seemed uncertain in the challenge and his willing running did not mask a lack of anticipation. But he tried and cared and, after picking up a knock, was clearly irritated by his substitution. His mother looked concerned.

Breiðablik retreated and allowed a dinked ball into the penalty area which Valur central midfielder Ingvarsson expertly controlled on his chest before volleying home with his favoured left foot. Breiðablik seemed reasonably content to play out a 1–1 draw. But four minutes into injury time, Ingvarsson floated in a free kick and Valur left back Eiríksson headed strongly in off a combination of goalkeeper and post. 2–1 to Valur and another away win.

'That's football', was Gunnlaug's retort. There was only moderate derision amongst the crowd. It was hard to get that upset when the best of the Icelandic summer was still to come and you were in such youthful company. The crowd dissipated with efficient ease. Breiðablik had an army of brooms to clear away the mild detritus of popcorn and coffee cups even before I had left the stadium. A point may have been lost but maintaining cleanliness was rightly imperative.

I found my way back to Stjörnuvöllur, just two miles to the south of Breiðablik, more easily the following evening. Victor had given me a Stjarnan gold card season ticket, worth around £480, after our conversation. 'What do you want me to do with it after the game?' I asked. Victor smiled knowingly. 'Keep it, you won't be back.'

Stjörnuvöllur had a ground floor bar. The four young barmen were interested in my story and tried charging me £27 for a beer. It was a joke. A Gull was only £6, cheap by local standards in a country where drinking beer was legalised as recently as 1989. The barmen pointed out a group of twentysomething Stjarnan supporters. They were the 'silver spoons', the sons of local businessmen. Stjarnan are based in one of the wealthiest parts of Greater Reykjavik.

I spoke to Elías and Jakob from the 'silver spoons'. Elías stood out in his curious baseball hat and brown trousers. His aspiration was a league title or cup victory, and to progress to the second qualifying round of European competition. Elías explained that the Viking thunderclap that backed the national team at Euro 2016 was fostered at Stjarnan. They had picked it up from Motherwell during their Europa League run. Twenty-two Stjarnan supporters had travelled to watch a 2–2 draw at Fir Park in 2014 and had been inspired by the Motherwell tradition of slow clapping to their club anthem 'Since I Was Young'.

Confidence was high amongst the Stjarnan fans despite the fact they had lost their previous game. 'We always score two', said the exuberant Jakob. Jakob was the originator of the 'silver spoons', a name clearly more tongue in cheek than derogatory. A six-foot silver spoon sat in the corner of the bar and was on show in the 2014 championship-winners' picture. I lifted the spoon with Jakob and Elías for a terrific photograph.

The crowd was smaller and more adult than at Breiðablik. The rock anthems kept giving, though, with a full six-minute rendition of 'Bohemian Rhapsody'. The Stjarnan hardcore also borrowed classic tunes, their version of Creedence Clearwater Revival's 'Bad Moon Rising' accompanied by a snare and bass drum. This added sharp percussion to key moments in the match, a hard tackle, a corner gained or conceded.

It was a messy start of straight, over-hit balls. Away side Vikingur took the lead after fifteen minutes with a close-range volley. Stjarnan right back Laxdal equalised a minute later as Vikingur began to make more mistakes. It was 1–1 at half-time. I had already scoffed a tasty £8 burger – 'the best in the Icelandic league' according to Victor – but flashed my gold card to enter the hushed church hall atmosphere of the Stjarnan members' room. Locals sipped glasses of wine whilst I picked up a chicken and avocado Ryvita and talked quietly about the game. It was a strangely angular football snack that I couldn't see taking off in England.

I moved to pitch level for a different perspective. Victor paced around on the sidelines as the visitors dominated the second half, Sveinsson firing in the decisive goal for Vikingur after seventy-three minutes. The artificial surface had a lower bounce than Breiðablik's grass pitch, which seemed to restrict long balls but not the mighty long throws that bombed into the Vikingur penalty area. These stimulated the chant of 'Inn Med Boltann' – 'get the ball in the net' – a rhythmic mantra that accompanied set pieces across Iceland.

There was little hope for the Stjarnan hardcore. The drums stayed silent for the remaining minutes of the match. The Vikingur players celebrated their 2–1 win in front of their fans, housed in one side of the darkening main stand, as I recorded my third straight away win. The Stjarnan players had not performed to the early levels of this season. Their fans' faces were even whiter than normal. It was through no lack of effort. Effort is mandatory in Iceland.

Valur won their first title for ten years, finishing twelve points ahead of second-placed Stjarnan. Breiðablik and Vikingur finished in mid-table.

3 Faroe Islands

There were not many flights from Iceland to the Faroe Islands. Only two per week. I couldn't miss this one. I bounced into Keflavik International Airport and looked up at the departures screen. My flight wasn't listed. 'Has it been cancelled?' I asked one man. I already had a deep sinking feeling before a second official informed me that I was at the wrong airport. My flight was departing from the domestic airport, over thirty miles away on the fringes of Reykjavik, in just over an hour.

There was no time to lose. It would be three days until the next flight to the Faroes. I jumped straight in a taxi minivan. We became stuck behind a budget hire car on the single-lane road. 'They stop and take photos on bridges', said my driver. His soothing voice helped settle my frayed nerves. He increased his speed, very deliberately, as the road cleared, and calmly called Atlantic Airways to hold my flight. I thankfully paid £135 and sped into the airport, from the car park to the plane in just four minutes.

'Would you like a drink?' asked the air stewardess. I very nearly ordered a vodka and coke until I realised it would probably cost me another tenner. I settled into my seat with my heart still pounding. I ran through, in my typically logical mind, how difficult it would have been to rearrange my trip to the Faroes. I already had many flights booked. And to visit this island nation, geographically isolated between Iceland, Scotland and Norway, later in the summer would have been hugely expensive and disruptive.

Arriving at Vágar Airport was almost as exciting as my plane chase. A low cloud often hugs these windswept islands, shaped like an arrowhead in the North Atlantic. The flight before mine had aborted a first attempt at landing as fog clung dangerously to the runway. I was just pleased to be here. 'It's Sheep and Easy by Bus', suggested an advertisement in the arrivals hall. The next bus to Tórshavn, the capital, was in two hours. My confidence and cash had been shredded by my near disaster in Reykjavik. Both were partly restored by a kind local couple, fresh from a Celine Dion concert in Copenhagen, who offered me a lift.

Davis drove me into Tórshavn. 'There are only two people called Davis in the Faroes and the other one is a girl', he said. He looked up my guesthouse owner, Pætur, on his phone. 'I used to work for him', he added. Iceland is small but the Faroe Islands is almost like an extended family. Knutsford, a potential football contact and a big fan of my hosts HB Tórshavn, had informed me he was out of town. 'Yes, he's out sailing', Davis confirmed.

Pætur was also out, but his front door was open. I tapped up a few notes on my laptop in the hallway until his dog started nibbling at my ankles. I spoke to a neighbour and he pointed me to the back door, where the guest rooms were open as well. Crime levels are very low in the Faroes. Everyone knows everyone. I heard that most convictions were either for drink driving or paedophilia. I wasn't sure about this combination, but would feel safer here than in any other nation.

The seas lapping Tórshavn harbour were red with the blood of whales. And the HB fans were hoping that this would be the only giant killing in town this weekend. HB were playing minnows Skála ÍF from the second largest island of Eysturoy. Dead whales apart, Tórshavn was a lovely town with beautiful turf-laden houses dotting its centre, still inhabited by local people, unlike so many European capitals today. The view from Skansin, a strategic fort for centuries, was inspiring. The offshore island of Nólsoy cut the cloud, and mist shrouded the surrounding hills.

I visited Tinganes, the jutting rocks that have housed a parliament since the ninth century, even longer than Þingvellir in Iceland. I bumped into two young American brothers, Alex and Peter. 'Did you see the whales?' exclaimed an East Coast accent. I explained my mission was football, not whale hunting. 'Are you Matt?' They were at the Stjarnan match and had met Jakob, one of the silver spoons. 'He said you would be on our plane, but we didn't see you.' I explained my problem. 'Yeah, like, an international flight going from the domestic airport!' They also planned to watch the match on Sunday.

The following day, I took a boat trip around the awe-inspiring Vestmanna bird cliffs, north-west from Tórshavn and, like the capital, located on the main island of Streymoy. The sheer cliffs crashed dramatically into the sea from heights of 700 metres, the puffins and guillemots mere flying specks against this magnificent backdrop. I stopped at Tórsvøllur, the compact national stadium, on the way back to Tórshavn. I spotted a black man in a tracksuit. He stood out against the Faroese chatting and chilling in the bright environs of the stadium café.

He was Bakary Bojang, aged thirty, born in Gambia and a Danish resident since he was thirteen. An attacking midfielder, he had made a few appearances for Tamworth in the English Conference, played for the reserves at OB Odense, the Danish Superliga team, and had an injury-ridden spell in Oman. Bakary now coached at B71, a club from the southern island of Sandoy. B71 were top of the Faroese third tier and Bakary was waiting for them to arrive ahead of their game against KÍ Klaksvík's third team.

I asked Bakary how he had ended up here. He had a Faroese friend from his time at OB Odense who had since joined B71 and asked Bakary if he was interested in moving to Faroese league football. Bakary visited and fell in love with the place, his Danish easing communication in this self-governing part of Denmark. 'It's very calm, people are friendly, life is easy-going.' B71 are unpaid amateurs, all locals. Promotion to the second flight would mean B71 could pay wages and recruit some international players. Bakary believed they would improve the standard.

A few days earlier, in Iceland, I had spoken to Victor about the small number of foreigners in the Stjarnan squad. He said that the club was focused on signing older Icelandic players to promote a more professional attitude. Foreign players often needed a lot of help: housing, cars, shopping, and if the internet breaks down they call the club to try to get it fixed. Stjarnan had a Jamaican international goalkeeper, Duwayne Kerr, who had to travel for two days each way to play for his national team and missed six matches the previous season. I was interested to see how the foreign players fared in my Faroese match.

I didn't have any local contacts after Knutsford had chosen sailing over football. My host, Pætur, made a series of calls, gradually spreading the word in the way familiar from the days before social media. I layered up at my guesthouse and strolled to Gundadalur, HB's ground, located next to the national stadium. I admired the interesting Scandinavian houses on the way, rarely two of the same design, some clad with darkened wood, others topped with traditional sod roofs. It was blowing a gale by summer standards and lashing with horizontal rain. I was soaked in seconds. 'Fifty-two to go' ran through my dampened mind. But with wind blowing the clouds swiftly across the sky, new weather is only minutes away in the Faroes. It brightened as I crossed a park filled with strongly scented pine trees and modern sculptures, in black and grey to match the clouds.

The café at the national stadium was strangely empty so I ventured to the HB club room that overlooks the Gundadalur. HB share their attractive stadium with more recent rivals B36 and each club has their own stand with its own club room. HB had a friendly feel. Players were beginning to arrive from both teams and greeted me as they passed the glitzy trophy cabinet and a dazzling football mural. Perhaps they thought I was a scout.

Turið, the club secretary, was expecting me. News travels fast in this small place. She worked part-time for HB, combining her duties at the football club with more formal caring as a social worker. She was also an Arsenal fan who had been to a recent match against Hull City. The attendance of 60,000 at the Emirates Stadium was greater than the population of the Faroe Islands – even including the tourists.

HB are the most successful club in Faroese football, with twenty-three titles to their name. But the team had been struggling, missing out altogether on European qualification for the 2017–18 season. This had a massive impact on their finances, as even losing in the first qualifying round, something that has happened in all but two European campaigns, considerably boosted their budget. HB had started the season in diffident form, drawing too many and crashing out of the cup. They were fourth and needed to finish third to guarantee European qualification. This was a big match.

Turið said that failing to qualify for Europe had been difficult for HB, taking a sharp intake of breath in a characteristically Scandinavian way. The club spent in the region of £250,000 per year on their academy, with around fifty coaches and sixty-five teams playing under the HB banner. She explained that HB may have to cut back should they miss out on Europe again. HB might stand for Havnar Bóltfelag, or 'Harbour Football Club', but Tórshavn didn't have the fishing money – fish products account for 97 per cent of Faroese exports – of other towns to support the club.

I spoke to Thomas Jule, a former reserve goalkeeper and lifelong fan of HB. He had an infectious smile, and loved HB and the over-achieving national team. The Faroe Islands had recently beaten Greece home and away and were seeded in the fourth-highest of six qualification pots for the 2018 World Cup. He looked as nervous as you would expect a loyal supporter to be. Thomas wanted more spectators at games but mentioned other diversions such as playing handball and going to the gym. He lamented that there were not many HB players from Tórshavn; local players were often lured to Denmark, and that meant players' families didn't attend.

Thomas pined for a better atmosphere at the ground to help inspire the players: more shouts, chants, maybe even a drum. He was also less than enamoured with foreign players' motivation. The highest paid international players earn around £5,000 per month in the Faroes. Thomas believed this is too high for the standard of football, which I would find noticeably lower than in Georgia and Iceland.

I was enjoying the rock classics before each Nordic match and was treated to a rare remix of Queen's 'I Want It All' at the Gundadalur Stadium. Most HB fans congregated in their own stand, with the seats of the B36 stand left empty, but a few families and a large dog assembled on a grassy bank overshadowed by a mountainous ridge. The stadium is well protected from the elements by Faroese standards and Thomas had explained that postponements were rare here despite the wild weather. Tórshavn had seen snow in every month over recent years.

The fans seemed cautious. There were a few gruff chants of 'Harbour' as HB dominated early possession on an artificial pitch that gleamed from the earlier downpour. Skála played ten men behind the ball, with Brian Jacobsen, one of four Jacobsens in the starting line-up and another two on the bench, leading the line. Pingel, the ponytailed Dane, latched onto some good left-wing interplay, controlled and turned a low shot into the corner to put HB into a 1–0 lead. The goal seemed to be in slow motion.

It was all HB. Skála had barely made it past the halfway line in the first twenty minutes. Frustration was growing amongst the middle-aged HB faithful as chances were wastefully spurned. Skála finally won a free kick twenty-five yards from goal and rushed away precious possession with a ridiculously quick set piece. 'This could be a massacre', I said to my American friends behind me. It wasn't, though. Skála had not managed a shot but then scored. A cross came in from the right and, with a suspicion of offside, the ball fell nicely for Brian Jacobsen, who slotted in for Skála. 1–1 was a truly audacious half-time score.

The HB club room was a welcoming hearth of discussion and sweet treats at the break. The typically friendly woman manning the café asked why I was here. I gave her my business card and she sold me a lovely homemade cake and a charming smile for £1. A windswept HB fan in the stand reflectively rued the missed chances. I said that I had watched three successive away wins. 'Go home', he joked, before posing for a photograph in his red and black HB shirt and scarf.

HB started the second half with purpose. But there were increasing signs that this would not be the HB victory that most predicted. There was no hiding the lack of quality. 'Please be better, just once', pleaded a familiar American voice behind me. The slow build-up play had been replaced by increasingly desperate HB long balls. 'Is this the worst football ever?' questioned my American friend. It wasn't quite; but it wasn't good.

Skála substitute Jakub Johansen was then played through. HB centre back Hansen was too hesitant in the tackle: the ball bounced into Johansen's path and he slotted the ball calmly into the corner. Faroe Islands international goalkeeper Gestsson disconsolately picked the ball out of the net for the second time. He had not made a save the entire match. This was the definitive smash and grab. It was Burnley coming from behind to beat Manchester United at Old Trafford.

Supporters of both teams spilled onto the pitch after the game. I saw the opportunity to play on a top-flight pitch during my travels. I politely grabbed a ball from a boy and took a penalty against his fortysomething father. It smashed against the crossbar. Perhaps some foreigners are best kept in the stands.

HB finished fifth and missed out on European qualification again. Skála, who won only one of their opening twelve matches, finished a respectable sixth. Bakary and B71 were promoted to the second tier.

4 Norway

I knew the numbers. Bergen receives four times more rainfall than London. And I had flown in from the Faroes during a very damp June, the wettest on record, with heavy rain falling every day. There's nothing quite as unwelcoming as arriving in a new city when it's dark or lashing down. I trudged around Bryggen, the historic trading hub of Bergen, bumping into hordes of cruise tourists with their sharp umbrellas and fierce determination. This was not a promising start to my Norwegian matchday.

I would normally have retired to a pub or a restaurant in such gloomy circumstances. But Norway is a ludicrously expensive place. I was still hungry after munching on a seafood wrap from a local restaurant, Søstrene Hagelin. I visited the KODE art museum, whose tickets were reasonably priced and valid for all three galleries over two days – useful in the likelihood that it would rain again the next day. The vivid artwork of Edvard Munch seemed less surprising in this tempestuous climate.

I had associated Norway in my teenage years not with painting or football, but its black metal scene, an extreme form of heavy music defined by tremolo picking, blast-beat drumming and harsh vocals. I tape-traded bootleg recordings of Bergen bands such as Burzum, Immortal and Gorgoroth by exchanging cassettes in the post with pen-friends. I still enjoying listening to Norwegian bands and, on this first visit to Norway, I made a pilgrimage to the Fantoft wooden stave church in the ghostly woods surrounding Bergen. It was a reconstruction after the medieval original was burnt down in 1992; its ashes tellingly featured on the cover of a Burzum release. The forests and darkness had inspired Norwegian bands, but the inclement weather wasn't helping me find football context.

I didn't have a contact in Bergen despite trying the club, Brann, and two newspapers. But Brann have their own pub, Footballpuben, in the city centre. And this seemed my best bet. The outside area was quite empty several hours before kick-off. The acrid smell of damp cigarettes mixed beautifully with Hansa, the local Bergen brew. I caught the eye of a middle-aged fan fiddling with the DJ decks as the rain bounced off the street. He was Gert Bøe, a bus driver and ardent Brann fan. 'Brann is my wife', he said with pride. Gert was wearing a bright red scarf, Brann colours, with white lettering that announced 'I'm from Bergen'.

Gert was too young to remember the club's heyday in the 1960s, but a perfect age to recall the club's only title since then, in 2007. A key striker in this era was Robbie Winters, a Scot who played for Dundee United and Aberdeen before his long spell in Norway. Gert said the players are close to the fans, staying in the same hotels, travelling and talking together. He had befriended Robbie and visited him in Livingston, a later club, laden with the local Norwegian sausages that Robbie and his children craved. The game was called off due to a waterlogged pitch; but Robbie got his sausages and Gert an exclusive tour of the unused stadium.

Gert took me on a tour around his local, the stark ground floor decorated with Premier League football shirts, the more tasteful basement partly designed by Gert himself. A realistic goal, complete with netting, framed the bar, and three of Gert's Brann shirts were proudly displayed. Gert, now in his fifties, said that the ground floor of Footballpuben was too rowdy for him these days. He suggested I stood with the younger hardcore Brann fans at the game in the middle of the Frydenbø stand.

Gert introduced me to Thomas, one of the leaders of this younger crowd, who was pumped by the announcement that Brann had a second qualifying-round Europa League tie against a Serbian or Slovakian team. 'We can fly to Budapest and drive!' Thomas looked like a fan leader: shaven head, wearing a black T-shirt with 'Ultras weekend' emblazoned in yellow below tongue-in-cheek logos of fighting, police and handcuffs. Nicely designed red T-shirts advertised the Europa League adventure that I feared would last one round.

Thomas and his friends help with the pyrotechnics that fire up home games. These are important to Brann; the team name means 'fire' in Norwegian. These flares are permitted by the authorities but banned by some other clubs. Brann have received considerable fines – after several incidents at away games – that the supporters helped pay. Brann clearly has a community feel, a strong sense of pride often found in regional hubs that seemed more pronounced in Bergen, surrounded by verdant mountains and bordered by the North Sea.

Thomas pointed out the stains on the pub ceiling. I nodded. Damp was understandable in such a wet place. 'No, beer, we celebrate after a big win', he explained. Gert had already described the misery of the Everton fans when they realised the price of beer in Norway before a UEFA Cup tie in 2008. These stains were Norwegian gold plate. Footballpuben serves the cheapest beer in town but when Thomas mistakenly grabbed my beer, I clasped it like a child would a new toy.

The operatic voice of Bergen-born singer Sissel Kyrkjebø hit the sound system that Gert was monitoring. He put his hand on his heart. This was 'Nystemten', the town anthem of Bergen, sung fervently at Footballpuben and at the Brann Stadium. After the distinct lack of crowd noise in Iceland and the Faroes, it was refreshing to hear a song that brought the city and its club together. I was enjoying my first true sight of football passion.

Footballpuben know their clientele and put on free bus transfers to the Brann Stadium. Thomas ushered me on board as cans of Hansa welcomed the fans, and excitement brewed amongst the hardcore. Traffic moves fast in Bergen, a spread-out city with a good transport system, and we arrived ten minutes later. The stadium was circled by heavily forested mountains, shrouded by low mist. A lone waterfall was gushing, a frayed white thread against a dark background. A duo of sea birds swayed in the light wind. Several days later the rain stopped, the clouds broke and I viewed the stadium from Fløyen, one of the seven mountains of Bergen. This highlighted its perfect location in a flat part of the suburbs and surrounded by dark peaks, green spaces and, closer to the city, the calm inroads of the North Sea.

Thomas took me into the tight supporters' club room underneath one of the stands. It had the feel of an Andy Warhol studio, a hub of counterculture with a paint-flecked floor and a toilet vaguely reminiscent of *Trainspotting*. Red and black stickers were everywhere. 'Pyrotechnics is not a crime', stated one. Thomas grabbed some banners but the fire-works were on hold. The game was live on Monday night television, convenient for a foreigner who had just watched Sunday afternoon football in Tórshavn, but less appealing to many Bergen residents. The crowd was several thousand below the season's average. Thomas and the Brann hardcore berated those that stayed away while four large flags protested against the Norwegian Football Federation's television deal.

I had already bought a seat in the Frydenbø stand. Thomas is well known by the Brann authorities, though, and took me into the standing area, housing around a thousand fans for league games. His Europa League T-shirts weren't selling well but the tension was building. Brann had the opportunity to top the table with a victory against Stabæk after leading clubs Rosenborg and Sarpsborg had unexpectedly lost at the weekend.

Thomas directed the hardcore from the front, one eye on the game, the other on the crowd. There was an impressive range of songs, some drawing on the forthcoming Europa League adventure, and references to Yugoslavia and Czechoslovakia were clearly provocative. There were plenty familiar to English football crowds, shaped around the tunes of 'Rule Britannia' and more recent refrains, 'Don't Take Me Home' and 'Take Me Back'.

I was enjoying the crowd more than the game. 'Sit down if you hate Rosenborg' provided me with a dilemma, laden as I was with camera and notebook. My companions compelled me to. Rosenborg had dulled Norwegian football with its dominance, winning the league for thirteen consecutive seasons from 1992. The most innovative lyrics were 'Niagara Falls, London and Paris, what are these compared to Bergen, the Nordic paradise.' Indeed there is a Bergen suburb, not far from the stadium, called Paradis. And it felt wetter in Bergen than at Niagara Falls.

Braaten was the key player for Brann. The thirty-five-year-old former Toulouse and, briefly, Bolton Wanderers winger with more than fifty caps for Norway was dubbed 'the old one' by Brann fans. He caused havoc mainly on the right wing, and settled Brann nerves with a low finish from a Nouri cross. The second goal was all Nouri. Brann's impressive right back won the ball back in the penalty area and drilled a left-footed shot inside the Stabæk goalkeeper Mande's near post. Moments later, Costa Rican defender Acosta headed a free kick into an empty net with Mande nowhere near ball nor goal-line. The Costa Rican in front of me, jacket adorned with the names of Brann's 'Ticos' Acosta and Vega, went mad.

It was 3–0 at half-time. There was no beer on sale and everyone was sobering gently under the grey evening skies. The stadium snack of choice was a tray of giant bacon crisps, salty and savoury enough to absorb the Hansa lingering on our tongues. I could see these being a hit in England.

The contest was over twenty minutes into the second half when Stabæk midfielder Ba needlessly nudged a Brann corner into his own net. Braaten was involved in Brann's fifth goal, starting the move that would feed Costa Rican substitute Vega. 'Sometimes he's brilliant, sometimes he's awful', said a nearby supporter. Vega was alone in the lush green grass and his controlled finish clipped the post on the way in. I celebrated with the fans behind, poking one of them in the eye in my exuberance.

'We win 5–0 and it has stopped raining!' exclaimed a Brann fan as my home team curse came to an end. I had even spotted some blue sky between the clouds during the game. Brann were top of the table for the first time in nearly a decade and seemed to have a real chance of securing a fourth Norwegian title. The team celebrated in front of the Frydenbø stand. Nouri, who had played well and knew it, danced and later tracked down my Instagram photograph of his jig to 'like' himself.

I handed my card to a couple of fans. Benjamin had travelled from Sarpsborg, near Oslo, with his grandfather to watch the match – a flight to Bergen, five hours in the city and an overnight train back. Gert had explained earlier, 'Brann supporters are the biggest ones, we have a lot of fans from Oslo who were born in Oslo. But they love the team.' Brann certainly draws you in: as does Footballpuben. Thomas and his friends celebrated until 3 a.m., and the ceiling stains surely darkened.

I chanced another message to BA, the Bergen newspaper, and switched the email subject to 'Brann 5–0 Stabæk'. It grabbed their attention and, three days after the game, I met Jan Gunnar Kolstad, a gnarled sports journalist with the look of a retired rugby player, at Brann's training ground. He introduced me to Lars Arne Nilsen, Brann's relaxed manager, and told him that my run of four successive away wins had been broken by their demolition of Stabæk. Lars laughed. 'I would have shot you had I known about this curse before the match.'

Jan explained that every Norwegian boy followed an English club. Liverpool were the best supported, with two generations of fans. Some fathers would threaten to throw their sons out of home if they did not follow in their footsteps. Jan had watched the 1982 European Cup final with his grandfather and had become an Aston Villa fan, though he was no lover of the West Midlands – 'I must say that Birmingham is no interesting city' – and preferred to watch Villa play away. He attended both the 2015 FA Cup semi-final and the final, which Villa lost 4–0 to Arsenal. ('I had a great time until the game started.') Jan and other Norwegians' love for English football may help explain the relatively sparse crowd at Brann for such a key game. The lowest ticket price, the equivalent of £18, was certainly very affordable by local standards.

Jan published a double-page spread in the Friday edition of *BA*. The headline translated as 'Project Ball Insane'. It was strange to see my name in print. I was a normal guy watching some football. But I was pleased that my first coverage was in Norway. I liked the Norwegians, reserved yet friendly, their pleasing regional lilts influenced by the English television programmes they watched. I stayed in an excellent Airbnb near the stadium, with an enormous cat called Hansi and an owner who knew black metal musicians in Bergen. We stayed up late into the night drinking cans of beer and listening to Alice in Chains and Opeth.

Norway attracts a well-heeled tourist set, ticking off a fjord and wondering why they are wandering around a reconstructed wooden wharf. As with Iceland, watching football in Norway felt the most local thing you could do on a wet summer evening. I had enjoyed my time in Bergen, but much of me was looking forward to the more offbeat, and affordable, destinations to come.

Brann Bergen lost their Europa League qualifier against Slovakian side Ružomb-erok. A downturn in form saw them finish the season in fifth. Stabæk finished mid-table.

Fixing my matches

I was regularly asked how I decided on my matches. There were some clubs I was keen to visit from the very beginning. IFK Mariehamn – shock 2016 Finnish champions from the Åland Islands – looked an attractive story in an appealing place; tiny Crotone was the romantic choice for Italy; and Trabzonspor are a relatively big Turkish name in an unheralded Black Sea city. I visited all three on my travels, but my plans didn't always pan out. I was in Kazakhstan for eleven days and neither Kairat nor Astana, the teams in the two best-connected cities, were at home. I took the train to Taraz instead.

A smaller club hosting a domestic giant often led to an intimate atmosphere and the hint of a shock. This was certainly the case when I watched Ufa against Spartak Moscow in Russia and Napredak Kruševac play Red Star Belgrade in Serbia. I occasionally had to choose a match that pitted a big club against a minnow knowing that this might – and sometimes did – lead to an absolute walloping. It can be fun to watch a 5–0 thrashing in Vilnius or a 7–0 demolition in Bucharest, but closer matches are normally more exciting.

I'm a fan of the underdog. Manchester United, Bayern Munich and Barcelona were not on my route. I would struggle to support the home team or find an angle that had yet to be exhausted. And it was my suspicion that it would be harder to meet people at massive clubs or in larger cities. I generally chose lesser lights in the bigger leagues, such as Montpellier in France and Málaga in Spain, whilst Bournemouth were my English hosts. My Premier League selection meant that I could watch matches at two top-flight outposts in Great Britain, the most northerly at Ross County in Scotland and furthest south in England, just three days apart.

It was much easier in smaller countries. I often had a choice of several games, and would see two top-division matches in the likes of Belarus and Luxembourg, three in Armenia, Cyprus and Gibraltar and an unforgettable five in Malta. There were relatively few midweek fixtures across Europe – most leagues are much smaller than in England – and I selected these slim pickings for my schedule: Croatia in April, Spain in February and the incendiary December derby between Cracovia and Wisła in Poland.

Beitar Jerusalem were the only club that I was actively looking to avoid, having watched Beitar fans abuse two of their own Muslim players in the award-winning football documentary *Forever Pure*. I spoke to Uri, from indie Israeli football website Babagol, over a couple of Malka beers in Tel Aviv. 'It was made to seem worse than it actually was', he said. I understood this: I edit words and photographs to enhance their impact. 'But the racism was still there', said Uri. And so in Israel I visited mid-table Bnei Yehuda and champions Hapoel Be'er Sheva.

A follower of my travels said he was inspired to try to watch a derby, or as close as possible, in all fifty-five UEFA nations over one season. This was a nice tweak and, with greater budget and flexibility than I had, eminently possible. He then added he would travel only by land. The vast distances between Kazakhstan and anywhere, and the difficulty of getting to Israel overland, sidelined any thoughts I might have on sticking to surface travel. He would need even more luck.

It was unintentional but, as I closed in on my target, I realised that I had not visited any of the stadiums before in my previous existence as a normal football fan. This was an exploration in the truest sense of the word.

5 *Sweden*

Sweden felt like a continuation even though it wasn't. I would have travelled directly from Bergen to Gothenburg were the Swedish league not in the middle of a month-long break. Instead I returned to London before journeying through eight countries: Sweden, Finland, Estonia, Kazakhstan, Russia, Belarus, Lithuania and Latvia. This was my longest single trip, in distance and duration, and promised to be one of the most challenging, with tiring travel and a substantial language barrier to overcome. I packed light, predicting warm weather and the accumulation of football memorabilia. I included my Russian phrasebook. This was a wise move as, somewhat surprisingly, Russian would prove the most useful foreign tongue across the fifty-five leagues.

It was clear that two football people were sitting next to me on my flight to Gothenburg. It was difficult not to listen. Players – first names only, not giving much away – were discussed; loans to League One and Two clubs evaluated. They were southern, clearly, possibly from London, definitely representing a club in the top two divisions in England. It certainly wasn't Fulham, but maybe West Ham. I introduced myself. They were from Brighton & Hove Albion, interested in my travels and relieved I wasn't a rival scout attending the same Halmstad youth tournament.

I was visiting Häcken, not Halmstad. Malin, Häcken's communications director and a former professional handball player, presented me with a club scarf, the first of my travels, when I arrived in Gothenburg. I normally sided with the home team and Häcken's underdog mentality appealed. Häcken are not a historic Gothenburg club. IFK are the most popular, with their eighteen titles and two UEFA Cups in 1982 and 1987. Örgryte IS and GAIS are older still, and both now plied their trade in the second tier. But Häcken do not even consider themselves a Gothenburg club. They are from Hisingen, the large island to the north of the city, an area previously heavily influenced by its shipbuilding and now home to Volvo. And Häcken.

Malin had put me in touch with the *Gothenburg Post*. I was fast finding that meeting the media helped publicise my travels, eased barriers with clubs and gave me alternative views on domestic football. Fredrik, another likeable Swede, was the first journalist to ask about my budget. I was keen not to quote a figure. I saved money by cooking my own pasta in Iceland and eating a frozen Tex-Mex pizza in the Faroes. But some of my costs were unavoidable, especially accommodation. Airbnb was working well in Scandinavia, its lodgings being cheaper than the bad-value hotels, and often closer to stadiums.

I was conscious that my social media streams were being advertised in the following day's newspaper and I had not taken a single photo of Gothenburg. I walked the quiet, windswept Sunday streets, the dipping sun adding an attractive glint to Sweden's second city. The late evening light is often the best for photography, with colour in the fractured skies, and I certainly have more energy for taking photos than during the other 'golden hour' just after dawn. I took pictures of the brooding crane silhouettes, a photogenic symbol of Hisingen.

Monday's *Gothenburg Post* included a double-page feature on my travels. I tucked a copy in my bag, still finding the limelight strange. I climbed Skansen Kronan, a seventeenth-century fortress built to protect the Swedes from invading Danes. It was never needed back then, but offered a fine modern-day view of the city's mishmash of architectural styles and the harbour that established Gothenburg as an important trading colony. The port remains, along with Bergen, one of the two busiest in the Nordic countries. I strolled the atmospheric Haga suburb below the fortress, where people sheltered from the wind and devoured enormous cinnamon buns.

I crossed the water to Hisingen and met Erik Ranesjö, from the Häcken supporters' club, at the Whoopsi Daisy, a pub located in a 1970s-style shopping centre. Erik explained that Häcken – 'the hedge' – were formed in 1940, near bushes along a Hisingen street. The island and club had never escaped the shadow of their more illustrious Gothenburg neighbours. They should play in green and white, but wear a bright yellow and black kit instead, the story being that one of Häcken's founders crossed to Gothenburg to buy green and white kits for the new club, but there were none, and not wanting to return to Hisingen empty-handed, he purchased yellow and black shirts.

You challenged the norm by becoming a Häcken fan. Erik explained that, unlike at IFK, there was no family tradition of going to matches. The Häcken fan base reflected the heavy immigration that Hisingen had experienced, and this diversity was something the club promoted.

A banner at the ground stated 'everybody is different, but that's okay'. Erik felt that Häcken should promote themselves more, but without losing the family ambience that had seen stranded away supporters given a lift in the team bus.

Erik had been to virtually all their home and away games since 2012, when Häcken finished in their best ever position of second place. The most unforgettable match was when Häcken won the 2016 Swedish Cup, their first major trophy, by beating Malmö on penalties. Erik said that this was the greatest moment of his life, ahead of his wedding, wincing at the response that gets from his wife. But you could see he was telling the truth.

Häcken play in a location that befits the club's working-class heritage. The new, hard concrete lines of the Bravida Arena were surrounded by five tower blocks, a roundabout and a drive-through. The grey stadium was brightened by yellow signs and a welcoming atmosphere. Children took penalties under the supervision of a giant wasp mascot called Stickan. Meanwhile, Erik's supporters' club sold offbeat shirts emblazoned with the charismatic Hisingen cranes just yards away from the official shop, a scene that you don't see in many grounds. The club marches at West Pride in Gothenburg every June and rainbow corner flags fluttered in the breeze.

There was a large contingent of Hammarby fans with green and white flags and drumbeats. 'Hammarby-la-la-la, Hammarby-la-la-la', they chanted, well before the teams walked on. I would chance upon Simon, a Hammarby supporter, in a Stockholm bar the following day. Hammarby had won their only title in 2001 but Simon said that might have been the worst thing to happen to the club. Hammarby were relegated to the second division in 2009 and frustrated fans displayed a flag that demanded, 'we start to deliver when you start to deliver'. Attendances, helped by a move to a new stadium, grew to the highest in Scandinavia, a remarkable feat for a second-division team, and Hammarby had been promoted back to the Allsvenskan in 2014.

Häcken and Hammarby, fifth and seventh respectively, still seemed to be on their summer break in the early stages, but Lindgren shone for Häcken in defence with good anticipation, a timely block and a fine header. Erik had said that Häcken's recruitment was more international than at IFK, and the home side fielded a Nigerian rookie, Egbuchunam, in place of the injured Sierra Leonean striker Alhassan Kamara. Björn, a Häcken diehard who had recognised me from the *Gothenburg Post*, was not bothered. 'I could score Kamara's goals. He's like an Andy Cole, a Pippo Inzaghi.' Egbuchunam struggled at first, dropping deep, chasing hopeful long diagonal balls, but worked tirelessly throughout and improved.

Häcken took a 1–0 lead into half-time when Egbuchunam flicked the ball to Farnerud and the former Torino midfielder dinked the ball over the advancing goalkeeper. I chatted to Björn at the break and asked about the difference between Gothenburg and Stockholm. 'This is Hisingen, not Gothenburg', was his friendly answer, and one I should have predicted. Häcken embraced the difference, and when the home fans sang a version of the Euro 2016 staple 'Take Me Home', the song ended with the addition of 'Hisingen', the island home of Häcken.

Häcken were the dominant attacking force in the second half. Paulinho was pushed over for a penalty after some incisive Häcken passing. The Brazilian placed the ball high to the goalkeeper's left. 'Paul, Paul, Paulinho', chanted the Häcken fans as I silently pondered whether the penalty conversion rate was higher on artificial pitches on which it is easier to strike the ball, and harder to dive.

Abrahamsson, the Häcken goalkeeper, broke a boot and trotted to the sidelines for a replacement. Hammarby fans howled at the wasted time, one throwing a shoe beside him to speed up his lace tying. After a fine home win, Abrahamsson picked up Erik's loudspeaker and led team celebrations in front of Björn and the standing home fans. The players seemed close to the fans at Häcken and not only because of their intimate stadium. Two children, offspring of a player, ran onto the pitch and between the posts. 'Goal!' responded the crowd. 'I told you it would be 3–0', said Björn. There was an inclusiveness that made this team different. A 2–0 win kept them as Gothenburg's, and Hisingen's, leading club. IFK would need to keep looking over the water.

The clouds, forever changing on a windy day, darkened and joined to reveal a yellow light. Thunder murmured, lightning crackled and a wide rainbow formed with the Bravida Arena underneath. It was a fitting climax to the Häcken experience. My train the following day passed through pleasant scenery of wood cabins in forests and beside lakes, before the Stockholm skyline came into view. I dragged my bag to an over-priced hostel room. Stockholm was undoubtedly a prettier city than Gothenburg, but I already missed Häcken and Hisingen.

Häcken only lost six matches all season, finishing fourth – fifteen points ahead of IFK – and qualifying for the Europa League. Hammarby stayed in mid-table.

6 Finland

The Åland Islands, a barely visible chain of islands in a treacherous stretch of the Baltic Sea, have a low profile. They are nearer Sweden than Finland, primarily Swedish-speaking and a self-governing region of Finland. IFK Mariehamn, from the islands' quaint capital, had shocked Finnish football by winning the Veikkausliiga for the first time in October 2016, six months after Leicester City had secured their own stunning debut title. I was keen to explore. I like islands and anomalies.

The grey Nordic skies gave way to a brilliant blue as I took the spacious ferry from Stockholm. My one-way ticket to Mariehamn, six hours away, had cost only £12. (Rather bizarrely, to encourage on-board spending, a return was £2.50.) We passed forested islands and clapboard houses in small fishing villages. I soaked up the warming sun on the top deck as we moved into a wider channel, and then hid inside as these innocent scenes gave way to the blustery Baltic. This was a tremendous way to travel. The lonely Lågskär lighthouse warned that we were approaching the Åland Islands.

I found a friendly face in Mariehamn's tourist office. It must be boring answering the same questions about ferry timetables and cycle routes. I asked where the local newspaper, *Ålandstidningen*, was based. I couldn't imagine asking this in many capitals. Their office was only five minutes' walk away. Everything was. When I got there, the junior sports editor interviewed me on the spot and we visited Mariehamn's stadium for photographs. A hedge slightly taller than me protected the Wiklöf Holding Arena from non-paying eyes.

I was introduced to Peter Mattsson, Mariehamn's affable director, in his office. He barked instructions to two juniors in the adjacent room without leaving his chair. 'Eight or nine years ago we only had one and a half people running the club. It is lucky there are twenty-four hours in a day', said Peter. Legia Warsaw were visiting for a second qualifying-round Champions League tie the following week, the biggest game in Mariehamn's short eight-year history as a professional club. Champions League accreditation passes were heaped untidily on a desk. There was tension and expectation. 'No one could imagine that we would play Legia a couple of years ago, especially fifteen years ago when we were in the third tier.'

I spoke with Peter about the divide with mainland Finland. 'Everyone wants to be identified as Åland Islanders. We have our own government, flag, stamps and domain name. We speak Swedish and Finland sends information in Finnish.' Swedish and Finnish are very different languages. According to Peter, around one-third of Åland Islanders felt culturally closer to Sweden and supported Sweden in sports.

Peter explained that the Finnish newspapers had predicted relegation for Mariehamn before the start of their title campaign. HJK Helsinki, perennial champions, had three or four times their budget. Mariehamn had been called 'the Finnish Leicester' by the sporting media, and this gave their achievement a point of reference, but, as Peter noted, Marie-hamn had been close to the top three for a while, finishing in the top six in the previous four seasons.

Air fares to the Åland Islands are high so, remarkably, Mariehamn travelled to every away game by ferry. 'We leave 11.30 the night before the game, then we are in Helsinki for breakfast', explained Peter. 'If we are playing in the far north we travel on Thursday afternoon for a Saturday match. It's a minimum thirty-six hours each way and you lose one day of training as you can't train on Monday.' Nevertheless, Peter believed that there was a better team spirit when players had spent so long travelling together.

Mariehamn were drafting in extra security for their Champions League qualifier even though Legia's infamous fans had only been allocated eighty-five tickets, 5 per cent of the seated capacity. I won-dered what damage Legia could do in a sedate holiday town. Björn, a Mariehamn fan and the owner of Pub Ettan, which he called 'the pretty okay pub', was taking no chances. 'I'm not opening. Sure, I lose some beer money, but this is my busiest season. I'm not risking it.' Björn, who also booked heavy metal concerts for the likes of Entombed, one of my favourite Swedish bands, had the rare talent of being intentionally funny in a second language. He had read the Legia forums. 'The Legia fans have been looking at the stadium on Google Maps and think they can travel without a ticket and watch the match over the hedge.' Little did they know that the hedge had since grown.

Björn gave me a shot of sour apple vodka. It was the same colour as Mariehamn's green shirts. His father walked in and started cutting his nails with a terrifying knife. Then the conversation itself became more bizarre. 'We had a Kenyan goalkeeper, who made some pretty crappy games. They said he picked up 50,000 euros in a plastic bag from a gas station for throwing two games. One game we lost 2–1 to a good shot and a penalty. The goal in the other game he threw in the net from a corner.' Peter Mattsson had been quoted in a Nairobi newspaper, the *Standard*, as saying, 'He was a good goalie. We wondered why he let in a couple of easy goals, but he just apologised and promised to try harder.'

It wasn't just Mariehamn who had been involved in the clandestine world of match fixing. Björn explained that a Chinese businessman, Ye Zheyun, bought AC Allianssi, another top Finnish club, in 2005 and changed the whole team for a match against FC Haka. They informed their regular goalkeeper, Finland international Henri Sillanpää, that he had been given a trial by Belgian side La Louvière. When Sillanpää arrived in Belgium, La Louvière were confused and said they had never offered the goalkeeper a trial. Allianssi lost 8–0 to FC Haka and went bust the following year. Mariehamn's goalkeeper was never seen in the Åland Islands again.

My hostel was hostile, busy and expensive. A single room with a bathroom shared by twenty others – seemingly staying for the annual door-slamming competition – was 54 euros. The curtain had never fitted the window and tea stains dotted the walls. At least I hoped that's what they were. I needed to escape and hired a budget Boris bike without brakes. The calm, wooded inlets and still beauty of the surrounding countryside were perfect cycling terrain. I cycled south until Arctic terns dive-bombed me on a bridge. I then cycled north to the Stallhagen brewery, my thirst growing from pedalling the bicycle equivalent of a baby buffalo for twenty-five miles.

I absent-mindedly checked my phone after stopping for directions.

There were dozens of new followers. Paul Doyle, chief football writer for the *Guardian*, had written a long article about my challenge. I considered my mild fame as I cycled the remaining few miles to the brewery. I sampled their entire range, the sun dying over an idyllic forested backdrop with a small stage lit in the foreground. I received a few messages wishing me well on my travels before my phone died. It was probably better this way as I could think about the publicity I had attracted without distractions. I was quite tipsy by now and there was no way I was cycling back to Mariehamn. I ordered a taxi and prepared to swallow the bill, before a Finnish couple approached me and we split the ride three ways. It really was my day. The baby buffalo bike sat sulkily in the boot.

I subsequently received a huge number of messages from all over the world: Thailand and Brazil, Bulgaria and Ukraine. Random football fans offered me beds, beers and friendly advice on which clubs to watch. I was even called 'their new hero' by one follower, although his previous idol was the man who ate ninety-two pies in the ninety-two English League grounds. My fame was still modest. It was great to have people following my adventure, admiring it even, some slightly envious. I smiled inwardly whilst I read their messages with the faux curtain flapping in the wind as I tried to air my scrappy room.

I digested an eventful day with dinner at Dino's Grill, and picked up an ice cream on the way back to my hostel. The vendor was closing up and gave me a large scoop in a small cone. The cone looked vulnerable. I licked fast but the cone collapsed and my scoop fell. I deflected it with my left arm, the scoop rebounded on my chest and I caught it with my right hand. This was deft but I didn't quite know what to do. I was carrying a cold scoop of ice cream and my cone had gone. I hid in a shop doorway, my back to passers-by, and licked out of my increasingly numb palm. It was a strange end to a memorable day.

Before leaving London for Georgia in June, I had sent a farewell email to my Ministry of Justice colleagues and asked if anyone had any European football contacts. Krista, a Finnish social researcher, put me in touch with her brother, an ice hockey coach who knew people at Mariehamn's opponents Ilves, better known for its ice hockey team than its football. A month later, I was speaking with the laid-back Ilves coach Toni Kallio, a former Fulham and Finland player nicknamed 'Bonecrusher' for his uncompromising defending, a few hours before his team's match. 'Talented players will choose ice hockey over football', said Toni. And it was easy to see why. Toni said that average hockey players earn 80–90,000 euros per year, with top players earning 150,000 euros. In contrast, Ilves' best player earns 35,000 euros per year, but the average is less than 25,000 euros.

I had to talk about his time at Fulham. He had loved London but hated the traffic. Although Toni only played a handful of times for Fulham, he was full of admiration for Roy Hodgson. 'I knew what the situation was, Paul Konchesky was ahead of me, but Fulham was still the highlight of my career.' He had been loaned to Sheffield United and then moved to Norway when his Fulham contract expired, which caused some regret. 'I had a few offers from League One clubs. I should have stayed in England. I loved the passion, especially in the lower leagues. Players are not the most skilful, but the attitude and determination are amazing. Whack the ball and fight.'

Toni had a short, unintentional spell in Thailand with Muangthong United. He was on holiday in Thailand when his agent called with an offer from Muangthong, then 2010 Thai champions and shortly to become Robbie Fowler's last club. Toni was initially sceptical but had a couple of spare hours in Bangkok, and Muangthong impressed him with a professional presentation. Toni signed for the club shortly afterwards but the problems started almost immediately. Muangthong went through three managers in quick succession. Toni twisted his ankle in pre-season, received no treatment, and Muangthong informed Toni they weren't going to pay his salary, as he was injured. Toni's contract was eventually paid up to the next transfer window and he returned to play in Finland with Inter Turku and then Ilves, where he now coached under Jarkko Wiss, the former Stockport County and Hibernians midfielder.

This would be one of the few times on my journey that I would speak to both the home and away camps. Toni explained that Ilves, with a distinctive badge featuring a wild-eyed lynx from which the club takes its name, had the biggest youth academy in Finland with about 4,000 junior players. The club ethos was to develop and sell players and aim for one of the four European places. Ilves attracted an average attendance of around 3,500 in 2017, the second highest in the league. 'We have live bands and happy hours. We need to build the family thing. In England, if your father is a Liverpool fan you are born a Liverpool fan.' He refused to blame ice hockey. 'Look at Sweden, they get good crowds at both sports.'

The attendance at Mariehamn was about 1,500 for fourth against fifth. It was a very congenial setting, many people drinking beers and eating excellent sausages on a terrace alongside the lone stand. After the media explosion, including an Ålands radio interview that was translated into Swedish, my Boris bike experience and ice cream hand, I was glad to finally get this match underway.

It was a scrappy first half where neither team settled into a rhythm.

Ilves struggled to pass the ball effectively and Mariehamn's build-up play was too slow and predictable. Sellin, a sprightly Swede, won the ball high up the pitch and crossed for Kangaskolkka, Mariehamn's leading striker, to shin a half chance wide. Mariehamn's captain then failed to emulate Marco van Basten's goal from the Euro 1988 final. The quality of play was low, a noticeable drop from Norway and Sweden. Mariehamn's goalkeeper Vaikla troubled the stand more than his waiting midfielders with two goal kicks, while Ilves forward Ngueukam overhit one pass by some twenty yards.

Arctic terns flew over the stadium, hopefully not in such a carnal mood as the previous day. The atmosphere in the stands was quite reverent, with very little noise from the home fans save the odd 'IFK' chant. I moved closer to a cluster of hardcore Mariehamn supporters with a drum and a young woman with a black poodle on her lap that was watching the game, or possibly the terns. I was getting used to some social media attention following my *Guardian* appearance, but the undoubted highlight was my poodle photograph being picked up by nonleaguedogs, the hit Instagram feed.

The second half was surprisingly entertaining, with even the poodle compelled to follow the action. Ilves midfielder Tamminen cut inside onto his right foot and hit an unstoppable shot past Mariehamn custodian Vaikla from outside the penalty area. The crowd was as restless as fallen surprise champions can be. Yet the Mariehamn faithful soon had something to cheer as current Kenyan Dafaa smashed a twenty-yarder in the corner. It was 1–1 and I had just seen two cracking finishes totally out of keeping with the rest of the match.

Ilves went 2–1 up through Ngueukam: the Cameroonian striker showed strength to make himself space and hit a right-footed shot that Vaikla should have saved. There were only minutes remaining when Mariehamn equalised, striker Kangaskolkka holding up a cross and lively substitute Sid scoring with a low shot. 'He scores when he wants' was sung for Sid in Swedish. Kangaskolkka, who battled hard throughout without ever looking like scoring, released Sid again but his late shot softly rebounded off the foot of the post and into the goalkeeper's hands.

It had been a decent second half. I returned to Björn's pub, dissected the 2–2 draw with some Mariehamn fans and waited for my overnight ferry to Estonia. Toni Kallio and his Ilves team were also travelling by ferry to Helsinki and he would be in Tallinn the following day for a short holiday with his wife. I asked if they would be checking out Infonet against Tartu Tammeka. 'Probably not', said Toni.

Ilves finished third and qualified for the Europa League. Mariehamn slipped to fifth and lost 9–0 on aggregate to Legia Warsaw. Mariehamn's Kangaskolkka was top scorer in the Finnish league with sixteen goals.

7 Estonia

I felt grotty after a night of snores and patchy sleep. I crashed around the tight ferry cabin to grumbled dissent, my cabinmates forgetting their own noisy entry a few hours before. I clambered up to the dining room and was greeted by a strange array of Baltic treats at the massive breakfast buffet: leek pie, Karelian pastries and haddock in mustard. I dodged sobering Finns on deck and gazed at Tallinn, the most magical old town in northern Europe. It was uplifting after my condensed cabin fever. The spires, new and old, jutted into the early morning light, the deep blue of the Baltic an entrancing foreground. Some of the modern constructions were barely on the drawing board when I visited a decade ago. But the Estonian capital is still a harmonious place.

The big four teams in Estonian football – Levadia, Flora, Kalju and champions Infonet, my hosts – were all based in Tallinn. Tartu Tammeka, Infonet's opponents that evening, were a typically non-Tallinn club as their much lower budget meant they could only afford younger players. Off the pitch they seemed notably progressive. They had the first ever joint managers in Estonian football and used crowdfunding to renovate their own stadium by allowing backers, including former national-team goalkeeper Mart Poom, to sponsor square metres of the new artificial pitch.

I met another Mart, a journalist from *Õhtuleht*, outside the charismatic thirteenth-century town hall. 'The style of football depends on the team', said Mart. 'Flora are more about technique and possession. Infonet will play from the wings and cross to the centre for the big guy.' Crosses for the big guy. It sounded simple at Infonet, a club that had equalled the largest margin of victory in a competitive senior match, set by Arbroath against Bon Accord in 1885, with a 36–0 thrashing of amateurs Virtsu Jalgpalliklubi in the 2015 Estonian Cup. I knew Infonet had been struggling but I could hardly predict the crisis I walked into. They had recently sacked Aleksandr Pushtov, their title-winning manager, and the assistant manager was suspended. Infonet were now refusing to talk to the media after it had apparently insulted their masculinity following a crushing 3–0 defeat to Maltese club Hibernians in the first qualifying round of the Champions League.

Mart explained that Soccernet, Estonia's biggest football website, had written a headline after the Hibernians match that had said 'third goal and impotent Infonet fell to the grass'. The main problem surrounded the medical implications of the word 'impotent'. Soccernet received an email from Infonet's press officer demanding an official apology and, when the website refused, their journalist was banned from visiting Infonet's home games or interviewing their players and management.

This was ridiculous. Mart thought so too. 'You can't ban journalism', said Mart, clarifying that the Soccernet headline was not insulting in Estonian. 'It was interpreted as more insulting than it actually was.

Infonet are a Russian club but not everyone in Estonia speaks Russian. I was born in free Estonia and don't speak Russian. It was only one word and everyone who saw the game thought it was accurate.' Infonet played as FCI Tallinn in European competitions, due to a ban on commercial firms. 'Now the "I" in FCI stands for "impotent". Other fans are chanting "impotent" at games but no one else will remember.'

Mart talked about the Estonian national team. 'Evolving' was a polite way to describe a side that had lost 8–1 to Belgium in November 2016 but, like other small nations, had a realistic chance of emulating Baltic neighbours Latvia and qualifying for a European Championship through the UEFA Nations League. I liked interesting rules. Estonia were boosting the chances of local players by only allowing five non-Estonian players and mandating at least one home-grown player on the pitch. This led to some strange situations. Mart recalled when Kalju substituted one home-grown player for another, but the second player was injured and they had to play with ten men. There was also discussion about where to play your home-grown player – central defence, winger or forward – as he would often be the weakest player in the side. I could see the dilemma.

The strong evening sun gradually deepened the shadows as my bus wound its way through Tallinn's eastern suburbs. I passed looming ten-storey high Soviet blocks. This journey could have been terrifying in the dark depths of winter, but I enjoyed the summer contrast. The juxtaposition between the medieval theme park of the old city, complete with archery range and locals dressed up in heavy cloth, and the residential suburb of Lasnamäe, just five miles away, was quite startling.

Mart had put me in touch with Dmitri, Infonet's technical director. He met me by the rustic ticket office, which consisted of a woman behind a fold-up table straight out of a village fête. Dmitri was instantly likeable. His English had a rough Russian accent that matched his dark stubble. We spoke in a Portakabin full of papers and cheap football trophies. Dmitri was in charge of contracts and organisation for Infonet, and moonlighted as head coach of Estonia's futsal team. He had also managed Infonet in their ill-fated Champions League second leg against Hibernians after their assistant manager was sent off in the first match. This was like Karren Brady managing West Ham.

Dmitri seemed relieved to be back in his Portakabin for this match. Infonet were already twenty points behind the leaders after seventeen matches, but Dmitri said that expectations were too high, as Infonet had never finished higher than fourth before their 2016 title. He was keen to talk about my travels – 'it's a good challenge, interesting challenge' – but was rather confused why I was not staying in the Baltics after my Estonian match. I explained that the Lithuanian and Latvian seasons were taking breaks during June and July, similar to my slight inconvenience in Sweden. I would be flying from Tallinn to Almaty in Kazakhstan, not a popular tourist route, to keep my challenge on track.

A man wearing a grey suit and holding a dead fish entered the Portakabin and interrupted our conversation. He turned around and left. Estonia was becoming ever more surreal. 'Estonian football needs money and time. We have only twenty-five years of independence', continued Dmitri. 'The Federation is making steps to make the league more professional by paying grants to players so that all ten [top-division] teams are professional.'

The transient-looking setting was not befitting of league champions. Guns N' Roses' 'Welcome to the Jungle' was belted out on speakers that sat on chairs behind the goal. Dmitri said that it was not really a stadium, just a pitch, and that the club had erected the small temporary stand. Infonet had played in Lasnamäe since they were founded in 2002 by a telecommunications company of the same name. A red demon mascot, Beastie – a slurred phonetic pronunciation of BSD, one of Infonet's first servers – looked hot in his costume. It was a delicious evening for a football match. The summer rays were still warm and the green artificial pitch contrasted beautifully with the grey apartment blocks.

Infonet started like a team that had been castigated in the media. Tammeka should have scored before the away side made numerous panicky clearances in an error-strewn first half. Kiidron, the Tammeka captain and their best player, cleared the low road-side stand with one hoof. Someone had brought along a klaxon and, although the crowd was only 200, it surely wouldn't be my quietest match. The horns sounded when Infonet's Kharin was brought down on the inside right of the penalty area. The referee, poor throughout, awarded a free kick.

Prosa, a bustling forward and the league's top scorer, effectively led the line for Infonet. He was 'a top striker' according to Dmitri. Mart was less convinced. 'It does not reflect his skill properly. He scored six goals against Vaprus, a schoolboy team, when Infonet won 11–1.' Prosa would be a curiosity, the only footballer I would watch play for two different teams during my challenge after his future winter transfer to Maltese outfit FC Valletta.

Infonet took the lead when muscular play from Prosa led to a spectacular own goal, with an under-pressure Anderson stretching and lifting the ball over his own goalkeeper. The ensuing injury, to mask the Tammeka defender's huge error, did not convince me or his teammates. The referee then awarded Infonet a penalty for a dubious handball and

Tumasyan scored a retaken spot kick, apparently unheard of in Estonian football. 2–0 Infonet and some sign of redemption.

A man behind the far fence put down his bike to watch more iffy refereeing. Tammeka's striker Jogi fell over theatrically and was awarded a penalty. Kiidron shaped up for a blaster over the Portakabins but steadied his run and side-footed home to make it 2–1.

Fans disappeared to a car park across the road to down shots of vodka at half-time. I overheard Russian voices and waved my beer as some sort of universal introduction. I complained about the generous penalty decisions. 'Estonian referees' was the gruff response. Surprisingly, I was not the only Brit in the crowd. I bumped into Mick, a groundhopper – the men, and it's virtually always men, who travel vast distances to watch matches at different grounds – who had heard about my trip after the *Guardian* article had been discussed on a non-league forum. 'Are you going to the big match tomorrow?' he asked. Levadia were playing Flora, two of the big four. I explained that I would be on my way to Kazakhstan.

Infonet missed a flurry of chances in the second half. The Portakabins may have exploded had they lost their lead, as Tammeka rallied towards the end. But Infonet hacked the ball away desperately and indulged in strategic, time-wasting injuries to hold onto their 2–1 advantage.

There was a pleasingly friendly feel come the end. Many Infonet players, faces showing relief at a narrow win, greeted the crowd. I shook the hand of Kruglov, a left back with more than a hundred caps for Estonia. The ticket woman helpfully arranged a taxi back to the old town as public transport seemed sketchy at 9 p.m. I wandered through the delightful warren of medieval streets and ate an enormous plate of sausages and potatoes. I needed sustenance ahead of what would be my longest single journey to a match.

Infonet stayed in fourth place but it would be their last season in the Meistriliiga as they merged with Tallinn rivals Levadia. Prosa was joint top scorer and left for Valletta in January 2018. Tammeka finished seventh.

8 Kazakhstan

The long horns looked lonely. Blood streamed from the once noble head of a ram, detached from its body in the centre circle. Home players soaked their shirts in the warm blood of this literal sacrificial lamb. It provided them with strength. Each spectacular horn symbolised a long-range volley that would crash into the defeated visiting team's net. The carcass was thrown to one side. Crows picked at the flesh as the game kicked off. It was a medieval scene. This was Kazakhstan.

It wasn't really Kazakhstan. It was Kazakhstan according to an article that the Sports Moldova website published about my travels later in the autumn. I never found out if Moldova – or only this Chişinău journalist – had a particular axe to grind or whether this was merely a rivalry between former Soviet republics. Horns or not, I was excited to leave northern Europe for Central Asia, a whopping 3,500 miles from London and the furthest east of the seven time zones I would visit.

I landed in Almaty, the country's largest city and its capital until 1997, a broken man following two overnight flights from Tallinn, Aeroflot's steely air hostesses having smashed their trolleys into my knee at every opportunity on the Moscow to Almaty leg. I arrived far too early to check into my downtown hotel, walked around in the sapping heat, ordered some breakfast and promptly fell asleep in the café.

Almaty grew on me when I woke up. The south of Kazakhstan felt very different from my home in the south of London. I liked Almaty's sophisticated cafés, stunning mountain backdrop and personable inhabitants. It felt slightly European, a mix of the Eastern bloc and the alpine, but certainly not a footballing hotbed. I spotted a young man wearing a Chelsea shirt in the evocative Green Bazaar. My presumption was that he could be one of the numerous players loaned out by the Stamford Bridge club. We chatted and he treated to me a 10p pot of tea. He was a sound engineer who knew more about music than football.

The Green Bazaar, with its piles of dried fruit, enormous meat section and fragrant local cheeses, was a fascinating slice of Central Asia. But photography was officially prohibited and I had to duck around the enormous structure to avoid the security man assigned to stop interested foreigners. Kazakhstan, despite its vast natural treasures, was not trying very hard to be an accessible tourist destination.

The world's ninth largest country, Kazakhstan has lots of land and a crucial sliver lies in continental Europe. This aided their switch from the Asian Football Confederation to UEFA in 2002, a move that had benefited leading club side Astana more than the national team. It was clear from conversations I had with several people that Kazakhstan also has lots of corruption. The country had been governed by Nursultan Nazarbayev since independence in 1991 and bribes seemed the norm under this authoritarian regime. Allegedly even a school cleaner had to pay a bribe to get the job. This corruption hindered football, as the rich reputedly paid the right people to get the best training whilst the talented poor remained underdeveloped. Boxing was more popular with the masses, with good coaching available for those without the means to influence.

I took the train to Taraz, eight hours west of Almaty. Public transport is very cheap in Kazakhstan, and I could afford second class, a four-berth cabin, where I met Eric, a Kazakh and sporadic Manchester United fan. I asked why. 'Why not?' he responded. I couldn't argue. Eric spoke good English, always qualifying his words with 'or something' at the end. I could instantly tell Eric was going to be more than an anecdote. He was thirtysomething and worked hard in the oil and gas industry in western Kazakhstan, a fortnight straight, and was returning home to Taraz. He looked shattered.

Eric rested as I explored the train. I don't envy those tasked with building trains for the climatic extremes of Central Asia, but no opening windows or air conditioning seemed a strange oversight. I was glad the skies had clouded after forty-degree Almaty, and enjoyed the relative airiness of the virtually empty buffet carriage. I ordered a lemon tea and a samsa, a folded meat pastry, and watched the endless steppe pass, mountains to the south marking the border with Kyrgyzstan and the Asian Football Confederation.

Eric had been away from his wife, herself an ethnic Russian, and their son for nearly three weeks. They were thrilled to see him arrive at Taraz railway station. His first concern was getting a haircut and he invited me along. I was looking even shaggier than Eric. My nervous barber did a reasonable job, well worth the £1.20 that Eric insisted he paid. Eric's second priority was more predictable: eating lots of meat. I was his guest at a steamy shashlik emporium where an enormous platter of horse, pork, lamb and kidneys – each the size of a pear – arrived. This was just my plate. I felt instantly defeated, but did my British best.

Taraz is a modern interpretation of an ancient Silk Road trading post. A horse statue sat in the central square, surrounded by administrative buildings designed to look much older than they were. As Alexandr, a football journalist for sports.kz, explained, the local team shouldn't even have been playing Premier League football. FC Altai, a new club who finished second in the First Division, won promotion by beating FC Taraz, who finished eleventh in the twelve-team Premier League, in a play-off. However, Kazakh rules dictated that a club needed to have existed for three years to play in the Premier League. Altai then played what Alexandr called 'strange games' by declaring themselves the successor of defunct club FC Vostok, who had been founded in 1963. But when they couldn't pay Vostok's debts Altai announced they were no longer Vostok's successors, and therefore not eligible for the Premier League. Taraz retained their place in the Premier League but the timing was awful. Taraz were informed of the decision in February and only had a month to prepare for the new season. 'It was a shock', said a Taraz official.

The following day Eric had one mission – to help me. We visited the local newspaper, where the sports editor was away, and it didn't seem to be anyone else's job to speak to us. We wandered into the deserted Central Stadium: good for photos, less so for football contacts. Eric found out that the club administration was watching a youth game at a nearby training ground. We scooted across. Eric explained who I was and, after a barrage of 'salaam alaikums' and strong handshakes, we had a club onside.

We visited a local market that wasn't going to make *Lonely Planet* any time soon, full of Uzbek vegetables, Chinese goods and a beautiful Kazakhstan national team tracksuit I would have purchased if it cost rather less than the extraordinary £47 quoted. Even Eric couldn't barter down the trader. I bought Eric lamb plov with horsemeat sausage, sweet fruits and yellow peppers in Zarashan, another excellent restaurant, and we then visited the car wash. Eric's other concern was cleaning his car, southern Kazakhstan being a dusty place in the height of summer. We later met Murat, the FC Taraz translator, at the club hotel, a gaudy affair overlooking the training ground. Taraz is a relatively small city of some 400,000 people and Eric knew Murat from his gym.

Murat introduced me to the laid-back Mohammed Diarra, one of the few English-speaking players and part of the Guinea squad at the 2015 Africa Cup of Nations, a tournament I would have attended were it not scandalously relocated to Equatorial Guinea, original hosts Morocco citing concerns about the Ebola virus outbreak in sub-Saharan Africa. Mohammed was a Paris Saint-Germain academy graduate alongside Celtic and former Fulham striker Moussa Dembélé – 'he was very good but surprised at his development' – and had then spent four years at OB Odense in Denmark. He came to Kazakhstan after injury had stalled his Danish career.

Mohammed's story was similar to Bakary's in the Faroes. 'I heard about Kazakhstan from a friend playing at OB Odense who was loaned to Astana. I like to take another challenge but I don't know where. When they say "Kazakhstan", I don't say no, I'm curious. I go to the training camp and the feeling of the coach has been good and they like my profile. I want to start a new feeling.' Diarra had originally agreed to join Altai, and switched to Taraz when Altai were denied promotion to the Premier League.

Taraz only won one of their opening ten fixtures but had since rebounded to seventh. Diarra said that it had been difficult for a set of new players to forge an understanding in the first three months but that things had steadily improved since. I had heard that it was particularly hard to build a team atmosphere in Kazakhstan, as domestic players came from all across this vast, traditionally nomadic country.

Eric was busy the next day – 'boring family stuff or something' – but met me before the game. He was watching his first match in fifteen years with some friends, supporting me and Taraz from the stands. The atmosphere was generated by an eclectic choice of music that ranged from Beyoncé's instructive 'Move Your Body' to Kazakh classics and the most inappropriate use of the Champions League anthem. More than a hundred police officers stood in front of the main stand, hands on chest, as the Kazakh national anthem was belted out. There was no sign of a blood sacrifice.

Diarra had told me not to expect a possession game against 2013 champions Aktobe. And he wasn't kidding. He might have likened his role to Claude Makélélé – 'to win the second ball, to help the defender' – but he barely touched the ball in a first half characterised by deep Aktobe possession and ineffective attacks down the flanks. Taraz's tactics were brutal, with long balls launched broadly in the direction of the willing front two: the strong Ukrainian Feshchuk and lithe Haiti international Maurice, another graduate of the PSG academy.

This was my first really poor goalkeeping display. Mande, Stabæk's goalkeeper in Norway, was certainly at fault for some of Brann's five goals. But his kicking wasn't as woeful as Taraz custodian Babakhanov, whose goal kicks regularly peppered the blistered athletics tracks surrounding the pitch. The pitch was rough and the grass rather long. Alexandr, the football journalist for sports.kz, said, 'The biggest problem in Kazakhstan is the small number of high-quality natural football fields due to difficult weather conditions.' Babakhanov could not really use the surface as an excuse.

A hardcore dozen chanted 'Taraz, Taraz, Taraz' to a lone drumbeat. The crowd were enjoying some highly optimistic long-range shooting. Aktobe's right back blasted wide from distance whilst the Taraz right back responded with an effort from fully thirty yards straight at the Aktobe goalkeeper. Mijušković, his fellow defender, then smashed one over the crossbar from even further out.

The referee controlled the game well, picking out genuine fouls from those Taraz were trying to draw. Alexandr explained that being a Premier League referee is a desirable and highly paid profession by Kazakh standards. The refereeing was certainly far better than in Estonia as Aktobe were penalised for a clear foul and, from the resultant free kick, Mijušković crashed home an unstoppable header to give Taraz the lead. Diarra then showed his Makélélé tendencies by making a crucial block after a left-wing Aktobe raid.

Aktobe dominated the second half. But their equaliser was a mess. Nane, the Cameroonian who patrolled the midfield well, squared for the marauding Valiullin and his left-wing cross was put into his own net – a third own goal in my last five countries – by a sliding Taraz defender. The crowd were livened by the sight of Senegalese striker Mané warming up. The rotund forward was top scorer for the nearly relegated Taraz team last season and had just returned from a spell playing for Inner Mongolia Zhongyou in the Chinese second tier. He was enormous.

Taraz striker Maurice was replaced by Seidakhamet, a seventeen-year-old winger inevitably dubbed 'the Kazakh Messi'. He looked like a frightened teenager running against such uncompromising defenders. There were a few dribbles and darting runs, but he was not quite Kazakh Premier League, let alone Lionel Messi. Diarra, something of a passenger for most of the game, had a good last ten minutes, tackling strongly and holding possession well as the match finished 1–1.

Eric and I sunk a few post-match beers, lamb skewers and cubes of kurt, dried cheese made from sour milk, at another eatery. 'Everyone thinks I'm your translator or something', he explained. Eric was just being hospitable, helping someone who would otherwise have blundered his way around with little Russian, no Kazakh and Google Translate. I shook his hand before leaving in the car he had arranged to take me to Shymkent, Kazakhstan's third largest city. I will never know what my Taraz experience would have been like without Eric, but it would surely not have been as memorable.

There was no reprieve for Taraz this season. They finished second from bottom after their survival bid was hit by a six-point deduction for unpaid debts to Odita, a Nigerian striker who last played for them in 2013. Diarra left Taraz and helped Vendsyssel achieve promotion to the Danish Superliga in 2018. Aktobe ended the season ninth.

9 Russia

Russia was the problem child of my early travels, having moved from a summer to an autumn league in 2012. I applied for my expensive visa before the 2017–18 fixtures were released, and my speculative route through Yekaterinburg and Kazan attracted the attention of the Russian embassy in London. They called with stereotypical suspicion. 'Why are you going to these unusual places?' said a chilling voice. I was honest. I was travelling from Kazakhstan to watch Russian football. This seemed suitably bizarre to satisfy the authorities.

Russia is massive. Everything is large. The roads and buildings, the men and their egos. I was keen to experience a more intimate slice of Russian life, and shunned the bright lights of Moscow and St Petersburg. It transpired that FC Ural of Yekaterinburg and Rubin Kazan, the easiest clubs to visit from Kazakhstan, were both playing away. So instead I watched intriguing matches in Ufa, a sprawling city near the Ural Mountains, and Tula, an industrial hub near Moscow, on consecutive days: Ufa hosted champions Spartak Moscow and Tula Arsenal played newly promoted SKA-Khabarovsk from the Russian Far East. I would also discover that I was not the only football fan completing this unlikely double of Russian Premier League matches.

I flew from the Kazakh capital Astana to Yekaterinburg and, the following day, took a stomach-churning propeller flight to Ufa. 'What is an Englishman doing in Ufa?' asked a Moscow-based teacher on the airport bus. I explained and asked if she knew any football fans. 'In Moscow, yes, but not in Ufa. This is a hockey town.' It also seemed something of a ghost town. Ufa is Russia's eleventh largest city but not many of the million inhabitants were to be seen on a bright Saturday afternoon. I doubted they had all gone to the seaside. I walked into Highlander, a strange Scottish-themed pub, where two burly barmen in kilts declared that 'football was fucking shit' before serving me a pint of local craft beer. They were fans of Ufa's successful ice hockey team, national champions in 2009 and 2010.

Ufa was founded on a dramatic bluff overlooking the languid Belaya River. It has a compact centre, where traditional wooden houses fill the wide gaps between modern buildings, yet is incredibly spread out, even by Russian standards. I visited the obligatory horse statue and the regional museum, chatting to two Spartak supporters as I waited for it to open. Nikita and his father were from Tula, over 700 miles west of Ufa, and season ticket holders at both Spartak Moscow and Tula Arsenal. It was an incredible coincidence. We were probably the only three football fans who would watch these two matches, and we had met at the unheralded National Museum of The Republic of Bashkortostan. We agreed to meet in Tula the following day.

I took a minibus towards the Neftyanik Stadium, ten miles north of the city centre. This was the equivalent of travelling from Trafalgar

Square to beyond Croydon. The endless concrete apartment blocks sent me into some sort of torpor. And I missed the stadium. Fortunately there are millions of buses in Russia, all of them cheap and clearly numbered. I took the same bus back and found the stadium, swarming with red-clad Spartak Moscow fans. Spartak are the Manchester United of Russia with fans spread across the country. It will take post-Ferguson United some doing to beat Spartak's sixteen fallow years, which instigated much mockery from Russian rivals, until their surprise title win in 2017.

A DJ blasted summer beats as Spartak fans congregated outside the organised ticket office. 'Since 2011', Ufa scarves unnecessarily advertised. Ufa were formed from the convenient embers of regional teams and financed to top-flight stability. This was their third season in the Russian Premier League and this would have been many Spartak fans' first visit to the ground. I explored the adjacent park where children clambered on tanks and military paraphernalia. And the big guns certainly were in Ufa on this hot Sunday afternoon.

This was a big game in a small football town. Two diminutive memorabilia tents were swamped, unused to such attention. I tried to buy a programme. The vendor spoke worse English than my limited Russian. I passed over a few notes that seemed to please her more than they should. As for the stadium itself, the Neftyanik was a low-slung affair with a blue running track separating the stands from the pitch. The booming voice of the announcer gave the contest an almost gladiatorial feel, emphasised by the mock Roman pillars at the northern end of the stadium.

The atmosphere was bizarre. Spartak fans were in every stand. The home fans, barely roused by a soft-rock Ufa anthem that has yet to go platinum, were indifferent. Nikita said he was saddened that Ufa had not sold out a home match against the champions. Spartak chants echoed as the teams lined up for a trio of anthems: first the Spartak song, loudly echoed across many parts of the ground, then the Russian national anthem and finally the state anthem of Bashkortostan as Ufa's youthful hardcore waved the state flag. A Spartak fan leapt over the barriers and was comically felled by a laconic steward. The intruder beat the ground in mock frustration.

A pleasing number of local couples attended 'Spartak day', some returning to their seats ten minutes into the second half as casual fans do. They watched the first goalless draw of my travels, as Ufa goal-keeper Belenov, once on the fringes of the Russia squad, made several great saves from Spartak's Cape Verde international Zé Luís. The home fans seemed impassive towards the action. This was like going to the theatre for them. I was hoping for more passion in Tula.

Ufa to Tula took ten hours by taxi, plane, train, Moscow metro and another train. It was long, tiring and linguistically challenging, the nadir being an attempt to buy a train ticket from Moscow to Tula, a simple transaction for the two-hour journey south. A helpful Ukrainian trans-lated and it emerged the sales person was confused why I did not want to take the cheaper, later train. I had a match to get to in Tula and an appointment with Nikita.

Nikita welcomed me at Tula railway station in his striking orange car. Russian cars are normally black. I could tell Nikita, who was twenty years old, but looked and acted older, liked to be different. He spoke Russian into his phone when he forgot an English word – politely stating 'one moment please' – and was frustrated when his phone responded with the answer. 'Spring', said the phone. 'I knew that!' said Nikita.

We drove to a cheap buffet restaurant attached to a massive super-market. Nikita was easy to speak to. His father was born in Kazan and studied in Moscow, watching football at all five teams in the capital before settling on Spartak. Spartak are Russia's most popular team, following 'Spartak time', a sustained period of success in the 1990s. Nikita wore a cute Spartak T-shirt covered with pigs. I had noticed the pig references in the Spartak crowd at Ufa. Spartak were founded in 1922 and supported by workers of the Moscow meat-processing plant, history still referenced in the chant, 'Who are we? We are meat, meat, meat!' I was enjoying a colourful salad known as 'herring under a fur coat' as Nikita chatted away.

Tula, an industrial centre with a fine revamped kremlin, was famous for its armaments and biscuit factory, reflected in the military-style badge and club nicknames of 'artillerymen' and 'ginger cakes'. Tula had played in the lower divisions until their first promotion to the Premier League in 2014. I asked Nikita what he did when Tula played Spartak, a clash between his £75 Tula season ticket, roughly the cost of one ticket to watch the other Arsenal, and substantially more expensive Spartak membership. 'I love Spartak but I also support Tula. I was born in this city and football being here is great. I enjoy that all the teams come to Tula and I can see these games live.'

Nikita might have more cause than most to own a half-and-half scarf. But he was really a Spartak fan. Tula hosted Spartak in the last match of the 2016–17 season. Spartak were champions and 'already on holiday'. Tula needed points to avoid relegation and won 3–0. Nikita still supported Spartak. 'I came out of the stadium upset but in my heart it is a good result for Tula.'

Nikita was definitely different. He loved all levels of football even though his friends were only interested in the elite game. Nikita preferred club to international football, citing more tactical play and greater scope for a coach to change a team using the transfer market. He watched Spartak away, thinking nothing of driving to St Petersburg or Krasnodar. (Nikita rated the Krasnodar Stadium, with its unique 360-degree video screen which wraps around the top of each stand, as having the best atmosphere, but the city, along with Yaroslavl, was disregarded as a World Cup host.) And his dream was to watch Spartak play away in the Champions League, 'maybe Sevilla'. His father had always wanted to visit Seville.

I am virtually never late for matches. But Nikita had to wait for his father, who was delayed, and this was the only match where I missed kick-off. The setting sun silhouetted cameramen perched precariously on the west stand. A gorgeous Turner palette of fiery horizontal streaks backed the action. 'Red and yellow', chanted the Tula faithful in the east stand repeatedly, creating an impressive atmosphere for a match against SKA Khabarovsk, a team with few fans, no rivalry and, according to Nikita, little hope. 'Let's go Tula, we're with you' followed. Tula were renowned for their noisy, die-hard support, regardless of whether their team played in the Premier League or First Division.

This was SKA Khabarovsk's first ever away match in the Premier League, 4,000 miles and seven time zones west of their home city. Russian fans mocked their isolation. 'We say that as soon as they get back from one away game they have to start their journey for the next', quipped Nikita. Khabarovsk is six days from Tula by train. The twenty-three away supporters were more likely to be based in Moscow. I wondered what impact playing a match at 2.30 a.m., Khabarovsk time, would have on their players.

Tkachev, the bright right-sided Tula attacker on loan from CSKA Moscow, hit a thirty-yard free kick with more power than precision after eighteen minutes. The Khabarovsk goalkeeper Dovbnya got his body behind the shot but the ball squirmed into the corner. Khabarovsk, who had struggled to attract many new players to the Russian Far East, looked shell-shocked and could have conceded again.

Dovbnya made another error, passing the ball straight to Rasik, Tula's lumbering Argentinian forward, who blasted it straight at the recovering goalkeeper. The Tula fans howled. It should have been 2–0. A half-time draw was announced for programme purchasers and a Rasik shirt was one of the prizes. 'I'll give it back', said one terrace wag. Rasik was replaced by Đorđević, a young striker on loan from Zenit. 'He's faster than Rasik', said Nikita. 'I'm faster than Rasik', I joked.

I was introduced to a few people. One, with very 1970s curly dark hair and wild eyes, couldn't believe I was English. 'He wants you to say a few words in English', encouraged Nikita. This wasn't difficult and I passed him a Russian version of my business card. He seemed very pleased. 'I can't speak English', he explained through Nikita, 'I can barely speak Russian!' He wandered out of the ground with fifteen minutes to go, happily waving his flag. Nikita explained that the 'intelligent' fans, the quieter set, sat in the west stand. He probably didn't mean to use that word but I could see where he was coming from. It was unpretentious and fun in the east stand, a fact highlighted when the second half started with a song about the streets of Tula, the crowd raucously shouting 'Arsenalskaya', Arsenal Street.

Tula played a defensive game, a familiar Russian tactic, and Khabarovsk enjoyed more of the ball in the second half. It was a dangerous game at 1–0 but Tula were rightly confident that Khabarovsk, where it was now 4 a.m., would remain comatose in attack. 'One day we will be as famous as the London Arsenal', sang the Tula fans as they secured a first win of the season. I doubted this would ever be true but the east stand will still be supporting their team, twirling their red and yellow scarves, regardless of fame or stature.

Ufa edged out Tula Arsenal for sixth place and qualified for Europe for the first time. Khabarovsk only picked up three draws from their fifteen long away matches and were relegated. Spartak finished third. Nikita was fortunate to realise his dream of watching Spartak play at Sevilla in the Champions League after he and hundreds of other Russians were sold fake tickets by touts.

10 Belarus

I was making all my own decisions on this trip. They weren't necessarily the right ones, but they were mine. I was keen to experience more of Belarus than the capital Minsk and had chosen mid-table Vitebsk against twelfth-placed Krumkachy as my match. It didn't look a cracker on paper. BATE Borisov, winners of the previous eleven Belarusian titles, read about my journey in the *Guardian* and tried to persuade me to visit them instead. I would be their special guest at the best stadium in Belarus. I politely declined. I was definitely visiting Vitebsk, the country's fourth largest city, and its understated football team.

'I'm on the nightrain. I can never get enough. I'm on the nightrain. Never to return.' I met John on the night train to Belarus. He used to be a defender for Vitebsk's second team. He had kind eyes and I felt safe with him in my four-berth compartment as we trundled out of Moscow. I was ready to crash and burn after another baking day. I never found out if he was a fan of the Guns N' Roses classic I hummed.

John bought me a green tea. Our conversation flowed better with pauses that gave time to phrase something for someone who spoke English as a second language. I asked about the difference between Russians and Belarusians. 'Very little', said John. He was born when both countries were part of the USSR. He worked in Russia and lived in Belarus. It was all one country to him. I woke up shortly before Vitebsk came into view, a startling red sky hinting at another fine day. John wouldn't take any money when our taxi dropped me off at my hotel. I was on a run of unexpected encounters that were enlivening my travels.

Belarus took a battering during the Second World War, losing around a quarter of its pre-war population, the highest proportion of any modern-day country. Vitebsk had been flattened. The buildings had been rebuilt yet the attractive riverside setting was the same. I visited the home of Marc Chagall, the city's most famous son, and went to a downtown restaurant for a pre-match meal. The menu was in Russian and nobody spoke English. I pointed at something and ended up with a chicken escalope covered with microwave-blasted cheese. It was just about edible.

I had been travelling in the blazing summer heat for three weeks. I was relieved that the skies had finally greyed, as I ambled towards the stadium between Soviet-style apartment blocks and encountered two bulls and a herd of grazing sheep. This was hardly Wembley Way. I was frisked by some terrifying police and wondered if I would ever meet anyone in Vitebsk. I was finding that, trains aside, the best way of meeting people was turning up *really* early. A group of tough-looking guys with sharply shaven heads somehow picked up that I wasn't a local when I donned some ridiculous Vitebsk headgear for the club photographer, and, rarely for Belarusians, they spoke some English.

Yury was from the Section 8 hardcore group. He had completed a 'golden season' in their 2014 promotion year – every game, home and away – and received a T-shirt from the club for his efforts. Yury's friend Oleg had hoped to complete his own 'golden season' with Vitebsk this year, but his plans had been crushed after Vitebsk scored a late winner at home to BATE in May. The Vitebsk team had run across to celebrate with the Section 8 fans who had piled down the concrete terracing. A supporting wall had collapsed and dozens of fans crashed several metres to the hard ground below, injuring seven or eight supporters. Oleg broke both his arms.

I was standing in that very same area now, two months later. Yury and I walked through an impossibly complex web of corridors underneath the only stand and entered Section 8 through a cracked concrete staircase. I fired off some harmless shots to prove my camera was nothing more sinister to an edgy policeman clearly not used to seeing a foreign photographer in Section 8.

Yury, the orchestrator, and his hundred-strong Section 8 hardcore were quiet as a highly entertaining match kicked off. Away side Krumkachy Minsk took the lead after only two minutes when Filanovich latched onto a long ball straight down the middle and the striker steered it over the advancing Guschenko. It was the sort of goal that Shane Long used to score. Yury and the drummer at the front of Section 8 weren't even watching when Vitebsk equalised: a loose ball in the Krumkachy penalty area fell to Kozlov, who slotted past goalkeeper Kostyukevich. A corner was then headed in at the near post by striker Vergeychik. Vitebsk had come from behind to lead 2–1 after just eleven minutes.

The small away support from Minsk had little to cheer. But Krumkachy had been causing waves in Belarusian football since a group of football enthusiasts from the popular internet forum Pressball, led by chairman Denis Shunto, founded the club in 2011. Krumkachy had become the hipster club of Belarus. They played in all black, were nicknamed 'the ravens', and their 'aggressive media campaign', according to English-language *Belarus Digest*, had attracted tech sponsors. This was very unlike the typical system of clubs being backed by state-owned companies. Yury and others were critical: 'Some things are fashionable; some things are forever', they chanted at the 'internet team'. Vitebsk were more traditional, and organised an annual work day where supporters could choose to donate one day's salary to their club.

Section 8 looked fearsome with their stoic faces and 'White Boy Vitebsk' T-shirts that drew on Vitebsk's blue and white colours. Vitebsk, with seven names since their foundation as Krasnoye Znamya Vitebsk, 'Red Flag Vitebsk', in 1960, had changed their colours to blue a decade ago. 'Red and black is in my heart', said Yury. The Section 8 drummer was clearly enjoying himself and added rock-style fill-ins to liven up his percussive beat. I spent half-time taking photos of his drum before Yury introduced me to his girlfriend over FaceTime as she cooked their dinner in a modern-looking kitchen. This was a brilliant encounter that would soon get far more bizarre.

Krumkachy started the second half brightly, dominating midfield possession after switching from a back four to the wing-back system widespread in former Soviet lands. Vitebsk had struggled against the lesser teams like Krumkachy yet no one could have predicted that a long punt out of goalkeeper Kostyukevich's hands would lead to a Krumkachy equaliser. The ball took a skiddy bounce off the turf on the edge of the area and soared over Guschenko. The Vitebsk goalkeeper vainly tried to get back but both he and the ball ended up in the corner of the goal. Krumkachy's players raced towards Kostyukevich in celebration. The twenty-seven-year-old had been forced to retire from football in 2009 due to ill health after a promising youth career. He only started playing again in 2015 and was now Krumkachy's second-choice goalkeeper and club videographer.

This was quite ridiculous. The only previous time I had seen a goalkeeper score was when Tony Lange converted Fulham's third penalty in a shoot-out victory at the Goldstone Ground after a goalless FA Cup second round replay against Brighton in December 1995. Kostyukevich had bettered that in front of around 600 fans and several rows of army personnel. And from the edge of his own area.

There was little criticism from Section 8 of their poorly positioned goalkeeper. Guschenko, one of Vitebsk's best players, was popular, and had visited Oleg in hospital several times after the wall collapse. The second-half goalkeeping drama didn't stop. Vitebsk's substitute Skurin latched onto a through ball and took the ball around the onrushing Kostyukevich, who hauled him down. Kostyukevich played the injured hero, writhing on the ground, but it was a clear red card. The visiting goalkeeper had scored from his own penalty area and been sent off twenty minutes later.

Krumkachy brought on their third-choice goalkeeper. Anton Shunto, the chairman's brother, who had started one game in the previous two seasons, didn't even look like a football player. He just about parried the resulting free kick wide. Three successive goal kicks skewed horribly out of play. Shunto flapped at several crosses and argued with the referee to deflect attention away from his ineptitude. He then made an unintentional late save when his head blocked a goal-bound shot.

Krumkachy celebrated an unlikely 2–2 draw with a slow, Iceland-style clap in front of their fans. Guschenko threw his unlucky gloves into the stand. Yury stuffed banners and flags into a car boot before leaving for dinner at home. I sat next to Anton, Yury's friend, in a big black car with heavily tinted windows. It felt very Belarusian to be driving down the roads of Vitebsk with Yury's friends and 'Personal Jesus' blaring out of the stereo. I arrived with cows, I left with Depeche Mode.

I asked Anton whether he knew about Fulham. 'Yes, that's the team that just transferred their French player to Marseille.' I thought it unlikely his memory would go back to Steve Marlet and 2003. The name of that player came to him. 'Payet, Dmitri Payet.' 'That's West Ham', I corrected. 'Oh, there's a lot of ham in London!' We drove to Vogel, a pub that overlooked one of the largest squares in Europe if you ingeniously included the part sectioned off by the main road. We chewed over the match with draniki: stuffed hash browns with richly flavoured mushrooms and ham. There was also a lot of ham in Belarus.

Anton, a professional gambler with a playing card tattoo on his arm, had mixed emotions about the result. He normally only bet on volleyball, basketball and handball but had won £350 by putting money on Vitebsk to score two or more goals. Anton knew that four of Krumkachy's best players, including their first-choice goalkeeper, had gone on strike after not being paid. He was happy after eleven minutes, less so after the second half. His optimistic aspiration was for Vitebsk to finish third or fourth to secure a place in Europe.

Anton was the world's slowest eater. I had never seen anyone take so long to eat a plate of shashlik. Or indeed anything. It must have been stone cold when he finally finished it an hour later. I wondered if this was the eating habit of a hardened gambler, unable to concentrate on something that was not going to win or lose him any money. We walked back to the centre with takeaway kebabs. Anton hadn't finished his when I wished him and Vitebsk goodbye.

I took another cheap train to Minsk, four hours to the south-west, and one of the cities I was most looking forward to visiting. A young waitress asked me to describe the Belarusian capital in three words. I chose 'green', 'classical' and 'clean'. It was incredibly clean; I saw only one piece of litter blowing away and felt like chasing after it like a demented labrador to put it in the bin. It was the most Soviet of cities, the centre brimming with brutalist creations – concrete monstrosities that seemed more innocent in the burning sky of high summer – and the most beautiful of opera houses. It was also orderly: so law-abiding that jaywalking on even a small, empty street is frowned upon. I transgressed, frustrated by the long waits at traffic lights that gave pedestrians seven seconds to scuttle across the road.

Dinamo Minsk were also playing at home, a temporary one until their Dinamo Stadium had been renovated for the 2019 European Games. I took the spectacular metro, all soaring torches and marble, to the dishevelled Traktor Stadium in southern Minsk. The atmosphere was sombre despite forlorn attempts to dress up concrete girders with blue and white banners and pictures of old heroes. Six cheerleaders waved Dinamo flags nearly in time to 'Enter Sandman' by Metallica.

I sat next to Peter, an ice hockey fan from Polotsk, close to Vitebsk in northern Belarus, who was watching his first ever football match. Peter was frustrated: the atmosphere was poor and the quality was low. Belarus was clearly struggling to make matches attractive. Several hundred people, some sitting down with a picnic under the trees, watched for free from the forested hill behind the far stand. Dinamo benefited from a dubious red card and penalty double and more dreadful goalkeeping to beat Dnepr Mogilev 2–1. Peter sloped away. 'This is my first and last football game in Belarus', he said, as 'The Final Countdown' boomed at the final whistle.

I returned to the Planeta, my gargantuan hotel with a space age theme. It was built in 1980 with the feel of the decade before. My beige and gold room was as retro as my football experience in Minsk, but whilst I quite enjoyed the old Soviet lines of the stadiums, I felt Belarusian football needed to make itself more appealing to fans. Sixteen top-division teams, the same number as in Russia where the population is fifteen times greater, felt too many, even with Krumkachy adding an unorthodox edge.

The Planeta offered a disastrous breakfast that included chicken and potatoes left over from the dinner service. I overheard a British boxing team toying with some old and very cold food. They were the first native English voices I had heard since Tallinn, over three weeks earlier. My most easterly journey was over.

Dinamo finished second, level on points with BATE Borisov, who won a twelfth consecutive title on goal difference after securing the draw they needed with a dramatic ninety-fifth-minute equaliser in their final match. Vitebsk were seventh, Dnepr twelfth and Krumkachy thirteenth. Krumkachy were relegated to the third tier after failing to clear player debts and changed their name to NFK Minsk in early 2019.

Contacting the clubs

I'm not Jonathan Wilson. I was not blessed with a vast array of football contacts across the continent. I actually didn't have a single one before this trip, aside from the usual football mates that everyone has in England. My travels were a balance of organisation and spontaneity. Some of my best experiences were random meetings with football people like the Brann Bergen fans or locals like Eric in Kazakhstan. But I didn't know how frequently this would happen. And it was hard work at my Georgian match finding anyone who spoke English. Fortunately, Nika was a true football enthusiast who wanted to help after the Georgian Football Federation responded to my speculative Facebook message.

Before these travels I had never used Facebook. I didn't look at Twitter and thought Instagram was only for food photos. I took social media advice from younger friends and signed up to the modern era. It was a good idea: different clubs were contactable over different channels. And fans as well. Tom, an Exeter City exile based in Malta, sent me a message over Twitter offering to buy me a match ticket and a beer. And I took him up on his pledge when I visited the following February.

I contacted virtually every club on my schedule before I visited. Some, like BATE, even got in touch with me. I started to receive responses to my cold calls, especially from mid-sized clubs, such as Häcken, who had more infrastructure than some, less stardust than others. The *Guardian* article became useful ammunition: every football club knew the newspaper and it gave me credibility. I handed out business cards, an important transaction, especially in eastern lands where they fawned over the quality of my English card. I sometimes listened to club propaganda and details about finances that I instantly knew would never make this book. But I was happy to sit and sift through it all as I received genuine insight from people who really knew their football. I also wasn't going to turn down free tickets, trophy room tours and cups of coffee. This was a self-funded expedition, after all.

It didn't work everywhere. I translated messages into Russian for clubs and didn't receive one reply. I even met, by chance, the Vitebsk administrator who had read my message. He just shrugged his shoulders. Perhaps it wasn't his job, maybe he didn't know what to do with it. I sent messages to all three first-division clubs I visited in Cyprus, and even telephoned one, all to radio silence. Clarity of response was a fair barometer of how organised the club was: confusing conversations with officials at Istra 1961 in Croatia and FK Sarajevo in Bosnia-Herzegovina were unsurprising given their off-pitch challenges, whilst all three Slovenian clubs I visited were wonderfully polite and helpful. My mission was too obscure for some: Brann Bergen and Borussia Mönchengladbach thought I was merely asking for permission to take my camera into the stadium (which the German club denied, but I smuggled my DSLR in regardless).

I didn't have time to harass clubs when they blanked me. Anyhow, it offered variety. I spoke to clubs in some countries, fans in others, journalists in many. I watched from press boxes on the halfway line, or surrounded by drum-beating ultras. It was never my ambition to watch every match from behind the goal with the hardcore. My photographs would be almost identical and I would be deaf in both ears.

BEER STICKS AND LIONS

11 Lithuania

The modern train from Minsk to Lithuania felt like a return to Western Europe. I wasn't even supposed to visit Vilnius. I should have been off the beaten track, by Lithuanian standards, watching Jonava host Trakai in a town better known for its fertiliser factory than its football club. But the match was rescheduled after Trakai unexpectedly beat St Johnstone and IFK Gothenburg to reach the third qualifying round of the Europa League. I quickly changed my plans to watch champions Žalgiris, arguably the best supported club in the Baltics.

I climbed Gediminas's tower, the highest point of the Vilnius castle complex, which was founded as a wooden structure in the fourteenth century. I had last visited Lithuania in 2006 on a random week-long holiday after spotting silly-priced flights to the second city of Kaunas. The old town panorama of red roofs was more pristine now. And I had not been attuned to the stadium views then. This time round, I picked out the old Žalgiris Stadium and the LFF Stadium.

The old Žalgiris Stadium was slowly being deconstructed to make room for apartment blocks to the north yet still oozed character, the terraces full of weeds, and two old floodlights and a scoreboard battling vainly for survival. Žalgiris now played in the LFF Stadium, visible to the south, owned by the Lithuanian Football Federation. It was not their real home. Vėtra, who lost 3–0 home and away to Fulham in the 2009 Europa League qualifiers before going bankrupt and folding the following summer, used to play at the LFF when it was known as the Vėtra Stadium.

The national team also played at the LFF. 'It's a shame that Switzerland and England players come to the stadium with 5,000 seats', said Karol, Žalgiris's lanky press officer. The 'new' national stadium, an abandoned site in the north of Vilnius, had become a painful symbol of mismanagement for Lithuanians. Building work began in 1987 and ceased when the Soviet Union collapsed. 'It restarted five or six years ago and has stopped again. I hope that my children will see the stadium but I and others are not so optimistic.' Žalgiris would have to play in Białystok, 150 miles away in neighbouring Poland, if they qualified for the group phases of European competition.

The golden era for Žalgiris was when they finished third in the Soviet top division in 1987, yet it was debatable whether this was even the same club. Žalgiris went bust in 2009 when Vadim Kastujev, their Russian owner, was arrested in Moscow, after which a phoenix club was set up with help of the Pietų IV supporters' group. The new Žalgiris started in the second division and paid for the privilege of taking over the original club's trophies and history. Karol pointed out that in countries such as Romania reformed clubs start in the bottom league.

I enjoyed the gentle stroll from the old town to the LFF Stadium rather than making an epic journey on public transport. Karol was right when he said I would have preferred to visit industrial Jonava, watching A Lyga football in their low-key Central Stadium, surrounded by a park and a hospital. I had even booked a strange hotel in Jonava for 2 euros per night. But this was the nature of my challenge. Things changed and I moved elsewhere. And I was content to be back in Vilnius, a pleasant city that sees fewer visitors than fellow Baltic capitals Tallinn and Riga.

The LFF Stadium offered cold beer, kvass (a low-alcohol beverage made from rye bread) and beer sticks, delicious charred rye bread fried in garlic and sesame seeds, whilst the DJ aired more renditions of 'The Final Countdown' than you could shake a beer stick at. The police were relaxed, leaning on the barriers overlooking the brightly coloured seats, a pleasant contrast to their stern presence in Russia and Belarus. The only problem was getting in. I looked around like a lion scanning the savannah. There was nowhere that looked remotely likely. A security guard eventually pointed me towards a parked Audi where a woman with a laptop, banknote scanner and printer swiftly sold me a ticket without leaving her seat.

Lithuanian matches are switched to indoor pitches when the weather is inclement at the beginning and end of a season that starts in March and finishes in November. This was not a problem on a beautiful Wednesday evening in early August. There were quite a lot of women in attendance, some accompanying their male partners, others attending with their female friends, as smartly dressed as if they were going to the theatre. The crowd of 700 was lower than Karol had predicted. Some spectators didn't like midweek kick-offs, others didn't like using up their weekend afternoons. The club couldn't win. It struck me that you were not a particularly ardent fan if you complained about scheduling in Lithuania. I doubted many fans had travelled the vast distances I had heard about in Russia and regularly witnessed in England.

Utenis Utena, the away side, were creating headlines. They had recently fielded a starting line-up without a single Lithuanian player. David Campaña, their Spanish coach since May, had brought in nearly twenty new players. There was debate about whether Utenis's fans would boycott. 'Some people feel that they would not cheer for a foreigner-based team', said Karol. But 1,100 had watched them play Atlantas at home in July, a record for the club. The curiosity factor was winning for now.

Utenis started another entirely foreign team against Žalgiris: eight Spaniards, a Frenchman, one Moroccan and a Colombian with a haircut straight out of their 1994 World Cup squad. I was excited when a Žalgiris official approached me as I swatted wasps away from my beer. He invited me, another foreigner with dubious football skills, onto the hallowed artificial pitch at half-time to take part in Top Corner, a competition to kick a ball through holes in a sheet that covered a goal on the sidelines. He clearly had not watched the footage from the Faroes.

The game had a pace that had been lacking from recent matches. Žalgiris took the lead when a shot from Togo-born winger Nyuiadzi was pushed by the Utenis goalkeeper into the path of Elivelto, the watchable Brazilian, who guided his header home. Utenis were being overwhelmed by the home side's sharper movement and minds. It was little surprise when Žalgiris striker Šernas, nicknamed 'the pitbull', finished off a sweeping move to make it 2–0. A trio of Žalgiris fans released a green flare, the first fireworks of my travels, as Lithuanian beer, Latin flair and Baltic sunshine mixed in a heady atmosphere. A

Žalgiris long throw was then flicked on by an Utenis defender and Nyuiadzi headed in at the far post, putting the hosts into a slightly flattering 3–0 lead at half-time.

I waited in vain by the corner flag for my Top Corner call-up. A long, thin inflatable footballer that looked more like Peter Crouch than me wavered in the wind, while Spanish and Brazilian fans ended up taking my place as token foreigners. Instead, I spoke to some Vilnius-based Spaniards who had been lured to the game by the Iberian influence at Utenis. They were unsurprised at the score as Utenis were a new team with some talent, but maybe a little callow for a game against the champions. Žalgiris showed their superior class in the second half. Lithuania international Šernas scored a fourth from a classic counter-attack and spurned chances for my first hat-trick before being substituted. Atajić, his replacement, completed the rout. 'Song 2' by Blur was aired for the fifth and final time.

It was a more competitive match than the 5–0 scoreline suggested. The atmosphere had been friendly and Karol said there was not much rivalry between teams. He supported every Lithuanian team that was in European competition, as performances affected the country's European ranking and therefore the number and seeding of teams that played in Europe. I couldn't imagine this in every country. Karol was confident that Žalgiris would win their fifth consecutive title. 'There are five or six players from national team. Salaries better, we can afford better foreigners. You have to be objective. It wouldn't be normal if Žalgiris didn't win.'

Just like Krumkachy in Vitebsk, Žalgiris celebrated with a slow Iceland-style handclap in front of the thirty-strong hardcore support. The crowd quickly evaporated and when I reached the Gates of Dawn, the southern boundary of the old town, there was little evidence a top-division football match had taken place just moments ago.

Žalgiris finished in second, four points behind champions Sūduva, and Utenis were sixth. Karol's other prediction came off. 'I know Fulham are in the Championship, but I think the supporters next year will support a team in the Premier League.'

12 Latvia

My Latvian match should have been Babīte against Liepāja in the pleasingly named village of Piņķi. But Babīte were thrown out of the Virslīga for suspected match fixing in late June, a fact I only found out after routinely rechecking kick-off times before I left on these long summer travels in early July.

I read the Latvian Football Federation's report with interest. Six Babīte matches had attracted unusual betting activity, including a meeting with Lithuanians Sūduva in the Winter Cup – a friendly tournament involving teams from Estonia, Latvia and Lithuania. This low-key match attracted suspicious wagers that there would be four goals and Babīte would lose the first half 2–0. Babīte lost 3–1 to Sūduva after being 2–0 down at half-time. The *Baltic Times* reported how, when Sūduva attacked to score the first goal, 'one Babīte player is busy tying his shoelaces' while two Babīte defenders 'make errors that are very hard to explain.' For the second successive Baltic nation, I was forced to switch my attention to the reigning champions, Spartaks Jūrmala.

Riga immediately felt grittier, more urbane, than the other Baltic capitals when I arrived on the bus from Vilnius. The grit was visible. Riga's drainage system was being replaced in the balmier summer months. Old drains were noisily deposited on the wasteland behind my apartment block and sandy channels were whipped by the wind. Riga has a cooler vibe than Vilnius or Tallinn and houses an amazing treasure trove of art nouveau architecture. The streets were a feast for my eyes, even if they were bleary from the sandstorms.

I scuttled on the suburban train to Jūrmala, a seaside resort popular in Soviet times and with enduring appeal nowadays. The train was painfully slow and painful, with plastic seats moulded to fit only a small portion of its passengers' bottoms. I couldn't imagine many people enjoying their fifteen-mile commutes to Riga.

The area around the Slokas Stadium was neither beach haven nor country retreat, with ugly Soviet-era buildings clashing with the deep forested backdrop. I waited for someone to arrive at a fold-up table, similar to my Estonian experience, and paid 2.50 euros to enter the stadium's only stand. There was nothing to do other than ponder which row of seats to commandeer. Nothing was on sale, not a beer, a bottle of water, chocolate bar or cheap memento. This was something of a theme in former Soviet states.

I was pleased when Sergey from today's opponents, FC Riga, found me asleep in my seat. FC Riga were brash and rich and not to everyone's tastes. Karol had expressed his concern in Lithuania. 'Riga make some strange moves not known in the Baltics. They make live messages on Facebook when they are at the airport or in a training camp.' Riga has a large ethnic Russian population and FC Riga often communicated in Russian. 'If I spoke in Russian it would be a big, big scandal', said Karol.

97

FC Riga were formed in 2015 after a merger of two clubs: Caramba Riga and Dinamo Riga. There was concern that their mysterious owner ('He is Russian but lives everywhere') might disappear, something Sergey was keen to diffuse. FC Riga were certainly ambitious, trying to sign players from major European leagues and wanting Ronaldinho to play a match in Latvia for children's charities.

FC Riga were trying to do something different with their marketing. They were the first Latvian club with an online shop, and had a striking club badge with a lion, the emblem of Riga, as well as roaming lion mascots that gave out gifts to children. The club even had a motto – 'football in families, families in stadiums' – to encourage attendance at live matches. FC Riga were also the only team in the Baltics to put together an original promotional video for every game. Sergey showed me the promo for their match against Liepāja, a team with a Georgian coach, Tamaz Pertia. Two giant FC Riga lions discussed cooking Georgian meat on a barbecue in a park. Georgian background music gave the video a faintly fantastical feel.

Spartaks Jūrmala's small hardcore arrived as we were talking and asked us to sit elsewhere. This was their spot. It felt rather ridiculous given the swathes of empty seats, most of which remained unfilled as the match kicked off. Spartaks were clearly the more accomplished team, holding the ball better and attacking directly down the wings. There was little evidence of the 'ground ball' promised by Sergey as passing exchanges between the FC Riga back four normally ended with Gorkšs, the former Queens Park Rangers and Reading stopper, launching a speculative ball forward. Spartaks took the lead when the dangerous Kozlov found space on the left wing and Kazačoks drilled his cut back past the FC Riga goalkeeper.

A small gathering of fans watched the match through the fence that surrounded the stadium. It was hardly worth coming in for the non-existent matchday entertainment, and the fence fans hid in their cars at half-time. 'Ice hockey and basketball are more popular than football. A lot of people like football but they don't go to the stadium because they think Latvian football is shit', said Sergey. 'Our football looks like shit because television shows football on two cheap cameras. If you film Fulham v Manchester City on this camera it looks shit.' He had a point, despite his strange choice of exemplar match. And the lack of anything to do or buy couldn't help either.

Spartaks played intelligently on the counter-attack after the interval. Kozlov was involved in the second goal, scored by Ukrainian midfielder Gabelok from twenty yards. Spartaks had the game won and Kozlov brought out some showboating flicks. This was a comfortable 2–0 victory. One of the fence fans started yet another Iceland-style handclap that wasn't, and didn't deserve to be, replicated. Spartaks had played like champions. According to Sergey, FC Riga had the best team in Latvia on paper. Fortunately, football isn't played on paper.

This was the end to my curious time in the Baltics. I was forced to change two of my original fixtures and visit Vilnius, a city that I would otherwise have skipped. I paid 12.50 euros to watch ten goals, a reasonable return. But only a thousand or so people had watched my three matches: the Estonian game of two dubious penalties, a dodgy referee and an own goal, Lithuanians Žalgiris swatting away the Spaniards of Utenis, and this slightly underwhelming contest in Latvia.

In 1989 the Baltic nations formed a 400-mile human chain, from Vilnius to Tallinn, of some two million people to peacefully protest against Soviet occupation. And their football leagues soon became symbols of newly gained independence. But I wondered if the lustre was waning. I could envisage some leagues, especially those in the Baltics where there were fewer political challenges than elsewhere in Eastern Europe and the Caucasus, merging for greater competitiveness, interest and financial stability. My challenge may not even be repeatable in the near future.

I had travelled long and hard on the hot summer road. I experienced the mass media outbreak in Finland, an endless array of forgettable hotels and an unbelievable match in Belarus. I was pleased to be returning home for a rest. And an interlude of familiar football across the Irish Sea.

Spartaks won the Latvian championship by nine points. FC Riga finished third. Ronaldinho was pictured with a Riga shirt, but didn't look likely to come out of retirement any time soon.

OVER THE IRISH SEA

13 Republic of Ireland

I had a blind date in Bray. Darragh had followed my travels on Twitter. He was wiry from swimming in the Irish Sea and cycling to work in north Dublin. His haircut was a sharp as his wit. We strolled from the station past holidaymakers laden with optimistic ice creams. Bray, a coastal town twelve miles south of Dublin, had been a popular seaside retreat in Victorian times, the Irish Jūrmala. 'Sinead O'Connor used to own a house here', said Darragh, filling the gaps in our hesitant conversation. It felt strange to be walking along a promenade with a random football fan. Maybe Darragh felt the same. We quickly retraced our steps and went to the pub.

The Harbour had recently won an award for best pub in the world. I could see why, with its snug bars, fish-and-chip shed, spacious outside area, craft beer and, of course, Guinness: lovingly poured, unlike the urgent pints of London. Darragh was an old-school football fan. He used to be a Bray Wanderers regular, but now preferred to watch Cabinteely, his local side, in the Irish second tier. Bray traditionally soaked up the talent south of Dublin, although Darragh said that Cabinteely now offered similar prospects.

'The League of Ireland is boom and bust', explained Darragh. 'A bit like the country', he added. The domestic league gets relatively scarce media attention and competes with 'Barstoolers' who watch their Premier League club, often Liverpool or Manchester United but also clubs from London, on television. Darragh himself was a Spurs man, a family loyalty formed when his grandparents had moved to Shoreditch in the 1950s.

The Republic of Ireland start their league season earlier than any other, and Bray against Drogheda United had been the first match I chose when planning my early travels. Bray had since nosedived into trouble. Paul Doyle in his *Guardian* article said, 'Even a match that Matt thought would be straightforward could turn out to be problematic, as the future of Bray Wanderers has suddenly been thrown into doubt by financial turmoil.' The owners had pumped in too much money, lost interest, wanted to sell the ground and, most bizarrely, had called the council 'the North Korea of business' in an open letter. Fans wore Kim Jong-un masks to their next match. The club might have fielded the North Korean leader and won no fewer points. Bray had lost five and drawn one of their last six, and they needed a win against bottom-placed Drogheda.

My host, Tony, was no football man but had sped up my journey when I arrived at his guesthouse. 'You better be quick or they may have sold the club by the time you get there', he quipped. I talked about walking the scenic route along the coast to the town centre. Tony took one look at the threatening clouds and said that he would be giving me seasickness pills the following morning. His neighbours saw me waiting at the bus stop and kindly gave me a lift into town.

The Carlisle Grounds has a long history as a sports arena and a fresh, seaside feel, being located just back from the Victorian promenade. An old iron sign spelt out the letters of the home team and a jackdaw rested upon it. A passing woman had spotted my gaze. 'I've never noticed that', she said. 'I'm not sure the bird is always there', I responded. 'No, the sign, I only moved to Bray last year.' I wondered if this was an indication of local feeling towards the club: something easily ignored or missed. I took a photograph of a memorial outside the ground. 'That's for those fallen in the Second World War', explained an elderly man. Two people had spoken to me in a couple of minutes. If this was London, I would have called the police.

The ground has made recent steps towards modernisation. Darragh and I sat in the low-slung west stand for the first half where a three-foot barrier, replacing a perimeter wall that collapsed in both 2009 and 2010, separated us from the action. I admired the setting. The sky was lit up by the dying sun, and clouds hovered low over the housing in front of me. Bray Head, a steep incline of dulcet colours, was visible to the south, a cross on its peak, a truly magnificent view eclipsed by a bowling alley.

Darragh picked out Drogheda's assistant manager. The face was familiar but I couldn't retrieve the name of Mark Kinsella, the former Charlton Athletic midfielder and Republic of Ireland international. Darragh was a big supporter of the national team, brought up on its success during his youth. The Republic of Ireland were eight minutes away from qualifying for the semi-finals of Euro 1988, reached the quarter-finals of the 1990 World Cup and beat Italy in their opening match at the next World Cup in the United States. 'I took this as a given', lamented Darragh.

Ireland didn't qualify for the next three major tournaments and when they next did, for the 2002 World Cup, it was with a Given: Shay in goal, accompanied by Kinsella in midfield and Damien Duff on the wing. Darragh had waited for this moment and, after his friends pulled out, travelled on his own. 'You're never on your own with the Irish.' He recalled Japan not knowing how to celebrate after qualifying from their group. They copied celebrating Europeans and drew concerned looks from bemused police. We had a mutual love for Duff. 'We were at Craven Cottage and shouted "come back to Bray" at him. Duffer turned around and gave us a smile. Pure class.'

The game started with some suicidal Bray defending. Cherrie, Bray's Scottish goalkeeper, made a hash of a clearance and Mulhall had two chances to give Drogheda the lead, left back Kenna doing well to clear both shots from near the goal-line. It was hardly vintage football but was at least being played on the deck. There had barely been a header in a match between two quite diminutive sides when the mighty Bray right back Douglas, all long mane and tree-trunk thighs, took advantage to power in from a corner. Douglas was visibly charged by the goal, roaming upfield shortly afterwards like a less mobile John Stones.

It was 1–0 to Bray at half-time. We queued in a Portakabin for a hot drink and Darragh proffered a note. The teas were free, completing the very non-league feel of this match. We moved to the east terrace for the second half. My experiences at Craven Cottage had been homogenised by sitting in the same Hammersmith End seat for over a decade. I fondly remembered our lower league days when I stood in the enclosure, now part of the Johnny Haynes stand, towards the end that Fulham were attacking. And then, along with a few sage others, switched at half-time to continue to be close to Fulham goals and further away from the frequent defensive disasters at the other end. I enjoyed the change of perspective at Bray, one of a number of grounds where I would alter my view during the match.

Bray started the second half well, exploiting spaces on the wing. The skilful McCabe was bundled over on the edge of the penalty area. Darragh and I were convinced that McCabe would take the free kick himself, being nicely positioned for a right-footer. But Greene, the best player on the pitch, confused both us and the Drogheda goalkeeper with a left-footer straight down the middle. It was 2–0 and Drogheda looked a beaten side. 'It's just like watching Brazil!' exclaimed a clutch of young Bray fans. It wasn't, much like it wasn't when Barnsley fans chanted this in the 1990s, but the precious points looked safe.

Drogheda then scored. A free kick was drilled into the Bray wall and the rebound squared to Mulhall, who converted and fell into the net after scoring. Cherrie made a move towards the ball, Mulhall pushed Cherrie and the goalkeeper retaliated, pushing him harder. Players from both teams ran to trade shoves. The crowd behind the goal got an intimate view of a scuffle and yellow cards for Mulhall and Cherrie.

Drogheda fans started a verbal altercation with Cherrie, some twenty yards away, voices clearly audible on the sea air. 'We'll see you after the game', an older fan threatened. The sun had set and the clouds were an inky black to the west, moving like a volcanic eruption away from the hilly County Wicklow backdrop. Ireland might be a series of ever-changing micro-climates yet it was hard to hide from the wind and I felt chilly without my jacket. I looked at the press boxes to one side. 'They didn't use to have Perspex', said Darragh. They must have been freezing in the winter, and I could see why the League of Ireland had switched to a summer schedule in 2003.

Bray felt confident enough to field their youngest ever player, six-teen-year-old Jake Ellis, as a late substitute. Drogheda, despite their bluster, didn't look like they could force a leveller, and it ended a nervy 2–1 win for Bray. Darragh realised that I had been recognised – unsur-prising in a crowd of 400 when laden with camera and notebook and wearing the same grey trousers featured in the morning's *Irish Times*. The young Bray fans came across. 'Are you the man from the *Guardian*?' I asked where they were celebrating. 'In the bowling arena, it's 10 euros and you can bring your own cans!'

Darragh and I left with 'Push It' by Salt-N-Pepa bouncing in our ears and went for a final pint. It had been good to watch a match with someone who, whilst interested, wasn't blinkered by passion. I went to pay my guesthouse the next morning. 'That will be fine', said Tony, as he took 25 euros less than the agreed price and gave me a lift to the bus stop. 'You've got plenty more places to go.'

Bray were relieved to end a chaotic season in mid-table. Drogheda finished bottom with twenty-two points from thirty-three games and were relegated.

14 Northern Ireland

I was tired after a four-hour bus journey from Bray to Belfast, but was nevertheless looking forward to my visit to the Oval, a classic old-style stadium, home of Glentoran. Declan Roughan, photographer for the *Belfast Telegraph*, picked me up from my Airbnb by Belfast's docks. 'Why are you going to that shitty ground?' asked Declan as, perhaps subconsciously, he drove in the wrong direction. Declan was not really a football fan. He was also a Catholic. 'No real reason to now, but I still get the shivers when I go east', he explained. The Oval is in staunch loyalist and Protestant East Belfast. Union Jack flags adorn the housing estates surrounding the stadium. I didn't actually know East Belfast was Protestant. I was always more interested in the place than religion. I might have just written my own epitaph.

I was glad to be featured in the *Belfast Telegraph* as we accessed parts of the ground not normally open to the casual fan. I enjoy wandering around the labyrinthine insides of stadiums and Declan photographed me standing in the players' tunnel, reeking of past games, with its

Anfield-esque 'The Oval' sign. A comment from 1967 by former player-manager John Colrain was painted underneath. 'The secret of Glentoran's success is sacrificing individual ability for the sake of teamwork and all-round effort.' Glentoran had won ten titles between 1970 and 2009 but no successive championships since Colrain's short spell in charge in the late 1960s.

Declan photographed me walking slowly towards him through the tunnel and onto the pitch, now being whipped by horizontal rain. We visited the tight home changing room, full of bouncing players in green and black, where a coach joked that Glentoran were after a new centre back. My family had sponsored the match ball in Fulham's fourth-tier days, for a 1–1 draw against Rochdale in 1997, and I smiled at the same joke that was made, twenty years earlier, by Alan Cork, then Fulham's assistant manager.

Declan took some photographs outside the ground, the exterior wall newly painted green, and a steward informed me that the Oval was used as a mock Maine Road for *The Keeper*, the film about the legendary German goalkeeper Bert Trautmann. The wall was painted blue for the film and there had been wild rumours that Manchester City were taking over Glentoran. Fellow Premier League club Cliftonville's ground, Solitude, was also used as a stand-in for Stoke City's now defunct Victoria Park in *The Keeper*. I visited the following day and the entrance fee for the match shown in the film, 3 shillings, was still painted on the conveniently red wall. Cliftonville fans had apparently asked to pay the decimal equivalent, 15p, for the first home game of the season. Stephen McKillop, Cliftonville's finance director, was sanguine about Belfast's old grounds attracting new money as film sets. 'We received a small amount of money we weren't expecting to pay a bill we didn't expect.'

I doubt that 'Holiday in Cambodia', a dark song written by the Dead Kennedys in the late 1970s, immediately lured visitors to Phnom Penh. 'Holiday in Belfast' could have been written about the decades that followed in Northern Ireland. But, like the South-east Asian country, Belfast had reinvented itself now the Troubles were over. Workers were relocating from the British mainland, the city's affordable housing more than compensating for the highest energy costs in the UK. I could hear the lilts of Spanish tourists in the bustling Crown Liquor Saloon. The docks, which were behind the city's remarkable population explosion from around 85,000 in 1851 to 350,000 in 1901, had been revitalised. I visited the impressive *Titanic* attraction, marking the site where the vessel was built over a century before. I flashed the *Guardian* article on my phone and the ticket office gave me an unemployed person's discount for the audacity.

I walked around the perimeter of the Oval, admiring the wonderfully photogenic and decrepit terracing in the fleeting sunshine. A club official told me more about its history. The Oval was in a strategic location near to Belfast's docks, and its grandstands had been destroyed and the pitch turned into craters by Second World War bombing. Glentoran played at Grosvenor Park, home of rival club Distillery, until the Oval reopened in 1949. The main stand was rebuilt in 1953 and the ground had not seen much renovation since. A smaller sister stand housed away fans and was dwarfed by the enduring yellow cranes of the docks. There had been talk about a move to a more modern ground for several decades, but I loved its retrospective feel, a bowl of a stadium that reminded me of the Traktor Stadium in Minsk, only with a precarious-looking main stand that loomed over the pitch.

Declan and I visited the well-stocked trophy room. I was photographed cradling the first ever European trophy, the Vienna Cup which Glentoran won in 1914, although not the original – a replacement was moulded after the first was melted down to assist the war effort. A picture showed George Best in Glentoran colours playing against Manchester United, reportedly the only time this ever happened. I also learned that Glentoran were the first team to stop Benfica scoring in a home European tie, although the 0–0 draw, after 1–1 in the Belfast leg, meant they also became the first side to go out of Europe on away goals.

I climbed the stairs up to the main stand. They felt like they had not changed since the Glentoran icon Sammy Hughes was banging in the goals in the 1950s, and a wonderful glass mural of Hughes was beautifully lit by the sun. I met Thomas, a groundhopping Kaiserslautern fan who had tracked my journey and, coincidentally, also been at Bray. We sat together in tight wooden seats amongst the home faithful, one couple recognising me from the *Belfast Telegraph*. I was getting used to moderate fame. An announcement reminded fans not to indulge in any racist or sectarian chants.

The weather, as changeable in the north of Ireland as the south, switched again to lashing rain. Scrappy long balls, with little thought given to their target, were launched by both teams into the wind. An overhit free kick from opponents Carrick Rangers rolled gently up the wide grassy bank behind the Glentoran goal. The atmosphere, muted at Bray, was more vociferous and informed at Glentoran. The Glentoran support, mainly middle-aged men, screamed as the referee, who had an awkward game, failed to play an obvious advantage after a Carrick foul.

Balls were going nowhere. Possession was passed around like an unwanted present, lost and gained six times in as many seconds in one comedic sequence. 'This is football in Northern Ireland', remarked

Thomas, who had watched matches in Belfast before. I had been surprised by some of the ambitious play, if not the execution, in Bray. But this was base football. Eamon Sweeney, a journalist I had spoken to at the *Belfast Telegraph*, had warned me about the lack of skill and ability. My German companion seemed appeased, probably by the amazing setting. 'Not my cup of tea to spend two weeks on the beach', he said.

The Glentoran strike force showed some signs of being on the same wavelength, but the overall quality of play was low. Carrick's left back tried a hugely optimistic long-range volley, one in a thousand in most games, one in a million in this. The Glentoran fans were strained. 'C'mon Glens, do something.' A cry of desperation. And it worked. Redman, the advancing Glentoran left back, hit a strong shot underneath the Carrick goalkeeper's body.

The home faithful seemed content with a 1–0 lead at half-time with hushed predictions of a two- or three-goal win. They shifted to the terraced curve behind the goal that would be the focus of Glentoran's second-half attacks. The weather was crazy. The sun reverted to rain. Clouds darkened and gathered on the attractive hilly surrounds. The fans trotted back to the main stand with knowing faces. I asked if it was always like this as I contemplated queuing for chips in the rain. 'Four seasons in one day' had never felt less like a cliché.

The indie slant on the tinny PA playlist didn't feel in harmony with the creaking stadium. I expected the classics, Elvis or the Beatles, and instead I heard the Dandy Warhols and Oasis. I would write a backpacker's guide to football for the French sports magazine *L'Équipe* three months later, and the Oval was featured under 'for lovers of all things vintage'. Glentoran reprinted the article in their Boxing Day programme against Belfast rivals Linfield.

Glentoran's optimism quickly evaporated. The Carrick winger Chapman headed past the home goalkeeper to equalise just seconds after the restart. The rest of the second half was terrible. There was more dissent from the stands but no supporting chants. The wind was now behind Glentoran and a dire free kick sailed into touch. 'Woeful', said the fan behind me. 'Useless' followed, as a long punt from Glentoran's right back exited the playing area. The highlights package broadcast on television later was brief.

The Carrick fans could tell a point was close. Cheers drifted across on the wind from the sister stand as their team slashed the ball down the pitch. I was hardly expecting a goal fest. Eamon at the *Belfast Telegraph* had joked that 'it takes six games to see six goals' in Northern Ireland. But this was a very scrappy 1–1 draw, an experience reminiscent of Fulham's toils in the 1980s and early 1990s. This had been the worst game I had watched so far, with no standout player, a chastening view on any match. The football would hopefully be more entertaining in Azerbaijan, my next stop.

The crowd drowned their sorrows in the strong community feel of the Glentoran bar. I bought a cheap pint of lager and spoke to Iain, a Glentoran season ticket holder who also supported Spurs and Glasgow Rangers. 'I'm rarely happy', he said. I wondered if occasions when all three of your teams win are sweeter than victory for your only team. I'm only Fulham. Iain couldn't convince his nephew to watch Glentoran as pubs showed English Premier League matches at the same time, a problem shared with the Republic.

Glentoran were a famous name, with twenty-three titles and twenty-two Irish Cups since their foundation in 1882. But I didn't get the impression they were buoyant in hope. I walked outside the Trautmann gates where several players and Gary Haveron, the manager, waved goodbye to me as they drove past in their workaday cars. I recalled Iain's words from the bar: 'Gary is a nice guy but he's not going to be here long'. He darkly suggested that the club's Christmas Murder Mystery dinner, advertised on posters on the bar walls, might have a certain managerial target.

Haveron survived the Murder Mystery but was sacked in February 2018. Glentoran finished a disappointing seventh out of twelve, still good enough for a Europa League play-off final against Cliftonville, which they lost 3–2. Carrick finished second from bottom and were relegated after losing a play-off to Newry City.

Challenge Europa

My journey through Europe was like a big board game, and I found it easier to break my immense challenge into smaller parts. I first concentrated on organising the twelve summer leagues. I had hoped for a systematic easterly sweep from Iceland to Kazakhstan, but fixtures in Georgia, Lithuania and Latvia made me deviate. The forty-three autumn leagues were even more of a test. I spent several days in August checking to see if my route was still feasible. It was strangely enjoyable seeing cities and clubs appear on my schedule. But I still had to overcome forever changing kick-off times and, in some later countries, waiting for top divisions to divide into championship and relegation play-offs.

I actually quite loved the logistics. A colleague offered to write me a computer programme that would work out the best route. There were lots of knowns and unknowns. But software could not emulate intuition and chasing a football story whilst being one yourself. I stuck pins in a massive map of Europe, each representing a top-division club, and followed the sun and my interests, spending longer in the Caucasus than the Alps. I had a narrow window for Moldova's short autumn season, which started in July and ended in November, before they too switched to a summer schedule. I always planned to end in the Balkans, a dense concentration of leagues that ran well into May.

The most important thing was not missing my match. Sometimes finding out about them was hard enough. The Kosovan fixture list was tricky to obtain; only a message in the week of the match from rival club Prishtina pushed me to see Drita in Gjilan. The kick-off time for my Macedonian match was changed just two days beforehand. Matches were moved for television, often at short notice. Every match in Romania and Portugal was televised with scant regard for fans. And Domžale, a sleepy commuter town in Slovenia, played at 4 p.m. on a Wednesday when most people were at work in nearby Ljubljana.

I researched when leagues typically played matches and planned weekends, like in Belgium, Germany and the Netherlands, where I could combine several. These were my most intense experiences, and I would be frazzled by the time I had covered the Czech Republic, Austria and Slovakia in three days. But the adrenalin running through my veins kept me enthused. I also knew I would need rest from the road and spent several weeks at home in August and December when many seasons were nascent or nearing their winter break.

The pace was unrelenting. I was often researching a dozen countries in a single day. I spent over 200 nights in more than 100 hotels, hostels and guesthouses. It was sometimes hard even to manage mundanities. I arrived in Armenia with a large bag of sweaty clothes. My cheap hotel said they would charge me £27 to wash them. 'That's more than they cost', I said, before negotiating a discount. But I didn't have the time to sit in a steamy laundrette. I had a new country to explore and three Armenian football matches to watch.

The travel was tough, especially for a man as tall as me. I took fifty-four flights and six ferries, drove in a dozen countries and squeezed into countless buses and trains. I spent a lot of time waiting around, frustrating for someone who normally arrives at the station thirty seconds before his morning train. Kars in eastern Turkey was a particular low point. I had an hour to kill. The inside of my parked bus was roughly the same temperature as the centre of the Earth. The bus station smelt strongly of stale urine and was full of shops selling nothing whilst a sliver of shade was populated by toothy old men chain smoking on a bench. I stood outside the bus and gently fried in the midday sun as stray dogs fought over scraps of food wrapped in plastic bags.

I would speak to Andrei from fourth-tier Carmen Bucureşti in Romania. He, quite rightly, said that with a greater budget it might be possible to complete my challenge in six months, nearly half the time. But for me the context was important. Spending an average of four days in a country felt about right to better understand the place and its people. And, of course, if feasible, watch more matches.

15 Azerbaijan

It was 2,700 miles from Belfast to Baku. I had more time than money and took a budget flight with crowds of drunken Irish from Stansted to Kutaisi, Georgia's second city. Kutaisi is home to Torpedo, one of the country's leading teams. There would be a remarkable last day to the Erovnuli Liga season several months later when second-placed Torpedo played leaders Dinamo in Tbilisi. Torpedo needed a win to secure the title whilst Dinamo only needed a draw. Torpedo were 1–0 up when they conceded a clear penalty in the ninety-sixth minute. It was the final kick of the season. The immense pressure affected Dinamo captain Otar Kiteishvili. He smashed it at the goalkeeper's legs and Torpedo won the championship.

'You chose the wrong game', Nika from the Georgian Football Federation would later say. It would have been a great match to watch. But I did visit the impressive Dinamo Arena, where this drama unfolded, for Georgia's 1–1 draw against the Republic of Ireland in a World Cup qualifier. I then rested in the spectacular Greater Caucasus Mountains at a guesthouse in Kazbegi with a lovely garden full of ducks. I returned to Tbilisi and flew to the Azerbaijani capital Baku, the landscape below becoming increasingly more arid and the brown outlines of houses barely visible against the dusty soil.

Azerbaijan is Turkey with oil. The people, language and food have many similarities. It is an archetypal crossroads state, trampled on by many, the cracks revealing the black gold that has been pouring out of its land and sea since the mid-nineteenth century. Azerbaijan wanted to be loved. It had sponsored Atlético Madrid and Sheffield Wednesday, attracted Formula One, hosted Eurovision and would be the most unorthodox of Euro 2020 hosts. Visa costs had recently been slashed from £100 to £18 to attract more than the current paltry level of Western tourists.

Azerbaijan is not a country with a rich footballing history. It's still probably best known in England for Tofiq Bahramov, the Azerbaijani linesman who deemed that Geoff Hurst's shot was over the line in 1966. But I still expected their football to be comfortably better than its neighbours in the Caucasus. The eight-team Premier League was sponsored by Topaz, a major energy company, and large commercial operations backed many of its clubs.

The Topaz Premier League featured Gabala, Kapaz and six teams from the capital, including the leading club Qarabağ, who relocated in 1993 when their home city of Agdam was abandoned during the conflict with Armenia over the disputed region of Nagorno-Karabakh. Armenia and Azerbaijan are still technically at war and their international and club sides cannot be drawn against each other in competition. The border is closed and I would need to travel through Georgia again to reach Armenia.

Baku, with its purple London cabs and audacious architecture, was intriguing and irritating when I arrived from Tbilisi. I fruitlessly dragged my bag around the searing streets of the medieval core, trying to find my hotel. A boy in a Messi shirt eventually led me to another hotel which explained that my original hotel was closed – indeed, I later found that even the sign had been taken down – and that they were full. Finally I found a third hotel and they were simply incompetent. The doorman turned off the water by mistake and I couldn't get a shower in a very dry city.

The following morning, a cat dropped in through the breakfast-room window and attacked a giant plastic-wrapped sausage. I let it chew away before the doorman ushered the cat – a respected animal in Islamic culture – down the stairs with a rare reverence. This seemed typical of how Azerbaijanis lived, a mix of the modern and the traditional in a cloud of cigarette smoke. Architecturally, the carpet museum in Baku was perhaps the epitome of modern-day Azerbaijan, a distinctive building shaped like a rolled carpet and housing ancient weavings.

I was a little sullen in Baku. I had planned to watch Sabail, a new team from the south of the capital, play champions Qarabağ. But the fixture was postponed at just three days' notice after the Azerbaijani Football Federation granted Qarabağ a rest before their Champions League match at Chelsea. Instead I watched a hastily arranged friendly between Sabail and First Division Bine at Dalga Beach, twenty-five miles north-east of Baku, with Ruslan Amirjanov, a former Azerbaijan international right back.

Ruslan, thirty-two, was expected to sign for Sabail in the coming weeks and gave me a lift back to Baku in his sporty saloon. Cheap potato snacks decorated the passenger seat and Ruslan offered me one. I knew

Azerbaijani cuisine was tastier than that. He opened a can of 'Hell', a local energy drink. 'What the hell are you doing?' he joked, when I turned it down. Ruslan was better company than he was a driver. Both hands strayed from the steering wheel to discuss carp fishing with his friend on his mobile or to gesticulate wildly.

After the Sabail postponement, I now had to find another Premier League match in Azerbaijan. I chose third-placed Gabala, around 130 miles to the north-west of Baku, against early leaders Zira. 'Gabala is the same as Austria. They have mountains, green things, the oxygen very good', said Ruslan. Ruslan had played for wealthy Gabala, his spell disrupted by a badly treated knee injury. He said that everyone wanted to play there as the best players earned three or four times the £7,000 monthly salary they would at a club like Zira. 'When you finish football everyone forgets you so you want to earn money.' Ruslan said that life in Gabala was boring compared to the capital. 'It's just hotel, training, hotel, training, maybe go to the mountains. Everybody misses Baku and their family.'

We were getting close to the city. The traffic became 'catastrophic', according to Ruslan. But it was hardly the M1 on a Friday. As we neared the city centre, Ruslan showed me a YouTube montage of sinuous dribbles, assists and goals on his phone. 'I am the same as Dani Alves. After this video, you think why he play in Azerbaijan, why does he not play for Standard Liège or Gent', said Ruslan, eerily predicting the two Belgian teams I would watch in November. Ruslan was amusing and his free kicks were good, although some of the clips were clearly several years old. I suggested his favourite current right back might be Kyle Walker and gave him my card. 'Now, that's why you say Kyle Walker, your name is Walker.' 'He's my brother', I joked, and left Ruslan to drive off into the Baku sunset.

The following day, I took a cramped minibus that charged from Baku's mammoth bus terminal through the desert and towards the mountains. I was wedged next to a man, overheating in a dark suit on a hot day, travelling to a wedding in the hillside town of Sheki, around fifty miles north-west of Gabala. He actually thought the driver was too slow and invited me along to the wedding. I politely declined as I had to get to Gabala for my match. I arrived and was stopped in the street by some young children. 'Are you Arab?' one asked. Direct flights from Dubai and Saudi Arabia to Gabala indicated where foreign tourists were coming from.

Gabala was one of the managerial outposts of Tony Adams. Adams's team finished seventh out of twelve in 2010–11, his only full season, with ex-Derby County striker Deon Burton making more of an impact for Adams than Collins John, the wayward former Fulham forward. I tried to get some stories. 'He was a keen skier', said a Gabala official. I tried again. 'He was very humble. He introduced himself to everyone as "Tony Adams" when he arrived. I was thinking, I know this player, he's played for England and Arsenal and he still says who he is.' Gabala were clearly honoured to have had such a famous ex-player working with them.

I walked from my hotel to the Gabala City Stadium as the sun tripped over the horizon and darkened green and brown mountains with a foreboding tint. I passed children playing at the back of unattractive four-storey housing blocks and noticed three Ladas spilling sugar cane, onions and potatoes out of their open boots. Old men sat by the road and nodded their heads at me as I contemplated bettering my Kazakh haircut in a bargain-basement barber's shop.

The stadium housed a glitzy club shop, a real rarity in the former

Soviet states, keeping the local populace well stocked in red and black Gabala mugs and babygros. I spoke to six under-worked workers. Their favourite player was Dion Malone, previously with ADO Den Haag, who would be my Dutch hosts in two months' time. They predicted a 2–0 home win in their game against Zira. I countered with a 1–1 to youthful disdain.

Anar, Gabala's press officer, led me onto the media balcony. I was greeted with tea, biscuits and passive smoking. Azerbaijanis love cigarettes; many buy singles from open packets in shops, either to cut costs or to deny their habit. I had heard that Qarabağ was also a well-loved brand across the country, representing the name of the disputed region, Nagorno-Karabakh, that had once been part of Azerbaijan. I asked Anar whether he wanted them to succeed in the Champions League. 'No, they are our rivals. You understand.'

Gabala is a small town of some 13,000 without a deep football culture. The club, founded in 1995, were trying to build their supporter base and the young-looking crowd was let in for free. Suno, Gabala's general manager, wasn't impressed. 'Still they don't come', he said. I thought the attendance, a shade over 1,000, was reasonable given that the match kicked off at 8.30 p.m. and the barber's shop was still open.

'Score, score, Gabala!' demanded Gabala's heavy metal anthem as Huseynov, the Gabala captain, passed the ball into touch straight from the kick-off. This was not a good start unless there was underground gambling on the time of the first throw-in. And it wasn't beyond reason that such spread betting could happen in the Azerbaijani Premier League if it occurred in the English Premier League, albeit in 1995, when Southampton played Wimbledon. Bookmakers had predicted that the first throw-in would take place around one minute into that match, and Matthew Le Tissier's plan was to kick the ball straight into touch and collect fifty-six times his stake. Unfortunately, his tentative attempt was kept in by teammate Neil Shipperley on the left wing. 'If there had been Prozone analysis back then my stats would have been amazing for the next minute as I charged around the pitch desperately trying to kick the ball out of play', Le Tissier reflected later.

Suno buried his head in his hands as his team lost the ball in midfield. Things weren't going well and I doubted it was due to gambling. Zira looked more threatening in the bustling and organised counter-attacking style Ruslan had predicted. 'Gabala, Gabala, Gabala' rang nicely off the tongue from three singing sections. 'Zira, Zira' was the retort from the small throng of away fans from Baku, corralled by a similar number of policemen and stewards. Gabala had been out-thought in a goalless first half.

The entertaining crowd were enthused by second-half substitutions. 'Goal, goal, goal', they predicted as a free kick failed to challenge Zira. The visitors took a deserved lead after seventy-four minutes when substitute Igbekoyi smashed home a loose ball from a right-wing free kick. The Gabala right back turned his back on Igbekoyi's shot. John Terry would have taken one for the team. Suno was a picture of despondency.

It looked unlikely that Gabala would equalise. The fans agreed and were streaming towards the exit when a long throw was handled in the Zira penalty area as the match entered injury time. Huseynov calmly slotted in the spot kick. I cheered the penalty as I thought I should on the media balcony, and felt rather awkward when no one joined in. Two cards were issued after an entertaining ruck in the net over the ball that reminded me of Bray. Gabala had sneaked a point.

The Zira manager was disgusted and complained to just about

everyone as the referee was shepherded away. It was harsh on his team. The marginal relief on Suno's face did not disguise that this was a game that Gabala expected to win. The atmosphere was black. I left promptly and was treated as a mystic soothsayer by the club shop boys as my 1–1 prediction had come true. I also predicted that it was going to take me some time to get to Armenia for my next match.

Gabala finished a distant second, sixteen points behind Qarabağ. Zira faded to fourth. Ruslan played two matches for Sabail and was released at the end of the 2017–18 season. Qarabağ's rest hardly helped as they lost 6–0 to Chelsea in the Champions League. Chelsea also prevailed in the all-London 2019 Europa League final held in Baku, beating Arsenal 4–1.

16 Armenia

Gabala looked close to Yerevan on the map, but it took me four days to travel between Azerbaijan and Armenia. I rested in a beautiful caravanserai, as traders would have done centuries ago, in the quaint Azerbaijani town of Sheki and rode three screeching minibuses to the border. A herd of cows lapped the Bneli Kheoba River that separated Azerbaijan from Georgia as I walked across the bridge and took a shared taxi to the picturesque hilltop town of Sighnaghi. I was looking forward to my stay in eastern Georgia, not least because my guesthouse promised free wine to every visitor.

It was not only free wine, it was unlimited. I sipped glasses of home-made red, white and throat-scarring chacha, a grappa-like spirit, on the vine-wrapped terrace. Two men in their twenties, clearly British, sat down at the adjacent table. Josh was undertaking a very different mission, to cycle 'from Cheddar to China' – later rebranded as 'from Bristol to Beijing', presumably because it sounded less cheesy – and his brother Matt was visiting him en route. We compared our travels, his more flexible and physically draining, mine more frantic and focused. His brother weighed up our unorthodox challenges. 'Matt's sounds more fun', he concluded. The three of us went wine tasting in the bountiful Kakheti region the following day and, as the English tend to, got gently sozzled on cheap booze.

Our routes would not cross again, but there was a mutual admiration of our challenges. Josh was cycling on to Baku and Almaty, earlier haunts of mine, whilst I was travelling on his cycle path through Turkey and Bulgaria. Josh was grilled about his Armenian passport stamp as he entered Azerbaijan, proving the advice I had received to visit Azerbaijan first was wise. We would both end up at the World Cup the following summer, Josh confusing an official at a remote Kazakh–Russian border post by turning up on his bicycle and with the fan ID that enabled visa-free travel in Russia.

I left Josh and hiked the desolate landscapes around the monastery of Davit Gareja, where faded ecclesiastical cave paintings peered out over the desert. The Caucasus is a wonderfully diverse region. I returned to Tbilisi for the final time and took the night train to the Armenian capital of Yerevan. Tbilisi had seen a rash of recent investment but not much had been spent on its railway. The station was described by the travel writer Paul Theroux as 'a tableau from the distant past, a scene from some dismal period in tsarist times', and little had changed since. Dimly lit platforms were connected by a tunnel that masqueraded as a sewer. Broken concrete and contorted metal chairs completed the post-apocalyptic feel. A gaggle of tourists and locals waited in the gloom for the train, which had laboured from the Black Sea resort of Batumi.

I was welcomed by fresh tea and friendly Armenian faces in my compartment. We shared delicious local fruits and joked at my phrasebook

Russian. These may have been my travel dreams, but the reality on board was somewhat harsher. 'You can't sleep here', said the father of the Armenian family. I rechecked my ticket. I was in the correct lower berth, although it seemed over-populated with toys and clothes. 'This is a women's cabin', said the father. I had travelled enough to know it wasn't. Two twentysomething women and a dozing child were my companions in the steamy cabin. They were jaded from their Georgian beach holiday and hardly overjoyed to see a foreigner add his personal pool of sweat to the floor. There were no other lower berths on the packed train. I bedded down with the scowls bouncing off me.

The night air freshened the cabin. I slept better than expected and woke with the spiritual Mount Ararat on the skyline. I was begrudgingly offered a breakfast biscuit by my cabinmates. 'It's been great to meet you', I said, leaping off at Yerevan station to catch the underground to my hotel. 'Metro not working', lied a taxi driver on the platform. I wasn't sure whether I was going to like, let alone love, Yerevan.

At least I felt rich. I received over 600 Armenian dram for each British pound, more than any other European currency, and paid the equivalent of 17p to be transported to the city centre. Yerevan shouldn't even have an underground system. The Soviet Union had decreed that only cities with a population of one million were granted one. Yerevan's population was around three-quarters of a million in the 1970s, but the Soviet leader Leonid Brezhnev was persuaded to disregard the rule. The Armenian Communist Party had argued that families were so closely knit that every Armenian who lived away from their parents were likely to visit them daily, increasing the projected passenger flow. As a result, Yerevan was the eighth Soviet city to have a metro system when it opened in 1981.

I was hot and tired when I arrived at my hotel, but the friendly owner gave me a free breakfast and put me in touch with his friend, Hayk Karapetyan, the media officer at the Armenian Football Federation. Armenia offered a rare possibility. I could watch the entire fixture list. The Armenian Premier League was the smallest in Europe, with only six teams, and all three matches were being played in Yerevan on consecutive days.

Hayk was downbeat when he spoke to me. 'The league has decreased to six teams [from twenty-four in post-independence Armenia] due to the war in the 1990s, the semi-war situation with Azerbaijan now, the poor socio-economic situation and the results-oriented nature of owners who want to gain revenue in their first year.' Oh. 'It was deliberate to play on different days to provide TV broadcasting for all the matches. But there is no interest this season from TV.' Oh. To encourage attendance the Armenian Football Federation had made league matches free for all. Yet I would still be the only football fan 'doing the treble' this weekend.

The domestic game was in crisis but Armenia attracted large attendances for their internationals at the Republican Stadium. They had been the closest of the three Caucasus countries to qualifying for a major tournament, scoring twenty-two goals when finishing third behind Russia and the Republic of Ireland in Euro 2012 qualification. Hayk described Armenian players as technically good yet physically weak. But they had a true idol in Henrikh Mkhitaryan. Replicas of his shirt were strung across market stalls. 'In all post-Soviet countries there is no one playing at his level', said Hayk. 'Ukraine used to have [Andriy] Shevchenko, Georgia had [Kakha] Kaladze, Russia maybe [Andrey] Arshavin for one year.'

My first match was Pyunik, where Mkhitaryan started his career, against Banants, winners of the 2014 title, at the Republican Stadium. The architecture is a triumph. It is built from the pink-hued stone that characterises the city, with artistic swirls, columns and a roof shaped like a family of Toblerone bars that glowed in the hot evening sun. I sat behind three Pyunik supporters making serious inroads into an enormous bag of blackened sunflower seeds. The stadium DJ rocked into action with Led Zeppelin. Bob Marley, Def Leppard and Guns N' Roses' 'Sweet Child O' Mine' followed. It was some playlist. I was probably not the only one in the 300-strong crowd disappointed by Axl Rose being cut off mid-track so the teams could be read out to casual disinterest.

A messy start to the first half improved when Banants scored twice through striker Gyozalyan. There was palpable half-time relief when the rock DJ played 'Sweet Child O' Mine' again from the start. 'It's not going well', I suggested to the man in front. He shrugged, offered me some more sunflower seeds and nodded along to Oasis and the Pet Shop Boys. Pyunik reduced the deficit when midfielder Minasyan half-volleyed into the corner to make it 2–1. Banants held on to pick up my first away win, after eight home victories and six draws, since the Faroe Islands.

I explored Yerevan, one of the oldest continuously inhabited cities in the world. It really was a curious place, easily the most Soviet of the Caucasian capitals, unsurprising given Armenia's continued reliance on Russia. Armenia's poor economy is hindered by the country's trapped geography: the border was closed with Turkey as well as Azerbaijan. I was in Alexander Tamanian Park taking a photograph of a bulbous cat statue by the Colombian sculptor Botero when I got a tap on my shoulder. A security guard straight out of the Soviet Union pointed out that one inch of my foot had strayed onto the grass.

There were pretensions towards development in Yerevan. Older buildings had been demolished and replaced with characterless apartment blocks, giving parts of the centre the feel of a low-grade Canary

Wharf. The outskirts were even more depressing, full of malignant factories that would be regenerated into arthouse bars in wealthier countries, but here were left as derelict reminders of when Armenia, an industrial hub, was one of the richest Soviet republics.

My second match was between champions Alashkert and leaders Shirak, the only team not playing their home football in the capital. I couldn't find the stadium, searching around the side streets before asking a sleepy security guard for directions. I had somehow got off the metro one stop early. I retraced my steps and found something vaguely Roman about the Alashkert Stadium with its single stand topped by narrow arches. I was sitting with a spare seat on either side when a big man in a sweaty red shirt plonked himself next to me. He last used deodorant in the Soviet Union. And this was a hot day. The match kicked off at 4 p.m. to compensate for the lack of floodlights. It was 32°C and felt even hotter with the armpits from hell next to me.

Alashkert wisely used early second-half substitutions in the sapping heat. A neat passage of Alashkert possession culminated in the Serbian striker, Nenadović, guiding a fine goal home. Shirak striker Muradyan was booked for a tetchy confrontation and then charged around the pitch like a bull on heat. There was little surprise when he was sent off moments later. The Shirak manager, wearing the casual jeans and polo shirt that seemed the norm for Armenian coaches, ignored Muradyan as he struggled to open a metal gate and stomped down the tunnel.

The Shirak goalkeeper saved a penalty, the first I had seen missed after seven successive conversions, before Alashkert were also reduced to ten men for the last few minutes. It finished 1–0 to Alashkert after a feisty and skilful match, the Shirak fans drifting off into an orange sky that matched their replica shirts.

The following day, I visited the Armenian Genocide Museum. 'Look at what those Turkish have done to us. They are animals', said an old woman to me. I didn't know how to respond. I needed to escape history for the present. My final match was Ararat against Gandzasar, and I took a taxi to the Mika Stadium, passing the vast Soviet half-bowl of the abandoned Hrazdan Stadium where Ararat beat eventual winners Bayern Munich 1–0 in the second leg of the quarter-finals of the 1974–75 European Cup. Arkady Andreasyan, the goal-scorer in 1975, was now the Ararat manager. A statue of Andreasyan scoring that famous goal was still positioned outside the Mika Stadium, a remnant of his short spell as FC Mika manager.

If the Republican Stadium was showy and the Alashkert Stadium gritty then the Mika Stadium, where FC Mika played before going bust in 2016, was desolate. The grass was patchy, the seats in the VIP area were ripped and the toilets had not been cleaned since the previous season. I met Davit, the burly young press officer for Gandzasar, a club from the southern city of Kapan who were playing home matches in Yerevan whilst their stadium was renovated. Davit showed me around the sad-looking stadium. 'This used to be beautiful', he lamented. There was a congenial atmosphere in the players' tunnel. Everyone knew everyone, hardly surprising when teams competed against each other six times in the league alone.

Davit commentated for Gandzasar's YouTube channel. I joined him in the open commentary box where green paint was peeling off the flimsy roof and the air was being squeezed by the afternoon heat. We had a fine view of a half-built lodge, unlikely ever to be finished but planned to accommodate promising young players from the provinces. A man climbed up the back of the giant scoreboard to switch it on. It flickered into life. The soft melody of the old Ararat anthem was aired, the male lead vocalist backed by female vocals that lingered on 'Ararat, Ararat, Ararat'. The dated music somehow reflected the feeling of sadness when the teams were led out into a virtually empty stadium. The crowd of eighty would be my lowest outside the micro-states. Davit's cameraman arrived just before kick-off and spent five minutes fiddling with his cables. The early action will remain a mystery to Davit's devoted audience.

Ararat, the league's bottom-placed team, had fallen far from their 1970s heyday. Gandzasar were 2–0 up in the second half when I recorded a fourth substitution for Ararat. I double-checked my scribblings to make sure I had not miscounted. There had definitely been four changes. Davit explained that this was permitted if the fourth substitute was aged under eighteen, a rule unique amongst European top divisions and an interesting method of getting young players precious minutes.

Andreasyan, the Ararat manager renowned for his arrogance, was sent off for verbal abuse in injury time and refused to leave the pitch. 'You're the one who should be sent off', he shouted at the referee. 'You fucking bastard.' The match was abandoned, the only time this would happen on my travels, and a 3–0 win was eventually awarded to Gandzasar. The Ararat legend trudged off the pitch as the few remaining spectators left the dilapidated stadium. It was a sad, but strangely representative, end to my trio of matches.

Alashkert won the Armenian Premier League. Banants were second, Gandzasar third, Shirak fourth (deducted twelve points for match fixing), Pyunik fifth and Ararat finished bottom but weren't relegated. The Armenian Premier League expanded to nine teams for the 2018–19 season.

EASTERN EUROPE KICK-OFF

17 Turkey

I stuffed millions of lira through some metal bars and a man let me in. The match between Fenerbahçe and Ankaragücü was seemingly sold out. But it didn't matter. I squeezed onto a row and stood with the fanatical support for a six-goal thriller, 5–1 to the home team, before taking the ferry back to Europe. This was seventeen years ago, the first match I saw in any UEFA nation outside my own. I would watch Trabzonspor play Alanyaspor this time, and it would be no less exciting.

Just getting to Trabzon was exciting. Anna and her ethnic Georgian father were waiting at the bus station in Yerevan, all of us thinking that the minibus to Georgia was leaving at the listed time of 8 a.m., not a hastily revised 8.30 a.m. We chatted on the seven-hour ride through undulating scenery scorched by the summer sun. Anna explained that Armenians were uncomplicated people, without the passion or patriotism of Georgians. Many Armenians wanted to leave their country, for Europe and particularly the United States, where a large diaspora already lived, and I had noticed the distinct lack of middle-aged people on the streets of Yerevan.

We shared cheese and delicious apricots. I circulated a printout of my *Guardian* article to much amusement from my fellow travellers. The minibus crossed the Georgian border in the middle of nowhere, the air reeking of asphalt from an untimely resurfacing of the road, and I thought of how congenial this journey was, a complete contrast to my unfriendly arrival into Armenia. We arrived in the Georgian town of Akhaltsikhe in the mid-afternoon. My guidebook said there would then be a bus to Ardahan in Turkey. 'No bus', said a taxi driver. I wasn't convinced. He dragged out the bus station manager. 'No bus.' Convenient. I got a third opinion from the tourist office. 'No bus.' Bugger.

I couldn't hang around in a Georgian town I couldn't even pronounce. The following day I found a likeable Armenian taxi driver with a Turkish permit and knowledge of a new crossing at Kartsakhi, a beautiful lake shared between Georgia and Turkey. We first drove to the fabulous cave city of Vardzia, clinging to a startling ridge in the mountains. I then photographed a rusting train carriage being used as a bridge across the Paravani River, later featured in the adventurer Levison Wood's television series *From Russia to Iran*. My driver filled his pockets with cigarettes and his car with petrol, both considerably cheaper in Georgia than Turkey, before we crossed the border and twisted through hauntingly barren and beautiful landscapes to the charmless city of Kars. I paid £65 for the nine-hour journey. My driver looked uneasy in Kars, previously part of Armenia, turning his car around and heading back towards Akhaltsikhe.

I wanted to explore this unique part of north-eastern Turkey, which saw few foreign visitors. I trampled around the crumbling medieval city of Ani, alone for several hours, and the remarkable landscapes around Çamlıhemşin, like a steeper Scotland with its pine trees, peaks and plateaus. I sat next to an extremely irritating man on the bus to Trabzon and tried to block his inane ramblings with my headphones. My phone had somehow deleted every song apart from Rammstein. The bus ducked and dived through the mountains to Germanic industrial metal.

Trabzon is hemmed in on a narrow sliver of land between the mountains and the Black Sea. It is a port city without pretensions. And people from Trabzon support Trabzonspor who, along with Bursaspor in 2010, are one of only two non-Istanbul teams to have won the Turkish Süper Lig since its foundation in 1959. Trabzonspor's Medical Park Arena is more atmospheric than its name suggests, built on reclaimed land and cleverly designed to represent the waves of the Black Sea. The locals joke that it will sink. The ticket office was positioned under a giant staircase, with no roof to shade fans who lined up in the blazing sunshine. The two men in front took forever. I joked with the queue that they were trying to buy Hugo Rodallega. The Colombian striker, who made his name at Wigan Athletic before being relegated at Fulham, was something of a Trabzonspor favourite for his goal-scoring exploits at the end of the previous season.

'Are you alright mate?' I heard a West Midlands-Turkish twang from the back of the queue. Laz had met his English wife in Turkey and spent two decades running a kebab shop in Worcestershire and watching Aston Villa, the team who inspired Trabzonspor's colours. In 2016 Laz had moved back to Trabzon, where his wife now taught English. I asked if there were many other English here. 'One or two mate.' He didn't miss anything about the West Midlands. 'The weather is bloody miserable just like here', he said, as sweat dripped down his brow. It had been a hot summer on the Black Sea. Laz kept me entertained as I waited to sort out football bureaucracy.

Turkey is the only UEFA member where all top-flight football fans need a membership card, a Passolig, a scheme comparable to Margaret Thatcher's foiled identity cards. It costs the equivalent of £8 and, in a drive to maximise profits and keep tabs on the populace, must be renewed annually. Turkey is a fabulous yet frustrating place where the transgressive websites Soccerway and LiveScore, mainstays of my football research, were blocked. And my bus to Trabzon was stopped twice by police, every passport collected and the details tediously typed into a tablet.

Ergin met me outside the stadium after I had procured my Passolig. He was a friend of someone I had met on an internet message board. We messaged each other before I arrived. His English was minimal; my Turkish was mainly limited to menu items. Ergin's thinning hair and sunken eyes reminded me of many football fans, and his sinewy build reflected someone who smoked more than he ate. We took photographs of one another, the new art of conversation.

I was baking on the exposed concrete, and Ergin could see I needed a cup of tea. Turkey runs on tea. We took a dolmuş, a shared minibus taking its name from the Turkish for 'seemingly stuffed', to Akçaabat, six miles further west along the urban coastal strip. Ergin ran a tea shop here with a chintzy pink theme in a quiet residential courtyard. I sat on garish furniture as he brought me lots of tea. It was rather surreal. A well-loved Trabzonspor flag appeared and Ergin presented me with a scarf. I was touched. You don't become rich selling 30p cups of tea.

We tried to talk football. Ergin was a leader of his local fan group and saw Trabzonspor play across Turkey. He hated Fenerbahçe more than any of the other Istanbul teams, understandable after the 2010–11 match fixing scandal that denied Trabzonspor their seventh title. I kept quiet about my first visit to Turkey. I asked Laz whether he thought it still happened. 'Maybe not for money, but sometimes a player will hear from his agent. A big club are interested in signing you this summer. Have a quiet game against them.' Away supporters were banned when Trabzonspor played Fenerbahçe, owing to the considerable threat of crowd trouble.

I returned to the city of Trabzon. Turkey was my seventeenth country but I had yet to buy a replica shirt, which were expensive in Scandinavia and non-existent elsewhere. I bought a faux Trabzonspor kit with a faded Barcelona look and strolled the streets in my new jersey. I asked a man for directions. 'Go down the street, turn right, come to the main square and ask someone else.' I laughed at his honesty.

It was an inspired choice to visit a city unified by one team. The shipping, the separate identity, the fervent fans and the sweeping mountains reminded me of a hotter Bergen. Friendly smiles followed me around everywhere. A carpet trader gave me a Trabzonspor flag; others presented me with more scarves. A man even served me balık ekmek – fresh fish in fresh bread – wearing trousers in an impossible shade of Trabzonspor turquoise. I ate well in Trabzon, and always Turkish. It was very rare to see other cuisines represented in provincial Turkey.

Atatürk Square was strung with maroon and blue banners. People in matching colours congregated in the shaded tea shops. It seemed unlikely that anything other than football was being discussed. A group of young Trabzonspor fans ignited a flare, jumped up and down and chanted as women in headscarves filmed on their mobiles. The fans set off on their procession to the ground, a tradition started when the club played at the old Hüseyin Avni Aker Stadium, much closer to downtown Trabzon. They now had to leave earlier.

The Medical Park Arena buzzed with excited fans and traders. Ergin accompanied me through four security lines into the stadium. He hid my pen down his trousers and cigarette lighters in his shoes. He got me some tea to sip. Men prayed on mats, their deep floral designs contrasting with the harsh concrete floor. There were lots of women, many young, others older, a claret and blue headband an essential accessory. Ergin knew plenty of people at the stadium, many of whom were familiar from my visit to Akçaabat. I recognised one man by his turquoise trousers. I shouted 'balık ekmek' at him and he replied with a thumbs up.

Ergin and I sat behind the goal in the south stand. The crowd were muted until they stood for the national and Trabzonspor anthems. No one sat down for the entirety of the first half. Five men stood with their back to the game and built the crowd into a caffeine-fuelled frenzy. They waved, banged the seats, whistled, jumped up like Slipknot fans on the count of ten and sang local refrains. 'Jingle Bells' was the one familiar tune, appropriate given that Saint Nicholas was from present-day Turkey.

Trabzonspor and Alanyaspor both fielded hugely experienced international forwards. Turkey striker Yılmaz had rejoined Trabzonspor after a spell in China and thirty-three-year-old Vágner Love, capped twenty times for Brazil, plied his trade for the visitors. The game took just ten minutes to get going. Trabzonspor midfielder Şahan played a neat through ball to Yılmaz. The forward flicked it into the path of the Slovakian Kucka, who finished truly with his left foot, to make it 1–0 to the home side. 'Kucka', shouted the crowd. The south stand had been so involved in the tumult of shouting and screaming that I'm convinced most had missed the goal. 'I come to the game and go home to watch the match later', said the fan next to me. The noise levels increased further.

This never looked like a low-scoring game. Yılmaz scored Trabzonspor's second, the ball ricocheting on the left wing and falling nicely for the striker, who strode into the penalty area and stroked the ball low into the far corner. Yılmaz then latched onto a perceptive Sosa through ball, fell over and side-footed the resulting penalty to the goalkeeper's right. It was 3–0 to Trabzonspor. The crowd were delirious and smoked more cigarettes, their heady smell ever more intoxicating in the humid evening air.

Esteban, Trabzonspor's second-choice goalkeeper, made his only save of the match, parrying a free kick to his left. 'Esteban', chanted the crowd. Love then collected the ball on the halfway line and charged through the inside right channel. His run attracted limited interest from Trabzonspor defenders and the Brazilian struck a hard shot through the goalkeeper's legs to make it 3–1. There was no 'Esteban' chant. Esteban was surprisingly replaced after this mistake and Çakır, the young third-choice goalkeeper, would take his place in the second half.

Everyone sat down for a rest at half-time. Ergin passed water and another steaming tea to me. There was excited chatter about this being a 'number-plate game', 6–1. 61 is the number-plate code for Trabzon and was proudly displayed on the back of many shirts. I was not so convinced. Trabzonspor had scored an unfeasibly high proportion of their chances, one aided by a dubious penalty decision, and their defence continued to push up and play risky passes.

Ten minutes into the second half, Alanyaspor's Greek right back

Maniatis exploited space on the wing and midfielder Fernándes headed his deep cross beyond Çakır. 3–2, and the crowd were getting edgy. Trabzonspor then had another problem when Yokuslu headed wide from a corner and landed awkwardly. The Trabzonspor defender was limping around the pitch when the bright Fernándes was brought down for a penalty. Love took a diagonal and deliberate run-up. Çakır didn't look capable of saving a Word document and was stationary as Love placed the ball to his right. A solitary Alanyaspor fan jumped up in the opposite corner of the stadium. It was 3–3 after only sixty-eight minutes.

Trabzonspor were rocked. Fernándes played in Love, hunting for his hat-trick, and his shot was cleared off the line. Rodallega warmed up to chants of 'Ugo, Ugo, Ugo' and arrived as the third Trabzonspor substitute. Yokuslu collapsed and Trabzonspor were effectively down to ten men.

Yokuslu was still struggling on the sidelines when Love picked up another loose ball in midfield and was brought down for the clearest penalty of the three. Love passed the ball into the opposite corner for the first hat-trick of my travels. The crowd was incendiary. 'Manager go home', they chanted. A tame Rodallega header was the nearest Trabzonspor came to equalising. Yokuslu collapsed again in pain. It was tragic and compelling. Alanyaspor had come from 3–0 down to win 4–3. There was even a flutter of excitement in the Ministry of Justice as my colleague who drew Turkey realised that a seven-goal game put him in an enviably strong position in my sweepstake.

This was a crushing defeat. The crowd were ruined. Ire, insults and items were thrown towards the manager, the scapegoat after some mysterious substitutions. I could see why programmes were not sold.

It was just something else that could be thrown. Ergin kept his calm and shepherded me through the simmering crowd. It was important that I was safe. Making sure I had a good time was more crucial than Trabzonspor, at least for this game. Laz informed me that a lot of bad words had been shouted in the north stand. I asked which ones. 'All of them', he said.

I retired to a kebab shop on Atatürk Square for a delicious Adana wrap. The feeling of despair was dripping off the walls. I paid and the man behind the cash desk gave me the equivalent of £40 back in change by mistake. He shook his head. The entire city was struck with disbelief.

It didn't get any better. Trabzonspor lost their next home match 6–1 to mid-table Akhisarspor – 'a reverse number-plate game', joked Laz – and Ersun Yanal, their manager, was sacked. They ended the season fifth, sixteen points short of European qualification. Alanyaspor finished twelfth and Love left for Beşiktas.

18 Bulgaria

Lokomotiv Plovdiv are the most dangerous club to own in football. Three presidents had been murdered in the mid-2000s. And now the fans weren't happy. 'Snakes in the boardroom, mice on the pitch', read the no-nonsense banner unfurled at the match against Septemvri Sofia. Bulgaria was not going to be boring.

Whether Lokomotiv or Botev, I was always going to watch one of the Plovdiv teams. Yet a Bulgarian follower suggested I would be arriving a week too late in Bulgaria's second city, as the fiery Plovdiv derby was the previous weekend. But it had been played behind closed doors after Botev fans had thrown water over the visiting players and referee at a recent match against Levski Sofia. Lokomotiv fans were no angels either, it seemed, and had launched a metal bar at Slavia Sofia goalkeeper Stergiakis at their last home match. Amazingly, Lokomotiv's current rumbustious owner, Hristo Krusharski, had defended the fans, saying, 'That keeper provoked us throughout. I quite fancied hitting him myself.'

I took a flight from Trabzon to Istanbul and a bus to under-visited Edirne, three hours north-west of Istanbul and home to the Selimiye mosque, considered the pinnacle of the architect Sinan's creations. 'What are you doing in Bulgaria?' asked the frosty border official as I re-entered the European Union on the bus to Plovdiv. I had indifferent feelings about revisiting a country where everything is just a bit rubbish. I think of Bulgaria and I think of budget beaches and cheap skiing. Its capital Sofia, once an important part of the Roman empire, can be seen in precisely four hours. I know because I've visited twice now. Even the locals were deserting in droves. Bulgaria is one of the fastest depopulating countries in the world, home to around nine million inhabitants when communism fell in 1989 and only seven million now.

Bulgaria was unlikely to be my favourite destination but the country had played an important part in my football life. I skidded across my lounge carpet when Yordan Letchkov headed the winner against Germany as the national team, with the superb Hristo Stoichkov as top scorer, were unlikely semi-finalists at USA 94, and unplanned experiences when I watched Fulham open their Europa League campaign at CSKA Sofia in 2009 helped shape my own European tour. Back then, I had bumped into a CSKA fan next to a communist monument near the National Stadium. We met his friends, drank cans outside side-street bars and took great pleasure in ridiculing city rivals Levski. This was not the archetypal European away day, although there was still time for post-match beers with Fulham fans and a Bulgarian barman who looked uncannily like Bobby Zamora. Fulham took home a point and I two decent bottles of red from Sofia airport, having not made much of a dent into the £50 I had changed into lev. Bulgaria was cheap then and still is now.

Along my journey, I would meet some very bland press officers at football clubs. It was, after all, their job to promote their club. Nikolay, a lifelong Lokomotiv fan, gave an honest and balanced view of the situation at his club. Surprisingly, he said that he had to approve match reports and photographs with players, even if they were from the youth team, before they were published. He was also a fan at heart. 'Most of the fans of Botev are not from the city, they are from small villages near Plovdiv. This is my perspective as a Lokomotiv supporter. If you ask Botev supporters they will say, "All Lokomotiv fans are from Turkey, they are all gypsies".' Bulgarians didn't like the Turks, after centuries of Ottoman rule.

I stopped at the sad concrete foundations of the new Botev Stadium on the way to Lokomotiv. The authorities had tried to cover up the stadium plan with a metal city map. Construction had stopped three years before and the unfinished stadium was now a tangle of weeds. Botev were searching for investors to find the estimated £13 million required to complete the build. Nikolay said that it was a Bulgarian tradition to destroy what had already been built and then say you have no money to build a replacement.

I chatted to Nikolay on the side of the Lokomotiv pitch. He helped translate some of the banners, one of which named three Lokomotiv board members and the coach. 'We want you out' was the stark exclamation. There was a boycott as fans demanded action following a string of poor results, including a 3–0 defeat in the previous week's derby. I had chanced upon Emil, a rare English-speaking fan, outside the stadium. He looked forlorn and said that continued disappointment was keeping many fans away. His father and grandfather were Lokomotiv fans. 'Love and heart makes me come to the stadium.' Both Emil and Nikolay fondly recalled Lokomotiv's last championship in 2003.

Nikolay went missing as kick-off approached. The PA announcer had been stuck in traffic transporting a Lokomotiv player back to Plovdiv from Sofia, and it had fallen to Nikolay gamely to take on the additional responsibilities, playing defiantly upbeat pop music and confidently announcing the teams.

Lokomotiv, struggling in tenth, and Septemvri Sofia, newly promoted and second from bottom, were both horribly out of form. I was not expecting to see a thriller in Plovdiv. Instead, I got an anti-crowd. The supporters were in a febrile mood from the very start. They howled at every decision, miscontrol or Septemvri move. Upton Park was hardly an encouraging place when West Ham were struggling but I had never heard this level of relentless derision against any home team. Lokomotiv looked nervous. Their centre back Markov nearly made a hash of a back pass and a defensive header. The crowd howled once more.

Right back Krumov, Lokomotiv's fourth captain of a season just ten games old, was given the first of a litany of yellow cards for a high challenge. Some glorious defensive hacks nearly entered orbit. Lokomotiv midfielder Velkovski took an almighty swing with an attempted shot and caught only the slightest part of the ball. The crowd jeered at their own player. Another Lokomotiv player miscontrolled the ball into touch. The crowd jeered again. They were furious that top goal-scorer and club legend Martin Kamburov had left Lokomotiv earlier in the season after a conflict with the owner, Krusharski.

Lokomotiv were not playing well against one of the weakest teams in the league. Septemvri, named after the month I was travelling in, started playing with more adventure. A training-ground corner targeted Sandanski a full thirty yards out. The Septemvri midfielder took a touch and tested the Lokomotiv goalkeeper with his shot. It was a slow-motion version of the Beckham–Scholes move against Bradford City. And the highlight of a desperately poor first half.

The boycott was half observed. One ultra group had brought their 'God with Us' flag in defiance, but the gate receipts from an angry crowd of around 400 probably didn't cover the cost of policing. An anti-Botev banner screened the ultras behind the goal from much of the penalty-box action. They didn't miss much. Nikolay explained that Lokomotiv were called 'Smurfs' by a radio commentator several decades ago 'as the players were very fast and brave like Smurfs'. The unusual nickname had stuck, but the current crop of players didn't look like they wanted to face such a hostile environment.

Lokomotiv went ahead just before the hour mark. Septemvri goalkeeper Georgiev flapped helplessly at a corner and pushed the ball into Marchev's path. He headed home from one yard out. It was a goal as poor as the game.

The referee handed out eleven yellow cards in a cynical match that never verged on being dirty. A red card was near inevitable and Septemvri defender Dobrev, already on a tightrope after an earlier block, received a late second yellow for an elbow. It was a red end to a grey 1–0 home win with a black atmosphere. The players didn't applaud the Lokomotiv fans after their palpable lack of support. Everyone went home not quite as unhappy as before. It had been a thoroughly dispiriting experience. I had missed my friend Tom's fortieth birthday in London and I know where I would rather have been.

I had earlier taken a free walking tour that ended at Nebet Tepe, one of the seven hills where historic Plovdiv had developed. I was distracted by an English woman who looked so London that I actually tried to work out which part of the city she lived in. Sue was from Streatham and took my photograph. I mentioned my challenge and she gave me her friend's email address at *Lonely Planet* and, one month later, they published an interview with me. I was hardly exploring lands as wild as Levison Wood and Benedict Allen, who were also featured in their 'Meet a Traveller' series, but it reminded me that I had a niche – something unique that others wanted to read about. I joked to Sue that her photograph would be used by the Bulgarian media. And *Meridian Match*, the sports daily, did, when they featured me the following week.

Plovdiv had been fine. The interesting Cabana district was a haven for independent shops and the old town was still more shabby chic than Disneyland. The Roman amphitheatre, only rediscovered in 1972 after a landslide uncovered part of the ruins, was now a restored hub for cultural events. Other Roman parts looked neglected, peppered with broken glass and enclosed by ugly fences. But there were hidden depths: the basements of shops revealed buried sections of the 240-metre-long ancient stadium. I had never been so excited in H&M.

There were similarities with the football match. Everything looked fine. The Lokomotiv pitch was a lush bed of lovely grass. The stadium was perfectly functional. But the management, players and fans were a discordant mess. And maybe, like the city, the best things about Lokomotiv Plovdiv, even Bulgarian football, were buried in history.

Septemvri, eighth, finished the regular season just ahead of Lokomotiv, ninth, in mid-table. Nikolay assured me later in the season that the Lokomotiv fans were now a little bit happier than when I visited.

Travel yarns and toads

Lonely Planet had been my backpacking guide and were now running an article that included my own travel tips. I did not have much wisdom to share – despite being labelled 'a veteran traveller' at the age of forty – but recounted visiting my sister, Claire, whilst she was teaching English in the Russian city of Novgorod. It was March, freezing, and I turned up without a coat. I missed my flight home and spent twenty hours waiting for the next Finnair plane, shivering on metal chairs in St Petersburg airport – which, in 1998, was a fairly rudimentary place – and listening to bootleg Nirvana and Judas Priest cassettes on my Walkman. 'I still don't understand why you came to Russia without a coat', said my sister.

These were the old days of travelling. It was me with a guidebook, film camera and, sometimes, a coat, a far cry from the tangle of tech and seven cables that joined me now. It's perhaps easy to get nostalgic: people talked more, places seemed impossibly exotic, and everyone rocked up at hotels without bookings. But there's no doubt that this spontaneity meant I stayed in some absolute dives. Every place in India seemed to have a resident mouse; the very cheapest, in the ramshackle town of Orchha, was a barn with mattresses piled on top of haystacks. A night cost the equivalent of 30p and helped me meet my generous £5 per day budget.

I was always attracted to the more unusual places, even when it didn't necessarily make sense to visit. I'm probably one of the very few Brits whose first Asian country was tiny Brunei. I am still not sure why I went to the Cook Islands before I could scuba dive. And my first long-haul holiday from work was a three-week visit to Iran where I watched, sadly only on television, the home country beat Guam 19–0 in a qualifier for the 2002 World Cup, a scoreline that remains their record margin of victory. I kept my eye trained on more bizarre places and celebrated my fortieth birthday by visiting Palau, an island nation with an amazing flag – a yellow sun on a turquoise blue background – but almost unheard of, unless you are a diver or interested in Pacific military history.

Football was sometimes part of the trip and I even played impromptu matches in Burma, Mexico and Ethiopia. I visited the fabulous rock-hewn churches of Lalibela, but almost as memorable was playing a game with hundreds of Ethiopian children, all shouting 'Crutch, Crutch, Peter Crutch' at their lanky new player. Everyone in Ethiopia wanted to know my own football team and, without a mobile phone or widespread internet, they found out scores earlier than me. A man outside my hotel in the southern city of Awassa bounced towards me. 'Fulham 6, West Brom 1. Chris Coleman very happy.' I couldn't believe I had missed a 6–1 home win. Or that he knew the then Fulham manager's name.

I still got a buzz from visiting the likes of Uzbekistan or Senegal. But my stays there were less about football, and more for taking photographs, absorbing the different cultures and collecting the odd unexpected anecdote. I crossed the land border between Karang in Senegal and Amdalai in The Gambia and spotted a large toad squatting in the corner of the Gambian office. I asked what the toad was doing. 'He lives there', said the Gambian official.

I definitely preferred to have a focus to my travels. I fulfilled my long-held dream of seeing the wildebeest migration in the Serengeti; carnival took me to Trinidad and Tobago, and a cat festival to Belgium. Yet I still found that it was football that broke down barriers more than any other mutual interest. I visited Luxor a few months after the Egyptian revolution in 2011. The amazing temples were empty and I stayed in the five-star Winter Palace for the cost of a hostel bed in London. But locals were desperate for business and, as just about the only tourist in town, it was impossible to avoid their clamour. It all changed when I walked into a smoky café, full of hookah pipes and local men, for the Champions League final between Barcelona and Manchester United. We watched the match and talked like friends. I was one of them, at least until I strolled the souk the following day.

19 Serbia

It was still goalless as seven minutes of additional time were indicated. The press box and Napredak home crowd were incredulous. It was maybe five minutes at best. Napredak were content with a point their defending had merited against a Red Star Belgrade side that had only conceded one goal in their opening eleven league outings. A free kick from Red Star substitute Milijaš was very close. The crowd whistled feverishly.

Plovdiv to Kruševac in Serbia is hardly a major route. My second Bulgarian bus of the day dropped me in Niš. A long-distance bus bound for Montenegro was about to depart via Kruševac. I was bemused that Niš, the third largest city in Serbia, did not have an ATM or moneychanger at its bus station. I was only carrying Bulgarian lev, British pounds and assorted shrapnel from the twenty-seven currencies I used on my travels. I had to get this bus, and jumped on knowing I had no Serbian dinars.

The ticket man looked concerned when I couldn't pay him the equivalent of £6. But, not for the first time, I had chosen my seat well. Stefan, my English-speaking neighbour, translated and reassured me that I was not about to be thrown off the bus. 'I'm 90 per cent sure there is an ATM at Kruševac bus station', he said, despite never having been there. I liked such reckless levels of confidence. We chatted for a couple of hours until a flashing ATM came into view as we drove into Kruševac station. I bounced off the bus and paid for my ticket.

As I dragged my bag through the growing hordes of Saturday night revellers in Kruševac, I must have looked a strange sight. This was not a city used to much tourism. I passed teenagers swigging cans of lager on the street and visited a kebab shop opposite a throbbing bar. I ate a pork kebab several hours earlier than the local youth. I may have merely been tasting the relief of making it to Kruševac, but it was delicious.

Kruševac was sleepy on a bright Sunday morning when I visited the small collection of historic sites. Worshippers congregated in a church with impressive brickwork and a cat lazily chased a surprised rodent in a ruined castle. I soaked up the sun in a quiet square and watched two young brothers kick a ball between tiny goals. 'Neymar, Messi, Benzema, Mbappé!' they shouted. This was a generation raised on the Champions League, not overly excited by domestic football. However, this was an important matchday for home side Napredak as Red Star, one of the two Belgrade big boys, were visiting Kruševac.

I visited the Mladost Stadium several hours before kick-off. Josef, a big Napredak fan, explained that during communism there were five approved stadium designs and clubs simply picked one of those five. The Mladost Stadium was neat, central and built in 1976 in just three months, with help from residents. Photographs showed locals looking happy next to their wheelbarrows, and I wondered whether I could see Chelsea fans upping tools for the rebuild of Stamford Bridge.

I walked down a desolate path behind the north stand that would have been frightening on a darker day. Metal bars around the entrances framed the enticing green of the pitch. 'Mentol Boys', proclaimed some pink graffiti. I walked into the shade of the east stand to chance upon an unexpected hive of activity Hundreds of police were milling around, many scoffing burgers, sustenance for the busy evening ahead.

The main gate was a heady mix of television people and yet more police. I wasn't quite sure how to find Valentina, Napredak's press officer, who had agreed to meet me following a friendly email exchange. I was on time, as I normally am, but everyone was concentrating on their jobs. The polite woman in the ticket office didn't speak English but knew Valentina's name. She pointed me towards the club building, a modern attachment to the stadium. I walked in purposefully, my business card in hand as a useful insurance policy.

Valentina was excited to meet me. I was intrigued to meet a woman working in football, the first since Malin in Sweden, the classy Italian style of her clothes standing out against the sportswear and military fatigues. Valentina had worked as a television producer for seventeen years when her hometown club approached her. She was nervous. 'When you work in television you are protected from the public because you are working with people with the same interests as you. You think everyone is nice.' She was scared of the 'Yakuza' ultras, Napredak's hardcore fans, and the people who worked at the club. But she took the job despite these concerns. 'Since I'm an Aries the great challenge for me was to succeed. I learnt everything about my job and after one year became a FIFA representative.'

'There are three things you don't touch in Kruševac', explained Valentina. 'The October 14th factory (heavy machinery), the Rubin factory (alcoholic beverages) and Napredak.' Jovan, a Belgrade journalist and Red Star fan, had called Napredak 'a solid club': a great compliment in a country where football clubs were often on the verge of disaster. Marko Mišković, the owner since 2012, had invested in the players and the stadium, including building floodlights, rather taken for granted now in mainstream English football. When Mišković took over, Napredak were struggling in the second division and they were now SuperLiga stalwarts.

The club had progressed, and I asked Valentina if attitudes to women working in football had changed. 'It's quite funny because we only have three women at our club including the finance director. We're always asked, "You are working at a football club? What are you doing there?" I always say that "I'm playing football".' Valentina showed me the press room. A dozen senior police and security officers were sat around a long table with stern faces. They were planning their tactics for the match with no less seriousness than the coaches. Valentina explained that I was English. 'As long as he can't understand what we're saying', said one of the chiefs, lightening the atmosphere.

I waited in the hallway where a nervous man in a blue suit with a laptop talked loudly about UEFA to a Napredak official. He pointed at me. He was either unhappy that I was not from UEFA or unhappy that I was. The suit stormed off across the bridge to the stadium. 'Welcome' was the unconvincing response from the official. After four months and nineteen countries, this was the first frostiness I had encountered anywhere.

The windows of Press Box 8 flapped open to allow in ambient stadium noise, errant footballs and wind chill. And let out cigarette smoke. I sat between two women in the press box: seasoned sports reporter Sanja and Vesna, a press officer from a second-division team. Sanja tapped away at her laptop. Vesna, all jet-black hair and perfume, took a plastic bag of hazelnuts out of her enormous beige handbag. This was so far proving to be a very different match experience.

The matchday DJ built an atmosphere by switching between club songs – Napredak have three, including a rather suspect rap – and classic anthems 'Eye of the Tiger' and 'We Are the Champions'. Napredak's stadium was built for football. The fans were close to the pitch and the noise was intense. Officials and players sidestepped security personnel, ball boys and cameramen as they exited the tunnel into the tight confines. Old photographs depicted the stadium with people standing behind the goal. Not much had changed.

Vesna lit a cigarette and held it delicately between her immaculate nails. The smoke mixed beautifully with the scent of the hazelnuts. The first Napredak chants were drowned by the drone from the Red Star fans. The game itself was technically better than in Plovdiv, if rather shapeless. Vesna seemed unimpressed by the contest. She entertained herself by taking selfies, pouting her lips, slipping her pink crocheted top slightly off her left shoulder. Sanja was making decent headway into her match report. As in Plovdiv, a red card looked more likely than a goal at half-time.

The second half started with a volley of fireworks and flares from the Red Star fans. Smoke filled the stadium and the game was stopped. Vesna was suddenly animated. 'Does this happen in England?' I shook my head. 'Always in Serbia.' The Red Star captain pleaded for the fans to stop. It was colourful for a few minutes, irritating afterwards. Firecrackers were thrown onto the pitch, some close to the Napredak goalkeeper they were doing their best to intimidate.

The Red Star fans started chants that followed the tunes of former England song 'Here We Go' and perennial favourite 'London Bridge is Falling Down'. The game was becoming a more enthralling joust. The Red Star fans quietened in anticipation as Stojković, their right back, fed left-winger Radonjić, who dragged a right-footed shot wide. Srnić then slammed the ball against the Napredak crossbar after a left-wing pull back from the sprightly Radonjić. There was a hubbub around the press boxes as they sought to confirm the player for their reports. 'Was that Srnić?' The journalists tapped away furiously.

Few were noticing the increasing chill in the October air as the match approached its climax. The Red Star fans became noisier, trying to inspire their team and hustle the Napredak goalkeeper, who clutched his head. It was an unforgivable coin.

The match was deep in injury time and Stojković was attacking like a winger. Napredak substitute Đerić broke down into left-wing space behind him, played the perfect pass to Mitrović and the midfielder chipped home brilliantly from outside the penalty area. Napredak had beaten leaders Red Star in the very last minute of stoppage time. Players and fans celebrated as if it was a title win. After the delirium had eased Valentina coolly invited me back for next season's Red Star match. I smiled knowingly. It was unlikely I would return to Kruševac. It had been hard enough getting there.

I melted into the evening after Napredak's late winner. It had been a great day. I was genuinely pleased for Napredak, who were very much the underdog. I stopped in a local tavern and dined on sarma – vine leaves stuffed with mince – meatballs and salad. My beer tasted good after an inspiring and interesting day. A second appeared. 'That's for you, man', said the burly man on the adjacent table before he sipped some terrifying-looking quince rakia. Kruševac had been the perfect choice for my Serbian match.

This was the only league match Red Star lost in their title-winning campaign. Napredak finished seventh.

20 Ukraine

I was getting used to delays in and out of London airports. But this one was serious. My morning flight from Heathrow to Warsaw was delayed and I would not make my connection to Ukraine. I sighed. I never like arriving late into a new destination and my re-routed flight via Istanbul meant I reached central Odessa long after nightfall. The neglected sign for my cheap hotel hung above an uncompromising dark alley. Two beggars approached me and I swerved into a prostitute who offered me somewhere to stay. I briefly wondered if this was a planned pincer movement. I didn't hang around to find out, plunging through a heady stench of urine into the alleyway. This was not a good start to my stay in Ukraine.

Odessa was founded on the north-western shore of the Black Sea just over 200 years ago by Catherine the Great. It has a cosmopolitan past and present that provokes pride in its population. 'At school, everyone doesn't say they are "Ukrainian", "Russian" or "Armenian". They say "I am Odessian"', said Grigoriy, an erudite young journalist for website Futbol 24. I remarked that the European-influenced architecture reminded me of St Petersburg. 'No, St Petersburg is the Odessa of the Baltic' was the response. I loved these local sayings.

Odessa was built from under ground. The beautiful Baroque buildings and solid residential blocks were constructed from the native soft rock that insulates sound and maintains warmth. There were holes both underneath the city and, so it seemed, in the home football team. Chornomorets Odessa were bottom with only one win from their first eleven matches.

I strolled past the magnificent opera and ballet theatre and down the Potemkin stairs, made famous by the silent film *Battleship Potemkin*. A grizzly man was selling old coins at the bottom. He was forthright about football – 'For me Ukrainian football is dead' – and the local team – 'Every few months they change half the Chornomorets team'. Football in Odessa felt as hollow as its mines, the mood at Chornomorets blacker than its sea.

Grigoriy from Futbol 24 said that the Ukrainian Premier League was getting progressively worse. Ukrainian football had been adversely affected by Russia's annexation of Crimea in 2014. Shakhtar Donetsk retained their squad of Brazilians – Willian, Douglas Costa and Fred had all passed through in recent years – but less powerful clubs could not persuade frightened foreign players to stay. Clubs, run by businessmen with commercial interests threatened by the crisis, were forced to promote untried young Ukrainians into their teams. Top-division teams Olimpik Donetsk, Zorya Luhansk and Shakhtar played matches outside their home cities in eastern Ukraine. It was no wonder the league was on its knees.

I walked through Tarasa Shevchenka Park, where low arches framed the city's busy port. The Chornomorets Stadium sits incongruously and unintentionally in the middle of the park. The authorities originally wanted to build a lake. A hole was dug but money ran out before work was completed. The empty space was turned into a football pitch and eventually the first stadium. Grigoriy was bemused why a lake was planned just 100 metres away from a great sea. The stadium was rebuilt in 2011 and retained some of the columns from the original. The imaginatively monikered Black Sea Hotel was located in the north stand. Sadly, rooms only had views of the water, not the pitch.

I bought a ticket for the Sunday evening match against Dynamo Kiev, bumbled into the main entrance and found a club official. I gave him my card and later received a bevy of messages as the club found out about my challenge. The most welcoming was from Nikolay, Chornomorets' translator, and we met in an underground bar that Saturday evening. Nikolay was probably in his late fifties but still had a joyful spring in his step. His English was passable, and excusable given that he spoke five languages more fluently: Ukrainian, Russian, Portuguese, Spanish and French. Nikolay's wife had wondered how he would communicate with an Englishman, and I hardly thought my rudimentary Spanish would be useful in Ukraine. But a combination of bad English and worse Spanish worked, given Nikolay's naturally inquisitive and welcoming demeanour.

Nikolay had worked in the army as a translator, his Portuguese invaluable in Angola and Mozambique during the dying days of the Soviet Union, and his job put him in some compromising positions. 'Sometimes I knew it was illegal to translate the document I was given.' But not doing so would go against the army. 'It was impossible', said Nikolay, who is immensely proud of his Ukrainian heritage; a blue and yellow flag was carefully positioned on his car dashboard. He spoke only Ukrainian in Odessa, which caused some confusion. A man asked in Russian if we were using a spare chair at our table. Nikolay replied in Ukrainian and the man responded, 'Don't you speak Russian?' It was unusual not to revert to Russian even in the current political climate.

Nikolay explained that the previous season was *too* good for Chornomorets. They finished sixth, narrowly outside the Europa League spots. Key players left for other clubs and Chornomorets didn't make any money from the transfers. The Ukrainian league has a particularly short turnover, finishing at the end of May and starting again in the middle of July. Chornomorets had started poorly with an almost entirely new team. Nikolay was upbeat about the match the following day, as players usually upped their game against Dynamo and Shakhtar.

Nikolay sedately sipped his beer and explained that he was playing football the following morning, a tradition followed by a Sunday barbecue. He invited me along, and ten hours later I found myself playing in borrowed trainers one size too small. The pitch was sheltered by a protective plastic dome and even had a small stand for spectators. I was impressed. 'Everything is better in Ukraine', joked Rob, a gnarled sea captain who spoke the best English and played the worst football. 'Football is the second most popular sport in Ukraine', he added. 'First is politics.'

Rob barked orders to play long balls to him and everyone fervently contested decisions, as they do at casual matches around the globe. Our goalkeeper was sixty-eight years old, whilst the youngest players were in their twenties. I hit a fine shot, low and hard to the other ancient goalkeeper's right. The glovesman got a slight touch and a teammate snaffled the goal as it crossed the line. I was left feeling like Jermain

Defoe after David Nugent poached his only England goal against Andorra. It was the perfect prelude to Chornomorets Odessa against Dynamo Kiev.

Nikolay introduced me to his friend Alex at the stadium. Alex remembered the old stadium fondly. 'If the match wasn't very good, you could turn around and gaze at the Black Sea.' Alex had been a fan since 1966. 'To be a Chornomorets fan is to suffer all life long. We have never ever won any great prize. We never won the Championship, never won the Soviet Cup, only the Ukrainian Cup. Every year, we strive to get something and every time something interferes with our wish.' Chornomorets had recently celebrated the fortieth anniversary of the team that finished third in the Soviet championship in 1974.

'Seven Nation Army' and 'Smells Like Teen Spirit' rocked the barely quarter-full stadium before we stood for the Chornomorets song. Two dozen female dancers entranced fans unused to such harmonious teamwork on the Chornomorets pitch, whilst bored teenage boys held a giant circular club banner. Chornomorets, not really known for its ultras scene, attracted a range of fans from hopeful youth to weathered sea dogs. Horns and a drumbeat felt sparse in a rather hollow atmosphere for a match against Dynamo Kiev.

Chornomorets were immediately on the defensive whilst Dynamo's full backs attacked and left spaces for eager counter-attacks. Chornomorets' midfielder Kovalets failed to take advantage on the break when he stepped on the ball. This was normal according to Alex. The home crowd erupted minutes later when Khoblenko, Chornomorets' lone striker, fed Kovalets, who steered a low shot into the far corner. Two flares were lit high up behind the goal and a warning followed on the PA system. Alex didn't care for the smoke and mirrors of the ultras' behaviour. 'I come to watch the beautiful game', he said, without irony or cynicism. Alex's dreams edged closer to reality when Khoblenko scored a passable replica of the first goal. 'Song 2' bounced around the stadium again.

Chornomorets were 2–0 up at the break, during which I turned down dried fish snacks that looked more like cat treats than a terrace staple and picked up a beer. I heard premonitions of a 3–0 win from barflies who had rapidly forgotten that the ball didn't leave the Chornomorets half in the last fifteen minutes. I predicted 2–1. The defensive masterclass continued into the second half and crosses from Dynamo's full backs were easily repelled. Alex took a photograph of the scoreboard. I warned that there were still thirty-five minutes remaining.

The sharp sound of a firecracker echoed around the stadium like a bullet. Pretty pink flares were lit amongst the small contingent of hardcore home fans. Odessa were now hanging on. The Congolese bruiser Mbokani, who had loan spells at Norwich and Hull City, used his strong chest to hold the ball up well for Dynamo, while substitute Kravets' shot was cleared from near Chornomorets's goal-line. It was starting to get a little desperate.

Dynamo pulled one goal back when Kravets converted from close range. Mbokani headed a cross wide as Alex looked increasingly anxious. Smoke from Dynamo flares occluded their own fans' view high up in the corner. Chornomorets' fans drifted away from the smoke into the many empty seats to watch the tense final few minutes.

Chornomorets clung on without fashioning a second-half chance. The players hugged one another. For many this was the first win they had experienced in Odessa. Chornomorets had not beaten Dynamo Kiev at home since 2003. I was greeted in Odessa by two beggars and a prostitute. I left with a fistful of new friends and a second shock home win in a row.

Chornomorets finished eleventh and lost a relegation play-off against FC Poltava. In a chain of events fairly typical of Ukraine, Poltava were dissolved in June 2018 and Chornomorets were chosen as their replacement in the 2018–19 Premier League. Dynamo Kiev were second.

21 Moldova

A key, a smile and a WiFi code. I only need three things when I arrive at a hotel. The Cosmos Hotel in Chişinău is an uncompromising concrete block, famous to every Moldovan. I had printed a very limited edition, of one, T-shirt advertising my travels and Anastasia, leading light in the Cosmos reception, immediately noticed my attire. 'Fooootball, I like foooootball', she said. Anastasia let me retire to my retro room before quizzing me further.

Anastasia had long dark hair and a glint in her eyes. 'I think you are very lucky because you came to the Cosmos. And I'm here.' She was right: some of my chance encounters had been more illuminating than others. Anastasia explained, with almost Latin animation, how her love for football had been heightened by the Cosmos being the base for Milsami, the only team to win the Moldovan championship apart from Sheriff Tiraspol, the club from the breakaway territory of Transnistria, and Zimbru, my hosts in Chişinău. A poster of the Milsami squad sat on the Cosmos reception desk.

'You understand it is so exciting, all this football. I know the most important fooootballers, yes, yes.' The Cosmos was cheap, very cheerful and an obvious choice for international fans watching their country play in Chișinău. Moldova had played Wales in a World Cup qualifier the previous month and the Cosmos was full of Wales supporters. 'We joked with them. They are surprised when we say, "Gareth Bale, we need his autograph".'

I left Anastasia to stroll around Chișinău, a capital hard to recommend unless you were a city planner with a black sense of humour. I visited the top three TripAdvisor sights: two parks, golden in their autumnal glory, and a brick-coloured war memorial. I walked through the very small Arc de Triomphe that marks the centre of the city. The rest of Chișinău was something of a mess: dilapidated communist buildings loomed over the main roads, the foundations of an unfinished building were filled with litter and a lonely rat scampered across broken glass in an underpass. Chișinău's harsh architecture was a throwback to a previous era.

I also had a culinary challenge in Chișinău. My friend, another Matt, visited Moldova in 2016 and had been very critical about the local cuisine. I wondered whether I could find anything tasty to eat in Chișinău. I used to review food and service in London restaurants as a mystery shopper, an undercover activity that heightened my observation skills and made me an expert in the menus of Italian chains. And, as I had a free meal for two, everyone's favourite dinner partner. The ping of a microwave in an empty Moldovan restaurant with an unfeasibly long menu didn't promise; some annihilated meat smothered in cheese sauce didn't deliver. Locals didn't want to eat Moldovan food when they went out for dinner. They wanted Italian, burgers and sushi. I joined them in Andy's Pizza.

I thought there might be hidden treats at the Cosmos. Two old women examined my breakfast token with Soviet-style scrutiny before crossing me off their guest list. I dined on stolid bread, sickly cheese pancakes and apple juice that looked and tasted like urine. The recycling was impressive. One of the women collected dirty plates piled with uneaten slabs of fat and pushed the meat back onto the buffet. I had four Cosmos breakfasts and ate progressively less each morning.

My journey from Odessa had taken me through Transnistria, a breakaway state that occupied a strategic slice of land between the Dniester River to the east of Chișinău and the western border of Ukraine. Transnistria had its own government and a currency, the Transnistrian ruble, which was worthless elsewhere. Apart from to coin collectors. Transnistria issued brightly coloured plastic coins in different shapes, including the quirky three ruble: a subtle nod away from western-leaning Moldova and towards the east, where many ex-Soviet countries had previously issued this unusual denomination. I stayed at the Hotel Russia in Tiraspol, previously a base for Tottenham Hotspur when they played Sheriff in the 2013–14 Europa League. The hotel name said all you needed to know about Transnistria's political alignment.

Sheriff have won fifteen titles and are the most successful team in the Moldovan league. The club, whose badge fuses influences from Clint Eastwood Westerns and the Champions League logo, were founded in 1997 by Victor Gușan, a mysterious ex-policeman who presumably made most of his millions from outside the police force. Sheriff were all over town in Tiraspol, with posters of their latest championship celebrations plastered on billboards. The overarching Sheriff company also runs Transnistria, operating supermarkets, petrol stations and telecommunications, and even producing the local beer.

I visited the hugely impressive Sheriff sports complex where the main stadium, with expensive car showrooms underneath, gleamed in the morning light. A second arena with a capacity of nearly 9,000 hid behind, while an indoor pitch with an enormous domed roof, swimming pool, tennis courts and a hotel for stranded foreign players completed the sparkling facilities. These monied structures felt out of place in one of the poorest parts of Europe. The appeal of living in Transnistria, heavily disliked by Moldova and Ukraine, was reducing, and thereby the population of Tiraspol, the capital still dotted with Lenin statues, was decreasing.

Sheriff paid better salaries than other teams in the Moldovan league, with foreigners earning around £8,000 per month, and local players less. I asked a Sheriff official what players thought about working in such a remote place. She was frank. 'We don't care what they think, we pay them money.' Players struggled to spend their salaries in Tiraspol, where the highest public-sector salary was under £200 per month. Transnistria's grey status encouraged a darker market in trade and earnings.

Sheriff's recent dominance had, surprisingly, been broken when Milsami, from the small town of Orhei, won their only Moldovan championship in 2015. Milsami had used the Cosmos as their Chişinău base, and Anastasia had motivated the team in different ways. For instance, Igor Banović, a Croatian midfielder, asked for a sweet from the Cosmos reception before every match as he believed that chewing a gum would bring Milsami a goal. Anastasia and her colleagues also had superstitions: one of the receptionists followed Milsami's progress on Moldfootball, a Moldovan football website, whilst Anastasia had to wait until the game was forty minutes old before opening LiveScore. This was a modern interpretation of my old habit of only flicking to the Fulham score on Teletext for the last fifteen minutes.

'I'm a little bit of a psychologist', said Anastasia. She was probably a better psychologist than me, despite my degree in psychology from Durham University. 'I'm a hotel manager. I have hundreds of guests with problems. Mentality is very important. Zidane said we are strong from the mind.' I couldn't imagine that Zizou had ever stayed in the Cosmos. 'We see it when the Milsami boys have problems. We see them every day, the sacrifices they make, their concentration. We encourage them. When they go to match we have to be silent. When they lose we say, "For us, you are the best players in the world".'

And in 2015, Milsami were the best players in Moldova. Anastasia showed me a video of her and the team celebrating with the championship trophy in the Cosmos. She unfurled a massive homemade poster, which included newspaper clippings and photographs of their triumph. 'Every player found himself in the poster. It gave them motivation for the Champions League.' It sort of worked. Milsami beat group-stage regulars Ludogorets before going out to Skënderbeu of Albania in the third qualifying round.

I wasn't able to watch Milsami, as they were playing Petrocub in the awkwardly located town of Hîncești, so left the Cosmos for Zimbru Chișinău against Speranța Nisporeni. The Zimbru Stadium looked rather like a half-built Carrow Road, only with neat rows of rubbish bins along the sidelines. It was overlooked by a mighty fifteen-storey block of crumbling Soviet flats, the devil child of the Gorbals in Glasgow. I took an empty seat and was immediately ushered onto another as police cordoned off an area behind the goal. I presumed this was in the interest of crowd safety, having witnessed spectacularly awful warm-up shooting pepper the green seats.

Zimbru were champions for eight of the first nine seasons following Moldovan independence in 1992. But Sheriff had spoiled their party. 'Zimbru have the most supporters and they are very angry because they lose and lose and lose', said Anastasia. She said that typical Zimbru fans were now forty to fifty years old and cling to their memories from twenty years ago. A man with fuzzy dark hair who met Anastasia's description sat down behind me. Vlad had been a Zimbru fan for twenty-five years. I looked at the team sheet and asked him whether there were any players to look out for. He shook his head slowly and deliberately. 'It's difficult to say', he sighed. 'It's my town, my team', was Vlad's explanation for turning up when many didn't. The rest of the modest crowd of 300 mainly consisted of old men and children clasping giant packets of crisps.

Vlad's perm was surrounded by youths with crew cuts under half his age. He looked strangely comfortable in such company, even when the teenagers playfully pushed each other around and indulged in a salute just low enough to avert controversy. A small girl with a pink bobble hat nodded her head in time. This was hardly a threatening group of football fans. 'Zimbru Chişinău' was their chant, and a drumbeat drone the soundtrack to a fairly uneventful first half. Zimbru left back Moreira's deep cross fell at the feet of midfielder Zagaevschi, who controlled and fired a strong shot beyond the Speranţa goalkeeper's flailing hands.

I noticed that the scoreboard had a clock, a match timer and a red number one in the centre of the screen. I was confused until the second half revealed that the number was a half indicator, something I had not seen before on my travels. Strange but somehow Moldovan. Zimbru were 1–0 up as the half indicator switched from one to two.

The sky turned a beautiful misty pink as the evening drew in. Faded lights were turned on in the enormous concrete tower block. Two girls with dark hair and ripped black jeans were having more fun watching Vlad and his bouncing ultras than the second half. 'Zimbru Chișinăuuuuuuuu' boomed the PA system during a break in play and, like an unwanted karaoke singer, stunned the hardcore into silence. The PA system reverted to announcing substitutes five minutes after they had taken place. The Speranța fans, lifted by their team's flurry of half chances, became more audible on the thick evening air and roared after a corner led to some frantic penalty-area pinball. The ball hit six or seven players in a faintly comedic sequence, the last being Speranța centre back Planić's unstoppable side-foot into the top corner to make it 1–1.

Earlier I had asked Anastasia for her prediction. She quoted injuries, coaches and Paulo Coelho. 'I think Zimbru will win. It will not be a big score. Speranța will also score. I think 2–1. I already know.' She shrieked when it matched my own forecast. Five minutes after Speranța's equaliser, bumbling Brazilian substitute Douglas side-footed home a rebound. 'Goallllll Zimbru' announced the PA system as Zimbru held on for a 2–1 win.

The next day I dropped by the Cosmos reception on my way to the previous morning's meat slice. Anastasia gave me a high five. 'I understand something in football I think', she said. Moldovan football and the Cosmos were in safe hands.

Speranţa and Zimbru finished sixth and eighth respectively. Milsami were second behind Sheriff, who won their sixteenth title in the last eighteen seasons. The Cosmos is still open for business.

Bloc party

Moldova was the last of the eleven UEFA countries I would visit that were once part of the Soviet Union. Meanwhile, my personal football empire was growing steadily and this felt like a landmark. I had spent two months in the very east of the European football map before the leaves had fallen or the temperatures dropped, and could now reflect on the best and worst Soviet-style moments from the road, the pitch and the dinner plate.

When I first travelled to Russia in 1998, my sister's hosts sponsored me for a business visa, offering more flexibility, but causing some confusion when I tried to stay at barren student accommodation in St Petersburg. 'I'm a student businessman', I lied. The hotels I stayed in two decades later were modern if featureless affairs, notable for their limited toilet roll, rationed as if in Soviet times. In Kazakhstan, the 'best hotel in Taraz' was expensive and slightly shambolic. Bathroom light fittings clattered to the floor as I attempted to sleep on a mattress made of wood. I was often joined at breakfast by grumbling businessmen, apart from in my Moscow hostel, where I ate alone until a rat the size of a small football joined me. I shrieked and soon learned from the hysterical receptionist that *krysa* was Russian for rat.

The stadiums were like digestives: crumbling and not a biscuit-tin highlight. The action was too far away from the stands in many. Cursed running tracks were a legacy of Soviet multi-use. Chornomorets Odessa in Ukraine was a rare exception. The stadium had a Black Sea soul and a motorbike shop, nightclub and hotel for all your post-match needs. Vitebsk in Belarus was my least favourite. I had a better view of the paramedic reading her magazine in an ambulance than the football. Yet it was my most entertaining match with Kostyukevich's antics and the Section 8 hardcore ingrained in my mind. There might not have been much atmosphere at my matches in Yerevan, but the Spartak Moscow and Tula Arsenal fans put on a good show despite iffy Russian Premier League games.

Defensive football was en vogue. I watched a relatively measly thirty-six goals in fifteen matches as teams often lined up with five at the back. Ufa went one further with a holding midfielder dropping very deep, good enough to counter reigning champions Spartak Moscow on a melting afternoon. Goals might have been in short supply but the football was ridiculously cheap: free entry for all in Georgia, Azerbaijan and Armenia and not much more elsewhere, my outlay averaging around £2 across former Soviet lands. And that included spunking a tenner on the suntan seats in Ufa.

I travelled on Russian trains that rumbled through the night, Azerbaijani minibuses that careered around every corner and a Kazakh airline called SCAT. It wasn't very comfortable. But the sights, away from the football, were astoundingly diverse. I enjoyed the individualistic cities: the unique mix of influences in Tbilisi, the dreamy Tallinn spires, the surprisingly green and unsurprisingly Stalinist Minsk and the graceful buildings of Odessa. I escaped the cities when I could for fresh air and amusement. I visited some of Azerbaijan's 400 mud volcanoes, the greatest number of any country, on a cursed group tour. The guide clearly explained in three languages – English, Russian and Azerbaijani – not to get too close to one particularly explosive volcano. Ten seconds after he had finished speaking, a burly Russian man started charging up said volcano. Sadly, it remained dormant.

Georgia was my favourite country of them all. Entry bureaucracy dictated that I visited four times, taking in its emblematic ancient churches, walking the majestic Greater Caucasus Mountains and drinking wines in fertile Kakheti. But the most beautiful spot was the unfinished Mausoleum of Khoja Ahmed Yasawi in Turkistan, near Shymkent in Kazakhstan, arguably more charming than the over-restored Timurid architecture I had once visited in neighbouring Uzbekistan. It was a blue-sky Monday when I strolled the peaceful gardens alone and admired the greatest building in Kazakhstan.

Moscow divided me. It was a brasher, more confident place than the brooding goliath I had visited twenty years earlier. I meandered around the magnificent Tretyakov Gallery, the vivid paintings of rural life more rewarding than wandering around a Red Square being polished for the 2018 World Cup. I spent hours in its capacious spaces, and the art nouveau-influenced paintings of Mikhail Vrubel in a large, dark room made me reflect. My mother, who studied history of art, would have loved the deeply coloured escapism. I sat down and suddenly felt alone. Mammoth cities like Moscow were not integral to my journey.

I ate better than expected: steaming horse and plov in Kazakhstan, the world's best chicken kebab at Sehirli Tendir in Baku and, best of all, delicious borsch, wild rabbit and chocolate dessert at Pashtet in Yekaterinburg. It all fell apart in Ukraine. I might have chosen poorly but nothing tasted good apart from the local craft beer. A dish of cold chicken livers, apple and mashed potato with blueberry sauce at Molodost in Odessa was knowingly retro and devastatingly awful. Chişinău might have been another culinary low point, but I escaped to the Château Vartely winery in Orhei where I sampled the fruits of Moldovan vines and was allowed to keep the freshly opened bottles. I was incapable of drinking six near-full bottles in two days so presented several to Anastasia and her Cosmos colleagues.

It was the people that really added spice and context to my eastern travels. Football clubs may have ignored my advances but I enjoyed the company and hospitality of Eric in Kazakhstan, Nikita in Russia, Yury and Anton in Belarus, Nikolay and Alex in Ukraine and Anastasia in Moldova. I was certain I would see better matches elsewhere. I would be fortunate to chance upon such big characters.

CHANGE OF IDEAS

22 Romania

Identity is everything to a football fan, at home and, as I would find out, in Romania. I had felt empathy with recent protests at Cardiff City (about the Bluebirds' controversial change from blue to red shirts in 2012, reversed in 2015) and Hull City (concerning the proposed rebranding to 'Hull Tigers'). And I certainly struggled to identify as closely as normal with Fulham during our two-year stint at Loftus Road until we returned to Craven Cottage in 2004, although not after seeking an alternative site, something rather forgotten by many, which may have stretched my allegiance.

In Romania, I would watch Juventus Bucureşti – who had been relocated forty miles away to Ploieşti whilst the club resolved land ownership issues in the capital – play Sepsi Sfântu Gheorghe. And the following day I would witness how FCSB, a team who had changed their name from the famous Steaua Bucharest, were struggling with their new identity in a match against Poli Timişoara.

I flew from Chişinău and had to get from Bucharest airport to

Ploiești, thirty miles to the north, for my first Liga I match later that afternoon. There was something *Fawlty Towers* about breakfast at the Cosmos Hotel on the Moldovan Riviera. The start of my time in Romania felt rather like another John Cleese vehicle, the film *Clockwise*. The clocks were all ticking. The city of Ploiești, after all, is famous for its clock museum, one of the few of its kind in Europe.

'Ploiești?' asked my taxi driver. I showed him a map on my phone. He was clearly unconvinced, either by my pronunciation or destination, and checked these unusual instructions with an airport supervisor before driving as hard and straight as the road. He wasn't happy. 'No return fare', he said, conveniently overlooking that I had paid twice the normal Bucharest city centre tariff. I was relieved. I had made it to Juventus București against Sepsi in time.

Juventus's move had not gone well. The club were failing to attract fans to Ploiești – this match had a pitiful attendance of 150 despite entrance to the 15,000-capacity stadium being free – and had drawn four and lost the other ten of their opening fourteen matches. Sepsi, who, like Juventus, had been promoted twice in the previous two seasons, were also struggling, positioned twelfth in the fourteen-team Liga I. This was a relegation battle in October.

Sepsi were enthusiastically backed by ethnic Hungarians who make up the majority of their Transylvanian hometown of Sfântu Gheorghe, once part of the Kingdom of Hungary. I watched a gaggle of travelling fans staggering out of their coach stinking of booze. 'Where is the toilet?' asked one Sepsi supporter, desperate after the long, beery journey from central Romania. Others clustered around a fan leader for their free tickets: one held a cigarette too close for comfort, another a sponge cake to soak up the alcohol, a third was a dead ringer for Derek

Smalls from Spinal Tap. The Sepsi fans proudly showed off their scarves and flags, Hungarian slogans scrawled on them. There was no doubt about their identity. They wanted their own country. Or to be part of another one.

Inebriated Hungarian voices were soon in some sort of separatist ecstasy when Sepsi striker Astafei scored with a low finish. Astafei had multiple personas: he moonlighted as a rapper with the stage name Asta ('This One') and was an internet poet with literary aspirations. 'My dream is to write a book and it will certainly become reality', he said in a recent interview. Sepsi's play was neater and their fans were also well co-ordinated, jumping up and down to celebrate and sitting down in unison precisely halfway through the opening period.

Juventus equalised later in the first half and took a 2–1 lead on the hour when Măzărache, their big number nine, slammed home a rebound. The Sepsi fans, suddenly as quiet as the empty seats, started solemnly taking their flags down, folding them carefully ahead of the long coach journey home. There was still half an hour left to play, but it proved an accurate prediction as Juventus held on for their first win of the season. The Sepsi fans sang a rousing song with a few minutes remaining, then trudged disconsolately up the steps and back in the direction of their coach.

The next day I took the train to Bucharest and visited a children's fair overlooked by former dictator Nicolae Ceauşescu's monolithic Palace of the Parliament, the world's heaviest building. I met Adrian, a follower of my travels and social media manager for Carmen Bucureşti, by the giant mushrooms that dominated this strange scene. Adrian was trying to forge a new identity for Carmen, who were formed in 1937 and folded ten years later after they failed to follow orders to lose a friendly against Dinamo Tbilisi when Romania was under communist rule. Carmen re-formed in 2017 and now played in the regional fourth tier. Adrian said that fans can pay what they want to watch Carmen matches. 'If you don't pay anything, you don't deserve to watch the game. Even two or three lei is more than nothing.' At another match every woman called Carmen got free entry to the game.

Adrian used social media to entice younger supporters and had intended to film a video of the Carmen team on a tethered hot air balloon at this festival. But there was a problem. It was too windy for the balloon to be unleashed. The players looked uncomfortable in their club tracksuits, pacing from side to side, as children ran around them. Airy folk music drifted on the breeze. This wasn't very cool, even for a fourth-division footballer.

I left the mammoth mushrooms for the National Arena, one of the host stadiums to be used in Euro 2020. The stadium was visible from some distance, a glowing circle edging above the trees. Up close, high grey arches contrasted beautifully with stairways brightened by soft yellow light. Inside, the view was astonishing from high on the halfway line, the pitch feeling closer than at other stadiums of a similar 55,000 capacity. Inoffensive mainstream pop bounced out from the sparkling sound system, and the teams were pictured on a floating giant cube supported by numerous metal strands. It was a fantastic modern setting with a fantastical theme tune. The teams walked on to the music from *Game of Thrones*, apparently a favourite of FCSB's owner.

I met another Adrian, this time from PRO TV, in the stands and we talked about FCSB, the army team who were European Cup winners in 1986 as Steaua. There had been confusion about the legal entity of Steaua following privatisation, and so the club had changed their name and symbol to FCSB. Steaua's ultras defected to a splinter team, Sporting Club of the Army, who played in the fourth tier and would attract an enormous crowd of 36,000 – easily the highest in modern Romanian football, but still below the European fourth-division record of 49,000 for Rangers against East Stirling in 2012 – when they played Academia Rapid later in the season.

Adrian blamed George Becali, the controversial owner unpopular with the ultras, for the Steaua split. Becali had said he was not interested in fans and that he only wanted to develop young players who could then be sold for sizeable transfer fees. Adrian was balanced enough to admit that some people liked Becali. 'He's the people's person. He says it like it is.' Becali's views had enraged an impressive range of people, including Europa League opponents Hapoel Be'er Sheva. The Israeli club, who would be one of my hosts when I visited the Middle East three months later, were owned by a much-admired businesswoman, Alona Barkat, who had seen her unfashionable club win two successive championships. 'Women can't be presidents or owners of football clubs because that's a man's job', said Becali.

Visitors Poli Timișoara sat with every player behind the ball. 'A goal will help this game', I said to Adrian and, seconds later, FCSB forward Gnohéré obliged with a confident left-footed finish after a perfect fifty-yard pass from Budescu. Gnohéré was a crowd favourite: the FCSB fans warmed to the passionate striker who had lost three stone but still looked a bruising competitor. Gnohéré was known as 'the bison', coincidentally also the symbol of Zimbru, my Moldovan hosts. 'Goal Steaua Bucharest', announced the booming PA system. 'Steaua, Steaua, Steaua', chanted the crowd, never acknowledging their team's current incarnation as FCSB.

Adrian told me more about Coman, the promising left-sided attacker signed recently from champions Constanţa, the club founded by Romanian legend Gheorghe Hagi. Coman's girlfriend was not a fan of his varicose veins so he went to see a faith healer, who recommended leeches. The leeches had not helped his veins, but seemingly sucked away Coman's power, and he had started the season poorly. Coman, wearing socks over his knees as he tried to forget his leech adventures, slotted in a second FCSB goal from a right-wing cross. Timişoara looked desperate and beaten. A tiny group of ten away supporters, marshalled by one policeman in swathes of empty seats, looked depressed, bodies slumped in their seats and heads in their hands.

It got worse for the away side. Gnohéré collected another brilliant Budescu pass through the inside left channel and fired home a left-footed shot. It was 3–0 at half-time and, shortly after the interval, Coman scored his second to make it 4–0. Centre back Larie headed in a fifth from a beautifully arced Budescu free kick. Gnohéré then fired an unstoppable shot into the roof of the net and celebrated his left-footed hat-trick with the FCSB bench. It was 6–0 and there was nearly half an hour left to play.

FCSB relaxed. Budescu pulled off an audacious curling pass with the outside of his right boot. It was the sort of flick you attempt when comfortably ahead in a kickabout with your friends. And it would get even worse for Timişoara. Substitute Tănase was going nowhere fast on the inside left of the area when Šoljić brought him down for a penalty. The centre back was given a harsh yellow card for the foul and then sent off for lamping the ball high into the stands. Tănase slotted home the penalty. It finished 7–0, FCSB's largest margin of victory since defeating the same opponents 8–1 in 2004, when FCSB were still known as Steaua.

The FCSB players celebrated in front of around 3,000 fans, a low attendance hardly helped by the match being televised – like all Liga I matches – and played at the 8.45 p.m. graveyard slot. Public transport finished at 11 p.m. on a Sunday, which made it tight for many fans to get home to the Bucharest suburbs. But more fans were turning their backs altogether on the clubs in Liga I.

Adrian from Carmen București had explained that fans were redis-covering their love for football by following splinter and phoenix teams in the regional fourth tier. Large groups of fans travelled to watch their team play away at small clubs deep in the Romanian countryside. Adrian said that it became something of a celebration having all these fans coming to your village. It also improved the relationship between supporters and their clubs. 'There are even fans who play in the fourth division, so basically you have an ultra in the field playing for a team he loves', said Adrian.

It was a nice story. But Liga I felt a confused place for the supporter. Bucharest, the largest city in Eastern Europe, was a muddled mix of Western and Balkan influences where old buildings creaked with their former grandeur. And Romanian football seemed to be another faded jewel, as it struggled with the identities of its clubs and their fans.

FCSB were runners-up for the third year in succession. Sepsi were ninth. Poli Timișoara were thirteenth and relegated. Juventus București were bottom, rel-egated and, after pressure from a Turin-based club no one was going to confuse them with, changed their name to the snappy Daco-Getica București.

FOOD HIGHS IN LOW COUNTRIES

23 Belgium

This was a blitz. I would watch matches in three different countries in an unforgettable forty-two hours. Belgium would be stylish and restrained, Germany organised and titanic and the Netherlands full of dope-smoking hooligans. It all started at Amsterdam's Schiphol Airport after a short hop from London City.

I surveyed my hire car in the Netherlands. I didn't know Fiat still made cars that felt this cheap. The chunky plastic interior was a grey remnant from the 1980s, and it handled like a small truck. I only had Dutch dance music, flat asphalt and dull scenery for company and started playing a counting game: windmills v wind turbines. The turbines were well ahead when Google Maps diverted me through backstreets I would struggle to retrace. 'Weekend Dating Party', announced a large purple sign in the shape of a curvy female figure outside a small village. Before long I was over the border in Belgium, a country with an intoxicating range of beers and a slight image problem.

Ghent looked beautifully autumnal. The colours of clinging leaves were reflected in the serene waterways and toned with the magnificent medieval buildings. I was in Ghent thanks to scheduling. There is always a televised First Division A match on a Friday night and I left my Belgian choice to the broadcasting gods. KAA Gent against Standard Liège, Ruslan's unintentional prediction back in Baku, was a match between two famous clubs that were struggling, placed twelfth and eighth respectively, after thirteen rounds of fixtures. I had last visited Ghent on my way to Kattenstoet, the triennial cat festival in Ypres. It seemed very Belgian to hold a cat parade and to do so every three years.

I searched Ghent for signs of a football crowd. There were plenty of cyclists and Spanish tourists but no indication that a major match was taking place. I foraged without success for somewhere cheap to eat. I reverted to British type and started eating a supermarket sandwich and a large packet of paprika crisps at the bus stop. I was close to salt overload when I spotted the blue and white scarf of a Gent supporter. Julie, a regular at the new Ghelamco Arena, had the pleasure of watching me wolf down carbohydrates on the bus.

We chatted over Jupiler beers outside the Chess Café, a modern bar on the approach road to the impressive stadium. Julie was in her mid-twenties and had been supporting Gent for six or seven years. She began following Anderlecht after they played a successful Champions League group phase against Manchester United in 2000, but started watching Gent with her uncle more than Anderlecht and therefore converted to her local club. It is easier to change your football team at a young age.

Gent had a relatively modest history, with only three Belgian Cups until they won their first championship in 2015. 'We had some beautiful years. The mayor is a big fan of the team and when we were champions the whole city was behind Gent.' I asked Julie how she had celebrated. 'It was great, it was epic. I went into the student area and it was a full house, music around the streets and seven in the morning when I got home. And when I saw it in the newspapers, I still didn't believe it.'

A mixed Gent crowd was growing outside the Chess Café, where men, women and children mingled. I asked about club songs. Julie first mentioned the goal celebration music, perhaps reflecting the reserved Flemish nature. 'When Gent score it's "Zombie Nation". I hope you're going to hear it', giggled Julie as she played a fuzzy rendition of the dance track on her phone.

The First Division A season was the longest – too long, according to Julie – amongst Europe's top divisions, at forty matches, and its structure read like a Brussels regulation: every team played fifteen matches, home and away, points were halved and the top six played another ten matches. It created more big games and more money. The system of splitting leagues was now used by fifteen nations across Europe; interestingly, none of them were summer leagues: Northern Ireland, Bulgaria, Serbia, Ukraine, Romania, Belgium, Denmark, Poland, Scotland, Wales, Israel, Cyprus, Andorra, Slovakia and Bosnia-Herzegovina.

I could see why such a system was growing in popularity as it gave mid-table teams a greater incentive to finish in the top half and secure more matches against the leading clubs. But I heavily disliked the halving of points in Belgium, which gave more weight to the final matches. Belgium also employed a devilishly complicated play-off system for the last Europa League place that, bizarrely, involved the second- and fourth-placed teams from First Division B. I could never live in Belgium. Even the second tier was called First Division B.

The Belgian league system might divide opinion, but everyone loves the Ghelamco Arena. Ghent did not host matches during Euro 2000 and, with an eye on Belgium and the Netherlands' joint bid for the 2018 World Cup, the Ghelamco Arena was commissioned, and eventually opened in 2013. Remarkably, the Ghelamco Arena was the first new football stadium in Belgium since the Jan Breydel Stadium in Bruges was completed in 1974.

It looked truly stunning at night. Stylish vertical blue strips gave it an almost ethereal appeal that reminded me of Santuário Dom Bosco, the beautifully blue church I visited in Brasilia before France's 2014 World Cup defeat of Nigeria. And there were lots of interesting stories that accompanied Gent's new stadium. The 19,999 capacity was devised to avoid higher taxation levied on stadiums with one more seat. There was the possibility to expand to 30,000 or 40,000 by lowering the pitch to the level of the access road that circles the pitch or building above the current single tier. It is one of the most energy efficient stadiums in Europe, and is home to Horseele, a Michelin-starred restaurant serving pheasant, king crab and scallops.

The overall ambience for the average punter was nearly as sophisticated. The open interior of the stadium concourse was a comfortable place to congregate, with floating irregular shapes breaking up the space between head height and the ceiling. A blue glow softened the light on photographs of old players, whilst automatic doors to the stands cleverly regulated the temperature. There even used to be white leather sofas to lounge on until they were deemed a potential blockage by health and safety experts and removed.

I tried some of the football food: fresh and crunchy *frites* with mayo were sublime. A *boulet*, sausage meat rolled in breadcrumbs, warmed my insides on a cool evening and was more appetising than anaemic-looking sausages. It was fairly painless to buy and charge a card for Gent's cashless system. The expression on the barman's face was more pained when I ordered a tasty Maes beer when my card had a balance 10 cents less than required. Belgians prefer rules to mild audacity.

I waltzed through the automatic doors to my seat and found an instant friend next to me. Marnix, a fortysomething wearing designer stubble and a quirky geometric shirt, was a new fan attracted by the sparkling stadium. He quite liked the league system. 'It gives teams a chance and the difference between teams isn't so great. Of course, the leading teams don't like it.' It certainly gave both Gent and Standard Liège a shot at European qualification, even the title, despite their poor starts.

Sá Pinto, the Standard coach, unnecessarily interrupted the early stages of the first half to complain about a non-decision and break up play. 'He is always doing this', said Marnix. The former Portugal forward was from the Antonio Conte school. His flowing locks nudged the shoulders of his natty suit. I watched the other Sá for Standard, Orlando, who had been out of his depth at Premier League Fulham and more successful at Championship Reading. His first meaningful touch was a weak shot that resembled a back pass to the Gent goalkeeper. Early Gent promise drifted away and the half ended goalless.

The second half started with a fine goal, out of the Gent blue, when new Ukrainian striker Yaremchuk bravely headed in a left-wing cross. The Gent fans enjoyed 'Zombie Nation' in their own restrained way. Moments later, a display of mobile lights on fifty-two minutes marked the age at which Luc de Vos, a much-loved Gent musician, passed away in 2014. It was touching, if slightly out of place. My eyes were distracted by electronic hoarding adverts for boilers, banks and insurance companies, cycling wear and Swiss watches. This was a wealthy part of Belgium and the crowd seemed only moderately roused by the prospect of a rare win.

The stadium was a pleasant place to mingle and linger after a 1–0 home victory. The late shuttle bus back to the city centre is free in a successful attempt to keep the stadium bars full. There was reserved chatter as fans watched the press conference on televisions and drank more Maes. Children played in a corridor while two women toasted the much-needed victory with glasses of cava. The good food, beer and company kept people coming back to watch Gent even if the team were struggling. This was a very modern football experience, the complete antithesis to my match at the Oval in Northern Ireland but, in its own way, equally enjoyable.

Gent finished fourth and Standard Liège sixth after the regular season. The controversial points-halving helped Standard, who finished second and qualified for the Champions League. Gent stayed fourth, enough for Europa League football.

24 Germany

I drove from the atmospheric centre of Ghent to harder-edged Germany, where I had decided to track Thorgan Hazard, the creative force of Borussia Mönchengladbach's attack, to give my Bundesliga match a focus. Thorgan, now twenty-four, was named after a Belgian comic character from *Tintin* magazine and followed his elder brother to Chelsea from Lille in 2012. 'Of course, it helped that Chelsea also signed Eden, but it is not like they just sign every player's brother. Lampard and Terry's brothers never played for Chelsea', said Thorgan. He didn't play for Chelsea either. Successful loans at Zulte Waregem in Belgium and Mönchengladbach followed before he signed permanently for the Bundesliga club in 2015.

Thorgan was a Belgian playing in Germany and living just across the border in the Netherlands. It was a triangle identical to my own weekend. I walked towards Borussia Park, Mönchengladbach's large, if rather bland, stadium, and asked fans about Thorgan, capped six times by Belgium. Marc, a gregarious man in his twenties, called him 'a China fake of the real Hazard'. His friends added, 'Not every game', hinting at unpredictability, and then forecast a 3–1 or 4–1 win against Mainz 05.

I asked a loitering supporter to take my photo outside the green and grey towers of Borussia Park. He shook his head and walked away, the only person who refused to photograph me on my travels. Taken aback, I tried again and found Eric. He looked like your typical German football fan with his matted dark hair and love for sausages. Sausages were still king in Germany; a simple *bratwurst* in a roll from a car-park stall was the pick of three I sampled. Small pizzas were also sold outside and inside the stadium. They looked awful. A young girl in the stand tried to eat one. She took several bites and fell asleep for the rest of the match.

Mönchengladbach were nicknamed 'the foals' for the fast, aggressive playing style, employed when they won five championships between 1970 and 1977. The club finished in the top four in both 2015 and 2016, but Eric didn't think it was possible to pip moneyed Bayern Munich and Borussia Dortmund to the Bundesliga title. Eric was proud of the club's history and explained that tradition was very important at Mönchengladbach, more so than at upstarts Leipzig and Wolfsburg. Eric's uncle, standing beside us, was keen to reinforce this, talking loudly and waving his arms. I understood his gestures more than his German.

Mönchengladbach is a relatively small city of around 250,000 people and home fans come from across the western part of Germany. The club also attracts supporters from the north-west of England. I noticed half-and-half scarves that were split between the green of Möncheng-ladbach and the red of Liverpool. A mutual respect had been fostered since the clubs played three European matches in the 1970s, including the 1977 European Cup final in Rome. Mönchengladbach supporters had donated money to the families of fans who perished at Hillsborough and the clubs made visits to their counterparts every season.

Eric was honest about Thorgan Hazard. 'The other brother is better. Both play in a very similar way, but Thorgan is a little bit slower and in front of the goal Eden is more dangerous. Mönchengladbach is the next step on the ladder for Thorgan. I think in a few years he will play in England for a bigger club.' I was interested to see how he fared against Mainz, the over-achieving club where Jürgen Klopp cut his managerial teeth.

The Mönchengladbach fans appeared late and many missed the overly choreographed pre-match build-up. Jünter, the foal mascot, romped around the pitch with a black and white flag to 'Go West' by the Pet Shop Boys. The crowd were prompted to wave their scarves enthusiastically. They obeyed. The club hymn, one of the best in the Bundesliga according to Thomas, the German groundhopper I met in Belfast, was belted out by the old woman sitting to my right. She lit the first of many cigarettes and the thick ash covered me.

An energetic and organised Mainz fired off four shots in the opening minutes. And it was no surprise when the away side took an early lead following an almighty hash from Switzerland international goalkeeper Sommer. A corner was headed sky high; Mainz centre back Diallo outjumped the advancing Sommer and headed the ball into the empty net. The home support vented their frustration.

Hazard, with his hunched frame and orange boots, was an easy player to track on the right side of Mönchengladbach's 4-2-3-1. His first touch was an ugly miskick, but he soon showed strong defensive play and close skill, although less guile in tight positions than his brother.

He drifted sometimes to the left, his movement often sharper than his teammates' perceptiveness. Mönchengladbach had barely threatened when Hazard had their best chance, collecting a pass in the inside right channel and attempting to chip Zentner when a low shot would have tested the Mainz goalkeeper more. 'Always the wrong decision', lamented the season ticket holder to my left. 'A lot of good chances he has missed this season.'

This match was mostly about Hazard for me, but will be remembered in Bundesliga circles for an astonishing mistake. The ball was rolling gently back towards Zentner. The twenty-three-year-old goalkeeper took a touch, looked up and attempted a pass that became a horrendous air kick. The ball had already rolled underneath his foot. Zentner frantically scrambled the loose ball away before Mönchengladbach striker Raffael could pounce. The goalkeeper later claimed he had mistaken the penalty spot for the ball.

Mainz then seemingly scored a second. The referee ran to a television on the sidelines for my first live experience of Video Assistant Referees (VAR), which were on trial across the Bundesliga. The goal was disallowed and I later found that VAR had correctly spotted a foul by a Mainz player in the build-up. The season ticket holder next to me wasn't impressed with VAR despite its goal-saving intervention. 'There are two or three in every game. And not always the right decision.' I was also a sceptic. I didn't like the break in flow and the stunted communication with the crowd of some 53,000.

This would be the largest crowd on my travels, unsurprising given the German top flight has the highest average league attendance in the world. The Bundesliga was also a commercial beast: the Mönchengladbach club shop was a warehouse, a car manufacturer sponsored the corner count and a Swiss clock company indicated how much time was left with an annoying ticking sound. The worst offender was the loud braying by Jünter the foal that signalled a goal at other Bundesliga games. It was backed by a bank, and was a particularly irritating distraction. I was similarly frustrated when animated advertising hoardings were introduced at Craven Cottage, but at least the audio there remains muted, for now.

Mönchengladbach switched to 4-3-3 as they chased an equaliser in the second half. Hazard was instantly more involved on the right side of the attacking three. The Belgian shot over from the edge of the area and soon after, picking up the ball in a great right-wing position, smashed the ball into the side-netting when a cross-shot across goal may have been wiser. Hazard then cut into the penalty area, but delayed getting a shot away with his weaker left foot. 'Always the way', chimed the season ticket holder.

Hazard did create the Mönchengladbach equaliser, with centre back Vestergaard heading powerfully into the far corner from the Belgian's out-swinging corner. Mönchengladbach fans celebrated in the way that bigger teams do when they finally break meeker opposition who have had the temerity to score first. Despite the assist, there seemed little love for Thorgan, who attracted the frustration of the stands again for giving the ball away, and then failed to control a throw-in with his knee under little pressure, something his brother would have nailed.

Hazard moved to the central attacking position. He lacked the physique for the role and shirked several challenges from muscular Mainz defenders. A mislaid pass from Hazard attracted a guttural 'Scheiße' from the volcanic woman. She and many Mönchengladbach fans streamed out of the stadium with the game still poised at 1–1 and five minutes left to play. It could have been even worse. Brosinski curled a free kick against the crossbar as Mainz missed several late chances. It had been a disjointed performance by the home side.

I had rather hoped that Hazard would have either an outstanding or appalling game. It was rather inevitable that he would have neither. The Belgian had rarely been helped by his fellow attackers, but his decision making had not been as refined as his touch. Hazard even ended up defending in the right-back position after taking a corner – not where Mönchengladbach needed their main attacking threat. And perhaps this was why their fans were frustrated. Hazard was their star man, and when things didn't quite come off for Thorgan, Mönchengladbach also suffered.

The crowd quickly evaporated from Borussia Park. The match had been consumed, if not overly enjoyed, by the Mönchengladbach fans, which was more than could be said for the pizza. I watched big-screen highlights outside the stadium with my third sausage of the day. There were chuckles at Zentner's miskick and nodded appreciation at the correct application of VAR. The wind whipped up, everyone left and I drove my Fiat through the rain to the Netherlands.

Mönchengladbach finished a disappointing ninth. Mainz were fourteenth and avoided relegation by three points. Hazard had his best season in the Bundesliga, scoring ten goals, and made two appearances for Belgium at the 2018 World Cup. He transferred to Borussia Dortmund in May 2019 for a reported £22 million.

25 The Netherlands

The air was thick with dope. A group of around 400 ADO Den Haag supporters gathered in a swimming pool car park. The tarmac was overlooked by a twenty-storey tower block. This felt far removed from the canal-strewn city centres that characterised the Netherlands of my mind.

The favoured attire was black coat and cap, set off with yellow and green ADO scarves and badges from sister clubs Millwall, Juventus and Legia Warsaw. But it was not that hardcore. The police watched from a safe distance. The crowd were predominantly young and male but mothers, children and a woman in a wheelchair joined them. The November skies were changing fast as we started marching. Several children stared at yellow and green flares through the swimming pool windows. This was not their usual Sunday morning swim.

The ADO hardcore were marching to celebrate forty years of Midden-Noord, the north stand in their old Zuiderpark Stadium. ADO's current home, the awkwardly sponsored Cars Jeans Stadium, was built in 2007 and Feyenoord were visiting for this lunchtime match. The Rotterdam club had secured their first Dutch title in eighteen years in 2017 but had been beaten 3–0 by Shakhtar Donetsk in their midweek Champions League tie. I predicted a 1–1 draw. 'Wash your mouth, say it again', said Jacco, with a laugh. James Montague, the investigative journalist and author, had put me in touch with Jacco van Leeuwen, the welcoming president of the ADO supporters' club.

ADO were comfortably mid-table in the Eredivisie. Again. In Dutch ADO is an acronym for 'everything through practice', and the club were certainly well practised in hitting the middle ground, always finishing between ninth and thirteenth over the previous five years. 'It's okay for now', said Jacco about the equilibrium, over a period in which Chinese investors had not always delivered what they had promised, a subject elaborated on in Montague's illuminating book, *The Billionaires Club*.

Football in the Netherlands, despite Ajax's defeat to Manchester United in the 2017 Europa League final, was at a low ebb. Scotland had provided two European finalists since Feyenoord, the previous Dutch club to reach a final, won the UEFA Cup final they hosted in 2002. ADO didn't seem to have their own European aspirations even though eighth place in the Eredivisie – normally good enough for a Europa League play-off – seemed a reasonable target when only the budgets of the big three (Ajax, Feyenoord and PSV Eindhoven) far outstretched the rest. But the feeling at ADO was one of contented stasis. Despite my best efforts I failed to find a parallel in England, where mid-table Premier League teams had European aspirations despite the perpetual threat of relegation.

The Hague would be the only city on my travels where I stayed with a friend. Doug, a bohemian with beautiful British Blue cats, asked me for a Fulham scarf to add to the football paraphernalia on the ceiling of his local hostelry, the Café de Malle Meid. Mark Rutte, the Dutch prime minister, was known to frequent another pub in the same narrow lane. But these atmospheric neighbourhoods, where centuries-old housing fronted quiet streets, contrasted with adjacent working-class areas, such as where the old stadium was located.

Residents of The Hague and Rotterdam are famous for being blunt. Jacco said that ADO and Feyenoord, only fifteen miles apart, were rivals, but that the clubs were both from the same gritty background. 'Ajax are both of our biggest rivals', added Jacco. Some ADO supporters only referred to Ajax as 'zero twenty' – the telephone code for Amsterdam – and others were in Rome to cheer on Juventus to victory against Ajax in the 1996 Champions League final.

The march was well choreographed. Loudspeakers kept us to one side of the road. A young girl lit a yellow flare as her parents looked on and firecrackers were released at intervals not regular enough to prevent a jump every time one went off behind me. Some fans downed cans of lager whilst most of us craved a Sunday morning coffee. We approached an underpass that contained the yellow and green smoke. 'Go through if you want to get lung cancer', said Jacco. Or burst your eardrums from the echoes of firecrackers.

Jacco held back, yet would have charged under the bridge several decades ago. ADO supporters had a fearsome reputation, but Jacco said that most arrests now were for fireworks and singing rather than fighting. An electric car in ADO colours kept this morning's marchers in order as Storky, the club's bird mascot, posed for photographs and hugged fans. As we approached the stadium, I noticed a banner for

Laurens, a key Midden-Noord figure who had recently passed away, which showed the ADO fans remembered their own.

I took some photographs at the front of the parade. 'Are you the police?' asked one fan wearing dark glasses. My business card came in useful again in a tight situation. The ADO fans were a little more sedate now, rather like Jacco and this march, but there remained a hard edge. Around twenty ADO fans received stadium bans after racist chanting at the Ajax midfielder Riechedly Bazoer in 2016.

We approached the Cars Jeans Stadium, entirely covered with riveted aluminium that shone in the low autumn sun. It looked like an elongated garage door. We entered the stadium to see Storky circumnavigating the pitch with two young fans, all three soaked by sprinklers that made the artificial pitch glisten. A large flag commemorated four decades of Midden-Noord and another banner proclaimed, 'Without fans no football'.

Yellow and green smoke bombs, leftovers from the march, were thrown onto the sidelines and gave kick-off an otherworldly backdrop. Feyenoord scored after four minutes when Jørgensen, their Danish centre forward, headed in a right-wing cross. The visitors spurned chances for a second before ADO scored a quite majestic equaliser. Left back Meijers picked up a loose ball after an ADO attack, and played in Bakker who instantly passed to El Khayati on the left side of the penalty area. The ADO midfielder instinctively flicked into the path of the advancing Meijers, who slammed home a left-footed volley from fifteen yards. 'Like Barcelona', said the fan to my right at the total touch football. The ADO fans rightly went wild.

I wondered how fans celebrated a goal as magnificent as this. With a *stroopwafel*, it transpired. Kiosks inside the stadium sold these: two delicious layers of biscuit filled with caramel that melted beautifully when heated by a steaming coffee from beneath. A fan walked enticingly close with an entire *appeltaart*, extravagant even for a match against the champions, but entirely appropriate for such a fine goal.

ADO went 2–1 up ten minutes into the second half. Brad Jones, the Australian goalkeeper previously at Liverpool, seemed inspired by the Borussia Park errors, missing a left-wing cross and leaving centre back Kanon to head into an empty net. The influential Feyenoord captain El Ahmadi, the former Aston Villa midfielder, made it 2–2 with five minutes remaining when he charged straight through the ADO midfield, attracting more shrugs than challenges, and slotted in a right-footed shot.

Doug's colleague – a Feyenoord fan who also watched ADO – had arranged our tickets and invited us to the players' lounge to digest an exciting 2–2 draw. And drink some Dutch beer: small glasses were carefully filled with Heineken, the beery froth swiped away with unerring accuracy. Lampshades at the stylish bar displayed images of past stars and I spoke to today's hero. Goal-scorer Meijers, who shares a birthday with me, still beamed from his screamer, only his third goal in over 150 matches for ADO.

I was introduced to Harm, a long-term fan who had followed ADO for fifty-one years. 'He's fifty-two', quipped another supporter. Harm was actually sixty-four. 'My wife is number one and after that football', said Harm. His favourite ADO memory was being one of thousands of fans who travelled to England by ferry for a thrilling European Cup Winners' Cup quarter-final against West Ham United in 1975. ADO had won 4–2 in The Hague and West Ham only progressed on away goals after a 3–1 victory in London.

Harm clearly enjoyed regaling us with these yarns but, as with Jacco, I detected reservations despite the recent modernisation of the stadium and the club. 'Eleventh or twelfth is the best we can reach due to our budget.' ADO last played European football in 2011, but I still thought that a Europa League play-off place was a target worth pursuing.

I left several hours after the match had finished. Two bars on the ground floor were still packed, music blaring and football fans stonily staring around. It was like All Bar One on a Friday with fewer suits. The grass outside the ADO supporters' bar was a sea of plastic glasses and heated discussion. I had marched with fans of all ages, fierce in their opinions and their support for ADO. They were partisan and proud. But there seemed little ambition. I expected ADO to finish around eleventh for the next few seasons.

I stuck around in the Netherlands with Doug. Paradise Lost, a doomy Yorkshire metal band I had seen live more than any other, were playing in nearby Utrecht, a relaxed city that gave me my canal fix. We walked into the Tivoli venue, a modern twist of escalators and music halls, and nearly gatecrashed a rival gig by American rock outfit the Doobie Brothers.

Paradise Lost played to a hushed, almost pop music audience upstairs. The most animated was a man who spoke to me in a stream of words I didn't understand. Apart from 'the Doobie Brothers'. I pointed him towards his correct concert. Amidst the confusion, I wondered if live music audiences were an accurate representation of national characteristics, more so even than football. The Dutch, habitually polite and orderly, were perhaps better embodied by gig-goers than ADO fans.

Maybe muted ambition was justified. ADO finished seventh and qualified for the Europa League play-offs, losing to Vitesse Arnhem. Feyenoord finished fourth.

Chicken Cottage and Salmon Kalou

I was pleased with my choice of Dutch match, an energetic game blessed with one of the finest goals I have ever seen. Indeed, the Netherlands had provided me with plenty of live football drama in the past. After Fenerbahçe, the second match I watched in a UEFA nation outside my own was Ajax 9–0 Sparta Rotterdam – still the highest-scoring match and the greatest margin of victory I have ever seen. 'We want ten, we want ten', was the chant from the Ajax faithful in 2001. And thirteen years later in Salvador, I watched the remarkable substitution of Ajax goalkeeper Jasper Cillessen for penalty specialist Tim Krul ahead of the Netherlands' shoot-out victory against Costa Rica in the World Cup quarter-finals.

I love the unpredictability that can make a football match memorable or forgettable. I will never forget left back Jon Harley's stunning forty-yard strike for Fulham against Aston Villa in 2003. But what made it even more special was that it was his only goal for Fulham. And that he had struggled since his £3.5m move from Chelsea in 2001, so much so that during his first season at Craven Cottage my father shouted out that Harley was 'a chicken', following that up with a walking chicken impersonation that seemed to transfix most of the standing fans in the Hammersmith End.

Sometimes the quirks of football are easier to appreciate when it's not your own team. It was hard personal viewing when Fulham's expensively assembled second-tier side drew four consecutive matches 0–0 and then lost a fifth match without scoring a goal in December 1999. (Paul Bracewell's underwhelming team actually went eight league matches without a Fulham player scoring, although during that spell we still managed to beat Tranmere Rovers 1–0 thanks to an own goal.)

It was the randomness of football that drew me to the 2008 Africa Cup of Nations in Ghana, a tournament I had always wanted to visit after seeing fans watching the 2002 edition from a cliff in Mali. According to the Ghanaian organisers, I was going to be amongst one million foreign visitors, a figure that would have looked overly optimistic even to a non-statistician. I enjoyed reading the *Daily Graphic* during my Ghanaian travels and, after the tournament started, they reported that the official estimate had been revised down to 7,000 visitors. (Other *Daily Graphic* classics included the insightful reporting that 'the reason that Mozambique did not qualify was because they did not qualify' and their insistence on calling the Ivory Coast forward 'Salmon' Kalou.)

There was nothing fishy when Salmon scored a fine winner against Nigeria in the first of two group matches that day in Sekondi-Takoradi. But Sekondi was a strange place, the stadium a flying saucer plonked in a mangrove swamp in the middle of nowhere. It was an obvious future white elephant. The *Daily Graphic* soberly reported, just six years after the tournament was held, 'that managers of the facility were grappling with a number of challenges which need to be addressed' with the fading stadium. There were challenges even when I was there. After the Malian and Beninese national anthems, we were plunged into total darkness for fifteen minutes when officials switched from the stadium's purpose-built generator to the erratic, but cheaper, mains supply.

Football fans tend to make wild predictions based on insufficient evidence. But I always thought that Ghana would be a heady mix of disorganisation and flair. I also believed that then-Benin striker Razak Omotoyossi was 'all pace, verve and just twenty-two years old; he will not be playing for Helsingborg [his club side] for very long'. I wrote these thoughts after their 1–0 defeat to Mali and, although he had an admirably globe-trotting career, he never quite made the big time.

Back at Craven Cottage, I was sufficiently impressed by a young Arsenal full back on loan at Crystal Palace when they played Fulham in April 2000 to predict that he was a nailed-on international. Ashley Cole, who had barely played ten first-team matches at the time, made 107 appearances for England. But I'm often quite wrong. I noisily complained about the hype surrounding an already balding French midfielder I watched at Euro 1996. Zinedine Zidane was so good that he went on to star in a ninety-minute feature film that just tracked his performance for Real Madrid against Villareal in 2005.

AUTUMN IN THE BALKANS

26 Kosovo

After my heavy metal diversion in the Netherlands, I returned to London and flew to Skopje's Alexander the Great Airport. I hired a cheap car and was upgraded to a Macedonian monster, an over-sized Citroën. Together we would criss-cross Macedonia, Kosovo, Albania and Greece over an unpredictable two weeks of drama, downpours and demonstrations.

The road wound its way through the mountains north of Skopje and across the border into Kosovo. Kosovo, the unlikeliest of twenty-three UEFA members to use the euro as their currency, looked notice-ably poorer than Macedonia, yet the ongoing construction of a new highway above the Lepenica River hinted at loftier aspirations. I took a sideroad where war memorials were surrounded by brick-red Balkan roofs, russet-coloured trees and Albanian flags. 'Two nations, one people' was the oft-repeated phrase about Kosovo and Albania, as would be demonstrated the following summer by two ethnic Kosovans, Xherdan Shaqiri and Granit Xhaka, celebrating goals for Switzerland with the sign of the Albanian eagle in their politically charged match against Serbia at the 2018 World Cup.

The low clouds made it difficult to locate the horizon. It was easy enough to find Gjilan, around thirty miles to the south-east of capital Prishtina, and one of the most unusual football towns on my travels. It was not as easy to find somewhere to stay. A major hotel booking website did not list a single hotel in this small industrial town in eastern Kosovo, home to tobacco and radiator factories and birthplace of Shaqiri. I found the Hotel Demi on Google Maps and reserved via Facebook. It looked a short walk from the Gjilan City Stadium, shared by fierce rivals Drita and Gjilani.

Hotel Demi's reception was a hot fug of smoke and my room smelled of bleach. Haris, a polite receptionist in his early twenties, had been a Drita fan since he was ten and was pleased that I had chosen his club. His brother was a Gjilani fan. The two teams were not cosy brothers in eastern Kosovo and Haris said that it was impossible for him to forge friendships with Gjilani fans. The top of the Kosovo Superleague was incredibly tight. I asked if Drita, currently fourth, were going to win their first title since 2003. '1 million per cent', said Haris, with a winning smile.

I walked towards the stadium past mounds of large cabbages, mostly green, some purple, being sold from open trucks and mini-vans. I noticed an ad hoc car park on an abandoned segment of land, which looked like it might be used for football traffic. A barbed wire fence circled the stadium and soldiers guarded access on the main road. I retraced my steps, tried the back entrance and found more strung wire. Google Maps was wrong. This was a military base, not a football stadium. I returned to the Hotel Demi in a slight panic.

Kosovo would be a difficult place to squeeze in later on, if I missed the start of the match.

Fortunately time was on my side. And so was Haris. He ordered a taxi and barked instructions at the driver. I was thankful that the actual stadium was only just over a mile away. The grey November skies somehow fitted the rundown setting, the stadium flanked by decrepit terracing and ringed by graffiti. I walked up the steps onto the first floor of a ramshackle clubhouse opposite the main bank of terracing. The minarets of two mosques poked over the roofs to my left. The right-hand goal was backed by an almighty building site where a four-storey construction was beginning to take shape. A young black man wearing casual clothes was on the clubhouse balcony. I assumed he was a footballer. He was.

Ernest Bonsu was a Ghanaian defensive midfielder who had played for Liberty Professionals in his homeland before a loan spell at Bloem-fontein Celtic in South Africa. He looked unhappy. His brother had paid for his air ticket to Kosovo and visa, but his agent had broken promises. Ernest had believed he was joining a Superleague club but his actual destination was second-tier Korriku. Ernest still wanted to play, but Korriku could not afford his food or accommodation. 'Yesterday I cried before sleeping', he said. Ernest's agent said he was looking for a club for him in Albania.

Ernest was here to see Sarpong, his former Liberty teammate and childhood friend, play for home side Drita. 'He didn't know I was here. Someone invited me to Gjilani, I trained with them and Sarpong saw me.' Sarpong wasn't happy either. Drita was his first club in Europe and the new coach wasn't playing him. He was on the bench today.

Ernest and Sarpong had given up comfortable lives in Ghana to pursue their international football dream and had ended up, unwanted, in an unknown city in eastern Kosovo. I felt sympathy for them, my emotions heightened by the easy affinity I found with Ghanaians. I had watched and supported Ghana at three tournaments: the 2008 Africa Cup of Nations and the 2006 and 2014 World Cups. I watched the cruellest moment on television, in 2010 when Luis Suárez's handball and the resulting penalty miss from Asamoah Gyan, a constant in all these tournaments, prevented Ghana from being the first African World Cup semi-finalists, villainy for which I still haven't forgiven Suárez.

I spoke to Feti, Drita's general director, who was attempting to recruit more Ghanaians. Drita paid for their accommodation, food and salaries, which I presumed would be amongst the lowest for top-division football in Europe. Feti said Drita were formed in 1947 and that the city rivalry dates from 1995 when unhappy Drita players formed a new club, Gjilani. Players from the town stayed with Drita and those from the surrounding villages moved to Gjilani. Drita fans – whose 'no one likes us, we don't care' slogan I had heard somewhere near my south-east London home – call themselves 'the intellectuals' to distinguish themselves from the country yokels of Gjilani. 'When the derby comes it is a crazy week. There are flags on houses. At least 150 special forces are around the stadium. There are always scuffles between fans', said Feti.

I watched from the clubhouse balcony as an enormous birthday cake for Drita captain Limani was delivered below us. 'He will eat it afterwards', said Feti. We talked about celebrations. Kosovo declared independence from Serbia in 2008 and had become the most recent UEFA member after a tight 28–24 vote in May 2016. It was never revealed which members voted for and against, but Spain and Russia were clearly worried that admitting Kosovo would set a precedent for other breakaway regions, and the Serbian authorities had not held back when referring to 'the self-proclaimed football federation of Kosovo'. The emotion was clear to see in Feti's excited eyes. 'Gjilan is crazy about football and we had big celebrations. We always support other Kosovan clubs in Europe. It is our country.' The symbolism is heavy in Kosovan club names: Drita means 'light', Liria, the visiting team, 'freedom'.

Drita and Liria both played 4-3-3 formations that, like at ADO, led to some fast, attacking play. Xhevdet Shabani, the thirty-one-year-old on the right side of Drita's three-pronged attack, was immediately targeted by a challenge straight through the back: a free kick that would have been accompanied by a yellow card in most other countries. Players from both teams were doing their best to sidestep a barrage of sliding tackles on the rough pitch.

The excellent Xhevdet Shabani was not deterred. He swung in a free kick from the left wing, goalkeeper Bakaj dropped the cross and Bujar Shabani nodded in to make it 1–0 to Drita. The holding midfielder celebrated as fervently as if he had volleyed in from twenty-five yards. Drita then scored a second that seemed to define the physical and skilful nature of Kosovan football. A couple of meaty Drita challenges went unpunished in midfield and the ball fell kindly for Xhevdet Shabani on the right wing. He raced free and chipped the goalkeeper with a sublime dink from the corner of the penalty area. Drita merited their two-goal lead, but moments later Liria were back in the game when Sefa, in too much space outside the penalty area, calmly placed the ball in the corner. It was a lively 2–1 at the interval.

'Have you seen any trouble?' a friend had asked me during a fleeting visit home. I was nearly halfway through my travels and, surprisingly, had yet to see anything, even in hardened Balkan and ex-Soviet states. I somehow didn't expect to see crowd disturbances in eastern Kosovo. However, the Drita fans used half-time to throw off their intellectual cloak, poured onto the pitch and started running towards the small group of Liria fans housed in a pen near the corner flag. One clutched an iron bar, others were content simply to use their fists. The police were dozing and took several minutes to stop fighting between the rival fans.

It then started raining rocks, as fans who had been watching the game from the building site started throwing meteors at the Liria fans. Pitch invaders and rock throwers were eventually cleared, but not before players had emerged to try to calm the mild warfare. A Drita fan leader was eventually frogmarched to apologise to his Liria counterpart. 'It was Gjilani fans', said Feti, alert to potential negative publicity. Gjilani fans had apparently decided to watch their rivals and cause trouble to blacken their name. This seemed even less likely when I checked my photographs and spotted a rock-throwing fan wearing a lightning-blue Drita hat. After the game, Drita asked me not to post any incriminating photos on my website. I was happy to oblige. I didn't want to get Gjilani fans into trouble.

The Liria fans were not subdued by their half-time stoning, and continued their assault on my right eardrum with chanting and a solitary drumbeat. Drita looked eager to score again after the break, and Xhevdet Shabani, inevitably, played a part in their third: his right-wing free kick was headed purposefully by centre back and birthday boy Limani before meeting a Liria defender's arm. It looked a harsh penalty. Liria argued before Gerbeshi, the other Drita centre back, stepped up and sent Bakaj the wrong way. Drita were 3–1 up and in control.

I was beginning to feel the chill and the match was meandering. I noticed that the building site crowd, cleared during the half-time ruckus, was gradually repopulating. With just ten minutes remaining, the game quickened and suddenly it was 3–2, with left-sided attacker Magani side-footing home after incisive Liria passing. Drita looked leggy. Liria captain Korenica whipped in a free kick, the Drita defence dozed and Magani shinned in a second at the far post. The Liria players went wild. It was 3–3 and Liria were in the ascendancy.

The tension was tangible. Liria won a late corner until nearly half the Drita team pressured the referee into reversing the decision. Three yellow cards were dished out, including one to an interested substitute warming up. A feisty game then reached an incredible conclusion. Xhevdet Shabani won a dubious free kick on the right wing. His delivery was good, but it was bundled into his own net by Liria defender Basri. The Drita players celebrated in front of the intellectuals, now safely back on their terrace library. The management went wild on the balcony as the Liria midfielder Gashi was sent off for harsh words. Drita had won 4–3 with virtually the last kick of a game full of controversy, action and no little skill.

Liria were understandably distraught, one player kicking out at the metal tunnel as he trudged to the dressing rooms. Feti was happier with the outcome from a thrilling match. '3–1 up and I said game over. Only football can give you these emotions. That's why it's the most popular sport in the world.' He invited me to celebrate with the Drita management and players in City Pub Café, a hostelry covering all bases.

It was good to be amongst the Drita team. Everyone had bright eyes and many players puffed on cigarettes. Feti picked up the tab for chicken sandwiches and one-euro bottles of Peja beer. Sarpong, an unused substitute, ate every meal here but walked around looking a little lost. He clearly didn't feel part of the winning team. Meanwhile, Xhevdet Shabani was clearly a charmer. 'Find me a club in England', he said. 'Fulham is too high a level, League One is okay for me', he laughed. My only day in Kosovo, which started with grey weather and an invisible stadium, had turned into an unbeatable combination of footballing drama and local flavour.

The cloud was continuous the following day. Kosovo was the only country I visited where the sun remained permanently shielded. Men tried to sell cabbages and gourds from roadside trolleys in the Sunday morning drizzle. Casinos and petrol stations lined the road. Neither was particularly useful to lone vegetable traders. It looked an unhappy sight from my over-sized Citroën. But I had found a heart in the people of Gjilan, one beating alongside the two football teams that kept its population dreaming. I was asked 'Are you from Kosovo?' in Skopje market, maybe because Kosovans are taller than Macedonians. Or possibly because I smiled like Shabani.

Drita were unbeaten in their last twenty-nine league matches and won the Kosovan title after a 0–0 draw with second-placed Prishtina on the last day of the season. Xhevdet Shabani scored ten goals and was called up by the Kosovo national team in January 2018. Liria finished fifth.

27 Macedonia

'The Barnsley girls are far uglier than the ones back in Skopje. Our women are much prettier. Besides, they don't drink as much beer as the Barnsley girls, which is something I don't like at all.' My awareness of Macedonia, the nugget of former Yugoslavia sandwiched between Greece, Albania, Kosovo and Bulgaria, was limited to not much more than the Barnsley forward Georgi Hristov's comments. Only four Macedonians had played in the Premier League and the Tykes' striker's outburst had stuck in my memory more than the exploits of Goran Popov and Artim Šakiri at West Brom or Goce Sedloski of Sheffield Wednesday.

Skopje is strange. The city was mostly destroyed in 1963 by an earthquake that left around three-quarters of its population homeless. Its outskirts are now ringed by typically clunky Balkan buildings and this harsh urban scene is lightened with a misty mountain backdrop. The city centre has undergone a substantial makeover. The historic stone bridge across the river Vardar remains the focus, connecting

Macedonia Square to the revamped Ottoman-era bazaar. But these are now overshadowed by enormous statues of historical figures, peasant women, stony-eyed lions and a man on a horse, presumably Alexander the Great. The new sculptures had not gone down well with the locals. 'Totally disgusting', said Dusan, a half-Macedonian, half-Serbian sports journalist, who had followed my journey from the very beginning.

'The statues are awful. The old government used these for money laundering', said Dusan. They certainly didn't look anything like the alleged £500 million they cost to build. Some were already showing signs of poor construction; others were daubed with paint from anti-government protestors.

Alexander the Great was born in the Greek region of Central Macedonia and Dusan said that naming the airport after the ancient king was deliberately provocative. 'The Greeks are very angry about these statues and the new name of the airport. It's some sort of propaganda to promote nationalism and keep people under your control.' A new government now wanted to either relocate or destroy some of the valuable statues.

Vardar is the name of Skopje's river and the leading club in Macedonia. Fans were marking thirty years of their 'Komiti' ultra group and the seventieth anniversary of Vardar with a march to the Philip II National Arena. It got off to an inauspicious start. Dusan and I watched a handful of Vardar fans drink cans of beer in Macedonia Square. A dowdy dog seemed at ease amongst some tramps as several smoke bombs were released. The Vardar support was swelled by the promise of free beer out of car boots, the vehicles strangely sponsored by a soft drinks giant. I noticed some Schalke 04 T-shirts, an affinity between Vardar and the German club having been struck after they had played each other in the 2004 Intertoto Cup. Schalke fans had travelled to Skopje for today's 'eternal derby' against Pelister, a team from Bitola, around a hundred miles south of Skopje.

Dusan explained that the rivalry between Vardar and Pelister began in the 1989–90 Yugoslav First League at a match between Vardar and Red Star Belgrade in Skopje. A fight broke out between Vardar fans and a few Pelister fans who had actually cheered for Vardar, the only Macedonian team in the Yugoslav top flight. Inevitably, there were more scuffles when the two clubs met in the Yugoslav Second League the following season. Nowadays, it seemed more a fan rivalry than a contest on the pitch. Pelister, fourth in 2017, regularly bounced between the top two divisions. Vardar had won five of the last six Macedonian titles.

Dusan and I joined the Vardar parade snaking its way out of Macedonia Square and past a dozen riot police protecting the old stone bridge. I was getting involved in more marches than Mao Zedong. We approached the Philip II Arena as autumnal trees shed leaves and raindrops. The laudable decision by UEFA to circulate the Super Cup around its member states, not hoard it in moneyed Monaco, ironically not even a UEFA member, had benefited Tbilisi, Tallinn and Skopje. Other Macedonian stadiums might have been called 'catastrophic', but the one nice one hosted the 2017 Super Cup between Real Madrid and Manchester United in searing August temperatures.

Vardar used to play in yellow and red, only adopting the famous red and black colours of AC Milan after the Italian club sent equipment to help them recover from the Skopje earthquake. There wasn't very much Italian style on show in a match where heavy central areas of the pitch hardly encouraged a sure first touch. The surface had been protected ahead of the Super Cup but had deteriorated fast owing to

1 – Georgia – my challenge kicked off at the Mikheil Meskhi Stadium. Not many joined me in the multicoloured seats to watch Dila Gori v Locomotive Tbilisi on 2 June 2017.

3 – Faroe Islands – my mission was watching football yet the travel context was always important. The magnificent Vestmanna bird cliffs reinforced the Faroes' dramatic isolation.

5 – **Sweden** – Häcken, based across the water from more traditional Gothenburg teams, embrace the difference in their rainbow flags.

8 – **Kazakhstan** – Eric, me and a whole load of meat in Taraz. Football was my beat, but the heart of locals like Eric made my journey even more memorable.

8 – **Kazakhstan** – the beautiful Mausoleum of Khoja Ahmed Yasawi in Turkistan. Camouflage clothing was not mandatory at this World Heritage site.

10 – Belarus – Krumkachy goalkeeper Kostyukevich is mobbed by his teammates after scoring from inside his own penalty area. He is sent off twenty minutes later.

14 – Northern Ireland – the Oval is the glorious home of Glentoran in Belfast, a city popular amongst groundhoppers searching for authentic football grounds.

16 – Armenia – the sad-looking Mika Stadium hosted my lowest crowd outside the micro-states. Despite free admission, only eighty people attended Ararat v Gandzasar.

17 – Turkey – young Trabzonspor fans congregate in Atatürk Square before their long walk to the Medical Park Arena. The match against Alanyaspor would be one of the most thrilling of my year.

24 – Germany – my largest crowd, of some 53,000, was at Borussia Mönchengladbach, but my journey was mainly about less-heralded clubs and leagues.

25 – The Netherlands – ADO fans march in yellow and green to commemorate the fortieth anniversary of their Midden-Noord stand. "You couldn't pick a better moment for visiting", said Jacco from their supporters' club.

28 – Albania – the over-sized Citroën gets stuck in some pre-match traffic.

30 – Denmark – I drank at least one beer in all 55 UEFA nations, but rarely during the match. These neat beers at Helsingør's rustic ground, where you could ring metal bells for refills, were an exception.

35 – Israel – I teamed up with Gad and Vadim from Kaduregel Shefel and presented Hapoel Yeruham captain Vasker with his Man of the Match award: an 'I love Yeruham' T-shirt.

40 – Andorra – it was a stressful drive into the snowy Pyrenees. It was all worth it when I chanced upon a top-division match at Encamp's picturesque ground.

41 – Gibraltar – I watched three matches, more than anywhere else on my travels, in the shadow of the 400-metre Rock at the Victoria Stadium.

49 – San Marino – I had visited San Marino once before. I really never thought I would return, nor appear on their national television.

52 – Hungary – The Pancho Aréna is a quite astonishing and audacious stadium. It really doesn't matter if the match is any good.

55 – Montenegro – it was the start of the second half in my final UEFA nation and I felt confident enough to pose for a winning photo. I completed my challenge on 28 April 2018.

My European map – where I started plotting my football dreams – was a confused mess of tickets, media passes and memories by the end.

tough weather conditions and a high concentration of games, including Vardar's reserve team and Macedonia's international fixtures.

Several thousand Vardar fans barged into the west stand as the match kicked off. Firecrackers and Vardar chants echoed around the stadium. A large banner labelled 'Megaphone of Society' and an array of red and black plastic cards were held up by the Vardar hardcore. Another banner read '30 years – when you have something against the eye, older than political parties and bastion of the Macedonian people'. This was strong stuff. Flag waving and jumping around were also sensible activities on a damp, six-degree evening.

Goalkeepers were rarely tested by errant attacking from players as sluggish as the pitch. Pelister, who take their name from the third highest mountain in Macedonia which overlooks the city of Bitola, played in green and white hoops. It was hard to distinguish numbers from high up in the south stand, and a goal didn't look likely from either team.

The Vardar fans turned their back, Poznań style, and called out to the south stand. The firecrackers and drumbeats were a welcome distraction from the turgid match. Chants of 'Gelsenkirchen Schalke' bounced around the arena. Another enormous flag, 'Vardar – Skopje – 70 years', was proudly displayed. The first half was nearly over when a hundred or so Pelister fans finally arrived in the east stand to inevitable whistles from the Vardar support. Dusan thought they had been delayed by the notoriously late Macedonian trains. I could relate to that. The attendance of around 4,000 looked modest in the 34,000-capacity stadium, but was far greater than the few hundred that normally attended league matches. Handball, not football, was the most popular sport in Macedonia, one in which the country consistently qualified for European and world championships.

Komiti Zapat displayed their name in the west stand. These were the Vardar ultras who took their name from the Komiti, Balkan rebels who battled against the Turkish at the end of the Ottoman era. 'Green Power' was the less than threatening response from the Pelister scribes. Bitola is the second city of Macedonia, a strategic junction that connected the Adriatic and Aegean seas with Central Europe. It was now dwarfed, in Macedonian terms, by Skopje. 'We've got McDonald's, we've got McDonald's', the Vardar fans used to chant at Pelister. Nowadays Bitola has a McDonald's, and so the Vardar fans chant, 'We've got an airport, we've got an airport'.

The second half started promisingly for Pelister. Vardar were still sleeping. Maybe, like most of the crowd, they were waiting for the planned and very pretty display of pink flares and smoke bombs from the west stand in the forty-seventh minute, marking the year the club was founded. The match was held up for nearly ten minutes as smoke thickened the atmosphere. It was a highly photogenic distraction. I remarked that the fans were better than the game. 'Always this is the case', replied Dusan.

A Pelister midfielder, indistinguishable with the added smoke, overplayed, lost the ball and his unattended teammate fell over on the uneven surface. The fans behind me laughed. They were clearly not expecting much. An older man in front scrolled through some dull-looking videos on his phone. The match was not engaging the crowd. And then, from nowhere, Vardar scored. Attacking midfielder Felipe launched a free kick into the penalty area, Velkovski headed back at the far post and fellow centre back Musliu headed in at the near. It was unconvincing defending but a tad harsh on Pelister. Dusan translated a Pelister banner, barely visible across the smoky stadium. It read

'We've come for your birthday party of thirty years. You were and still are cunts.'

The game had all the look of a dull 1–0, although Vardar's Blazhevski, the best player on the pitch, curled an audacious shot onto the top of the crossbar with the outside of his left boot as the match petered out. Pyrotechnics apart, it was the finest piece of skill on show. The Vardar fans raided the pitch at full time, racing across the grass with their flags to confront the Pelister fans. The away supporters jeered and looked out of reach halfway up the stand. Some spare flares were launched towards them as the police moved in and we moved out.

Dusan and I retired to a nearby tavern for meaty ribs, dubious jokes and football songs. 'Oh, Wilfried Bony, score a goal for Swansea', sang Dusan for no particular reason. It was a good atmosphere, the sort of ambience that makes you lose track of time. Or humour. We compared Macedonian mountains with English peaks. 'Do you know what the highest mountain is in England?' I asked. 'Peter Crouch.' The Stoke City forward always got a sure-fire laugh regardless of context. 'Peter fucking Crouch', laughed Dusan hysterically. The evening became hazier than the Skopje stadium. But it was one of the best nights of the trip.

Vardar finished second, a whopping thirty-five points behind Shkëndija. Pelister finished bottom and were relegated. The eternal derby is on hold. The country was renamed North Macedonia in February 2019 and dropped the reference to Alexander the Great by rechristening its main airport Skopje International.

28 Albania

I drove the over-sized Citroën from Macedonia to Albania. Beautiful autumn weather accompanied stunning scenery, through the alpine environs of Mavrovo National Park, past gorgeous lakes surrounded by snowy mountains to the mysterious waters of Lake Ohrid, the deepest in the Balkans and shared between the two countries. Concrete bunkers, a legacy of the dictator Enver Hoxha's paranoiac reign from 1944 until his death in 1985, welcomed me into Albania, where the roads were rougher and more likely to be populated by goats.

I followed the shore of Lake Ohrid, where vendors optimistically raised large, silvery fish as I drove past. I stopped in the unassuming town of Elbasan, forty miles west of the lake and home to one of the largest stadiums in Albania. I thought I might be able to watch a bonus Europa League match between Skënderbeu, playing in Elbasan rather than their normal base of Korçë, and Dynamo Kiev, Chornomorets' victims in Ukraine. But the match was being played behind closed doors after undercover observers had recorded Skënderbeu fans chanting,

'Serbs must be killed, destroyed, slaughtered' in their Europa League match against Partizan Belgrade. Enxhi, an Italian-based Albanian journalist for *Sport Ekspres*, could not open any doors for me after all the media passes had been snaffled by Kiev-based broadcasters.

I settled down with Enxhi and a beer in an Italian restaurant, tantalisingly close to Elbasan's stadium, to find out more about Albanian football. Initially it felt positive. Enxhi said that Albanian football had never been in such a good position. Skënderbeu had reached the group stages of the Europa League in 2015 and 2017. 'For a country like Albania it is unbelievable, incredible.' The national team had also unexpectedly appeared at Euro 2016: they were one of three countries, along with Iceland and Northern Ireland, to qualify from the fifth lowest of six seeding pots. They had benefited from incredible events during qualifying when Serbian fans invaded the Belgrade pitch in October 2014 after a drone carried a pro-Albanian flag over the stadium. Fighting broke out between players, fans and officials, the match was abandoned, and Albania were eventually awarded a 3–0 win. Albania certainly didn't disgrace themselves at the tournament, losing narrowly to Switzerland and France before beating Romania. Enxhi said that when the Albanian prime minister met the returning players the scenes were as if Albania had won the World Cup. Football is not all about winning.

Our conversation became darker. Kukësi, the reigning Albanian champions, had surprisingly broken Skënderbeu's run of six consecutive titles. The championship was decided when Kukësi beat Skënderbeu 2–0 in the penultimate match of the previous season. Enxhi explained that the Kukësi president had wanted to win the league to help shore up support for his campaign for mayor and many refereeing decisions had gone against Skënderbeu. I later watched the highlights of the crucial match. Skënderbeu had two men dubiously sent off, one after just ten minutes, and were denied clear penalties, while Kukësi were awarded a non-penalty when the match was goalless. It was either the worst refereeing display in history or rigged.

But it was hard to feel sympathy for Skënderbeu, as they themselves had previously been deducted twelve points and stripped of their 2016 title by the Albanian Football Association. Match fixing had raised its ugly head in the Baltics and was hard to avoid in Albania. 'A lot of smaller clubs that reach the Superliga don't have interest to stay in the league, only to fix matches and make money', said Enxhi. Albanian football fans preferred to watch the national team, or Italian and German football. There aren't many days when I don't discuss football. But this doesn't happen in Albania. 'There is not this culture about talking about football. When a team loses a game here the first thing a person thinks is that the match is fixed.'

I retired to a friendly local bar and watched the Europa League match on television with 65p beers. Skënderbeu won an entertaining game 3–2 to give themselves an outside chance of qualifying from their group. The atmosphere was probably better in the bar than the stadium, as only a few hardy Dynamo Kiev fans, their team safely through before this match, and considerably more journalists, looked on.

I drove through more herds of goats to Berat, only forty miles south of Elbasan but a journey of several hours on rough roads. The city would become one of my favourites in the Balkans, located dramatically between two mountains, with squat Ottoman-era houses sitting on narrow, cobbled lanes either side of the gurgling river Osum. The elevated Berat castle, founded by the Romans and rebuilt several times since, provided dramatic vistas in gorgeous weather. 'Welcome to the

Albanian winter', said an old man in a cap as I soaked up the sun. Another man surreptitiously skinned a dead dog on a wall outside one of the city's mosques.

I reluctantly left Berat's charms for Vlorë, several hours south-west, where home team Flamurtari were playing Teuta Durrës. Vlorë was where Albanian independence was declared in 1912 as the Ottoman empire fragmented. There seemed little chance of anything revolutionary happening on a sleepy Saturday afternoon. People sat sipping coffee, rarely with any food, at pavement cafés on sunny streets lined with beheaded palm trees. I lapped up the last of the late autumnal warmth.

There was no missing the Flamurtari Stadium, a striking fusion of red and black, colours of both the club and the nation, located just off the main drag. The hard surfaces and strong colours felt like a Ferrari showroom. Flamurtari knew that I was visiting, and I approached the main entrance with a knowing stride. Yet the caretaker seemed confused by my visit. I became worried when he said 'No fans', but he showed off the stadium's gleaming interior nevertheless.

Gimi, Flamurtari's Facebook manager, arrived, and took me for a coffee. The coffee was good and strong. Gimi informed me that the match against Teuta Durrës was being played behind closed doors after crowd trouble at their previous home match against Skënderbeu. I wondered whether these doors were as closed as they were in Elbasan. My contingency plan would be a mad dash to a match in Tirana, the Albanian capital I wasn't planning to visit, three hours' drive to the north.

Gimi deflected my concern with talk about Barcelona. Flamurtari played Barcelona twice in successive years in the 1986–87 and 1987–88

UEFA Cup. They were only knocked out on away goals in the first match, with Mark Hughes and Gary Lineker playing up front for Terry Venables' team. These halcyon days had long faded in all but locals' memories. Flamurtari won their only title in 1991 and they had been deducted points in three of the last four seasons for financial problems. It was something of a standing joke in Albanian football that Flamurtari started nearly every season on minus points. They also had problems with referees. Gimi lamented that in the first eleven matches of the season Skënderbeu had been awarded seven penalties and Flamurtari not a single one.

Gimi showed me the highlights of Flamurtari's recent match against Skënderbeu. The referee failed to give Flamurtari a penalty, but the critical error was a disallowed goal when Flamurtari were leading 1–0. Skënderbeu's goalkeeper flapped at a cross, pushed it against a Flamurtari forward and the loose ball was thrashed in. It was a terrible decision not to allow this to stand. Skënderbeu scored an uncontroversial late equaliser and a plastic bottle thrown by an irate home supporter struck the referee's head. In response to this, the Albanian Football Federation had banned all fans from their next home match, my game against Teuta Durrës.

I nervously stood pitchside as both sets of players milled around. I still had not received the necessary clearance to watch the match. I attracted the attention of Flamurtari's friendly Macedonian right back, the bearded Goran Siljanovski. He said that the Albanian league was more competitive than the Macedonian league, with the teams at the bottom of the table offering more of a challenge than in Macedonia where Vardar and Shkëndija were a long way ahead of the rest. I admired the excellent pitch, one of the best I had seen, and Goran told me there were only two or three pitches like this in Macedonia. Maybe one fewer, I thought, given the current state of the Phillip II Arena in Skopje.

I found out that I would be able to watch the match an hour before kick-off. A fair few other people were also let in through the not-so-closed doors: journalists, club officials, players' partners, ball boys who sprinted to take up their positions, and a disabled fan, deemed not be a threat. There were around sixty police spread around the surrounding concrete wall, presumably to prevent fans breaking into the stadium. They need not have worried. Fans on the balconies of surrounding apartment blocks didn't look like they wanted to leave their homes.

The match was about to kick off when the stadium was plunged into darkness. The floodlights had failed, reminding me of Mali against Benin in 2008 and provoking more thoughts about a lunatic trip to Tirana. Fortunately, the delay was only four minutes, after which relief surged through me for the second time.

Teuta Durrës had the better of the opening exchanges. There was audible concern from an apartment block balcony as players' voices echoed eerily around the stadium. Flamurtari played a defensive 4-1-4-1 with Alves, their bustling Brazilian spearhead, often surrounded by two or three Teuta players. There was little flair or incision and the left boot of Juffo, Flamurtari's other Brazilian, looked the most likely source of excitement as the first half ended goalless.

There was not much to do at half-time other than drink espresso and smoke cigarettes. And keep warm. The temperature was plunging. There were murmurs of discontent from Flamurtari officials. There had been no contentious decisions, but this was clearly a club ill at ease with referees. The second period regressed into a series of high balls swallowed up by the centre backs. It was a throwback to a League Two match of yesteryear, only with less action. A multitude of free kicks broke up what fluidity remained.

There was normally something intriguing in a match. But not today. No fans, no real chances. I practised taking photographs of headers with twenty minutes of surely goalless football left to watch, the game looking destined to finish in a mess of half chances and substitutions. But there was a late controversy. A Flamurtari corner was dropped by the Teuta goalkeeper before a defender hacked the ball away from on the goal-line. It might well have been a foul. It might not have gone over the line. Flamurtari certainly didn't deserve a winner. 'Why didn't you see it?' shouted Juffo – in English, strangely – towards the linesman. Flamurtari officials kicked the plastic seats in frustration.

Flamurtari played a defensive formation against weaker opponents, and the ensuing goalless draw was the most tedious match I had seen in years. The highlights package that was broadcast later contained so little action they lingered on the teams coming out of the tunnel and lining up. 'That's football', said a Flamurtari fan after watching the match on television at a streetside bar. At least he had a beer to numb the pain.

Flamurtari had a point. Four months after my visit, Skënderbeu received a record ten-year ban from European competitions for match fixing. Flamurtari and Teuta Durrës still couldn't be separated at the end of the season, both finishing in mid-table on forty-six points.

Recording my matches

It became a pre-match ritual. I wrote down the previous matchday line-ups for the home and away sides in my notepad, the squad numbers and surnames an exciting foretaste of every step of my almighty challenge. As a result, I would always favour a quiet opening to the match itself, with the ball being gently passed between centre backs, whilst I adjusted my note of the starting elevens and attempted to identify the formations deployed.

My already terrible handwriting became a whirl of scribbled shorthand. I documented what I saw and heard, but also estimated the air temperature at kick-off (the mean of 15°C across all my games was, pleasingly, the same as the world's average climate) and the attendance. Before the game, I would examine teams' form – it was always important to gauge the mood of the fan base – research key players and, occasionally, even watch highlights of recent matches. I was often mistaken for, and sometimes felt like, a scout.

I looked for patterns and idiosyncrasies. I noticed a numerical oddity when watching Engordany in Andorra: their three attacking midfielders were numbered 17, 18 and 19. Numbers 17 and 19 switched wings regularly, but 18 kept central, almost as if to maintain the sequence. Engordany's 3–0 win was also a curiosity. All three goals were scored from outside the penalty area, a statistical rarity given that only 3 per cent of shots in the English Premier League are converted from that range.

I loved my nine notebooks – apart from the sparkly one, which left glitter all over me. They were a throwback to the travel diaries from my backpacking days, something that a mobile phone will never replace, useful though it was for recording conversations. I typed up my notes after each match and transcribed every discussion. Inevitably, large swathes of text and entire hour-long interviews didn't make this book. Neither did planned sections on the best mascots (the yellow rooster I would see in Israel was clearly the finest), most rousing club songs (maybe one for the audiobook) or tastiest terrace food (there really wasn't that much to savour).

Apart from watching the game, the only other thing I *had* to do was ask someone to take a photograph of me at every stadium. I posted a mugshot alongside a very short match report on Facebook, a website I was taking quite literally. These photos proved particularly useful for publicity. *Record*, a Portuguese newspaper, actually requested one from all forty-three countries I had visited at that stage (they would eventually settle for my best ten matches). I varied my poses: inside the dugout in Kazakhstan, pounding a drum with Section 8 in Belarus and, my favourite, pictured in a questionable floral shirt bought from a Turkish market alongside the Serb painting the halfway line in Kruševac. The slight kink in his otherwise immaculate white line was entirely my fault.

I recorded an array of detail about each match, including the current and final league positions – I would watch thirteen champions and nineteen relegated teams - whether beer was served and when the matches kicked off. There were twenty-five different start times, with 4 p.m. and 5 p.m. the most popular, and only four matches – in the Faroe Islands, Northern Ireland, England and Portugal – that commenced at the traditional, at least in my home country, 3 p.m. A comprehensive list of line-ups enabled me to concoct statistics of dubious value. I observed that three left-sided centre backs scored over one weekend in Germany and the Netherlands, and that 82 per cent of teams used at least three substitutes, with Ararat in Armenia being the only top-flight team to field a fourth.

I also subjectively ranked things based on my own experiences. Long before my travels commenced, I devised a spreadsheet where I rated non-European countries I had visited on a dozen factors, from weather and food to value for money and perceived friendliness. (Sri Lanka and South Africa remain the top two.) I tried something similar on this journey, rating each match for its skill, player fitness, excitement and atmosphere. My system was biased towards the big leagues – matches in Turkey, Spain and Portugal would own the top three spots – but it was no surprise that my goalless draw in Albania was lowest for excitement and atmosphere. I knew that my next fixture in Greece really couldn't be any worse. And it wasn't.

Match ratings, comprehensive team line-ups and more detailed statistics are published at 55footballnations.com.

ISLAND NIGHTS AND FESTIVE LIGHTS

29 Greece

Greece had been an awkward country from the very start. I could only target Super League clubs located in the northern part of the country, closer to the borders with Albania and Macedonia. I had debated travelling to Greece before Albania, Macedonia and Kosovo to visit Larissa, formerly managed by Chris Coleman, or Giannina, from the city of Ioannina, before I decided to visit title chasers PAOK in Thessaloniki.

I had contacted PAOK a few weeks in advance of their fixture against Atromitos, only to be informed the match was being played behind closed doors after recent fan trouble. I would need to find another game in Greece. PAOK would then cause incredible controversy at the end of the season when Ivan Savvidis, their Russian owner, charged onto the pitch with a gun during the dying moments of a game against AEK Athens. The Balkans were undoubtedly fiery: three matches I tried to watch in Albania and Greece were played without any fans, and there was crowd trouble in Kosovo and Macedonia.

I switched my route and my attentions to Kerkyra, the club based on the island of Corfu. It was a push to get to Corfu in time. My over-sized Citroën raced along the sun-kissed seaside road south of Vlorë and up a surprisingly steep incline into Llogara National Park, home to wildcats and wolves. My frantic travels were sometimes under-researched and I was hardly expecting to drive through pine forests, past alpine-style lodges and over the kilometre-high Llogara Pass, providing an epic view over the Ionian Sea. I twisted through more clusters of Hoxha's bunkers, a stone castle and quiet villages full of Sunday churchgoers, sleepy cats and the odd optimistic vendor.

There was only one ferry from the Albanian port of Sarandë to Corfu, at 1 p.m., with the alternative a rush to Igoumenitsa, the Greek port that sounded like an Argentinian defensive midfielder. The nuclear option was a mammoth 350-mile drive to Athens to watch AEK in action the following evening. The roads were thankfully clear, and I arrived in Sarandë and promptly drove over a hidden roundabout. I was relieved to ditch the Citroën and take the fast hydrofoil to Corfu. The seas were smooth, a false dawn given the rough conditions that followed. The Greek transport gods were on my side.

I had been fortunate with the weather on my trip so far, one of my biggest potential obstacles having been the havoc the winter might play with scheduling, football and travel. It had been a fine summer and a warm autumn, and I had been blessed with comfortable temperatures at most evening kick-offs. And very little rain, aside from the odd downpour in Northern Ireland. However, the clouds now looked to be changing. A storm was brewing over Corfu and it would strike during my match between Kerkyra and Olympiacos. The conditions may have affected my hosts, or even my receptiveness towards them, as positive vibes would prove hard to detect in Greece.

I visited the Kerkyra Stadium several hours before the evening kick-off and paid 30 euros for a ticket in the covered main stand. This instantly felt like a wise choice, as the sky was already darkening with threatening clouds as I walked away. Police-car sirens flashed like predictions of lightning. A small group of chanting ultras in Olympiacos red and white approached in the centre of the road. I instinctively raised my camera, the flash fired and this attracted one animated fan's attention. He danced towards me waving his fists. 'Hey, I'm English', I said. I was not certain this phrase would get you out of many tight calls, but it seemed to work in Corfu. The threat was diffused when he was restrained by a fellow ultra. I was surprised they were concerned about being photographed ahead of a televised match. But I took the unsubtle hint and hid my camera.

I retreated to a nearby bar. Old men were settling down to watch the match in comfort on large screens. One made some noises about me sitting in the wrong place. I wasn't being made particularly welcome; perhaps an out-of-season holiday island just wanted to forget about foreigners in damp November. I walked towards the away supporters and caught the eye of a young Olympiacos fan. He had obviously seen me take photos of the parade. 'Don't put it on Facebook', he warned. It was proving hard work meeting a friendly local in Corfu.

The Kerkyra Stadium is rather shambolic. The rickety main stand is held up by rusty blue girders, and a strong wind was making fans feel less comfortable than an air temperature of 14°C would otherwise suggest. Neither did the journalists look very happy in their rudimentary media area, clutching plastic cups of hot liquid on wobbly wooden desks rejected by a local school. A hefty gust blew over a substitutes' bench as Kerkyra's cheerleaders entered the pitch in sea-blue tops and maroon leggings. The Olympiacos fans opposite didn't look impressed by the dancers' haphazard routine. They probably knew that they were going to get soaked.

It was clear that many of the home crowd were not regulars. They were here to see Olympiacos, the best-supported team in Greece. Seat numbers had long been eroded and late arrivals caused confusion by trying to take their allocated places. I was sitting next to Ron, an Albanian with a pleasant smile that took the edge off some of the blank faces. He was, coincidentally, from Vlorë, my hosts the previous day, and lamented recent development in his hometown – 'There are no plans, just building' – before, inevitably, mentioning Barcelona. Ron had been at one of the two famous matches. 'We were there from 9.30 a.m., just to get a seat' he recalled. His son had been born in Greece and was a goalkeeper at the Kerkyra academy.

Monotone advertisements were still being played loudly over the PA system long after the game had kicked off. There was a murmur of discontent from the crowd until the adverts were paused until half-time. There was thunderbolt and lightning and it was a very, very frightening first few minutes from Olympiacos. A volley from the sure-footed Fortounis, one of only three Greeks in the Olympiacos line-up, was well saved. The drums of the Olympiacos fans from the lower stand were audible over the rumble of the storm. A brass duo from Kerkrya could not compete with either.

Kerkyra began to settle, playing 4-1-4-1 with an entirely Greek line-up apart from one German and a Cypriot. And the home side took a shock lead when centre back Gromitsaris struck home a firm volley from a nicely worked free kick. The sound of 'Goal goal goal Kerkyra' lifted the heavy air. I wondered which was older, the scratchy club song or the ancient audio system. Most of the main stand seemed happy, if not overly jubilant, in the way of occasional fans.

This was an elemental affair with lashing rain and grumbling thunder-storms. The monsoon conditions were not helping the more celebrated team. A simple pass by an Olympiacos midfielder slid harmlessly into touch on the sodden surface. Ron explained how, like the majority of Corfu residents, he used to support Olympiacos. 'Always the referee gives them decisions. This is why I am now Kerkyra, not Olympiacos.' Olympiacos's popularity had been cemented in Corfu after they had loaned players to Kerkyra when they were a lower-league team. It had been a determined first half from the underdogs, who fully deserved their 1–0 lead and hearty applause from the main stand. There were murmurs of a major upset.

The unmistakable mop of the French 1998 World Cup winner Christian Karembeu, now coaching at Olympiacos, was visible under a large umbrella. A classier Steve McClaren, he didn't look concerned by the weather or the scoreline as Olympiacos brought on two substitutes: Đurđević became the second striker and Chelsea reject Marin played attacking midfield as the visitors shifted from 4-2-3-1 to a diamond-shaped 4-4-2. But the biggest tactical curiosity was Olympiacos pushing centre back Cissé up front straight from the kick-off, a move that paid off when Cissé slammed in a close range rebound seconds after the restart. He celebrated and trotted back to his place in the back four. Job done and 1–1.

Olympiacos kept creating. Đurđević had a shot blocked, Marin fired over the rebound and midfielder Romao stuck the crossbar. This was as unrelenting as the downpour. Olympiacos finally took a 2–1 lead when Đurđević volleyed in a left-wing cross. The Serbian, who made a difference with his power and skill, then held the ball up on the left wing for Marin, who sealed the match with a low curler into the far corner. Kerkyra toiled for a way back, looking tired on a heavy pitch lashed with torrential rain. 'Olympiacos, Olympiacos', chanted the ever-dampening home ultras as their team came from a goal behind to win 3–1.

Kerkyra deserved their acclaim from the crowd, who were still divided between their home island and the Greek champions. The rain had finally ceased and the crowd dispersed swiftly to 'Smells Like Teen Spirit'. A friendly Kerkyra steward asked if I had enjoyed the game. It had been good. There had been skill and endeavour, crazy weather and the hint of a shock. 'They did well. Normally we don't even score against Olympiacos', he said.

Corfu Town was bright, blustery and blissfully rain-free the following day. I climbed the old fortress and admired the town's Italianate buildings, picturesquely hemmed in by the newer sixteenth-century fortress and the sea. The Kerkyra Stadium, visible on the horizon with the airport behind, looked less incongruous from a distance. The fish market, full of lithe cats admiring the haul, made me hungry. I dived into Rouvas, an authentic tavern dotted with old pictures, for a delicious slab of moussaka.

The owner was both a Kerkyra and an Olympiacos fan. I grabbed a few words between orders. 'I am from Kerkyra so Kerkyra is first for me. Kerkyra is now in the Super League but not always. A lot of people they grow up with Olympiacos, it's normal', he said. 'You know more about football than me', he smiled as I regurgitated some facts about Greek football. His chef cooked a much better moussaka than I could. We all have our strengths.

Olympiacos were one of the most dominant teams in Europe, having won twelve of the last thirteen domestic titles. But still the Olympiacos fans were not happy. 'They don't spend anything to make a good team. And now people are dissatisfied. That's why if you go to Piraeus the stadium is almost empty.' Oympiacos had been outplayed in the Champions League by Barcelona, Juventus and Sporting. But at least they were the best on their own patch. For now.

The hydrofoil back to Albania was cancelled because of the blustery weather, and the ensuing ninety-minute rollercoaster ride on the slow ferry was a passable metaphor for my Greek match. I began to regret the mini chocolate croissants I had guzzled in more placid waters, whilst neighbouring Albanians relived their own breakfasts. I was relieved to complete the choppy crossing to Sarandë and be reunited with the oversized and fully visible Citroën. I once parked my battered Honda next to the Thames before a Fulham match in the mid-1990s and returned to find only an aerial. The rest of the car was underwater. I found a telephone box and called my father. 'Wait for the tide to go down', he advised. I did, and the ancient Honda started first time. The river smell lasted as long as the car.

I clambered into the Citroën, approached the hidden roundabout from the opposite direction and completely missed it again. I motored to the pretty Roman ruins at Butrint before leaving Albania for Greece for the second time. The Greek motorway rose steeply through vertiginous mountains and ever-lengthening tunnels. I lapped up European Union tarmac after my adventures around Albanian potholes. *Once More 'Round the Sun* by Mastodon looped on the CD player. 'You take the high road down', urged the third track. My Corfu experience had certainly not been the pinnacle of my travels. The game was engaging, but I found it hard to find open people to talk to. And this hadn't really been due to any language barrier.

My Greek highlight was neither the football nor my moussaka. I had long wished to make a pilgrimage to the monasteries of Meteora, impossibly perched atop huge rock pillars nearly a hundred miles east of Corfu on the mainland. They pierced the searingly blue sky on a perfect November morning. I'm not a religious person but these were special – spiritual, even. Monks had built these hermitages long before mechanisation. My challenge seemed modest in comparison, and suddenly more achievable.

A giant yellow and red flag and friendly border officials gave the Citroën a rousing welcome as I returned to Macedonia. The immigration man complained about his League One bets. 'Peterborough away at Charlton. So sure', he lamented after two late goals at the Valley had denied him a win. 'I'm Chelsea', said the burly customs man. I groaned and drove away from him and his over-attentive sniffer dog. 'Ingerland, Inger-land, Inger-land', chanted the customs man, his dog yapping in unison beside him. I was glad to be back in Macedonia for my flight to London. My next destination could hardly be more different.

Olympiacos wouldn't need to worry about Champions League embarrassment. They ended the Super League season in the relative ignominy of third place. Kerkyra finished second bottom and were relegated.

30 Denmark

I was either getting jaded or conserving energy. Arriving at my Helsingør guesthouse, I had received a charming welcome from a large ginger cat. Margaret, named after the queen of Denmark, curled around my legs and leapt on my bed. It wasn't late and I wasn't tired, but I didn't feel like heading out into the dark and cold to eat an expensive dinner on my own.

Margaret was there again in the morning. She sniffed at the meaty remains of my takeaway pizza and lolled on my pile of jumpers. It was difficult to motivate myself. I layered up and walked around Kronborg Castle, the setting of *Hamlet* at the turn of the seventeenth century and a UNESCO World Heritage site since 2000. The mighty structure overlooks the Øresund, the strategically important stretch of water that separates Denmark from Sweden. The shoreline, sea and sky were a flat grey; a sign warning against swimming was entirely superfluous.

Helsingør had recently added a silver statue, Han, to its waterfront. It glittered against the subdued winter colours, a little merman to compete against the more famous mermaid in Copenhagen, only twenty-five miles to the south. I enjoyed wandering around the compact city, with its interesting churches, narrow lanes and maritime history, more than I perhaps thought I would. Denmark, organised and polite, was very different from the Balkans: I didn't miss swerving around Albanian goats in the Citroën. Plus this was another milestone. Denmark was the last Nordic country I would visit and had a league regarded as the best in Scandinavia, helped by tax breaks offered to overseas players for their first three years in the country.

Helsingør had a football tale more recent, but no less glorious, than something from Shakespeare. The club was founded from five local teams in 2005 and changed its name from the snappy Elite 3000 Fodbold to FC Helsingør seven years later. Helsingør were playing in the third tier as recently as 2015 and had shocked Danish football with their promotion to the Superliga the previous season. This weekend would see the last round of fixtures before the mid-season break. I thought it would be a fine winter's tale to watch romantics Helsingør against fellow strugglers Lyngby and, the following day, watch leaders Brøndby against old rivals AGF.

Helsingør had advertised a Christmas party it was hosting before the match. I arrived two hours before kick-off and surprisingly few fans were taking advantage of cheap beer in a tent that rocked to 'We Are the Champions' and the Helsingør anthem. I sat opposite Anders, a season ticket holder, on a wooden bench, as he told me about the thrilling promotion play-off against Viborg the previous season. The first leg had been 1–1. The second leg also finished 1–1 and had gone to extra time, in which Viborg scored first and Helsingør went through on away goals after making it 2–2 with eight minutes to spare. I thought there might be goals today. 'Helsingør does not make many goals and Lyngby have a very good defence and don't let in many goals', said Anders. I predicted a 2–2 draw. Anders seemed convinced and bet on the same scoreline.

The stadium was in a strange setting. An old wooden stand, seating just 282 spectators, was backed by a railway track and a densely wooded hill. There were two, very temporary, metal stands and a large, covered area behind one goal that was used for grilling sausages, reputedly the finest in Denmark's top flight. It had taken forty-nine applications to deviate from league rules just for Helsingør to play Superliga football in their own stadium.

I spotted a line of pint glasses neatly strapped to the back of advertising hoardings with metal bells fixed underneath. 'Don't touch those', warned Thomas, a Helsingør fan, first in Danish, then in English. 'Don't worry, I'm English. I don't steal beers', I said. The bells were sounded at corners or when a glass was empty. Thomas was a long-term Brøndby fan, but also supported Helsingør, his local team, and we would both attend Brøndby's match the following day. This was the third occasion, after Russia and Northern Ireland, that I had met someone watching the same two matches on successive days.

Thomas introduced me to the city's mayor, Benedikte Kiær, who lived close to the stadium and was a Helsingør regular. 'The most important thing about Helsingør being in the top division is awareness', she said. I wouldn't have been in Helsingør were it not for their new status. 'Exactly.' Benedikte explained that the new floodlights were one of the many changes that Helsingør had to make. They looked very temporary. And they were too short, as the view of Kronborg from the wooded hill was protected.

Helsingør had won four and drawn one of their opening eighteen matches, a reasonable return for a team that had lost four of its best players in the summer. They started well against Lyngby and were deservedly two goals up at the break. Winger Christensen side-footed a cross neatly into the far corner and, minutes later, crossed for central midfielder Basse to convert with his instep. Thomas and his rabble were suddenly over-optimistic. 'It's going to be 6–0.' Helsingør had only scored thirteen goals this season prior to this game.

A warming cup of tea helped combat the nose-diving temperatures at half-time. 'Why do you come to Denmark in December?' asked a woman behind the goal. I explained that I had to go somewhere or I would not complete my challenge. Pom-pom girls danced vigorously to the Helsingør anthem and tried not to look too cold whilst Holger Danske, the fearsome Viking warrior mascot, wafted his sword rather too close to them.

The second half started with two curiosities. First, ghostly figures waved red flares on the hill behind the wooden stand. 'It's not in the stadium so that's okay', said Thomas. A two-carriage train then trundled past and Helsingør winger Christensen was put off his touch by a beep from the driver. 'It's a tradition', said Thomas. Ten minutes after the restart, the Lyngby midfielder Rygaard curled a free kick over the wall and beyond Bruhn, Helsingør's goalkeeper, to make it 2–1. Rygaard then smashed a penalty over the crossbar. Helsingør struggled to get out of their own half but held on for the win. 'I'm glad it was not 2–2', said Anders, who, feeling confident, then bet that Helsingør would stay up at odds of 5/1.

I retired to the VIP cabin for spiced mulled wine. The barwoman presented me with a Helsingør-branded bottle of Chilean Cabernet

Sauvignon. 'This is for you', she smiled. I wasn't sure what I was going to do with it. We moved to the tent, now something of a Christmas disco, serving free beer as several players celebrated with increasingly inebriated fans. I spoke to Bruhn, the home-grown goalkeeper who had played for Helsingør since their third-division days. Sponsors had even paid for a helicopter to take Bruhn from his carpentry examination to a midweek match at Nykøbing during Helsingør's promotion season. He was sensibly grounded. 'We have to give something back to the fans', he explained, as beered-up males greeted him enthusiastically. Thomas and I retreated into town for more beer and mulled wine.

The next morning, I took the train to unglamorous Glostrup, on the western outskirts of Copenhagen. I felt a bit rough. My guesthouse owner kindly gave me a lift to the Brøndby Stadium. I gave her a Helsingør bottle of wine that I was never going to drink. I approached the slightly dilapidated blue and yellow cabin that housed Brøndby's supporters' club, a few minutes' walk from the stadium. 'I'm looking for Peter Nielsen', I said to a gaggle of smokers outside. They looked confused. 'The Peter Nielsen with the belly?' They laughed and pointed me inside.

Peter had invited me to join Brøndby's supporters' club for a Danish Christmas dinner. I was intrigued. I wondered whether it would be venison or goose. Instead, I ate rye bread with fish, prawns and various pork products. 'Is this vegetarian?' I asked. 'Everything', said the fan opposite. The Danes were friendly and funny, and celebrated Christmas with copious amounts of alcohol. Savouries were washed down with schnapps that took the enamel off my teeth. We hunted around a bowl of *risalamande*, rice pudding with cherry sauce, for five lucky almonds.

I spoke to the Father Christmas sitting next to me. Dennis had always been a Brøndby fan despite annual reindeer-steering and present-giving duties. He grew up just one mile from the stadium when Brøndby were in the midst of their first period of success in the mid- to late 1980s. Dennis, a ship's captain, wore his yellow Brøndby shirt whilst he watched streams of matches from the North Sea. Brøndby seemed to embrace all social classes. I also met a salesman, shop worker, IT technician and a sous-chef who worked in Surrey. I asked him what he thought of English people. 'Honestly, the people I meet around town are really nice. But the English workers in the pub are so bloody lazy.' This made me laugh.

Brøndby were top and had won their last nine league matches. They hoped for a tenth win in the 'old firm derby' against AGF, the Aarhus team. Dennis explained that there used to be a big rivalry between the clubs when AGF were successful. But Brøndby had won nine titles since the Aarhus club's last success in 1986. Hatred was now reserved for FC Copenhagen, the new and successful kid on the Superliga block. There were regular problems between the two sets of fans and the Brøndby clubhouse had been attacked. Dennis was fair enough to admit that the reverse had happened when Brøndby visited FC Copenhagen. Or maybe it was just the schnapps talking.

I had loved the local feel at Helsingør. Brøndby was very different. They were a big Danish club, as scarves from European ties strung around the cabin – including several from a devilishly difficult 1998–99 Champions League group that contained both eventual finalists and Barcelona – testified. I stood on the tightly packed Sydsiden stand as a volley of flags, streamers and fireworks announced the start of a match I could barely see. The east stand applauded the south stand for a vibrant display that had been partly funded by over £1,000 collected by Brøndby supporters' club.

Helsingør had deployed orthodox wingers whilst Brøndby played the same 4-4-2 formation with a midfield diamond. It worked. Tibbling cut in from the left wing and curled a right-footer into the top corner. It was a special goal and celebrated with another flare. The crowd jumped up and down and the stand shook. The crowd were high from the pre-match display, a fine goal and a five-Carlsberg-for-£24 offer. They laughed as a clearance was smashed straight into the referee. A deluge of leaflets was dropped from the heavens: fans were concerned that not everyone knew the words to Brøndby's staple 'Stoltheden er Kolossal' and were helpfully circulating lyrics sheets.

I took a freezing Carlsberg at half-time. This made taking notes and the odd photograph, waving flags, singing songs and retrieving streamers even more difficult. I was beginning to feel the cold in the second half. Fortunately, midfielder Halimi warmed everyone with a fantastic left-footed half-volley that crashed in off the bar and doubled Brøndby's lead. The Brøndby fans celebrated with a version of 'Macarena' that switched seamlessly between the sides of the stand. It was surely all over at 2–0. Brøndby would be top at Christmas. But Sana, the mercurial Swedish midfielder, whipped in a free kick and AGF left back Møller headed in. It was 2–1 with nearly half an hour still to play. AGF were back in the game and the Brøndby fans knew it.

There was a noticeable lull. A few yellow and blue flags still fluttered and reminded me of the dismal Ukraine v Poland match I had watched in Marseille at Euro 2016. This was much better. But it got worse for Brøndby. Captain and right back Larsson gave away a penalty and Sana, as cool as the weather, confidently dispatched the spot kick. I was surprised that large screens showed replays of the, admittedly uncontentious, penalty decision.

'Attack, attack, attack, attack, attack' was the familiar refrain, interestingly in English, from the Brøndby fans. The first snow of my travels, a fortnight before Christmas, started falling during injury time. The crowd whistled in frustration as AGF had the better of the late chances. A lone plastic glass was thrown at the irritating netting that masked our view of an entertaining 2–2 draw.

There was a feeling of drunken deflation back at the clubhouse. I took off my coat and a large bacon crisp fell out. I presume it hadn't been there since Bergen. I placed the crisp on the table in front of me and an inebriated Brøndby fan opposite picked it up and ate it. The Danish were good at recycling. I munched on Christmas lunch remnants and chatted to the dregs of the crowd before leaving.

It was bone-chillingly cold as I waited at the bus stop. A drunk Brøndby fan approached me and asked if I could look after an even drunker Brøndby fan. We took the bus back to Glostrup station and I left him circling the bus shelter. He may still be there.

Brøndby only lost three matches out of thirty-six but couldn't regain the Danish crown, finishing second behind Midtjylland. Helsingør and Lyngby were both relegated, making this the only time I would watch two relegated teams compete against one another.

31 Poland

'I'm the one who's got a lot to say when particular teams are playing', said a leading sports commentator from Warsaw. 'If you tell me you want to see Legia on Saturday evening we can make it happen.' Polish television had expressed an early interest and, although I wasn't sure about the morality of a league fitting its fixtures around my travels, Poland was going to be fun. It was also my final country before Christmas, even though I wouldn't get to sample the traditional Polish Christmas Eve spread of twelve meat-free dishes, representing the number both of the apostles and the months of the year.

I flew from Copenhagen to Kraków, not Warsaw, as the midweek derby between Cracovia and Wisła held more appeal. The last time I visited the cultural capital of Poland was with thirty-five men dressed as Santa Claus for a friend's stag do in 2008. It had not been a very cultural weekend. Nine years on, Kraków felt more mainstream, but the old town still oozed charm. The charismatic Rynek Główny was a bevy of festive stalls, selling cheap decorations and over-priced food, underneath a mighty Christmas tree. Bright lights and festive bon-homie cut through the dark streets, buskers playing Chopin and Oasis to passers-by. Kraków, now well connected to much of Europe, was a honeypot for visitors. The locals seemed, like in Tallinn, somewhat jaded by the masses, but still helpful, even when I experienced the conveyor-belt tourism of the unique Wieliczka salt mines.

I walked up to Wawel, the imposing royal castle overlooking the river Vistula, certain you could see Cracovia's stadium when I was last here as a Santa. Seemingly not now. Cracovia's revamped Marszałek Piłsudski Stadium is a lower-slung affair with floodlights bent over the roof. It was located next to a design workshop and some of its neighbour's élan had rubbed off on the minimalist lines. 'Some people say it looks like a supermarket', said Paweł, the sinewy television producer for Canal+ sent from Warsaw to cover my visit. I actually quite liked it.

A few fans scuttled around the ticket offices. This wasn't the weather for lingering, but there was little sign that the derby would be played later that evening. 'It's normal just to wear shirt and scarf in the sta-dium', said Paweł. 'Maybe in Warsaw, Legia are present on the street because they are so big people are not afraid to demonstrate they are fans.' It certainly wasn't like England, but the intense rivalry between Cracovia and Wisła was one of the oldest in Europe. Ludwik Gintel, a former Cracovia defender, labelled it 'the Holy War', which in turn set the thrashy Megadeth track of a similar name racing through my mind.

Paweł met me outside my guesthouse in Kazimierz, the historic Jewish district sandwiched between the old town and the river, with his cameraman and soundman. We relocated to a nearby tapas bar to film. The restaurant manager was nonplussed when we took over half the tables for the cost of two coffees and a plate of slimy pierogi, filled dumplings that normally taste much better. Paweł had done his homework and had plenty of questions. He kept mashing his intro, miscounting the number of UEFA members. 'Fifty-five nations', I shouted in encouragement.

It felt strangely natural to be filmed. I was being asked about my travels, my passion. I reeled off some familiar answers. I mistakenly said that Turkish fans were high on alcohol, not caffeine, but it was one quick take. The light was fading as we filmed me pretending to walk into my guesthouse. A stray football bounced towards me and I instinctively kicked it back to a young girl. The cameraman was excited and, after a quick spot of negotiation with the girl's father, we staged a kickabout until the father lamped the ball over the building in the centre of the square.

This had made me nervier than being interviewed for television. My football skills, or lack of them, were on show, and I played it safe in my winter shoes and hoped one flailing attempt at a flick would be edited out. We relocated to the stadium, where I was filmed picking up the tickets from the club shop. The brunette behind the counter was still doing her hair for the cameras as I approached. This was all quite amusing. We then approached the stadium slowly in a car, pretending to arrive for the cameras, as Paweł asked me about the cost of football tickets.

Paweł and I retired to a nearby arthouse cinema. 'The best thing about the Polish league is how this league has changed when it comes to stadiums', he said. Kraków had not been a host city at Euro 2012 but the tournament had improved infrastructure across Poland. And the players no longer creaked like the old stadiums. 'This league used to be related to corruption, alcohol, players who don't live properly.

Now the attitude of young players has changed a lot. We have a player like Robert Lewandowski of Bayern Munich and everybody wants to be like him.'

Paweł said that the Polish league was 'a little closed' and had almost become hipster football. Everybody was interested in the national team and knew leading players such as Lewandowski, Grzegorz Krychowiak and Wojciech Szczęsny. But the majority of Poles were not interested in the Ekstraklasa, the Polish top division, which was only broadcast on satellite television, too expensive for most locals. 'Most normal people watch Bayern Munich, Barcelona and Real Madrid on the internet', said Paweł. This was a common theme, even in a country that aspired to have a top flight that was on a similar level to those in Belgium and the Netherlands. I could envisage the national pride in seeing your best player lead the line for the perennial German champions, but supporting moneyed elite teams whilst living in Poland just seemed wrong.

Paweł was a touch hopeless and had left his coat in Warsaw. This was Kraków in December. It was a still night, but the temperature was a chilling −2°C. He also wasn't sure where our seats were and bounded down a tunnel to the corner flag. A large woman in a bib strode purposefully towards us and asked him to go through the usual turnstiles, which cued another film opportunity. I was quite relieved when the barcode scanner worked first time.

Cracovia's most famous supporter was Pope John Paul II, who had religiously followed the team's results until his death in 2005. I looked for modern Cracovia fans to speak to. Three young guys behind me in the south stand looked ripe. I introduced myself. One of them said, 'There is a problem'. It wasn't their English. They supported Real Madrid.

A colourful display of fireworks from the north stand marked the start of the derby. A stray red firework fell just short of the Wisła fans. It wasn't a coincidence. A massive Cracovia shirt appeared in the east stand before the match and would reappear several times during the game. The Icelandic slow clap made yet another incongruous appearance. The Wisła away fans, restricted to only around 400, were muted. 'Wisła is shit' and 'Shit tifo' chanted the Cracovia fans. The Wisła fans replied with something similarly derogatory. Paweł did not want to translate every obscenity. 'It's simple stuff', he said.

As was the football. The game had an old-school English feel to it, with no-nonsense defending and energetic pressing. Cracovia had the opening chance when defensive midfielder Deja, who in my dreams was playing alongside fellow holding player Vu, had an instinctive twenty-yard shot tipped over. The hosts had edged a contest of set pieces until, three minutes before the break, Wisła scored from one. Carlitos ignored debris being thrown at him and struck a low corner. Wasilewski, the former Leicester City title winner (albeit as a reserve behind Wes Morgan and Robert Huth), moved cleverly to the near post and volleyed home with his right foot. Cracovia were stunned, and Wisła scored twice more through the bright Spaniard Imaz either side of half-time. It was 3–0 and all over.

Cracovia fans in the opposite stand spent ten minutes under an over-sized black cloak. 'They're planning something', said Paweł. The unveiled fans innocently waved pretty pink flares before unceremoniously shooting fireworks at the Wisła fans. Some fell short, others struck stewards, some unerringly hit their enemy targets. This was like Kosovo with arrows. Wisła fans advanced up their stand to try to get out of range. But there was no escape from the fiery shafts, which arced into the away supporters, some hitting the underside of the roof with an ugly clang.

Smoke from the fireworks enveloped the pitch, and the goal in front of the Wisła fans was barely visible. The referee took the teams off and a line of riot police with large Alsatian dogs entered the fray. Several policemen were hit and the smell of tear gas drifted across the pitch. The smoke eventually cleared and fireworks were extinguished by firemen, by which point the derby had been delayed for twenty minutes. Paweł had received a volley of messages from television viewers confused by the pause in live coverage.

The PA system warned that if there were more pyrotechnics the match would be forfeited in Wisła's favour. But it was already 3–0 to Wisła. Cracovia fans responded with a brazen display of pink flares behind the Wisła goalkeeper that thankfully stayed in their hands. The game continued. I breathed a sigh of relief. I didn't want to test my definition of watching a top-division match.

Cracovia didn't seem to want to be on the pitch and hid from the ball. 'This is a dead game', said Paweł with twenty-five minutes left to play. 'Fuck on Cracovia', chanted the Wisła fans. Cracovia conceded a free kick twenty yards out and Carlitos, a growing second-half influence, curled a right-footer into the top corner. Cracovia's Helik headed in a late consolation to make it 4–1. There was a murmur of celebration from the home faithful, but most had missed the goal by participating in a backs-to-the-disaster-on-the-pitch Poznań.

Paweł offered me a lift, saying this was not a good time to be alone in Kraków, and I scuttled back to Kazimierz for a burger and bed. The night's events led to some soul-searching by Polish football experts. 'Some parts of fans didn't change. It's a big problem. We have attitude from eighties, nineties. We have different times, modern times now', said Paweł. The Cracovia fans' actions felt almost as historic as the city of Kraków.

Wisła finished sixth and Cracovia ninth. Carlitos was top scorer in the Ekstraklasa with twenty-four goals and moved to champions Legia. Cracovia's fans were banned from away matches for the rest of the season.

Top of the hops

The two words football and beer are often intertwined, and both were integral to my travels. I set myself an arduous additional challenge to drink at least one beer in all fifty-five nations. I actually managed to quaff a *domestic* beer in each, with the exception of Andorra and Gibraltar, where most things are imported. It was a fun task to research the current European beer scene, and try to find out which country was top of the hops.

Europe's fine beer tradition had been strengthened in recent years by a pleasurable plague, the craft beer movement. Sappy lagers were still popular, especially around the Mediterranean in Cyprus, Greece and southern Italy, but interesting brews had been breeding across swathes of Eastern Europe. My head had hurt from beers resembling rocket fuel on previous visits to Kraków. But Poland is now a two-tier beer nation, where heady lagers are countered by more complex brews that lean on Anglo-American techniques. Moscow has led a Russian beer revolution that had spread to Ufa – where I even found an American

Pale Ale called Great Britain Pound – and across former Soviet states. I encountered ales made from Armenian apricots at Dargett, Yerevan's leading microbrewery, drank a refreshing wheat beer in Georgia and a reasonable dunkel in Azerbaijan.

Beer prices varied as wildly as the quality of football. It was hard to get drunk in Norway: I paid an eye-watering £14 for a pint of delicious Norwegian craft beer and made it last for hours. My favourite Bergen barman then poured me a free half when I ordered a glass of water with an expensive plate of meatballs. My cheapest ever beer – 5p for a bottle of St George at a bar in the Ethiopian metropolis of Arba Minch, back in 2006 – will never be beaten. But drinks in Albania and Kosovo were amongst the most economical in Europe; 65p gets you a big beer in Elbasan.

It would have been an impossible task to drink at every stadium, as beer was sold at fewer than half of my matches. And that beer often wasn't very good. Maes, one of the better offerings, is hardly one of the truly great Belgian brews, but it somehow suited the comfortable surrounds of the Ghelamco Arena in Ghent. Meanwhile, beer at Häcken was only 3.5 per cent, the alcohol content being restricted by Swedish law. There was no beer for sale at matches in Spain or France, and the Mexican midfielder Corona was the closest I came to beer in Portugal.

I became over-excited by a beer sighting at ADO Den Haag, but it turned out to be non-alcoholic in the Netherlands. This was possibly a good thing. I already had enough things to do: take notes and photographs, speak and sing with the locals and celebrate when the home team scored. It was often a refreshing reward to savour a beer after a match, when I could collect my thoughts, on my own or with others.

I drank many enjoyable beers, but my favourite at the football was a sweet Vilniaus as the sun set on my summer match in Lithuania. There was nothing for sale, not even water, at Spartaks Jūrmala three days later, but Latvian beer was arguably the most interesting in Europe. I visited the taproom of the funky Riga brewery Labietis – blessed with a very heavy metal logo – and savoured how they used unusual ingredients like catnip and juniper berries to spice up their excellent beer.

The very worst beer was in Belarus. I tried mainstream and micro-brew, cheap and moderate, bottled and draught. It was all an unsavoury assault on the taste buds. 'Why are you drinking Belarusian beer?' asked Anton after we had watched the visiting goalkeeper score in Vitebsk. 'It's all awful. We drink German beer.' A bottle of Paulaner never tasted so good.

HOME FOR CHRISTMAS

32 Scotland

I'm not very non-league. I occasionally visit Dulwich Hamlet, my local team, and Harrow Borough, where my friend Simon compiles the matchday programme. Simon put together some jaunty reports based on my travels for Harrow Borough and asked if the stories could be republished by fellow Isthmian League Premier Division outfit Dulwich Hamlet. Why not? It might get me a couple of followers. They turned out to be BT Sport and the BBC.

I met Erik, an affable Canadian sports cameraman, in a Peckham coffee shop. His teenage son had read about my travels in the Dulwich Hamlet programme. Erik thought the story had potential, knew plenty of people in the industry and, unbelievably, pushed me into spots on *Scottish Football Extra* and *Football Focus*.

It was the day after Boxing Day. I took a 4 a.m. taxi through London, a train from St Pancras and the bus to Luton Airport. This was a jolting start to my trio of British games in Scotland, England and Wales. My plane sat helplessly on the tarmac as the flurries of snow thickened in the dark. The runway was closed and the aircraft needed to be defrosted. I was getting worried. I did not want to be late for my first UK television appearance or have to travel to Scotland in the New Year. After a two-hour delay, we took off into a snowstorm and my trip was alive. I was relieved to be on the early plane to Inverness as all later flights were cancelled.

I had never been this far north in the United Kingdom. I looked down to see snowy mountains peeking through the clouds like an Alpen packet. I have some Scottish roots. I've played Carnoustie (well, the putting green), where my grandfather was born. But this was an alien landscape. The plane circled over the inky waters and a grey sandwich of sea, town and sky. I took the train from Inverness around Beauly Firth to Dingwall, not as direct as the bus across Kessock Bridge, but more relaxing after my melange of sharply stressful transportation.

Ross, a London friend visiting his family in the Black Isle village of Rosemarkie over Christmas, joined me for Ross County's match against St Johnstone in Dingwall. The town took its name from *Þingvöllr*, a local assembly, preserving connections to its Viking history and my own travels in Iceland. Ross said that Dingwall, a small town of 5,500, had always been in the shadow of Inverness. The town had particularly struggled when the Kessock Bridge opened in 1982, replacing the ferry that had plied the Firth's waters since the fifteenth century and encouraging shoppers and workers to favour Inverness.

Ross is a music lover with a keen ear for an entertaining anecdote. He told me that Dingwall Town Hall was the second date on the Beatles' five-night Scottish tour in January 1963, just months before they hit the big time. But they only attracted an audience of nineteen as the Melotones, a local band, played the same night at nearby Strathpeffer

Pavilion, and drew a crowd of over 1,000. The Beatles never played Inverness though.

I met the Glasgow-based BT Sport crew, Steven and Stephen, at Ross County's Victoria Park, its 6,500 capacity the second lowest in the Scottish Premiership after Hamilton Academical's home. The ground was now sponsored as the Global Energy Stadium, reflecting the business interests of its chairman Roy MacGregor. Nothing lasts for ever but I was, not for the first time, thankful I supported a team that still played in its historic stadium with its traditional name.

BT Sport were creative. I sat in different east-stand seats and shouted out the names of places I had been to. Maybe I was a bit too precise. 'I think Kazakhstan is a few more seats to the left' didn't help continuity. I was filmed pretending to arrive on a train at Dingwall's diminutive station. Steven, the producer, said he was happy with the content after a quick chat overlooking the pitch. He explained that it was much harder with players, as they often had to run interviews for half an hour before they said something interesting.

Stephen, the cameraman, was a Rangers fan and nicknamed Darth Carlsberg, presumably for his love of lager and science fiction. He spoke with a genuine passion for the game. Stephen had filmed at the 2014 World Cup in Brazil. 'I couldn't believe I was at the World Cup final in the Maracanã. I spent the first half hour crying.' Steven and Stephen zoomed back to Inverness, their base until the evening's match. They were pleased that Ross County's rivals, Inverness Caledonian Thistle, had been relegated in 2017 as it meant fewer road trips from Glasgow. Ross County were bottom after twenty games and needed to beat seventh-placed St Johnstone.

Ross County were promoted from the Highland League to the

Scottish league system in 1994. I spoke to Graham, a fan since those non-league days, at the Staggies Bar. Graham lived on the Black Isle, the nearby peninsula that was neither black nor an island. Its name was rumoured to derive from a dark past steeped in witchcraft. Other Ross County fans travelled hundreds of miles from across the Highlands, as far north as Orkney, Stornoway and the Western Isles, to watch the team. As in Mönchengladbach, Ross County seemed to represent a region more than a town. The club had reached the Scottish Cup final in 2010, losing 3–0 to Dundee United, during which Dingwall was apparently a ghost town. It hardly felt like a metropolis during my visit.

Graham joked that St Johnstone were now Ross County's local rival despite Perth, the away team's base, being three hours' drive from Dingwall. He echoed the views of the BT Sport crew by saying that the big Glasgow clubs didn't enjoy travelling to play at Ross County. I asked Graham whether Dingwall's isolation helped attract players. 'I know a few of the players quite well and they love it up here. Other ones who enjoy the city life may not want to come. A few of them haven't settled and have had to go back but not many.' There was nothing really to see in Dingwall, but I liked the low-key atmosphere after Kraków.

Graham explained how Ross County would be nowhere near the Scottish Premier League without the investment from their chairman. MacGregor, listed fifth in *Management Today*'s Top 100 British entrepreneurs in 2014, spotted the BT Sport crew filming me outside the stadium in the snow. He stopped for a chat, an amiable man, easy to warm to, even with white stuff piling down in the pitch black.

I may have spoken to the chairman, but there was no chance of meeting Rosco, the club's stag mascot, who was presumably tired from his recent masquerades as a reindeer. My disappointment quickly evaporated with a rousing rendition of 'Christmas Time (Don't Let the Bells End)' by the Darkness just before kick-off. The Ross County players might have still been singing along to the opening words – 'Feigning joy and surprise at the gifts we despise' – as Johnstone headed in a left-wing cross for St Johnstone after just two minutes, the ball dribbling apologetically through the home goalkeeper's legs. It was particularly ragged defending. Ross County fans in the Jail End, so called because the old county prison and court were located behind it, looked less than impressed.

St Johnstone were neater and more compact, and deserving of their 1–0 lead. Chris Eagles, the ex-Burnley and Bolton winger brought in by ex-Burnley and Bolton manager Owen Coyle, was the only source of Ross County guile. The Ross County natives were restless. Young men in fresh suits jumped up in the south stand and shouted something I didn't understand. Ross County's tactics were crude: long balls launched down the middle for flick-ons, or increasingly distant crosses angled into the penalty area. It was physical and aerial football, and I counted a bout of five consecutive headers that brought back memories of Iceland and the Faroe Islands. I gazed at the advertisement for a local butcher, Scotland's Black Pudding Champion for 2010, and started dreaming of hot food.

I'm not really a pie man at English games. They're often overheated to disguise the thin taste and pastry. My friend Ross picked up four Scotch pies at half-time for us two, Stephen and Steven. But the BT Sport crew had already scarpered. Their material was secured and no doubt they were more enticed by a warm Inverness hotel room than the second half. This left me with an additional pie. This was no hardship as the pies were good. I had eaten my first and was contemplating the second when Ross County equalised. Eagles was tripped on the inside edge of the penalty area and Schalk stroked the penalty home.

It was 1–1 and suddenly we had a game. St Johnstone's chances were blocked by the Ross County defence as snowflakes fluttered like feathers from a pillow. Schalk struck the post and the rebound was repelled twice by Clark in the St Johnstone goal. Ross County's Merseyside-born Taiwan international Chow drove forward and shot straight at the increasingly busy Clark. The game was winding down to inevitable parity. Ross County left back Van Der Weg looked an unlikely hero as he charged into the penalty area. 'He's terrible', said Ross before the left back sliced horribly wide. Chow then conceded a foul on the edge of the area. I was relieved when the St Johnstone midfielder Craig hit the free kick wide with the last kick of the match.

It felt very northerly when I woke up the next day. My hotel coffee tasted so awful it could have been brewed in a cauldron. 'Dingwall is the sort of place you just want to get out of', said Stephen, his lowland roots coming to the fore. I didn't linger either and took the bus to Inverness over Kessock Bridge. I noticed that the snow had not settled on the Black Isle: its name is also derived from the climatic quirk that snow will often lie on the surrounding hills, but not the peninsula itself.

Eagles and Coyle both left before Ross County were relegated to the Championship after another 1–1 draw with St Johnstone on the last day of the season. St Johnstone, Ross County's not-so-near neighbours, finished in eighth.

33 England

This felt strange. I rarely watched a football match in my own country that didn't involve Fulham. But there was familiarity in everything else, two days after returning from Dingwall. My train from Waterloo zipped past an old family home in Surrey. And Bournemouth was very close to where my grandparents used to live. The pretty English countryside contrasted with the dingy train on a bright Saturday: perhaps not as dramatic as driving through undulating Albania or cruising the inlets of Norway, this was still more interesting than the flatness of Belgium or Latvia.

Conor, a contact at the supporters' club, met me at Bournemouth station in his ridiculously retro 1970s Volkswagen. I could barely fit in and nearly gave myself an injury opening the door with my shoulder. We drove to the Cherries' café for builders' tea, a soft bacon bap and hushed football chat. Conor had moved to the south coast from Northern Ireland in 2005, after which Bournemouth became his team. Conor volunteered for Dorset Children's Foundation, a charity supported by the club and represented at Bournemouth matches by the Dorsey Bear mascot. I was about to make my debut on live national television on *Football Focus*. Conor was about to wear a giant bear costume for the first time after the original Dorsey Bear had called in sick.

Bournemouth were very broke for very many years. Premier League status was not even a dream in the 1980s. It was all about survival. The club had needed a mascot and, according to legend, a local bowling alley had a discarded bear suit. There were no links between bears and the town, but the club decided moth-eaten fur was better than nothing and the bear was revived to become Bournemouth's mascot. The current bear had a fully furnished coat although Conor said there is a room in the Vitality Stadium with all the old bear heads.

We talked about Bournemouth's past. Much of it was familiar but comforting to our ears as we prepared for our unusual respective days on television and inside a giant bear costume. Steve Fletcher, scorer of the late winning goal against Grimsby Town that prevented the club from dropping out of the league in 2009, was now immortalised in a stand. We talked about James Hayter's 140-second hat-trick, the fastest ever in the English Football League, after he came on as a late substitute against Wrexham in 2004; and how his parents, convinced Hayter wasn't going to get a run out, left before his goals to catch a ferry home to the Isle of Wight. Bournemouth won that match 6–0. But they lost a friendly against Real Madrid, to mark the completion of the current stadium, by the same scoreline in 2013, in a match best remembered for Cristiano Ronaldo breaking a young fan's wrist with an errant free kick.

Eddie Howe had masterminded Bournemouth's promotion to the Premier League in 2015, thrashing a Kit Symons-managed Fulham 5–1 at Craven Cottage along the way. The scoreline was chastening, but the match was unique as I had watched Howe and Symons play out a goalless draw for the very same clubs in August 1998. Injuries forced Howe to end his playing career at the age of twenty-nine in 2007 and he became Bournemouth's manager the following year. Few managers are as loved. Howe even had a chant. 'He went to Burnley and then he came back.' One of the only reservations amongst fans seemed to be a reluctance to use certain players – young midfielder Lewis Cook had been ignored for most of the previous season, for example – until they learned to play Howe's system. Bournemouth were in the bottom three but I couldn't see them staying there.

I later watched the match against mid-table Everton with Richard, a long-term supporter, and he was also fully behind Howe. 'Eddie is quite unique in that he's very passionate about Bournemouth, about the town, about his roots. He's taken us as far as he can but that's further than anyone has ever taken us. The Steve Fletcher stand will soon be the Eddie Howe stand.' There was even a nice story from the Caucasus. Nika, from the Georgian Football Federation, had been impressed with Eddie during a training programme when he had worked for Dinamo Tbilisi. Dinamo had played Gabala in the 2015–16 Europa League. Nika bet Tony Adams, then their sporting director, a Gabala ski pass that Eddie Howe would keep Bournemouth up in their first Premier League season. Bournemouth were now in their third top-flight season. Nika never received his ski pass from Adams.

Conor and I walked from the café over a slightly sodden King's Park. The cricket pavilion dominated the horizon almost as much as Bournemouth's Vitality Stadium which, with its 11,000 capacity, was by far the smallest in the Premier League. Bournemouth were struggling when the stadium was built in 2001, at a 90° angle to the original Dean Court pitch. Supporters tried to secure the ground based on a fans' pension scheme, with thirty people putting in £50,000 of their pension funds to take out a commercial mortgage, buy the stadium and pay back £100,000 per year. It didn't work out, yet seemed to sum up Bournemouth. Audacious and quite affluent.

My television time was nearing. Conor was bearing up well ahead of his appearance as the charity's mascot. We chatted nervously outside the vividly green Jubilee Gates, a pleasing remnant from Dean Court. Conor said that most people preferred the old Bournemouth and that his charity had previously been granted more freedom. They were now forced to follow Premier League rules, which made it difficult to get permission for Dorsey Bear to run on the pitch before televised games.

Conor talked about the players who had risen up the divisions with Bournemouth. He recalled standing in the queue at Natwest with midfield stalwart Harry Arter and 'no one bothered him because he was just Harry Arter back then'. Fellow midfielder Mark Pugh visited a care home during a mid-season break rather than holidaying in Dubai like his peers. Conor had a signed shirt that was going to be auctioned for charity stolen. 'Steve Cook, our defender, heard about it and said, "I'm going to come down to the shop, give you my own shirt, have it signed by all the players and we're going to tell everybody to raise as much money as possible".'

Conor remarked that his charity was closer to Howe and his Bournemouth players than would ever be possible at the likes of Manchester United. But things were changing. 'All the good stuff still comes from the old guard who know what it's like not to have any money. The newer players are less willing. They've grown up in academies and always had the Bentley.' I spotted former goalkeeper Jimmy Glass, famous for scoring a late goal to keep Carlisle United in the league in 1999, drive up in a fast car. He was now one of the many ex-players employed by the club.

I picked up my media pass from the BBC. The name was correct. The photo wasn't. A young man in his twenties with a student fop wasn't me. I walked onto the pitch with a BBC microphone and earpiece. 'Do we call him "Matt" or "Matthew?"' I heard. 'Matt', I said, hoping I was not live. Dan Walker, the presenter, mainly kept to the script with questions about planning and the best and worst matches I had watched. Klan Kosova television later heard that I chose the Drita match as my highlight and invited me onto their channel. There was normally one rogue question. 'Has this trip changed your perceptions of European football?' asked Dan. I highlighted the competitive nature of the Polish and Armenian leagues without mentioning the fireworks in Kraków or the red cards in Yerevan. After the interview, the pundit Mark Lawrenson asked who was paying for my adventures. Dan said it was self-funded. 'Good lad', said Lawro.

I was relieved to be off screen. Conor and I walked into the spacious club shop and he changed into his bear costume. He was immediately asked for autographs. This was a different type of pressure. Dorsey Bear waved a Bournemouth flag as the players funnelled their way through a guard of honour before the match, while Conor would do well to let in goals during the half-time penalty shoot-out as his bear costume filled most of the goal.

The Bournemouth team posed for their matchday photograph on the sidelines. This was another Eddie Howe idea. I liked it. It was distinctive, it promoted team unity and young players could dream of appearing in their first starting line-up photo. I worked out the formations. Sam Allardyce's doughty Everton midfield trio of Gueye, Schneiderlin and McCarthy was short on guile, especially with out-of-position Sigurðsson and the inconsistent Lennon flanking the young Calvert-Lewin in attack. Richard, the long-term fan sitting next to me, was impressed that I tracked both teams. 'I've only ever noticed two players: De Bruyne and Willian. I'm so focused on Bournemouth.' It was certainly much easier at Bournemouth than tracking twenty-two unknowns with dodgy italic numbers in Belarus.

Not everyone was happy that Bournemouth were in the top division. 'The FA don't like it, other clubs don't like it, the Premier League don't like it. They would rather have a Derby County, Forest or Villa', said Richard. I thought the same about Fulham. Bournemouth joined the Football League in 1923 and spent almost all their subsequent seasons in the third and fourth tiers. 'We're a lower-division football club. No one in this ground would be overly disappointed if we went down to the Championship', said Richard, adding that people might take Bournemouth a little more seriously if their stadium had a 25,000 capacity. Richard, a property developer, had courted controversy by buying land behind the east stand to help his then cash-strapped club. The housing development meant that Bournemouth, with no means of expanding, were now looking to build a new stadium nearby.

It was not the most electric of first halves, hardly helped by a pedestrian Everton content to pass gently between Schneiderlin and England centre backs past and present, Jagielka and Keane. The busy Scottish midfielder Fraser volleyed in a right-wing cross to give Bournemouth a 1–0 lead at the break. Rooney joined the fray in the second half, in what was probably the last time I would see the former England player live. Fraser lost the ball to Rooney and his left-footer was turned wide by Begović. A clever flick from substitute Niasse then released Gueye, who scored Everton's equaliser. 'Oumar, Oumar', chanted the Everton fans at the creator as players celebrated in front of a seething mass of middle-aged men. 'It was like they were fighting to be fed a fish', commented one Bournemouth fan.

'We're AFC Bournemouth, we come from League Two', encouraged the faithful. Bournemouth looked the more likely winner. A cracking reverse pass from left back Smith released Fraser on the left wing. His shot, heading for the near post, looped off an Everton body, over the stranded goalkeeper Pickford and into the far corner to make it 2–1 to the home side. Richard said he would give me a love bite if Bournemouth held on for the remaining few minutes. They did with ease. I escaped, neck intact, and caught up with Conor. 'How was the bear?' 'Hot. I could only see through the mouth.' The club bar was light relief for us both. I chatted to Ciaran, a fan who had worn his Bournemouth shirt when working in Brazil. The locals had thought it was a Flamengo shirt for many years, but now recognised it as Bournemouth.

Bournemouth were more synonymous with their manager than any other club apart from Arsenal and Wenger. 'He said he will stay here until he can't take us any further. He is the club. The whole ethos of the club is built around his ethos', said Dave, a season ticket holder since 1987. 'Some of our players are League One and Championship players who are playing out of their skin for Eddie.' He would surely leave one day, for a bigger challenge. He was only forty and still learning. Both Nika in Georgia and I tipped Howe as a future England manager.

Conor gave me a lift back to the station in his Volkswagen. My door mistakenly swung open as we drove around a roundabout. 'Losing a door wouldn't be a good story for the book', I said. Bournemouth and Eddie Howe were.

Bournemouth and Everton finished five points apart in mid-table. After Arsène Wenger's retirement, Howe was the longest-serving Premier League manager as the 2018–19 campaign started. Allardyce was sacked by Everton in May 2018.

34 Wales

'Do not flush away your hopes, dreams or goldfish', chimed the Virgin train toilet. Llandudno Town, based thirty-five miles west of Liverpool on the North Wales coast, had never hoped or dreamed of playing Swedish big fish IFK Gothenburg in the Europa League. But they had in 2016. They lost 7–1 on aggregate, but the match raised the profile of the seaside town. Llandudno was no footballing hotbed and there was a distinct underdog theme to my Scottish, English and Welsh hosts.

My train crossed into Wales and followed the coast, where the grey mouth of the river Dee looked unenticing. Sheep grazed next to stone walls on fields dotted with puddles from recent storms. Clustered caravans were angled against the Irish Sea and, if buildings can have emotions, the derelict Colwyn Bay pier looked depressed. A three-carriage train took me from Llandudno Junction and past the chunky Conwy Castle to Llandudno, the 'Queen of the Welsh resorts'.

The faded architecture felt more striking than in Bray. Georgian housing fronted the gentle curve of Ormes Bay and framed a well-kept pier and the looming Great Orme headland. Llandudno's Giant Hospitality Stadium is set well back from the sea, next to a coach park and industrial buildings. The stadium's appeal increased when inside. Great Orme was visible behind one goal, and the frosted peaks of Snowdonia National Park added a mysterious backdrop to the south.

I spoke to Grant Montgomery, Llandudno director and a former player, about the piecemeal stadium from a clubhouse overlooking the artificial surface. It used to be a bumpy grass pitch and Chris Coleman, then the Wales manager, opened the 3G surface in 2014. 'What a nice guy. There is no façade. He is what he is', said Grant. I didn't need convincing. Coleman led Fulham to the Premier League for the first time. I still wished he could have played in that debut 2001–02 season. Coleman's slightly unfulfilled playing career was prematurely ended when he suffered serious leg injuries after crashing his Jaguar in January 2001.

The clubhouse was originally intended to be a café. Grant explained that Cyril, a bricklayer and Llandudno fan, used to lay a few bricks and then watch the match. The walls were nearly head height when Cyril, in his early forties with five children, passed away unexpectedly. Friends from his local pub donated labour and materials and finished it for the price of a pint each evening. Ambitions were raised and the café ended up a two-storey clubhouse with a balcony. A plaque and photos showed that Cyril would be remembered by his football club.

It was a poignant story and Llandudno had their own fairy tale. They were promoted from the Cymru Alliance in 2015 and, remarkably, finished third in their debut Premier League season after keeping faith with many of their Alliance players, and qualified for Europe after TNS completed a Welsh League and Cup double. Llandudno had reached the Europa League with a mainly home-grown squad who could hardly have dreamed of playing in Europe.

Grant sat next to the managing director of IFK Gothenburg at the Europa League draw. It was a premonition. Llandudno ended up playing the Swedish giants in Bangor, twenty miles west, as their home stadium had not been assessed by UEFA the previous January. Grant explained such preparations had been far from the club's thinking, as they were just happy to stay in the Premier League. He was still visibly thrilled by the memory of an experience that would be hard to repeat.

Despite its name, I wasn't sure whether to expect a friendly welcome at the Giant Hospitality Stadium. I am very English and decidedly not Welsh. Llandudno and visiting Bala Town fans mixed seamlessly in the Crossbar, appropriately located behind one of the goals. I introduced myself to a cluster of Bala fans who were poring over the team sheet. Bala, on the eastern fringes of Snowdonia, regularly qualified for Europe and had lost every tie. Arwel, a big Bala fan and graphic designer at the town's chocolate factory, enthusiastically recounted matches against Differdange 03 from Luxembourg and FC Vaduz from Liechtenstein. 'How were they?' I asked, interested in two countries I had yet to visit. 'Very hot', said Arwel. The first qualifying round of the Europa League is played in the height of summer. It would not be so balmy when I visited in March.

I was becoming an expert in league formats. The Welsh Premier League involved twelve teams who played each other twice before the league split into a top six and bottom six for ten more matches. Every team in the top six – and the top team from the bottom six – was guaranteed at least a play-off for a Europa League place. At the time of my visit, there were two matches left to play before the division in the division. Llandudno, in eighth, were one point off the top six. Bala were better placed in fourth. Nigel, Bala's general manager, liked the format, noting how not every league had games that continued to be crucial deep into the season.

Nigel and Grant were consistent in their admiration of TNS, now The New Saints, previously sponsored as Total Network Solutions, who confusingly play just across the invisible English border in Shropshire. They said that their teams aspire to match the standards that TNS, the only full-time team in the league, set. There was no evidence of the jealousy I expected. TNS had won the last of their six consecutive titles by twenty-seven points.

I stood between the clubhouse and the main stand. Both Llandudno and Bala have black and white home strips and it was hard to tell whether the scattering of seated fans were supporting the hosts or the visitors. 'Big winner' and 'Second ball' were clearly audible calls on the pitch as Llandudno played some neat football and created several early chances. Llandudno's two strikers combined for the opening goal. Marc Evans, returning from New Zealand to the club he played for in their promotion season, pulled out onto the right wing and his looping cross was headed home by Marc Williams. Llandudno had defended stoutly, attacked brightly and deserved their lead.

I was enjoying watching a sporting scene very different from the English Premier League in December: the light was fading, the temperature dropping and a flock of several dozen seagulls were attracted by something over the Llandudno goal. They got a good view of the best Bala chance as forward Davies flicked over a through ball. 'We might as well have stayed in the changing room', said Arwel about Bala's first-half performance.

I headed into a Portakabin at half-time for a cheese triangle, mince pie and warming cup of tea. Grant introduced me to Russ Austin, the club chairman, who was happy with the way Llandudno had played. Steve Lewis, a journalist from the *Daily Post*, overhead us and sniffed a story. He was disappointed I was from London, which was not the local angle he wanted. 'Our readers are more interested in stories about car crashes and a dog chasing a sheep', said Steve. I didn't want to get involved in either of those.

I relocated to the Snowdonia side of the ground, where I noticed the strange spiky floodlights. Llandudno received an unusual source of income from telecommunication companies, and the lights were actually attached to mobile phone masts. Meanwhile, the conditions were becoming more typical for January: the sky was burning red behind me, the wind whipped and my hands were numb. 'Everywhere We Go' and 'When the Town Go Marching In' sang the away fans as Bala restarted with more verve. I asked a nearby Llandudno man what he thought the final score would be. 'What is the score?' he said.

Bala were looking more dangerous. 'A goal is coming', I said to the man who didn't know the score. A Bala corner was flicked on and Disney headed in at the far post to level the score and send headline writers in North Wales into dreamland. Llandudno barely threatened in the second half and the match finished 1–1. Bala were pleased with an improved second half after a dire first, Llandudno content they could still secure a precious top-six spot the following weekend.

This was English non-league football with the carrot of European competition. Supporters were small in number, just 257, and reserved in nature. Grant informed me that Llandudno have a Danish fan who takes his annual holiday in the town so he can squeeze in two matches whilst his wife goes shopping. There certainly was a very friendly feel that reminded me of Helsingør. It was detectable in the Crossbar, where fans and players from both teams mixed after the match. The away team wolfed down nachos provided by Llandudno whilst leftover mince pies loitered on the bar.

The League of Wales shared similarities with the League of Ireland, where rugby and televised English football affected crowds. But Welsh football was determined to remain a winter sport, something that artificial surfaces, more common in Wales than in the Republic of Ireland, pointed towards. Arwel was relieved. A switch to summer football would clash with his commitments watching the Llandyrnog and District Summer League, a minor football competition that has been running since 1926.

I took the train back to London that evening, munching on a takeaway pizza in Chester station's freezing entrance hall. I enjoyed the pizza and my Welsh experience more than I thought. The football was fair, but the instant community feel was not something I had experienced everywhere. I noticed a sign in Crewe station that warned against over-enthusiastic train spotters and sat opposite a man happily dozing with his *Rail* magazine on the train. We all have our obsessions. I was becoming obsessed with watching football in strange places, even so close to home.

Llandudno missed out on the top six and ended in tenth place. Bala Town made the top six, finished fourth and qualified for the Europa League for the fourth consecutive season. TNS won the title by fourteen points.

Cost of football

The Belgians seemed particularly interested in how much my travels cost. The Danes came up with a wild figure. 'If every country was as expensive as Denmark you wouldn't be far out', I joked. My spending in Scandinavia was especially prudent as my travels were entirely self-funded. I had thought of sponsorship and even asked a camera company, who refused cheerily. I could have earned a few pounds by plastering brands on my website. But I had saved for a long time. And it would somehow be forever purer if I was independent.

You can't Google 'How much does it cost to visit fifty-five UEFA nations in one season?' Well, you can, and it comes up with my *Guardian* article. My overall budget was calculated from three separate outgoings: living expenses (accommodation, surface travel and food), flights and football tickets. I used an approach that estimated my living expenses based on typical accommodation costs, by far my greatest outlay, in each country. It transpired that the Faroes were the priciest place to stay, at £70 per night for a room with a shared bathroom, whilst my

Åland Islands hostel was hideous value during the height of summer. I knew that sometimes I would have to pay more than I envisaged, but that was balanced by cosy £25 rooms in out-of-season Italy and Spain.

It was quite straightforward to research flight prices. I took more planes than I expected (fifty-four flights with twenty-five different carriers), but the expansion of budget airlines meant that my average flight cost not much more than £60, despite some being bought at short notice as my plans changed. (A £9 flight from Luxembourg to Stansted, the lowest I paid, was predictably delayed.) My most expensive journey was, surprisingly, the train from Montpellier in France to Córdoba in Spain. But I benefited from some cheap car hire, paying just £3 per day for a spring drive around Slovenia, Hungary and Croatia.

I was slightly over budget for living expenses and flights, but well below my estimate of £14 per match ticket. I paid only £400 in total, an average outlay of a fiver for the seventy-nine top-division league matches I would watch in the fifty-five UEFA nations. I was helped by some free tickets. Victor started it all by gifting me a season ticket at Stjarnan in Iceland, and other clubs in mid-sized leagues such as Sweden, Serbia and Slovenia were equally amenable hosts.

My media links helped with hot tickets. A Belgian journalist secured me a ticket to Gent and television crews found me opportune seats in Poland and Scotland. And fans like Nikita in Russia and Conor in Bournemouth kindly bought or arranged tickets for me. Furthermore, football was free for everyone at fifteen of my matches: in Georgia, the Faroes, Azerbaijan, my trio of Armenian matches, Juventus in Romania and, later in my travels, in San Marino, Andorra, Gibraltar, at Čelik in Bosnia-Herzegovina and in Montenegro.

Everyone knows that football in England is expensive. I paid £22 to get into League Two Luton Town and £18 to watch National League Woking before my challenge kicked off, a sharp reminder why I didn't watch many non-Fulham matches in my own country. On the road, I only paid more than my original estimate of £14 on nine occasions: Bundesliga football in Germany cost £36 for a good seat, La Liga only slightly more, and my most expensive ticket was £57 for seats on the halfway line at Porto in Portugal. Most other places were very cheap: atmospheric seats at Turkey's Trabzonspor were £5 plus the cost of the Passolig membership card, Belarus and Moldova were less than £2, and the very cheapest ticket was 70p for adults and 12p for children in Kazakhstan. Meanwhile, arguably the worst value ticket was the £13 I paid to watch some fairly turgid fare in the Republic of Ireland.

Overall, I ended up only 2 per cent over my initial budget and was inwardly content with my forecasting skills. But my budget was just a number, an amount that I could afford. It was harder to predict whether this would be a wise use of money. As my travels progressed, I realised that this was a unique experience that would be hard to repeat, and impossible to value.

NEW YEAR IN THE EASTERN MED

35 Israel

It was mid-January. I had spent nearly a month in Great Britain, and I was keen to make some serious headway into my remaining twenty-one nations. I received a message from Kaduregel Shefel shortly before I departed for Israel. 'Do you want to leave Tel Aviv at 6 a.m. on your first day to watch a fourth-division match in the middle of the desert?' it asked.

There is an underground football culture in Israel that reminded me of England in the 1990s. Kaduregel Shefel means 'low football' in Hebrew and was about unheralded Israeli football, mainly of the fourth and fifth tier. Kaduregel Shefel, which started as a photographic project in 2013, had a cult following for their irreverent short films that mocked Israeli culture and showcased unlikely football destinations. This wasn't the Premier League, but it was going to be unique. And I was thrilled to be appearing in their short film about football in Yeruham, a town of some 10,000 inhabitants deep in the Negev desert. My mission had already been featured in newsprint, on radio and television. I was about to hit the silver screen.

I experienced divided emotions after reading Kaduregel Shefel's invitation. Part of me thought, 'Shit yeah!', whilst my more logical side persuaded me to check they were filmmakers, not mass murderers. Kaduregel Shefel are Gad Salner and Vadim Tarazov, the two stars of the films, and producer Doron Shahino. Their backgrounds reflected Israel's hotchpotch of influences. Gad is from Romanian stock, whilst Vadim had Ukrainian heritage and Doron Syrian.

Vadim, the joker, explained that he felt that everyone took life too seriously in Israel. Kaduregel Shefel had visited Arab areas where locals were worried they were going to film something politically correct. Instead, their slogan was 'Fuck coexistence. I just want to watch football.' They filmed at a match in Sha'ab, an Arab town in the north of Israel, in December 2017. As locals left the match to watch Real Madrid against Barcelona on television, the Clásico particularly favoured by Israelis, Vadim dressed himself as Santa and started throwing sweets at the retreating home support to get their attention.

Gad was our driver as we headed nearly a hundred miles south from Tel Aviv towards Yeruham. He wore a mid-1990s Derby County shirt and had been a Rams fan since he played *Championship Manager* in his youth. Kaduregel Shefel had exhibited photographs in Derby and Gad was in awe of the pictures of Mart Poom and Paulo Wanchope when he visited Pride Park, although he was hitherto unaware of the 'Poooooooooooom' chant that used to follow the Estonian's every save.

We drove south through stark landscapes that became progressively beiger. 'Beware of camels', flashed a road sign. Yeruham, our target, was one of the development towns founded in frontier areas in the 1950s to provide permanent housing to Jewish immigrants from Arab countries. We tried to find a British parallel on the periphery. Grimsby, not renowned for its arid environment, was as close as we got. I asked what the main industry was in Yeruham. 'Unemployment. They are very good at it', said Vadim. Yeruham had even mocked itself when an Israeli film called *Turn Left at the End of the World* was released in 2004. 'End of the world is here', said some graffiti.

We filmed at Lake Yeruham, where locals fished next to 'No fishing' signs. 'We live from the heart, not from signs', explained Vadim. A group of men were unpacking what looked like a morning picnic on some wooden tables. 'What are they doing?' I asked. 'Unemployment', said Vadim. We drove past a market. 'People open shops just so they can close them', said Vadim. It wasn't quite one joke a minute, but it wasn't far off.

We filmed a pastiche in a cactus-strewn square. Vadim was pretending to run tourist trips, 'Tarasov Free Walking Tours', around Yeruham every Friday. Gad and I were shown brown apartment blocks and local women feeding stray cats with cuts of meat. After the tour, we were presented with 'I love Yeruham' T-shirts. A red heart against a white background stood out against the taupe of the town and the bright blue of the sky.

We had pre-arranged a 10 a.m. lunch at a family home in central Yeruham. Mazal, the cook, was confused why we wanted to eat so early, but we were ravenous and piled through delicious salads, hraimeh fish, home-cooked bread and couscous fluffier than the lightest Dingwall snow. I showed my North African-Israeli hosts a photograph of my Scottish pie. 'I don't eat yellow and brown food', said Mazal, while her husband shook his head in genuine horror. Mazal stood around awkwardly as we polished off her brilliant food. Doron asked why she couldn't join us, and her husband replied that she had to get the food. Some traditions ran deep in the Israeli hinterland.

Mazal's husband told us his story. He had travelled across the Mediterranean from Libya to Israel by boat in 1951, boarded a bus and been
dropped off in Jerusalem in the middle of the night. At least that is
what he was told. He woke up to find himself in Yeruham. 'This is the
Israeli way', said Vadim. 'We say one thing and do another.'

We left Mazal's house for the nearby Municipal Stadium where the
ticket office, a dark hole in a sandy-coloured sporting mural, did not
look like it had been used for several decades. The view was extraordinary from high up in the solitary covered stand: a yellow brick wall
circled the pitch and behind it there was only desert and mountains.
The match, between Hapoel Yeruham and Bnei Yechala, a team of
Ethiopian Jews, kicked off at high noon in startling winter sunshine
that pushed the temperature to around 20°C. I felt warmth at a football
match for the first time since Romania in October.

Yeruham captain Vasker opened the scoring following some nice
touch football involving four players. The home crowd, which had
swelled from twenty-three at kick-off to seventy-five by the end of the
first half, was still nervous at 1–0. 'Don't give them a gift', shouted one.
Yeruham's chunky goalkeeper, Afik, something of a local hero, made
a clawing save to stop a far-post header. His watching father seemed
happy when I said it reminded me of Gordon Banks against Pelé at
the 1970 World Cup. 'You are writing more notes than I did for my
degree', said Vadim as I scribbled away, treating this match as I would
any other. He and Gad played the fool but were certainly not stupid.
They were software engineers, whilst the quieter Doron worked in
television production.

We piled into the changing rooms at half-time to film the Yeruham
coach laying into his team. This was basic psychology. Yeruham were

the better team, but there was no point inflating their egos by telling them so. Vadim said I would need to pick a man of the match. This could prove tricky as I had no team sheet and both sides could field a mind-boggling five substitutions in the Israeli fourth tier. With half an hour left to play, Yeruham were awarded a dubious penalty that Vasker converted to secure the award. The captain looked rather overawed as I presented him with his prize – an 'I Love Yeruham' T-shirt – after the 2–0 home win.

Vadim took me through some Israeli chants. The Yeruham and Yechala coaches were in heated discussion, and stopped to look up at Vadim singing 'All team come here' in English. Vadim was undeterred. 'Another popular chant is "Your mother is a prostitute" and this song is an inter-team, inter-league song. It basically means the mother of all the people here is a prostitute, which, of course, is not true. It's important to know that this is not true.'

We drove into the mountains to film the final scene of the day. I pretended to take photographs like a true tourist whilst Vadim and Gad staged an argument. 'This is where we kill you', Vadim said to me. The day had far exceeded my expectations. I had travelled to a unique place and watched offbeat football. I had learned and laughed about Israeli culture in a way that would have been impossible on my own. Doron presented me with a rare shirt from Bnei Sakhnin, the most successful Israeli Arab team who lost 7–1 on aggregate to Newcastle United in the UEFA Cup after winning the 2004 Israeli State Cup. 'That's great, I'm short on clothes. I'll wear it around Jerusalem next week', I joked. 'I don't think you should', said Vadim. They were the first serious words he had uttered all day.

I returned to buzzy Tel Aviv, a honeypot of Bauhaus architecture situated on a long sweep of the eastern Mediterranean. I strolled from the southern outpost of Jaffa along the coast, past countless tiny dogs being walked, cyclists, surfers and a middle-aged couple drinking a bottle of wine at 10 a.m. I enjoyed Tel Aviv, a liberal place with excellent food, more than I had envisaged.

Kaduregel Shefel had been fun. But I still had two top-division matches to watch. The first was mid-table Bnei Yehuda against bottom-placed Hapoel Acre. The match took place in the Petah Tikva Stadium, located on the fringes of Tel Aviv and shaped like a metal potato peeler. Bnei Yehuda won 2–1 in a match I remember best for their amazing yellow rooster mascot, who wore a striking red headband and an orange Yehuda shirt. Avner, a Bnei Yehuda fan, explained that an old fan, also called Yehuda, started bringing his live rooster, Rambo, to games in the 1980s. Rambo was considered lucky and was dressed in a Yehuda scarf for important matches. A later version of Rambo, 'Rambo IV or Rambo V', was released onto the pitch during the derby match at Hapoel Tel Aviv in 2014 and became a YouTube sensation when burly security guards slid around the wet pitch trying to catch him before he stalked down the tunnel, never to be seen at a match again.

The following day I took the train to the desert city of Be'er Sheva, sixty miles south of Tel Aviv, with a lot of guns. It was a Sunday and youthful military conscripts – service is mandatory for men and women at the age of eighteen – were returning to their army bases in the south after weekends at home. Soldiers looked bored as they played with their phones, rifles casually slung into the aisle. I wasn't sure if I felt protected when surrounded by such heavily artillery.

Hapoel Be'er Sheva, nicknamed 'the camels', are the success story of Israeli football after businesswoman Alona Barkat had taken over the club when they were in the second division in 2007. They were promoted two years later and won their first Israeli championship in 2016, repeating the feat in 2017 and breaking the stranglehold of the Israeli big four – Maccabi Tel Aviv, Beitar Jerusalem, Hapoel Tel Aviv and Hapoel Haifa – who had won all but one title since the Premier League's formation in 1999. Be'er Sheva are the most southerly club to play in the Champions League, a record unlikely to be beaten unless Canary Islanders Tenerife recapture their 1990s heyday.

The Turner Stadium, named after the city's former mayor, was another distinctive affair. Palm trees and the flashing red lights of Be'er Sheva's club colours gave the exterior the feel of a Las Vegas discotheque. Inside, an enormous banner covered the bottom of two stands. 'Always keeping going for more. This is not the time to get tired. After the final whistle your legs should fall off', it read. I filmed it left to right. 'You should do that the other way', said Yossi, a local who worked for the indie website Babagol and had found me a spare ticket for this sold-out match. Hebrew was going to take some getting used to.

Yossi wasn't watching when Hapoel Haifa kicked off against Be'er Sheva. Haifa played the ball down the inside left channel and Be'er Sheva's right back headed the ball tentatively. Haifa striker Ben Basat pounced, controlled and rifled an excellent shot in the far corner. Seven seconds were on the clock. It was the fastest goal I had ever seen. Ben Sahar, the former Chelsea forward, replied for Be'er Sheva as they drew a high energy match 1–1.

I took the bus to Jerusalem and watched Maccabi Tel Aviv play Maccabi Haifa, the last of the weekend's fixtures, on television. Maccabi Tel Aviv scored after eleven seconds. Israel had given me fast goals, stadiums unlike any others and an unholy Middle Eastern scrum to buy tasty za'atar bread, covered in oregano, thyme and sumac, at half-time.

I didn't wear my Bnei Sakhnin replica around Jerusalem. Instead, I wore my 'I Love Yeruham' T-shirt. Jerusalem was rather rainy so it stayed mainly under cover until I dived into a tour around the tunnels under the Western Wall. An American tourist took one look at my shirt. Then another. Then a third. 'Is that your name?' he asked. 'No, it's in the south of Israel', I said. 'I got it free with Tarasov's Free Walking Tours.' 'Wow' was his reply.

Hapoel Be'er Sheva won their third consecutive title. Hapoel Haifa finished fourth and Bnei Yehuda sixth. Hapoel Acre were bottom and relegated. Yeruham and Yechala were mid-table in Liga Bet South B. Tarasov's Free Walking Tours are still not in business.

36 Cyprus

I'm more of a football traveller than a groundhopper, enjoying the culture and context around games as much as visiting new stadiums. Unexpectedly, the four matches I watched in Cyprus would demonstrate how forays to foreign football fixtures can be experienced in different ways. I planned to watch three first-division matches over a long weekend, but belatedly realised that I could squeeze in a Friday evening match. I took the bus from Solomos Square in central Nicosia to the southern suburb of Lakatamia for local club THOI's second-division game against syllable-crushing Podosfairikos Omilos Xylotymbou. I wasn't sure how many others would be there.

I had low expectations and no bus back. Things would work out. Ticket prices were rather steep for such modest fare but I was hardly going to turn around. I entered the blue and yellow striped stadium and immediately spotted a man with white hair standing on his own. 'Do you come here often?' sounded stupid the moment it was uttered. 'No, I'm from Birmingham', came his response in a very West Midlands accent.

Stephen was a West Brom season ticket holder and a seasoned groundhopper. He had framed a short holiday around new grounds in Cyprus. And it transpired that he knew Mick, the groundhopper I had briefly met in Estonia. It's a small world when you have a niche hobby. We watched a frantic first half, shrouded in steam from the stadium's restaurant. The shrieks of the players were louder than anything coming from the assorted rabble of old men, women and children in the stands. I wondered how many had paid 10 euros to get in.

Stephen went to find a team sheet at half-time. He religiously recorded the line-ups at every match he watched. I asked the man behind what he thought of the game. 'I'm not a fan.' Vasilis Papafotis was a Cyprus Under-21 midfielder on loan from leading Cypriot club APOEL Nicosia to Doxa, who were coincidentally the first-division team I would watch the following day. He also looked rather like a smiling Emre Can. 'Everyone says that' said Vasilis. 'He's worth 350,000 euros', said Panayiotis, his agent, showing me the Transfermarkt value on his phone. 'Actually, 35 euros will do', he joked.

There are a lot of foreigners playing in Cyprus. Vasilis was honest. 'The foreign players don't like the Cypriot players. They think we're lazy.' The league insisted that each team fielded two Cypriot players in their starting line-up but many clubs were happy to pay the fine of 1,500 euros per player if they didn't. I asked if foreigners had improved Cypriot football. 'Sure, look at Cypriot teams in Europe', said Panay-iotis, referring mainly to APOEL's Champions League success, which included reaching a quarter-final against Real Madrid in 2012. Does it help the national team? 'Not at all, the Cypriot players don't get many minutes.' There was even an ancient Paraguayan striker, Adorno, playing for Lakatamia, and he converted the first of two second-half penalties.

Panayiotis drove Stephen and me back to central Nicosia after the 1–1 draw. He predicted a bright future for the promising Vasilis, who was out of contract at the end of the season. 'Good for us.' I expected to see Panayiotis at Vasilis's match at the Makario Stadium. He wasn't there and neither were many others. Doxa didn't have any fans and, according to a football source, their mid-table match against Alki could be rigged. UEFA provided evidence in 2016 to the Cypriot Football Association that seventy-five Cypriot matches had been fixed since 2011.

Vasilis waved at me as he walked down the players' tunnel into the decrepit former national stadium. It must be harsh playing in front of no one who cares. I looked for signs that the match might be fixed. Ba, Doxa's lumbering French right back, hit an ambitious cross-field ball that sailed into touch. It could have been deliberate. Or merely a reflection of his lack of quality, as he gave away a clumsy foul and rarely helped Vasilis on the Doxa right. Alki left back Ruca then curled a delicious free kick into the roof of the net that would be near impossible to stage. 'Alki, Alki', chanted the smattering of away supporters.

I watched Vasilis closely. His build-up play was neat and he attempted to release the Doxa forwards with early passes but didn't stretch Ruca with his pace. Vasilis punched the ground with frustration after another clipped through-ball didn't quite work. Sissoko replaced Vasilis at half-time. The Ivorian, a squat left-footer who drifted inside, was a different type of player. He was worse. My notes consisted of 'Sissoko gives ball away' and ditto marks. Alki spurned several good chances on the counter-attack for a second and deserved their narrow 1–0 win.

My weekend was divided between matches. Cyprus has been divided between the Greek south and Turkish north by a demilitarised buffer zone, also known as the Green Line, running for 112 miles and patrolled by the United Nations since 1974. It wasn't possible to cross Nicosia when I last visited in 1992 – I remember staring through bleak barbed wire – but the border at Ledra Street, where passports were briskly examined, had been open since 2008.

It was one of the most interesting borders in Europe. The difference was striking. Greek Cypriot café culture merged into Turkish teashops, Keo lager became Efes, euros were replaced by Turkish lira. Meaty kebab-shop smells, reminding me of Trabzon, infiltrated the air. There were noticeably more men and cats on the Turkish streets, more old buildings in need of repair. A mural of a whirling dervish, representing the mystical side of Islam, had been painted on a concrete block shelled with bullets. I visited the Selimiye mosque, its awkward exterior revealing that it had been converted from a Roman Catholic cathedral. It was a fascinating contrast. The people of Northern Cyprus have their own league. Perhaps I would visit and watch some football one day.

The big game of the weekend was APOEL against AEK Larnaca, first against third in one of the closest-fought European leagues. Ground-hopper Stephen wasn't there. He had already been to APOEL's GSP Stadium so watched a match in Larnaca instead. I couldn't quite fathom this. This was the match that everyone was talking about and tickets were only 10 euros. And it would turn out to be the best match of the four I saw.

Cypriot football has had problems with crowd violence as well as match fixing, with a ball boy amongst those injured during clashes between APOEL and AEL Limassol fans in December 2017. APOEL now required fans to buy tickets through a free, yet controversial, membership card system. I procured mine from the club shop in central Nicosia, a painless process compared to Turkey, but one that the hardcore fans were protesting about. The APOEL ultras marched outside the GSP Stadium, the largest in Cyprus, its twisty concrete access paths giving it the feel of a 1970s car park. They weren't going in. And neither was my camera, banned along with all bags. I tentatively left my expensive photographic sidekick with an elderly security guard manning a cupboard.

I could hear the distant horns and chants of the boycotting APOEL hardcore during a first half that AEK dominated. They opened the scoring when the league's leading scorer, Taulemasse, smashed in a left-wing cut back. APOEL had not looked convincing. But it was soon 1–1 after Nsue, the former Middlesbrough full back, was brought down. Morais, the ex-Chelsea midfielder who had made more than 300 appearances for APOEL, slammed home the penalty.

AEK fielded eight Spaniards and there were only two Cypriot players in the starting twenty-two: Merkis of APOEL and Laban of AEK. APOEL brought on another, the Cyprus international midfielder Efrem, with twenty minutes left to play. He glanced at Pablo loitering on the AEK penalty spot and hit a magnificent lob from the halfway line that arced over the goalkeeper into the corner of the net. Efrem tore his shirt off and celebrated with the main stand. It was one of the most audacious goals I had ever seen. Efrem's left-wing cross was finished by Nsue to make it 3–1 in injury time. But it was his terrific goal that had won the game for APOEL.

My final match was in stormy Larnaca, an hour's bus ride from Nicosia. The rain poured down and lightning flashed. It was like

Corfu all over again: the Greek gods were seemingly against my eastern Mediterranean travels. My taxi pulled up outside a battered kiosk and Stephen appeared. We walked across a car park that separated the AEK Arena, home of AEK Larnaca, and the GSZ Stadium, where we watched strugglers Ermis Aradippou and Olympiakos Nicosia. The two stadiums were just fifty yards apart. I wondered aloud whether there were two closer top-division stadiums in Europe. Stephen liked the poser but couldn't think of two.

Stephen was a real live football man. He didn't even watch West Brom on television. There was no competition or bragging with Stephen. Inevitably, we had both been to some of the same matches: Zimbru in the purple Chişinău mist, soulless Juventus Bucureşti in Ploieşti, the 2008 Africa Cup of Nations in Ghana and even a New Year's Day visit to Dulwich Hamlet.

We both had our rituals. I looked for photo opportunities, worked out the formations and then adjusted the squad numbers on my notepad. Stephen listed the shirt numbers and diligently noted the times of goals and substitutions. Our trust grew and we shared findings. The big leagues have saturation media coverage that can make the viewer lazy, yet it is more difficult researching and writing about lesser leagues. You become better at it. Orange boots playing behind the lone striker. Frizzy hair in defensive midfield. African winger. This was a tricky game to record. The main stand was set thirty yards back from the action, numbers were italicised and Olympiakos Nicosia wore black with gold writing.

The conditions were appalling. Heavy rain swirled in front of us and the match would have been postponed in many countries. The pitch held up better than the PA system as rock classics 'Paradise

City', 'Livin' on a Prayer' and 'Eye of the Tiger' were drowned out by the unrelenting rain. The slick surface added a certain gloss to the game. The Ermis centre back Taralidis opened the scoring with a free kick that dipped over the wall and skipped past the Olympiakos goalkeeper. Ermis's Ukrainian captain Martynyuk then curled two beautiful left-footers into the far corner either side of a goal by Alfonso. It was 4–0 to Ermis at the break and at full time after a remarkably uneventful second half.

Stephen was apparently 'not a number cruncher'. But you are always going to be with this sort of hobby. We both rated matches. I awarded this match six out of ten for entertainment. Stephen was rather aghast – 'Not a seven?' – but saw the logic: eight for the four-goal first half, four for the total non-event of the second. Stephen had some impressive numbers: over 1,200 matches outside England in more than 90 countries, he had completed the 92 English league clubs in 1976 and visited 190 new grounds in the 1994–95 season alone. His eyes lit up when he talked about his month in Buenos Aires, where he had seen thirty-two matches in almost as many stadiums. And, although he would never undertake my challenge – too few matches to make some countries worthwhile – he was only Kazakhstan short of watching football in all fifty-five UEFA members.

But we differed. People do. Even nuts like us. He had rescheduled a trip to North Korea in 2007, at considerable expense, after their international match against Turkmenistan was relocated to China. 'I'm not going to North Korea when there is no football.' I would have gone anyhow.

THOI survived in the Second Division by the slightest of margins over relegated Xylotymbou. APOEL won the title, AEK were fourth, Ermis eighth, Doxa ninth and Alki eleventh. Olympiakos were twelfth and relegated as the First Division reduced from fourteen to twelve teams. Vasilis made his debut for the full Cyprus team in March 2018 and signed a three-year contract with AEL. Stephen visited Kazakhstan in July 2018 to complete his fifty-five.

SMALL ISLANDS AND BIG LEAGUE

37 Malta

The match was in injury time. Valletta's Michael Mifsud, the former Coventry City forward and one of Malta's greatest ever players, collected the ball in space on the right side of the area. I visualised the ball nestling low in the far corner. Mifsud sliced it into the side-netting.

Second-placed Valletta and leaders Balzan had drawn 0–0 in a match the *Malta Independent* called 'positively stodgy'. I had experienced the dubious pleasure of watching two consecutive 0–0 draws on a sunny Sunday at the National Stadium in Ta' Qali, a former British Royal Air Force airfield in the centre of the island.

My goalless run was now 243 minutes. I watched two Saturday matches at Hibernians' stadium, the second decided by a single first-half Floriana goal. On Friday, I had watched a mediocre 1–1 draw between Gżira United and St Andrews on the artificial pitch of the Centenary Stadium, also in Ta' Qali. And then waited half an hour on the blustery main road for the bus back to Valletta. I wondered if watching five Maltese matches in forty-eight hours with a winter cold, probably picked up in the Larnaca downpour, was an early sign of madness.

Cyprus and Malta both have strong English influences and the cheapest way to travel between them was to fly via London. I was immediately struck by how unique the Maltese language, a fusion of Italian and Arabic, was in a country that had the vibe of both cultures. Malta has a growing population of just under half a million. Only Iceland, Andorra, the Faroe Islands, Liechtenstein, Gibraltar and San Marino amongst UEFA members have fewer residents. But Malta's inhabitants are football fiends. The country boasts four divisions, with fourteen teams in each. Even the neighbouring island of Gozo, with a population of around 30,000, has two divisions and their own cup competitions.

I didn't expect Malta to be so urban, with cars everywhere and districts around the capital of Valletta merging into an amorphous sprawl. Surprisingly, of the fifty-five UEFA nations, only Gibraltar is more densely populated. I escaped most of the traffic and people by walking the soaring roads of wonderfully compact Valletta, absorbing spectacular views from its fortifications. Renovation was rapidly beautifying them for the city's role as 2018 European Capital of Culture. I wandered into the Pub, where the actor Oliver Reed supped his last drink in 1999. A newspaper cutting marks its infamy.

The burly Australian barman didn't like football. 'Rugby is my sport. It's a man's game, none of this falling down clutching their face.' Fair enough, but it was the most popular sport in the world. 'Nah, rugby is number one.' He listed the major and minor rugby-playing nations. 'What about Africa?' I asked. 'Nah, rugby is number one, it's even taken off in Kenya now.'

I left faulty Australian logic in search of football history. Clubhouses were the traditional home of Maltese football supporters. I visited Valletta's clubhouse, a retro mix of mirrors and faded photographs, for a coffee. Paul, the barman, introduced me to two cousins who were old enough to recall much of the club's history. 'We have the first football anthem in Europe. Or maybe the second oldest after Catania', said one cousin. 'Forza Valletta City' was recorded in 1959, and sounded like it. 'Valletta was the first club to wear tracksuits', he continued. 'We had substitutions in Malta before England', said the other cousin.

I wasn't sure about the veracity of these claims. But Valletta were certainly one of the most successful Maltese clubs, along with Sliema Wanderers and Floriana, and it showed in the glistening trophy room upstairs. A plaque in the centre of the capital commemorated all six Maltese trophies that Valletta won over the 2000–01 season. 'When we used to win the league, they gave the other clubs a trophy', said a cousin. One cousin was going to the match against Balzan, the other wasn't. 'I'm not going to the game. I've got bronchitis from watching Manchester United play Stoke City in January. It was too fucking cold.' The links to English football were clear and, inevitably, Manchester United were the best-supported team. The Salisbury pub in nearby Sliema housed an impressive array of Old Trafford memorabilia.

Rivalries are close in Malta. Floriana is just outside Valletta, its clubhouse a few minutes' walk from the walled capital's entrance gates. Alan, the club's social media manager, called Floriana a suburb of Valletta and said that derbies between the two teams used to be quite fierce, warning that it was still dangerous to wear the green shirt of Floriana in Valletta. Floriana had faded since their glory days in the 1970s. Alan said that Floriana were like Liverpool. Both teams had suffered over twenty years without a league title.

Maltese clubs were all privately backed, there being little income unless a club qualified for one of the four places in European competition. Floriana received some additional money from an unusual source: their old training ground was now used for car parking. Space was hot property in Malta's tight streets. Floriana planned to build a multi-use stadium that included a shopping complex, parking, a gym and office space. And a football pitch. So Alan was hopeful that Floriana's finances would not be so reliant on benevolent owners in the future.

We watched Floriana, who were not quite as good as their name or history, toil to a 1–0 win over ten-man Hamrun Spartans. The long locks of Hamrun's Italian right back, 2006 World Cup winner Cristian Zaccardo, were not the only familiar sight for Alan. Only three clubs – Mosta, Hamrun and our hosts Hibernians – had their own stadiums in Malta, and so he regularly watched Floriana play here.

Hibernians' stadium sits in the humdrum industrial suburb of Paola, part of the urban sprawl that radiates from Valletta. I earlier clambered around warehouses and discarded rubbish to reach it. I had to decide whether to support Senglea Athletic and Floriana or Tarxien Rainbows and Hamrun Spartans. Eight euros bought me a ticket to both matches. The one covered stand was split into designated home and away teams. I virtually always supported the home team, so chose Senglea and Floriana.

The stadium was lower-league English from the outside, very Maltese from the inside. The solitary stand offered a peerless view of Senglea, one of the Three Cities around the Grand Harbour. The soft colours and graceful roofs clashed with the mechanical yellow of the harbour's cranes. The cranes moved, sometimes edging forward as if to meet a corner. A battered scoreboard in one corner reflected a scoreline from a past season.

My most entertaining Cypriot match had been the table-topping clash at APOEL. Unexpectedly, tenth-placed Senglea Athletic against Tarxien Rainbows in thirteenth was the best match of my Maltese five. I was enjoying the contrast of colours – yellow and blue of the shirts against the verdant grass – when two of Senglea's Argentinians combined, defensive midfielder Garcia flicking in a header from Paz's whipped corner. Tarxien midfielder Cipriott then kicked out at a Senglea player, threw himself to the ground in pretend agony and was shown a red card for his awful acting. Oliver Reed would not have been impressed.

Tarxien made it 1–1 through their Brazilian player, Wellington, before Senglea's own Brazilian, Gregori, embarked on a tremendous left-wing run to set up the Maltese forward Vella, inexplicably wearing gloves in 14°C, with the simplest of finishes. Tarxien, who had played almost the entire match with ten men, secured a deserved point when Romanian midfielder Calin scored a left-footed screamer with ten minutes remaining.

It was a strangely compelling 2–2 draw. I was never going to see South Americans, Eastern Europeans, Africans and Maltese – at least four in every starting line-up were mandated – play in gritty Paola again. Floriana fans drifted in during the second half. They watched the Senglea match with an eye on their team warming up on the far training pitch. I had only previously experienced double matchdays at the Africa Cup of Nations. It was different in Ghana, where fans routinely turned up thirty minutes late.

I supported Mosta and Valletta at the National Stadium. Valletta fans arrived early and quickly outnumbered the few Mosta fans who watched their team play a good defensive game against champions Hibernians. The fanfare from Valletta's support was rousing after four Maltese matches with a fairly tepid atmosphere. Giant red flags were waved and then carefully stowed. Confetti was launched into the air. The famous Valletta song was gallantly sung with a brass-band backing that barely ceased.

It felt a positively regal affair. Valletta, the most successful team in recent years, were trying to regain the crown that Hibernians had stolen. The match was niggly and uneventful. I watched Prosa, the striker I had previously seen play for Infonet in Estonia, flounder up front for Valletta. The game finally livened with a remarkable six cards in injury time, including two reds. I prayed for a goal in Italy, my next nation, to break my drought.

I had watched some fairly drab football with a lingering cold. There might not have been swathes of exciting attacking football, but four red cards in five matches at least showed that players were committed. There were some urgent shouts from the stands, but supporters seemed rootless. Clubhouses were not the social hubs they were decades ago and, if football is about representation, teams like Floriana needed their own grounds. I found that Maltese top-flight football, whilst undeniably fiery, was an uncomfortable mishmash where foreign players played other foreign players in neutral stadiums. At least it was sunny.

All ten teams I watched stayed up. Valletta won the title, Balzan were second and Gżira third. Hibernians and Floriana missed out on European qualification in fifth and sixth. Hamrun and Senglea were mid-table in eighth and ninth. Mosta finished in tenth, St Andrews in eleventh and Tarxien in twelfth, avoiding relegation after winning a play-off.

38 Italy

I had always wanted to visit Mount Etna. The blanket of snow on its volcanic peak contrasted with the brilliant blue skies. The heavens suddenly darkened. It started snowing, then hailed and the mist enveloped me. I approached a hazy figure. He was piling rocks onto a large plastic tray. 'What are you doing?' I asked. 'For remember', the man replied. And his patio. I patted two smaller rocks in my pocket. They were also keepsakes from my Italian sojourn, which would turn out to be one of the most unexpected turns to my trip.

Sportweek, the Saturday supplement of *La Gazzetta dello Sport*, had published two articles based on my earlier travels. I imagined James Richardson discussing my adventures over a coffee and an improbable cake on *Gazzetta Football Italia*, my favourite childhood football programme. *Quelli che il Calcio*, live every Sunday when in football season, then unexpectedly invited me to appear on Rai 2, the national television channel.

Marco and Giovanni flew from Milan to Catania to put together a video about my journey to Crotone for Rai 2. I had travelled by ludi-crously expensive ferry from Malta to the southern tip of Sicily, and then by train to wonderfully out-of-season Syracuse and the island's grungy second city of Catania. 'We thought about joining you in Malta', said Marco, a Turinese television producer, 'but it would take too fucking long'.

Marco and Giovanni were an entertaining duo. Marco was all shaven head, sharp wit and dark glasses. Cameraman Giovanni was worldlier and more laid-back. They specialised in offbeat football stories: Italian players in Estonia, Zaccardo in Malta and the Isles of Scilly champi-onship. They were to film the Royal Shrovetide match, a throwback to the ragged medieval tussle over an inflated pig's bladder, in the Derbyshire town of Ashbourne the following week. I laughed as they planned, desperately trying to avoid spending Valentine's night together in romantic Birmingham, the nearest city.

I asked Marco how many people from Milan took the train from Sicily, the largest island in the Mediterranean, to Calabria, the region in the toe end of Italy. 'Just me and Giovanni', he said. 'Some will take the boat with the car. But train. No.' Our slow travel had a beat and a purpose. We switched between filming, coffee, cigarettes and chat. The train trundled onto one of the few train ferries in Europe, and crossed to the Italian mainland. It took far longer to load and unload the train than the swift, five-mile journey across the Strait of Messina.

I had planned to visit Crotone ever since they escaped relegation in 2017 with the lowest budget in Serie A. The small southern city, once home of the mathematician Pythagoras and founded by Greek settlers in 710 BC, had richer ancient stories than footballing history. Marco explained that if you asked an average Italian about the town before their recent success they would have mentioned the Mafia, but now they associated Crotone with their over-achieving football team. 'It makes you understand how important football is in culture', said Marco, likening Crotone reaching Serie A to Ipswich Town winning the UEFA Cup or Watford's success in the 1980s.

'They had a terrible start', was a serious understatement by Marco. Crotone accrued fourteen points from their first twenty-nine matches in their debut Serie A campaign, hampered by playing 'home' matches 300 miles north in Pescara for the first two months of the season. There was a parallel with Castel di Sangro, the tiny club who played early 'home' matches in their debut Serie B season near Pescara and whose 1996–97 adventure was chronicled by the late American author Joe McGinniss in *The Miracle of Castel di Sangro*.

Crotone's Ezio Scida Stadium needed to be upgraded to meet Serie A rules. 'They find some ancient stuff when refurbishing the stadium. But they say, "What the fuck, we don't give a shit about this"', said Marco. 'It's amazing because in other countries they would say, "Oh no, there is some ancient Greek stuff, stop everything". In Crotone they said, "We've got enough of this shit, go with the stadium!"'

Davide Nicola was the Crotone coach the previous season. His son had tragically died in a road accident in 2014. 'The miracle of Crotone is also a rebirth of Nicola', said Marco, with true Italian passion. 'With this pain for his son in his heart he found something to believe in, which was Crotone.' Nicola made a bet that he would cycle from Crotone to his birthplace of Turin if his team stayed up. Crotone picked up twenty points from their last nine matches and Nicola cycled 800 miles north.

It was a miracle. But things were perhaps not always as they seemed in Italy. Crotone needed to overtake an Empoli team who lost eleven of their final fifteen games and duly received the maximum 25 million euro parachute payment for playing in three consecutive Serie A seasons. Empoli didn't seem that desperate to stay up. Marco said that he preferred to believe in a miracle rather than the conspiracy theories. Nicola had since resigned following criticism this season, despite Crotone being out of the relegation zone, and been replaced by legendary former Inter and Italy goalkeeper Walter Zenga.

The train stuttered its way through Calabria. Marco, with his northern Italian humour, said that agriculture and drug trafficking were the region's main industries. I spotted a series of unattractive concrete edifices around an inviting strip of sand hugged by low mountains and a flat grey sea. Calabria would be ripe for tourism if development was as refined as on the Sicilian coast. There were also lots of half-finished houses. Marco explained that the second storey of each would remain uncompleted until the family's son needed it; conveniently, the owner can meanwhile inform the authorities that the house is still being built and thus avoid paying tax.

We changed at Lamezia onto a one-carriage train. It hurtled like a bullet through olive groves, past scattered sheep and misty mountains. Marco and I chatted as we passed a darkened Catanzaro, the regional capital of Calabria, towards Crotone on the sole of Italy's geographic boot. Francesco, a railway worker wearing a red puffer jacket and designer stubble, pulled out his earphones to listen to us and asked what we were doing.

It turned out that Francesco was a Crotone fan. 'The football club and the sea are the only two things that work in Crotone', said Francesco. This was nearly true. The *Financial Times* had recently reported from Crotone, the epitome of Italy's struggling south with unemployment just below 30 per cent, ahead of the following month's elections. Francesco said that the team was grounded in its modest roots and wrote down a chant. 'Oi ma mammice chi de stu Cutroniii', slang for 'Look what a team Crotone has', made the Rai 2 video cut.

I met Marco and Giovanni for dinner that night. Everyone in Italy seems to be a foodie, and these two were no exceptions. We walked around Crotone for an hour as they compared TripAdvisor restaurant reviews on their phones. We settled on an empty hostelry with no menu. It was a good choice: anchovies with chilli, spaghetti with clams and chocolate orange fondant were washed down with two bottles of local wine for an agreeable price. Max, the owner, lamented in the local dialect about the total lack of jobs in Crotone before driving us home. 'I can understand Matt more than Max', joked Marco. 'You won't get a lift home from a restaurant owner in Montpellier', shouted Marco as I tried to find my guesthouse. 'They're too posh in France.' France would be my next destination.

It was another torrential matchday, even wetter than in Larnaca and Corfu. Whipping wind and horizontal rain made it impossible to explore Crotone. Instead I ordered a metre of pizza from a takeaway, whose box was a useful umbrella. A man bought a fist-sized calzone and a bottle of beer, looked at the wicked weather and shook his head. He thought that the game might not take place as the pitch could be waterlogged. I started to worry. I was due to appear on live television in Milan the next day and might have to duck out for Inter against Bologna. I retired to my guesthouse and dried my jeans on the air conditioning system.

'The match was one step away from being called off', said Marco. This meant it was happening. The rain had eased slightly, alongside my relief, as we approached the stadium. A policeman diverted us through a large gravel car park that had begun to form a map of the Great Lakes. 'Fucking hell', said Marco as he was soaked again. Giovanni continued to put together a roll-up. Nothing got between an Italian and his cigarettes.

The Ezio Scida Stadium was named after a former Crotone captain who died in a car accident when travelling to a friendly match in 1946. And the stadium looked like a horrific accident. The upper half of the main stand was a complicated web of scaffolding poles and metal steps that resembled the Industrial Zone from *The Crystal Maze*. AC/DC played over the sound system but it didn't feel like the game was about to rock: the ball was just about rolling in the slushy grass. Visitors Atalanta, a mid-sized club whose pinnacle was arguably reaching the Cup Winners' Cup semi-final in 1988 when competing in Serie B, looked poised in the 3-4-3 formation that had brought them a remarkable fourth place the previous season. They had sold three key players – Andrea Conti and Franck Kessié to AC Milan, Roberto Gagliardini to Inter – but were still seventh.

Only short passes and long punts were going to succeed in such wild weather. A heavy touch from Crotone's Trotta, the former Fulham and Brentford forward, span twenty yards in front of him to Atalanta defender Masiello, who promptly miscontrolled the ball out of play. There was a haunting cackle from behind me. The conditions were quite amusing. Crotone defender Toloi launched into a perfectly executed sliding tackle, water spraying in all directions, that reminded me why grass beats artificial. At least when the game takes place.

The Curva Sud, Crotone's hardcore fans, were wearing a colourful array of fashionable plastic macs and supported their team with a shrill drumbeat. They may have gazed wistfully up at the hospital to their right, its upper windows clouded with the grey outlines of spectators. It was good to be ill in Crotone, at least for ninety minutes every other week. The Curva Sud whistled as Atalanta's small clutch of fans chanted 'Crotone fuck you'. There was no real beef between two teams that had barely played each other. And there were no first-half goals. My goalless run now stretched to over three matches since Floriana's first-half strike in Malta.

Marco, Giovanni and I searched for a half-time beer in the VIP area. There was more action around the antipasti than I had seen in either goalmouth, an almighty scrum forming around several long tables dressed with mini panini, local ham, cheese and sun-dried tomatoes stuffed with tuna. The only available drinks were espresso, water and wine. I filled a plastic glass with local red and a man clasped an entire bottle as I looked for a refill. The highlights were shown on big screens. It really was slim pickings.

The start of the second half was even worse. I counted four fouls in five minutes. The Curva Sud echoed the maritime conditions with a rendition of 'Yellow Submarine'. Giovanni looked at his phone and laughed at a message from the man who would provide him highlights for the Rai 2 video. 'What am I going to send you from this shitty match?' it said.

The faster Ricci replaced Trotta up front and the switch seemed to inspire Crotone. A left-wing cross was launched into the area, the Atalanta goalkeeper parried and Crotone midfielder Mandragora arrived at the far post. 'Forza Crotone', I shouted as the Curva Sud went as wild as they can when soaked through. My personal 322-minute goal drought was over.

Crotone immediately retreated. Atalanta probed and a corner fell nicely for Masiello, whose shot was blocked but squirmed into the path of Palomino, and the Argentine defender converted another tap in. There were just two minutes left. Ricci fell over on the soaked right wing and the final whistle sounded. It was a fitting end to a messy match.

The next day a blacked-out Mercedes took me to the Pils Pub in Milan. I was hungry and jaded after an early taxi from Crotone to Lamezia, the nearest airport, and two flights. I needed to find some energy for my live appearance alongside charismatic Rai 2 presenter Federico Russo, wearing a battered black leather jacket and turquoise T-shirt. *Quelli che il Calcio*, a light-hearted mix of pop culture and Serie A, was billed as 'everyone drinking in a pub watching football', but I seemed to be the only one drinking. I ordered a Meantime Pale Ale. 'Don't you like Italian beer?' I was asked. I diplomatically lauded Italian pasta, pizza and wine as Federico took sultry selfies for his Instagram followers.

Giovanni and Marco's brilliant video crashed its way through a punky two minutes that featured the Cockney Rejects and 'Banned from the Pubs' by Peter and the Test Tube Babies, the Brighton-based band I watch every Christmas at the New Cross Inn in south-east London. I alerted Peter, the lead singer, that he would be receiving an unexpected royalty from Rai. 'Wow, nice clip and what a brilliant idea', he replied. Punk and Crotone were forever twinned.

Mia Ceran, the glamorous studio host, visited our pub many times over the next three hours. Federico planned to question me about my travels. But I was never spoken to again as the focus of the programme was on the Sanremo festival, a traditional music contest that has run since 1951. Instead I watched Inter struggle to their first Serie A victory for two months against Bologna and grimaced as Totò Schillaci, the former Inter and Italy forward, was featured learning to ski in a comedy sketch backed by a mariachi band. I self-consciously picked at chips, trying to look less glazed than I felt in front of the live cameras. My wooden chair became increasingly uncomfortable. I was glad to dive back to my hotel. I was in a city I didn't really want to be in.

The following day, my flight to London City was cancelled, the only such instance over my entire trip, due to an unexploded Second World War bomb in the Thames. I had the unexpected choice of visiting the San Siro or the Duomo before my new flight. I chose the cathedral of religion, not football. The Duomo was magnificent: the detail of the gargoyles, the incredible carvings on its enormous green doors. The San Siro could wait for a better-planned visit. Marco had summed it up. 'It was a bad pitch with good teams. Now it is a good pitch with bad teams.' Crotone was a bad pitch with a bad team. But it was an experience I would never forget.

There was no second miracle for Crotone as they were relegated on the last day of the season. Atalanta finished a creditable seventh and qualified for the Europa League.

SNOW WAY

39 France

Marco wasn't quite right. I may not have got a ride home from a restaurant but I did get a lift to Montpellier. Byllel, with dark eyes and
a friendly smile, picked me up from Marseille airport. I was hardly
looking my best after photographing a friend's wedding in Dorking the
previous day and taking an early Saturday morning flight from nearby
Gatwick. I was irritated that the flash had somehow become stuck on
my camera, and slightly daunted about squeezing France and Andorra
into one February weekend. I needed good weather and energy. It was
raining and I was knackered.

Byllel, a Marseille fan of Tunisian descent, was trialling a new website that helped visitors arrange to watch football with a local fan. This
interested me. It was sometimes hard to get tickets to big matches.
And even when you could, seats were often in inopportune places and
surrounded by other football tourists. I had experienced the top row
at Barcelona. Byllel wanted me to watch French football with a true
fan, Alex of Montpellier.

Another Montpellier supporter had read about my travels in *L'Équipe* and invited me to lunch before he realised my match against Guingamp clashed with his skiing holiday. This felt very French: in England you go for a beer and a curry, in France you go out for lunch and ski. Instead, Byllel and I dined in his hometown of Aix-en-Provence. I was a bit edgy. I wanted to get to Montpellier. Byllel wanted me to see Aix, which was looking its very worst in fine February drizzle. But my eyes lit up when I saw a glass of red wine was cheaper than a Coke, and my taste buds were invigorated by the delicious gooey depth of a chocolate fondant. France, like Italy, cared about its cuisine. I had, however, wondered whether it was really bothered about football.

I was left unconvinced from my six matches at Euro 2016, where the vivacity of travelling fans in the stadiums seemed countered by ambivalence from locals outside. Nevertheless, the absence of profiteering had been refreshing after my stays in over-priced hotels at the 2014 World Cup in Brazil. My Bordeaux guesthouse owner charged me 2015 rates because that was when I had booked; I was shunned by a Lyon guesthouse who informed me that they were closed in July 2016 because the weather was too hot. I was welcome in their other B&B in Burgundy, several hours away from Lyon. I laughed at the lack of opportunism. It was almost as if a major football tournament wasn't happening.

The stereotype of the typical Frenchman – more philosophical than an Englishman, preferring the arts to football – seemed to have some truth. Byllel believed that football was only really popular in grittier cities, such as St Étienne, Nantes and Marseille, unlike in England, where it was no longer just a working-class game. He said that in the two biggest cities, Paris and Lyon, many locals only follow football because others talk about it.

Byllel, 'the bible of football' as he joked, really loved football. He was friends with Youssef Msakni, Tunisia's best player, who would miss the 2018 World Cup through injury, and had played semi-professionally in France for FC Martigues, one of Eric Cantona's early clubs, and in the Australian second division. A skilful player, Byllel recalled being deliberately tripped by an opponent after scoring an audacious goal in a minor London tournament. He asked for a yellow card. 'Welcome to England', said the referee.

We drove towards Montpellier, eighty miles to the west of Marseille. Montpellier shocked French football with their title win in 2012: Olivier Giroud top-scored, the Moroccan Younès Belhanda pulled the strings and John Utaka, fresh from his disastrous spell at Portsmouth, stretched defences. Byllel said that Montpellier had never paid more than 5 or 6 million euros for a player and that their top salary was around 40,000 euros per month. Montpellier were very poor compared to PSG. Byllel might have joked that the people of Montpellier are 'like farmers' but Marseille fans were ecstatic when Montpellier pipped PSG to their only championship. Montpellier played Marseille at the Stade Vélodrome in April 2012 and Marseille supporters, who wanted Montpellier to win to deny their Parisian rivals, applauded the away side's 3–1 victory.

Montpellier was buzzy and endearing, with a youthful vibe from the large student population. The city is the fastest-growing in France after more than doubling in size from only 120,000 in 1962. The barman at the Egg, a craft beer haunt named after the city's ovular main square, talked about the nightmare of the windy streets, virtually all of which were pedestrianised. It might be bad for beer deliveries, but it was a joy to meander without traffic. The cars had their fun driving through Montpellier's mini Arc de Triomphe. You can't do that in Paris. I walked to the open Promenade de Peyrou and admired commanding views over the eighteenth-century aqueduct and the western suburbs. Louis XVI, the last king of France, said that no construction in the city could be built higher than this park. The Stade de la Mosson, a clunky over-sized beast used in the 1998 World Cup, was a rare exception. The medieval rules in Montpellier.

We met Alex, who had crazed eyes, a loud voice and an enthusiastic handshake, outside the stadium. He was good-humoured and called me 'Tour Eiffel', a refreshing slant on the usual 'Peter Crouch'. Alex had been a Montpellier fan for thirty-three years and particularly hated Nîmes, the club based thirty miles away. He ran a delivery company and once found he had to deliver a box of replica Nîmes shirts. He returned them to sender. Alex was sanguine about this season. Montpellier had an outside chance of qualifying for the Europa League but it was boring to watch the team play with five defenders. Fans wanted success and appeal. Montpellier were sixth and expected to beat mid-table Guingamp.

Byllel was filming a promo for his website. He asked Montpellier fans outside the stadium whether they knew their club's all-time top scorer. A klaxon sounded if they answered incorrectly. I knew the answer: Laurent Blanc. Blanc was a defender for Marseille, but played as an attacking midfielder for Montpellier between 1983 and 1991 and took the penalties. It confused Montpellier fans as some of Blanc's goals were in Ligue 2, and because Souleymane Camara, a former Senegal international who had played at the 2002 World Cup, had recently overtaken Blanc as Montpellier's record scorer in Ligue 1.

The top two tiers of one stand were closed, with pictures of fans covering the seats. This seemed strangely appropriate. Byllel had joked about Montpellier only filling the Stade de la Mosson during their unexpected success in 2012. 'It was amazing. The stadium was full of Footix.' Footix, a giant blue cockerel, was the mascot from the 1998 World Cup. But it was not part of French footballing culture to have mascots, and so a 'Footix' in France was a 'plastic fan' in England: new-wave supporters who know little about football. 'Plastic fan!' exclaimed Byllel in a thick French accent, laughing at the new term.

The Montpellier hardcore from the hardened Paillade district livened up the stadium with drums, giant flags and 'if you don't jump, you're not Paillade' chants. The rest of the crowd were mixed: dark-haired women hid under a black blanket, older men in hats looked uninspired by the action and one woman left with three bread batons under her arm. 'Come for the baguettes, you've only come for the baguettes', I chanted, to Byllel's amusement. He had complained of the paucity of imaginative new chants at French stadiums.

We talked about the opposition. Guingamp were one of two clubs to have won the French Cup, in 2009, as a Ligue 2 team. They now seemed to finish tenth every season and had an impressive reputation for developing players: Florent Malouda, Laurent Koscielny and Didier Drogba had all played for the Brittany club. Guingamp now played Marcus Thuram up front, a lithe version of his father, Lilian, the powerful defender who won 142 caps for France. Thuram wasn't going anywhere fast when he collected the ball on the inside left of the penalty area. Hilton, the veteran Brazilian twice his age, clumsily brought him down. Congolese midfielder Ngbakoto, previously with Queens Park Rangers, slotted in the penalty to give the away side the lead.

Montpellier were struggling to stretch Guingamp. Alex was incandescent when a Montpellier player took a bad touch and gave the ball away. 'I can't translate that', said Byllel. We rushed to the bar after a half of slow, defensive, football. The beer was non-alcoholic and as tasteless as the match. 'I have nothing to say', said Alex when I asked him about the game. He shook his head with the slow despondency of someone who really cared.

Montpellier missed a host of chances early in the second half. The series of long, hopeless balls that followed was easy for Guingamp to defend. Montpellier midfielder Lasne then claimed he was felled in the penalty area and the referee showed him a deserved yellow card for diving. 'The referee is from Nîmes', shouted Alex, piling down the steps to remonstrate. He was suddenly placated. Lively Montpellier right wing back Aguilar hit a strong drive that the Ivorian striker Sio turned in to make it 1–1.

There was a moving tribute to the former Montpellier chairman, Louis Nicollin, after seventy-four minutes. Nicollin had passed away the previous summer at the age of seventy-four. 'Lou, Lou', chanted the crowd during a minute's applause. 'He built Montpellier', said Byllel. 'His company is a famous recycling company and people joked about it by saying "You're rubbish!"'

Rustic cardboard signs were held up by children after the match. 'Dolly your jersey please', said one. Players obligingly trotted over in a quaint, family scene. I grabbed a baguette stuffed with sausage and chips that challenged my gums before saying goodbye to Alex in the car park. 'I'M NOT PERFECT, BUT I'M A MONTPELLIER SUPPORTER. IT'S ALMOST THE SAME', said the back of his shirt.

It had been a strange experience, watching my Ligue 1 match with

Alex, a true devotee, and Byllel, a Marseille fan. But it had certainly enlivened what would otherwise have been a rank average 1–1 draw. I returned to my guesthouse for not enough sleep before hitting the road to Andorra.

Montpellier and Guingamp finished tenth and twelfth in mid-table. Montpellier drew eighteen of their thirty-eight matches and only conceded thirty-three goals. Nîmes, Alex's nemesis, were promoted to Ligue 1.

40 Andorra

I had never visited Andorra. I had never really wanted to. Andorra also
represented one of my biggest risks. Public transport from Montpellier
was not going to get me to my 4 p.m. Primera Divisió match in time,
and I knew I would have to drive into the snowy Pyrenees the morning
after the match at the Stade de la Mosson. I prayed for good weather.

Andorra is around a 200-mile drive from Montpellier. The skies were
bright and the Sunday morning roads clear as my Peugeot motored
towards them. I drove past the medieval town of Villefranche, which
brought to mind a past family holiday, but there was no time to stop.
The road narrowed through villages where old houses clung to the side
of pavementless roads. I swung around hairpins as a dog bounced in
the back of a pick-up and a bird of prey circled in the mountains. The
driving was tough. A lunatic overtook on a blind corner.

The altitude increased and the outside temperature nose-dived from
10°C to –1°C. The snow was over a metre deep next to the road and
several inches covered the tarmac. I was desperate not to skid off. I had

an £800 excess and a mid-afternoon football deadline I didn't want to miss. I wasn't sure if snow-tyre signs were advisory or mandatory, but every other car seemed to be a chunky four-wheel drive. I drove slowly and gladly paid the Envalira Tunnel toll to avoid more switchbacks. I was relieved when I reached Andorra. I really didn't want to have to come back.

The scenery was beautiful and serene until I entered my latest new country. There were still snowy mountains, but there was traffic. And lots of it. Andorra, a principality slightly larger than the Isle of Wight, attracts millions of tourists each year, though not many for its football. My eyes were distracted by strange dark spots tumbling down a mountainside, an avalanche perhaps. It was the first time I had seen skiers whilst driving. More were standing in the slush outside their hotels. My favoured adventure sport is tropical scuba diving: the waiting around is warmer.

I drove through Encamp, fifteen miles from the French border, and spotted people watching a match. I had stumbled upon an earlier Primera Divisió fixture between Encamp, the only Andorran team with their own stadium, and Penya. I ditched the Peugeot. The scene was spectacular. The winter sun reflected off the artificial pitch and a mountain dominated the horizon. The match was goalless when a Penya defender handled on the line. It was a great save. He was sent off and Encamp's Sosa converted the penalty. This was, in some ways, a perfect ten-minute dose of stunning scenery and eventful football.

I drove on five miles to Andorra la Vella, the dispiriting capital, full of workers drawn to its relative riches who would rather be elsewhere. It was the Middle East of Western Europe. The city centre was a thoughtless tangle of concrete, a building that resembled a mini

Shard and expensive car parks. Its tax-free shops were chock full of clocks and razors I'm certain you can buy in France or Spain. Andorra is heavily influenced by and reliant on its neighbours; its official language is Catalan and the primary export is strong tobacco, a fact as depressing as the cold streets. I drove further down the valley to the suburb of Santa Coloma, home to umpteen motorcycle shops and the communal Centre d'Entrenaments ground, a humdrum affair with an industrial-park backdrop.

I approached an older man with thinning hair and growing worry lines. He looked like your archetypal football fan. Pedro Santos, a Spaniard from Alicante, lived in Andorra because his twenty-four-year-old son, also called Pedro Santos, now played for Santa Coloma after infrequent appearances for Valencia Mestalla and Córdoba B. Pedro explained that the Andorran Primera Divisió was, football-wise, similar to the third or fourth tier in Spain. But the money was better in Andorra. Santa Coloma had won the last four titles and received precious income from annual adventures into European competition.

Pedro said his son used to train five days per week in Spain. But most Andorran players were part-time and only trained three times, late in the evenings after they had finished work. Pedro was a proud father and, naturally, believed in his son's potential. Norwich City were reportedly interested when he was at Valencia. Cyprus, Japan and Cardiff City were mentioned. I looked at the snowy Andorran mountains in my five layers of clothing and thought those destinations would surely be warmer places to play football. Pedro came across and greeted his father. He seemed to be carrying a bit too much weight for an elite sportsman. Other family members braved the February chill to support him.

Santos was never going to make the Championship. There was something Danny Murphy about the way he dropped deep to dictate play and took all the set pieces. But there was not enough athleticism alongside his flickering skill in central midfield. There were cries of encouragement from the Santa Coloma family after a good left-wing cross, never part of Murphy's armoury. His lashed clearance then hit the crossbar of an unused goal on the side of the pitch with a clunk.

There was a pleasing pace to this encounter after a glut of uninspiring games in France, Italy and Malta. I had watched Spanish players in balmier Lithuania and Cyprus and was intrigued to see their honed technique on an artificial pitch surrounded by piled ice in Andorra. The level of skill was certainly higher than in Wales or the Faroe Islands, two of the lowest-ranked leagues I had watched. Two successive flicks on the Santa Coloma right wing would have looked out of place in Tórshavn. But Santa Coloma and opponents Sant Julià would lose every header in Llandudno.

Sant Julià moved the ball with alacrity and opened the scoring with a fine counter-attacking goal from Vinasco, the fifth and final goal I would see scored by a right back during my trip. Santa Coloma were soon 2–0 down when a left-wing cross was slammed home by Luque. Santos was then mobbed by his teammates when he scored a Beckham-esque free kick on the stroke of half-time to reduce the deficit for Santa Coloma. 'Calm, calm', said his father. 'Good Pedro!' encouraged his mother as he shepherded the ball out for a goal kick.

I asked for my photograph to be taken at half-time. This normally broke down barriers. Annabel, a Spaniard in a stylish fur coat, introduced herself as Santa Coloma's general manager. We had something in common. We had both been to Alashkert in Armenia this season.

Annabel sighed. Santa Coloma had played Armenian teams three times in the last four seasons in Champions League qualifiers. I got the impression that she may not have appreciated repeated doses of Yerevan's post-Soviet charms.

About sixty supporters watched a match that was brighter than the weather. 'When it's a sunny day, this is full', said Annabel. Postponements, my worst nightmare, were fortunately rare here. Annabel explained that the Andorran Football Federation planned to build pitches with undersoil heating in La Massana, a few miles to the north. 'The idea is to get one team per stadium. It will be difficult with all the mountains here.' The electronic scoreboard read 'Local' against 'Visitant' for every match at the ground. 'We always play here', said Annabel. 'It's funny for the Spanish players when they arrive as they always play at the same pitch, home and away matches.'

Sant Julià seemed to lack their first-half composure and clearances were lashed anywhere. I pawed one away. 'Now you're part of the game', laughed Annabel. 'Too much space', I said before Pi, every mathematician's favourite midfielder, made it 3–1 to Sant Julià with a left-footed shot. A fading Santos switched to right back as the game, a good contest until now, disintegrated. 'I'm sorry that I didn't bring you luck', I said to Annabel following this defeat. She apologised for Santa Coloma's worst performance of the season. Neither comment was necessary, but football was polite in Andorra.

I was cold after watching Santa Coloma and frozen after sitting through a second Primera Divisió match, Engordany against Lusitanos, on the same pitch. I visited a desolate pub and ordered an over-cooked burger and my first and last beer in Andorra. The beef and beer were imported, like everything else. I cheered for Real Betis as they lost 5–3 to Real Madrid on television. Unsurprisingly, my waiter was Spanish and a Real Madrid fan. The chef slumped his head on the counter in the kitchen for some time; he might have fallen asleep. Andorra was sucking his life force, and mine.

The weather worsened overnight. The skies were grey and the roads black with ice, giving me nightmares of being trapped in Andorra. I followed the grit lorry out of the mountains, and signs outside the Puymorens Tunnel suggested I should dress my Peugeot in snow chains. Instinctively, I detoured on the lower-altitude road, circumvented the snow and stopped at the spectacular castle of Carcassonne. I was relieved to be back in France, though it turned out my driving was not snail-like enough for the French. I later received a speeding fine for driving 98 km/h in a 90 zone: my one night in Andorra had cost me nearly £300. At least the football was free.

Santa Coloma won their fifth successive title. Sant Julià finished third and qualified for the Europa League.

Kit out my wardrobe

My travels were colourful slices of football life, and I wanted to honour the nattiest shirts worn by the 156 teams I saw in top-flight action. I've fitted my best eleven jerseys into the Southgate-style 3-5-2 that would define England's World Cup campaign in Russia.

My goalkeeper is Krumkachy. The self-styled Minsk club have a terrifying logo: a massive black raven looms over an evil red sky and a giant retro football. They wore a controversial all-black outfit with hideous italicised numbers. But it's the all-red goalkeeper shirt that gets the nod, modelled by the legendary Belarusian Kostyukevich in red boots, which matched both his kit and his dismissal.

My three centre backs have a yellow striped theme. Sweden's Häcken's yellow and black stripes were vividly different – even their shirt sponsorship deal screams 'BRA' in red – especially given they should have been playing in a more sedate green and white. Senglea Athletic in Malta wore yellow and red stripes that matched their gloriously 1970s logo. And ADO's unusual yellow and green colours looked particularly fetching when modelled by their mascot Storky and unleashed from flares by Sunday morning marchers in the Netherlands.

Sant Julià in Andorra and Maribor from Slovenia line up at wing back. The Andorrans played against Santa Coloma in a fetching strip that looked like a paint advertisement, with its hazy shades of green. Maribor's purple colours were partly inspired by Fiorentina and Gabriel Statistuta, my Monday night five-a-side team back in London. I liked the striking difference. Most other teams in their league played in red, white and blue, the colours of the Slovenian and Yugoslavian flags.

I've chosen a dazzling central midfield in shades of Scorpio blue. Drita in Kosovo will captain my side with their sparkling outfit, the azure shades getting lighter towards the socks. I do love a turquoise top and Luxembourg's F91 Dudelange are the only club to make my selection with their away kit, stunning against their black shorts. Helsingør's subtle horizontal light blue and white stripes, which complemented the Danish team's striking modern logo, completes my midfield.

I've gone for a simplistic strike duo. The classic thick white and black stripes of Lokomotiv Plovdiv, strangely similar to a certain Italian giant's current attire, were arguably the highlight of a horrid match in Bulgaria. And my final choice should probably be Celje in Slovenia, the only team I saw wearing the same kit twice (I watched Sevilla play in different colours in their two matches), were it not rather marred by unsightly blue triangles. Instead I've elected for the pure, unsponsored white shirts of FC Taraz in Kazakhstan, exhibited perfectly by the hefty Senegalese striker Mané. Even the club badge, which reads like 'Tapas' in Cyrillic, makes me hungry for a return to this Silk Road city.

Kits XI: Krumkachy (red); Häcken (yellow/black), Senglea Athletic (yellow/red), ADO Den Haag (yellow/green); Sant Julià (green), Drita (blue), F91 Dudelange (turquoise), Helsingør (blue/white), Maribor (purple); Lokomotiv Plovdiv (black/white), Taraz (white).

IBERIAN HEAVEN

41 Gibraltar

I was relieved to be zipping past the Pyrenees on the train from Montpellier, not driving through them hunched in a hatchback. Low clouds welcomed me into Spain and I supped a free glass of cava to commemorate the tenth anniversary of the high-speed rail link between Barcelona and Madrid. The stark Spanish landscapes, where castles clung to cliff faces overlooking small villages, were brightened by vivid purple blossom. The evening skies opened up as I left Madrid for beautiful Córdoba, where I spent several days with friends before travelling south through the wild forested hills of central Andalusia. My near 1,000-mile train journey ended in Algeciras, a busy port located across the bay from Gibraltar, my next UEFA nation.

As with my travels to Germany and Wales, I didn't stay overnight in Gibraltar. Instead I resided in the Spanish town of La Línea de la Concepción, considerably cheaper than anything across the border. I dumped my bags and walked from La Línea to Gibraltar and into British territory. It felt idiosyncratic traversing a frontier on foot, especially as the Friday evening traffic was all the other way. Gibraltar relies on thousands of Spanish workers, including dozens of footballers, all of whom are seeking better wages and content to disregard the stance of the Spanish government, who have long disputed Gibraltar's status since it became British during the eighteenth century. Gibraltarians seemed happy to be a British Overseas Territory, a highly conclusive 99 per cent of voters having rejected the proposal of shared British/ Spanish sovereignty in a 2002 referendum.

Gibraltar became the smallest UEFA member in 2013, and FIFA membership followed in 2016. Playing in the Champions League and the World Cup was very different from competing against Rhodes and Menorca in the Island Games. All ten Premier Division teams play in the Victoria Stadium, Gibraltar's only arena, sandwiched between the Mediterranean, the Rock and the airport. I walked down Winston Churchill Avenue and over one of Europe's most testing airports. The short landing strip, challenging air currents and football fans crossing the runway to return to La Línea after watching a Premier Division match were unusual hazards for pilots.

Gibraltar was a fusion of the familiar and foreign. I strolled around the marina to find beery English voices enjoying a typical Friday night out but with better weather. English football was shown in pubs that looked more English than many pubs in England. There was even novelty value paying with British pounds in southern Europe.

I entered the Victoria Stadium bar and photographed a signed Trevor Brooking shirt from the 1980 FA Cup final. 'Are you a West Ham fan?' asked a voice behind me. Desmond Reoch was the former vice-president of the Gibraltar Football Association. I loved these impromptu meets. Desmond was a Hammer and a Gibraltarian. I immediately noticed his accent. He spoke in Llanito, 'little plain', a language which he called 'Spanish and English words prostituted'. It was fun to listen to.

'Gibraltar is football crazy and has always been football crazy', said Desmond. He explained that around 10 per cent of the 30,000 population is involved in football, as registered players, officials, administrators, futsal players or referees. UEFA funding had enabled more coaches to undertake their badges and for the Gibraltar Football Association to purchase the Victoria Stadium from the government.

There were similarities with Andorra and the likes of Pedro Santos. Young Gibraltarian players were being kept out of first teams by professional Spanish players, who could earn much more in Gibraltar than they would in the Spanish fourth tier. The majority of Gibraltarian players had full-time jobs whilst many Spanish players only earned their money from football and could train more often. 'Brexit might be good from a pure, selfish, Gibraltarian football point of view', said Desmond as he bought me a beer from the Spanish bartender. Adam, a journalist for the Football Gibraltar website, later commented that Jeff Wood, the previous national team manager, had to pick a twenty-three-man international squad and sometimes there were far fewer than twenty-three Gibraltarian players starting Premier Division matches.

UEFA had increased professionalism and interest in Gibraltarian football. Adam described the media storm when Gibraltar lost 7–0 to Germany in Euro 2016 qualification. 'All the journalists wanted to speak to us because they couldn't get over the fact that there were policemen, customs officers, firemen, students and teachers playing for Gibraltar.' Goalkeeper Jordan Pérez saved a penalty from Bastian Schweinsteiger and journalists reported that a fireman had just saved a penalty from one of the world's greatest midfielders. An even more thrilling moment followed in 2016 when leading club side Lincoln Red Imps beat Celtic 1–0 in the second qualifying round of the 2016–17 Champions League. It was Brendan Rodgers' first competitive match in charge of the Glasgow club and was dubbed the 'Shock of Gibraltar'.

I met with Paul, the Gibraltar United president and another West Ham fan, before their match against Lions. He explained that Manchester United were the best-supported club in Gibraltar 'by a mile', echoing my Malta experiences whilst quoting a very British measure of distance. There is an official Manchester United supporters' club in Gibraltar with around 400 members, over 1 per cent of the Rock's population. There were only twenty-two members at the West Ham equivalent. 'Quality not quantity', said Paul.

Gibraltar United were founded by servicemen stationed in Gibraltar during the Second World War. They played against other military teams and called themselves 'Gibraltar United' because they were united in the war cause. After the War, players had gelled and didn't want to leave so Gibraltar United was formed. The club won eleven titles, the latest in 2002, but harder times led to a merger with Lions.

In 2014, Paul and his friends re-formed Gibraltar United, independent from Lions, in the Second Division just as Gibraltarian football began to change. At that time, there were three Gibraltarian teams owned by Spanish businessmen, who were trying to get their sides promoted to the Premier Division and into Europe. Their players were arriving in a bus from Spain, playing football and then leaving. There was concern as to whether young Gibraltarian players would ever get a chance. There were no rules back then. Teams now had to have a minimum of one Gibraltarian or British player on the pitch and two on the bench. It still didn't seem much.

Gibraltar United had an interesting history and a potentially fascinating future. They were partly owned by Míchel Salgado, the former Real Madrid, Blackburn Rovers and Spain defender, himself now based in Dubai. This gave the club credibility and Salgado added his expertise and contacts. 'Salgado is very involved – during the game I will send thirty messages to him and he will send thirty messages back', Paul told me. He had brought in Fernando Hierro's brother, Manolo, who played for Valladolid and Tenerife, as director of football.

I had known about Salgado. But I hadn't known about *The Victorious*, an X-Factor-style television gameshow that Salgado ran for up-and-coming footballers across the Middle East. The prize for completing a series of tasks, including trying to kick a ball with a giant elastic band restricting your movement, was $100,000 and the chance to play for a Spanish club. Gibraltar United had two players from the competition through the Salgado link. The Moroccan Idouaziz was runner-up in *The Victorious* and, appropriately enough, on the bench against Lions. Elghobashy, an Egyptian striker, had won the competition, and started.

It was fascinating stuff. Yet I sort of knew the match would be anything but. Gibraltar United dominated a game littered with a ridiculous fifteen yellow and red cards. Lions had two coaches sent off from their bench in the first half for protesting against a decision. A Lions midfielder and Gibraltar United defender followed after the break for second yellows. Jonathan, Gibraltar United's secretary and a history teacher who actually knew where Ufa was in Russia, was more entertaining than the match. He gasped and clutched the bar at the top of the main stand. This was his lucky spot. Jonathan used to sit, or probably stand, on the far side but Gibraltar United kept losing, so he moved. I listened to his charming mix of English and Spanish with a heavy dose of slang in a contorted South African accent. 'Tranquilo', 'tarjeta' and 'vamos' were interspersed with 'Come on ref' and 'Take a shot'. 'Siempre falta, every time' was a winning combination of both languages.

I admired the impressive gathering of seabirds clustered around the Rock. Jonathan was less impressed. 'They shit on your car and keep you awake in summer.' Gibraltar United missed the better opportunities. Elghobashy was a handful up front but misfired in front of goal, striking one chance wide, unleashing a strong shot against the crossbar and forcing Lions' goalkeeper González into an excellent close-range block. It wasn't quite his day.

The national team had previously played all their matches in Faro, five hours' drive away in southern Portugal. Adam, the journalist for Football Gibraltar, explained that teams in Spain had offered their stadiums, with a close eye on some easy extra income, only to be predictably quashed by the Spanish Football Federation. Internationals could now be played on the recently relaid pitch at the Victoria Stadium. I had noticed the two-month break earlier in the Gibraltarian season. 'It affected my plans', I said. 'It affected my plans as well', said Jonathan. 'We were bored shitless.'

I walked across the runway, through the border and past seedy apartment blocks to my Spanish shoebox. 'Dope? Marijuana?' asked some Spanish boys. I crossed back into Gibraltar the following day, took the cable car up the Rock and photographed semi-wild macaques. I gazed across at the African Football Confederation: Morocco and Ceuta, a Spanish possession, were clearly visible across the Straits of Gibraltar. I strolled Cannon Lane and Crutchetts Ramp, streets brimming with military history, and ate fish and chips with a side of casual racism. 'Are there any white faces left in Lewisham these days?' said the expat owner. Fortunately this was the only bigotry I encountered on my travels. I hoped for a goal at my next two matches at the Victoria Stadium. I didn't want Gibraltar to join Albania as a goalless league.

I didn't have to wait long in the first of two Saturday matches. Ríos crashed a shot home off the underside of the crossbar to give Glacis United a shock early lead over Europa United. Europa were reigning champions, a surprise after fourteen consecutive titles for Lincoln Red Imps. Liam Walker, Europa's best player last season, had left for Notts County. The Gibraltar international, previously with Bnei Yehuda, one of my Israeli hosts, 'was a different level to everyone else' according to Adam.

Lawrence, Europa's social media manager who worked at Gibraltar's only hospital – 'We get lots of monkey scratches and bites' – was still living off their triumph. Europa won the treble last year: the Premier Division, the Super Cup and the Rock Cup. 'We won every competition we entered apart from the Champions League', said Lawrence. Second-half pressure eventually told against Glacis, when Belfortti bundled in from a corner and a left-wing cross was perfectly headed home by Méndez. Europa edged to a 2–1 victory.

Leaders Lincoln Red Imps comfortably beat struggling Lynx later that evening. The Imps had a certain grace to their appropriately diminutive midfield and scored from two sweeping attacking moves. I had watched three matches at the Victoria Stadium, more than at any other venue on my travels, and found Gibraltarian football to be a friendly curiosity. The Victoria Stadium was its lone symbol until a new arena and training facilities were built at Europa Point. Gibraltar United currently trained in Spain and many teams seemed unsure how to integrate foreign players into their league. Gibraltarian football was between a Rock and a hard place. It will be interesting to see how politics and football develop in this European outpost.

Lincoln Red Imps regained their title. Europa were second and Gibraltar United just missed out on European qualification in fourth. Glacis were seventh, Lions eighth and Lynx ninth. Gibraltar United hit the headlines in July 2018 after becoming the first club to pay its players in cryptocurrency.

42 Spain

'Don't eat the oranges', said José, my friend from Córdoba. They looked so appetising, dangling from almost every tree. 'They are very bitter and can give you stomach trouble. Only good for marmalade.' I sampled two different branches of Spanish football in Andalusia. I watched Sevilla play Atlético Madrid and, three evenings later, rock-bottom Málaga host Sevilla on Andalusia Day. It is one of Spain's pleasing peculiarities that each of the seventeen autonomous communities has its own public holiday. Andalusia Day didn't help fix my camera though. Málaga's electronic shops were closed and the flash was still comically stuck on.

Seville wasn't my sort of place. Theoretically, it should be in many ways. The food is very good, the weather is even better and it's a proper football city where locals support either Sevilla or rivals Real Betis. But I had been trying to avoid the bigger cities and clubs. Sevilla were pretty big, winners of the Europa League in five of the previous twelve seasons. Málaga, meanwhile, is sometimes misunderstood. Andalusia's second city is certainly not as attractive as Córdoba, Granada or Seville, but had changed since my last visit. Street art now decorated the Soho district and a multicoloured cube marked a branch of the Pompidou Centre on the revamped marina. Its football team was no Sevilla either. Isco might have starred for Málaga as they reached the Champions League quarter-finals in 2013, but the Qatari-owned club had sold its best players, not won since December, and looked doomed.

I had visited both cities before in November 2010. I enjoyed the Alcázar palace gardens in Seville more in sunnier weather this time around. But the tiles around the nearby Plaza de España seemed faded and cracked now. Seven years ago, I climbed the Castillo de Gibralfaro, the tenth-century ruins that dominate the Málaga skyline. Back then, I admired the views of the old town and the sparkling Mediterranean and took a photograph of La Rosaleda, Málaga's stadium, nestled beneath the mountains a couple of miles away. I never thought I would return to Málaga and visit La Rosaleda, but I was gradually revising my opinion on repeat visits. Places changed and so did I. And my double-header in Andalusia gave me the opportunity to compare matchday experiences at Sevilla and Málaga.

Sevilla's Ramón Sánchez Pizjuán home was pleasingly walkable from the city centre. The stadium, originally a bowl for some 70,000, had been redeveloped since the 1982 World Cup when it hosted the legendary semi-final between West Germany and France, in which the Germans prevailed on penalties after a thrilling 3–3 draw. It was a pleasing mix of influences. The traditionally steep incline of the red and white stands featured a striking memorial for Antonio Puerta, the Sevilla left back who collapsed on the pitch and died at the age of twenty-two in 2007. His face was flashed up on the big screen after sixteen minutes, his squad number: a poignant reminder.

It had been quite civilised around the stadium. A young couple, he Sevilla, she Betis, posed for selfies with their Sevilla-supporting dachshund. Fans clutched gin and tonics in glasses, a scene far removed from the English pre-match norm. I bought a beer from a streetside bar and chatted to Peter, a doctor and long-standing fan of the club and the city. 'Seville is full of oranges, sun and pretty girls', he said, with a dash of pride. And Betis? 'They have no money', he said, with a touch of arrogance. There was excitement amongst the growing number of Sevilla fans when they spotted what they thought was a weakened Atlético line-up on my notepad – no Griezmann or Diego Costa – until they realised I had merely written down the Atlético team from their last match, a routine Europa League win over FC Copenhagen for which they had rested their star players. Inside the stadium, lights were dimmed for the evocative Sevilla anthem, fervently sung by all with scarves outstretched.

Málaga's attractively open stadium, La Rosaleda, sits next to a dead river and grungy apartment blocks. Málaga fans are known as 'boquerones' for their immense consumption of anchovies. Inevitably, the club mascot was a giant anchovy. I grabbed a San Miguel for 1.20 euros, cheaper than in Seville, from a bar outside the stadium and chatted to an anchovy. Eduardo, who worked in IT support, taught me some Málaga songs outside the stadium. 'The shirt I wear is attached to my skin. I wear it, I wear it. And never take it off' was catchy. 'Málaga, Málaga' was another. 'I can probably remember that one', I said, before leaving for the match. Rain drenched my unoccupied seat in the open south stand. Instead I stood under cover at the back of the more expensive western tribune, while big screens showed stock footage of a sunnier, happier Andalusia. The hardcore waved soaked plastic flags in the gloom: green and white for Andalusia, blue for Málaga and purple just to be pretty.

'Giuri Army' was plastered over a large England flag. Eduardo had explained that the 'Giuris' were a group of expats, mostly English, but also Finnish and Danish, who lived in the Málaga area. They supported Málaga, often with more fervour than the locals, and Eduardo assured me there was no conflict between Spanish and foreign fans. The slightly subdued, very damp crowd and 'Seven Nation Army' welcomed Málaga onto the pitch for this Wednesday night match.

There was a noticeable juxtaposition as the Sevilla–Atlético match started. The 'Biris' – named after the cult Gambian winger Alhaji Momodo Njie, better known as 'Biri-Biri', who played for Sevilla in the 1970s – created all the atmosphere, waving flags, beating drums and clapping in unison. The rest of the crowd were really quiet. There were no songs. They were absorbing and watching and seemed knowledgeable. Good play was accompanied by 'bien, bien'.

A pigeon flew out of a tunnel during the first half. It looked at 38,000 Sevilla fans, gripped by the action below, and flew back. The pigeon missed Diego Costa imploding. The striker fought for a ball down the Atlético left, lost it, pushed a Sevilla defender over and pretended to be struck himself. The big Spain international collapsed on the turf. The referee had seen Costa play before and brandished an inevitable yellow card. Costa felt wronged and charged around the pitch. Sevilla midfielder Banega picked up the ball in front of his central defenders and didn't hear his pounding paws. The Argentinian playmaker was unceremoniously barged off the ball and Costa finished past Sevilla goalkeeper Rico's right hand. Atlético had had little early possession but were 1–0 up.

Griezmann was initially quiet, giving the ball away twice in midfield and trying a rabona, only to fall over. He then became the star. The France international picked up the ball outside the penalty area and, following a few sure touches, blasted the ball beyond Rico with his weaker right foot. It was Sevilla 0–2 Atletico at half-time.

Málaga's boquerones certainly showed more first half encouragement than the Sevilla fans had against Atlético, clapping heralding every
promise of a good early move. Málaga were clear underdogs against
Sevilla. Nolito – Sevilla's best player on the night with the best chant,
his name repeated to the beat of 'No Limit' by 2 Unlimited – brilliantly chipped the ball over the flat Málaga defence, and Correa hit an
unstoppable low shot in off the post. Málaga 0–1 Sevilla at the break.

*Three days earlier, Sevilla's fans had voiced their vitriol against Vitolo. The
Spain international had left for Atlético in acrimonious circumstances after it
had been announced he had signed a new contract with Sevilla. 'Hijo de puta',
'cabrón' and the simple 'puta' were shouted at the second-half substitute. But it
was already all over by then. I love the bizarre side of football, your Andorras and
Gibraltars, yet it was a pleasure to watch the understated quality of Griezmann,
one of the most valuable players in world football. He coolly converted a penalty
won by Costa to make it 3–0, beautifully flicked the ball into Koke's path for a
fourth and anticipated Saúl's pull back to put Atlético 5–0 up. Griezmann had
his hat-trick, and would also go on to score four in Atlético's next match, giving
him a total of seven league goals in four days.*

*Sevilla's Biris hardcore maintained a steady drumbeat as the goals rained in. I
wondered whether they had noticed the disaster on the pitch. The percussion and
chants, if anything, became louder as the fans around me disappeared home. It
was drum defiance against a killer scoreline. The stadium was emptying as Sevilla
midfielder Sarabia eased the ball past the Slovenian goalkeeper Oblak. And
many fans missed the second consolation. Nolito cut onto his right foot and beat
Oblak from twenty yards with a low shot. The final score, Sevilla 2–5 Atlético.*

Half-time was a depressing scene in Málaga where Sevilla were 1–0
up. The concrete concourse of La Rosaleda was being lashed with rain-
water. Two boys played football with a plastic bottle behind the stand

and unappetising *bocadillos* remained unsold. The rain had finally eased and I watched the second half from high above the corner flag. Málaga's performance seemed very English. There was no guile from the central midfielders in an old-school 4-4-2, and their fans and players seemed to have long accepted their fate. Sevilla probably knew the game was won as Málaga became reliant on long throws from their Venezuelan right back Rosales and brought on a substitute optimistically called Bueno. Málaga were fortunate as their former striker Sandro, on loan to Sevilla from Everton, missed the best opportunity of the second half. The game ended Málaga 0–1 Sevilla.

After the match in Seville, I gave an interview to Radio MARCA that was later dubbed into Spanish, and spoke to their journalist David about the strong links between the Spanish and English leagues. David explained that Spanish players don't go to England only for the money. Spaniards prefer the atmosphere of the Premier League and 'they also have more space' there. He didn't mean on the pitch, where the Premier League is noticeably faster than the technical Spanish game. He meant in the media, where Spanish players, with a few exceptions, were left alone compared to the extreme scrutiny they would receive in Spain. David said that players only return home to Spain when they aren't playing. We talked about a few flops, including the unused Sevilla substitute Roque Mesa, for whom Swansea City mysteriously paid £11 million in July 2017.

Both matches had boasted a considerable ex-Premier League presence: Costa and Brazil left back Filipe Luís had recently played for Chelsea, Navas and Nolito for Manchester City, Nzonzi for Stoke City and Blackburn Rovers, Layún and Success for Watford, Brown Ideye for West Brom and Sandro for Everton. Costa and Filipe Luís had excellent matches for Atlético and I liked the industrious Nzonzi and his nickname, 'the octopus'. But Success was anything but for Málaga. His crossing was poor and ball retention worse. The crowd whistled their displeasure as the Nigerian threw himself to the ground searching for a penalty he was never going to win. He was hauled off after thirty-four minutes and seemed to be the physical embodiment of Málaga's declining fortunes.

Sevilla finished a disappointing seventh, below their city rivals Betis. Atlético won the Europa League and were second behind Barcelona, ahead of Champions League winners Real Madrid. Málaga were last and relegated.

Expectation and realisation

I would see some good matches and some instantly forgettable ones. There would be sublime summer weather and shocking downpours. I would visit places to cherish and others to forget. This was inevitable when travelling across fifty-five nations over eleven months. But how did my travels match up against my own expectations?

I envisaged that every match would be merely another step towards achieving my challenge. But I underestimated how friendly clubs and supporters would be to a random Fulham fan who had turned up in their town. I hoped to speak to football people in around half of my countries. I actually managed to find someone in every one, both random encounters like with Nikita in Russia, Pedro Santos in Andorra and Vasilis in Cyprus, and those who contacted me such as Kaduregel Shefel in Israel and Conor in England. I developed an unlikely affinity with some clubs: Drita in Kosovo, Tula Arsenal in Russia and Chornomorets in Ukraine. I continued to look out for their results and would have loved to watch their campaigns unfold.

339

The big leagues, admirable Atlético apart, disappointed: three 1–1 draws in Germany, Italy and France demonstrated that a higher level of technical ability did not necessarily make for a more entertaining match. I wasn't initially thrilled to be visiting Denmark and Poland in freezing December. But I met welcoming Helsingør and Brøndby fans, and was warmed by fireworks and filming at the Kraków derby. It was a sharp combination of the planned and unplanned that turned into one of my favourite short trips. The Czech Republic to Liechtenstein leg across the Alps in mid-March looked cold and arduous, five countries in ten days, but the football turned out to be an unexpected highlight, helped by a diverse range of football people, three of whom had found out about my travels through very different means: English television, my own website and a Belgian newspaper article.

Before my travels, I was most looking forward to visiting Georgia, Armenia, Kazakhstan, Albania and Israel, five countries I had never travelled in before. I spent over five weeks soaking up their unique cultures, watching football and visiting eight UNESCO World Heritage sites. Georgia and Israel were my favourites. Tel Aviv and Jerusalem might just be the most interesting twin-centre break within range of home. I would have preferred fewer than eleven days in Kazakhstan and more than four days in Albania. But I had to fit my schedule around fixtures.

Undoubtedly, the biggest surprise was becoming a minor football celebrity. I had previously only been featured in a crowd shot used on the cover of 1990s Fulham stalwart Simon Morgan's book *On Song for Promotion*. My travels were slightly more mainstream, and I predicted a mention in the odd football magazine, or a few local newspapers, yet hardly expected to be penning the answers to interview questions on flights, or for my story to be covered more than eighty times in forty-five countries – including by big names such as *GQ* magazine, *Lonely Planet, La Gazzetta dello Sport, talkSPORT* and *L'Équipe*. On several occasions, I was even asked by some media outlets not to talk to their rivals until an 'exclusive' had been published. It opened doors. I spoke to people I wouldn't have otherwise met. But it certainly ate into my time.

I needed to strike a balance between experiencing and writing, meeting journalists with an eye on a story and developing my own, updating followers and following football clubs. It was both exhausting and exhilarating.

GROUNDHOPPING WITH MIGUEL

43 Portugal

Miguel and I drove through darkening skies to a second-division match on the northern coast of Portugal. He was an inoffensive sort: average height and build, his dark hair flecked with grey. But Miguel was doing something special. He was on a mission to watch a match at every stadium in Portugal's top two divisions this season. Miguel had been listening to M80 Radio when they mentioned my travels. 'I said to myself, I must do something like that.' His challenge encompassed thirty-eight stadiums, including four in the Atlantic islands of Madeira and the Azores.

I had flown from Málaga to Porto via Madrid, which was cheaper and quicker than the train. But Portugal was no drier than southern Spain. The seaside resort of Póvoa de Varzim was a Portuguese Llandudno, with modern residential buildings in the place of faded period features, rain instead of bright Welsh skies. The waves were whipped by the wind and seagulls circled apartment blocks overlooking the stadium. A Portuguese saying was quoted to me: 'Seagulls inland, storm in sea'.

Or maybe seagulls inland, lots of rubbish around apartment blocks. Mid-table Varzim hosted Santa Clara, surprise promotion chasers from the Azores, one of the outposts of Miguel's challenge.

My biggest challenge was getting into the Varzim Stadium with my bulky camera, flash still attached like a limpet on a rock. Unbelievably, although not a single professional photographer was amongst the crowd of 700, Varzim were not letting me in. Miguel intervened, proffering my ever-valuable business card and mentioning the four-page article that the Portuguese newspaper *Record* had written about my travels. Varzim hastily printed a media pass. My camera, often my best friend when travelling, was becoming a hindrance in some countries. The suspicion it provoked was a clear reflection of authoritarian regimes in the likes of Russia and Turkey.

Bahia powered a header in from a free kick to give Varzim a first-half lead before Thiago equalised for Santa Clara in the second half. Thiago celebrated in front of an Azores flag displayed by the youthful gaggle of away supporters. Incredibly, some Varzim fans took exception, leapt over a modest metal fence and confronted the ten Santa Clara fans. Policemen belatedly woke up and separated crowd trouble even more ridiculous than that I had witnessed in Kosovo. Miguel said that it was difficult to control crowds in the cooler north of the country and that fans were calmer in the south. Miguel was well placed to gauge as a Benfica fan who lived in Coimbra, slap bang in Portugal's middle. I enjoyed watching this 1–1 draw with Miguel and his trained eyes. But this was Miguel's quest, and it was time for me to focus on top-division football.

Porto, the country's second city dramatically set on the banks of the river Douro, had become fashionable. A crowd of cranes cluttered the skyline as the centre was renovated for a barrage of city breakers. More people were taking photos of São Bento Station's stunning blue and white tiled interior than taking trains. Porto is a distinctive and likeable city, even in the horizontal rain that blasted sightseers crossing the charismatic Dom Luís I Bridge, their umbrellas fruitlessly angled against the deluge. I visited a local bakery for a drier and more genuine Porto experience. Hard surfaces bounced the voices of people talking loudly over one another. Locals downed an espresso and a *pastel de nata*, a sublime custard tart, standing at the bar in a very southern European way.

Everyone loves *pastéis de nata* in Portugal. And virtually everyone loves FC Porto in Porto. The impressive club museum was hauntingly empty on a damp weekday in March. I delved through its weighty history. Few trophies were as imposing as the enormous Arsenal Cup, nine feet tall and containing 130 kg of pure silver. I smiled at the dearth of references to arch-rivals Benfica and tried to ignore the copious Chelsea links of Ferreira, Carvalho, Deco, Mourinho and Villas-Boas. A video showed Porto's players celebrating a title with Bobby Robson. A few tears dripped onto the screen. I doubt I will remember Sam Allardyce with such fondness.

My first choice in Portugal had been Vitória against Belenenses in Guimarães, a city I had heard was passionate about its team. But, when the fixtures fell in my favour, I was hardly going to turn down leaders Porto against third-placed Sporting in a packed Estádio do Dragão. I sat near the halfway line surrounded by fellow foreigners: a father and son from Paris to my left and a German couple in front, the woman distracted by unappetising hot dogs. The front row was taken by a young Japanese girl and her mother, both with expensive-looking jackets and matching ponytails. Her father was on camera duty. This was the football tourist in Old Trafford or the Emirates experience. I far preferred watching a match with someone like Alex in Montpellier; perhaps Byllel's idea stood a chance.

I was covered by an enormous flag and reappeared, like a badger after hibernation, to smell fireworks from blue pyrotechnics. Portuguese football is a mix of the familiar and the future. Casillas, Coentrão, Mathieu and Ruiz had played for Real Madrid, Barcelona and Fulham. And there were chances for young forwards Marega of Porto and Leão of Sporting as four regular strikers – Aboubakar and Soares of Porto, Dost and Martins of Sporting – were missing.

Porto took the lead when their Spanish centre back Marcano powered home a far-post header. There was more blue smoke from the Dragão. I had seen Rooney play for the last time at Bournemouth. This would probably be my final flicker of Ruiz. I had seen him play more effectively for Costa Rica than at Fulham, despite some delicious cameos and a truly brilliant first goal against Everton in October 2011. Ruiz started centrally for Sporting, shifted to the right and looked less comfortable, without the pace to beat the youthful left back Dalot. But Ruiz was intelligent. He drifted inside and played a perfect pass to Leão. The young Portuguese forward struck his shot through Casillas's legs to make it 1–1. Fireworks and, as in Spain, a song with the same tune as 'Rivers of Babylon' were aired by the Sporting fans above me.

The second half opened with a short sharp shower. And a second Porto goal. Paciência advanced down the right and his cross fell to Brahimi. The nifty Algerian smashed the ball into the roof of the net to make it 2–1. The Dragão behind the goal waved dozens of flags. Coentrão, the target of Porto ire in the far stand, pushed a paramedic on the sidelines and her male colleague shoved Coentrão to the floor in retaliation. Blue plastic cards rained down from the stands onto the Sporting left back. The atmosphere was turning incendiary. Sporting pressed. Coates, the former Liverpool defender, headed a free kick onto the roof of the net. Ruiz was closer still when he headed a corner against the post.

'Porto, Porto', rallied the crowd. The excitement was too much for the Japanese trio, who left five minutes before the end. No one else did. It was only 2–1 and Sporting were pressing. A perfect left-wing cross was met by Leão, presenting him with a late chance. The Porto fans fell silent. Leão volleyed over the bar. He was disconsolate at the final whistle. The Sporting and Portugal midfielder Bruno Fernandes, still only twenty-three himself, offered encouragement. This had been the biggest match of Leão's young career.

'Nice game', said Miguel, who had sat elsewhere. It was. It meant a lot, there were good chances, some sparkling midfielders, especially Brahimi and Fernandes, and a crackling atmosphere in a perfect modern arena. Miguel's favourite stadiums were the impressive homes of the big three: Benfica, Porto and Sporting. But outside those, he liked Braga, a remarkable construction in a quarry, and Vitória's stadium in Guimarães for their atmosphere, architecture and perfect sight-lines.

I took the train from the lavishly tiled São Bento station to Guimarães, the small city twenty-five miles to the north-east, which became Portugal's first capital in the twelfth century. I met David Silva for a drink in the well-preserved historic centre. Not *the* David Silva, but a follower who had noticed I was visiting his hometown. David explained that everyone in Guimarães supported Vitória, the city's only professional team. 'It's common to have a supporters' club for one of the big three in every city. We have nothing like that here. Only Vitória and that's our club. If you go to the Algarve you still find supporters of Porto but good luck trying to find some Vitória supporters.'

Vitória finished fourth in 2017, but were struggling this season. They finished bottom of a tough Europa League group that included semi-finalists Salzburg and finalists Marseille. Vitória had picked up an unwanted record against Salzburg by being the first club to field a team in UEFA competitions without a single European player. I asked if Vitória could ever break the strangle of the big three; apart from them, only Belenenses in 1946 and Boavista, the second team in Porto, in 2001 had previously won the Portuguese championship. David said that there was a lot more money in Portugal than there used to be and 'if the stars align' it may be possible for Vitória or another team to be champions.

The following evening, I left my troublesome camera at my hotel and walked to the Estádio D. Afonso Henriques, built for Euro 2004 and named after Portugal's first king. Vitória laboured against a less-than-title-vintage Belenenses. I wrote down passes rather than chances during the sodden first half. Even the drums and chants of the Vitória support merged into a malignant noise beaten by the battering of the heavy rain. The second half was only marginally better. Miguel pointed out Mattheus, son of Bebeto, who had been immortalised shortly after his birth in the former Brazil forward's baby-rocking goal celebration against the Netherlands at the 1994 World Cup.

Mattheus was on loan from Sporting and had a couple of hopeful shots. Miguel, who had seen him play recently, said that Mattheus was technically good, if rather slow. He toiled in the centre of an attacking three behind Vitória's lone striker. Mattheus moved to holding mid-field, a position that suited him even less, and played the full match, much to Miguel's bemusement. I presumed being owned by Sporting

347

and having an influential father might help his career. A pitiful match ended with 'I Predict a Riot' by Kaiser Chiefs. There was no riot. There was more rain. Miguel was a little downbeat when I rated the match two out of ten, a far cry from the excitement in Porto.

Miguel went on to watch a match at thirty-seven of the thirty-eight stadiums in the top two divisions. The exception was Nacional of Madeira. 'The fog was crazy. You could see the corner flag, but not the goal. The game was called off, but for me being there on the day of the match is enough.' Everyone had their own rules and their own dreams. Miguel's was to watch five matches in five continents in one season. He had already chosen the five countries: England – 'where football was born'; Brazil – 'the home of football in South America'; Mozambique – 'home of Eusebio and Mário Coluna, another great Portuguese player'; New Zealand – 'because of the All Blacks'; and South Korea – 'to go to the border with North Korea'.

I asked why there were so many British expats in Portugal. 'It's cheap for them, the food is good, the people are nice and the weather is good', said Miguel. 'Not today', he corrected with a laugh. Portugal had been wet and wild. And I still couldn't get my camera fixed. But I had enjoyed my second-division experience in Varzim, the sparkling lights of the Dragão and the good company of someone who had a heart for football beyond his own club.

Porto won the title and Sporting were third. Vitória were ninth and Belenenses twelfth. Santa Clara were promoted to the Primeira Liga and became the most westerly top-division club in Europe. Varzim finished in mid-table. Dalot, the Porto left back, was transferred to Manchester United in June 2018 for around £20 million. Miguel was saving for his ticket to South Korea.

THE EXPAT AND THE AUSTRIAN

44 Czech Republic

I fervently read *Fever Pitch* on the bus from London to Prague.

This statement doesn't feel right nowadays. Why would you get a bus to Prague? And surely I had already read Nick Hornby's book? But it was true when I last visited the Czech Republic in 1994. This time, I was pleased to complete the London airport sextet – Heathrow, Gatwick, City, Luton, Stansted and Southend – on my football travels by taking a bargain flight from Southend to the Czech capital. On the short bus ride from Prague airport to the city centre I noticed that several Czech passengers took out weighty paperbacks, a marked difference from southern Europe, where I had seen only one person reading a book.

Prague was placid after a stormy end to my Iberian travels. I strolled around its glittering centre, admiring the phalanx of gorgeous architecture, stopping at every gargoyle and Baroque statue on Charles Bridge. My bag felt light after a London shop had removed the stuck flash from my camera in minutes. There was a spring in my step and in the temperate weather. I climbed the Petřín Tower, a miniature

Eiffel that wavered in the slight wind and offered sweeping views of the river Vltava and the castle. I'm always drawn to stadiums. Sparta's Generali Arena was clearly visible near the river. The floodlights of Stadion Juliska, home of Dukla, my hosts that evening, peeked out of the northern suburbs. But my eyes were distracted by the monolithic Great Strahov Stadium to the west.

The Great Strahov was enormous. It was originally constructed with wood in 1926 and has been rebuilt several times since in sterner stuff. 'Is that a football stadium?' asked a tourist at the top of the tower. It was far too big, the playing field the size of eight football pitches and mainly used by communist Czechoslovakia for nationalistic rallies and gymnastic displays. It had a seated capacity of 220,000 and was one of the largest sporting venues ever built. It took me nearly half an hour to walk around its decrepit, yet strangely fascinating, exterior. The concrete was decaying and unlocked doors led to curious dark corridors. It dwarfed the neighbouring Evžena Rošického Stadium, home to the 1978 European Athletics Championships.

'The compound is an enduring if not endearing testament to Czech history', said the *Prague Post* about the Great Strahov in 2003. There had been some recent attempts to renovate for capitalism: a wine bar, a driving school, a gym. U2 and the Rolling Stones had played and Sparta Prague trained there. But the vast open terraces are a symbol of communism that Czechs would prefer to remove were it not so expensive to do so. 'If this is what you call a good life I want better', screamed some graffiti along one of the stadium's giant sides.

After some dark tourism, it was time for some light beer. Graham, an expat with typically downbeat English humour, had lived in Prague for thirty years but couldn't kick his *Football Focus* habit. He had watched my BBC appearance and invited me out for a beer at the Golden Tiger, a classic Czech pub with deep wooden interior, big cat paraphernalia and fresh pilsner. We talked about stadiums. Graham recalled that Slavia Prague needed to win their crucial last match of the season at home to Zbrojovka Brno to secure the 2016–17 Czech championship. There was a problem. The authorities had booked Depeche Mode and Rammstein to play at their Eden Stadium. Slavia searched for an alternative: playing at rivals Sparta was inconceivable and the crumbling Evžena Rošického, in the shadow of the Great Strahov, was their unlikely salvation. Safety officials closed the top tier and there were not enough seats for season ticket holders but Slavia won 4–0 in their adopted home.

Graham talked about how Prague had changed, lamenting that locals now only ventured to the tourist-dominated city centre to work or go to a concert or the theatre. He said that there were only so many times you could see the old town square and the famous astronomical clock. But Graham liked Prague's agreeable size: the city was an overgrown village large enough to have everything you might need. He once had his own football project – I was beginning to think everyone had one – to watch all sixteen top-division teams in one season. There are four main clubs in Prague: Slavia, Sparta, Bohemians and Dukla. Graham fondly recollected drinking all night with friends, watching a 10.30 a.m. kick-off at Viktoria Žižkov, a fifth Prague club, and then going to bed. This sounded like an Englishman in Prague.

Prague's public transport is swift and cheap. We travelled towards Dejvice, a district in the north-west known as the home of Dukla Prague, famous for eleven Czechoslovak titles and a Half Man Half Biscuit song I didn't know. But was I seeing the real Dukla? Probably not. The original Dukla, the army team, had merged and lost its name in the 1990s. The new Dukla had inherited its colours and traditional Juliska Stadium. It was a story similar to many across Eastern Europe. We saw two young boys wearing Dukla yellow and red on the bus as we approached the stadium. The match was free for children and women to mark International Women's Day.

The Juliska was unique, with its one giant stand built into the side of a hill. The rest of the stadium was very modest. Low-slung terracing attracted a cluster of fans who stood next to mounds of cleared snow, an indicator that I had narrowly avoided the bone-chilling winter weather. Graham and I circumnavigated the stadium before sitting at the top of the looming stand behind a group of two dozen footballers from Minnesota. They had all bought Dukla scarves. The shop must have sold out but the profits may have paid for a player's wages that week.

Graham and I settled into our seats, high above the pitch and clad in faded, luxurious red velvet. They were wide and, unlike their plastic cousins, felt more comfortable as the material warmed and fitted around you. The small group of hardcore Dukla fans far below us had a better view of the action. But less padding. They were making some noise with a drum and distorted Dukla chants. There were a dozen fans supporting opponents Vysočina Jihlava, from a small town in the countryside between Prague and the second city of Brno, cordoned in the far side of the stand. Four bored-looking security guards ensured the Americans didn't hurl their popcorn at them.

I had expected huge defenders and powerful centre forwards in the Czech First League; my judgement was clouded by memories of Tomáš Skuhravý and Jan Koller. Graham had seen enough Czech football to know otherwise. He was right. Football was played on the ground. And Jihlava, bottom during the long winter break, moved the ball like a team who had won their last three matches since, including wins over champions-elect Viktoria Plzeň and Slavia Prague. Latvian forward Ikaunieks opened the scoring for the visitors after ten minutes, and then intelligently laid the ball off to Zoubele, who smashed the ball in off the crossbar to make it 2–0 to Jihlava.

Dukla took their name from a 1944 battle on the current Slovakia–Poland border. Their past connections to the military and communism counted against them. 'The young fans all support Sparta or Slavia. Most of Dukla's old fans are dead', said Graham. The crowd of just over 1,000 was an unusual mix: there were certainly more older fans, but plenty of women clasped International Women's Day gifts of red and yellow tulips. There were a few other English voices and some Germans were taking photos of Dukla's strange stadium. Possibly they were here to watch young German full back Till Schumacher, the former Borussia Dortmund youth captain who had moved to Jihlava for first-team football. Or perhaps they were just groundhoppers.

My attention drifted to our dramatic setting. Three bright fairground rides stuck up like candy sticks in the darkening skies. A chimney from a local heating plant smoked behind the far terracing. And cheeks were puffed out from the minority of the crowd who seemed to really care. The others were perhaps used to such mediocrity, or here just for a night out. There was some unexpected first-half entertainment when Dukla right back Kušnír took a throw-in against his teammate Holek's back and then collected the rebound off the midfielder. It didn't lead to anything but was purely intentional. Dukla trailed 2–0 at half-time.

'Do you often come to Dukla?' asked the Minnesotan coach. I explained. They were also on their own football trip, but their visit to the Milan derby had been cancelled. All Serie A fixtures had been postponed in the memory of Davide Astori, the Italy international defender who was found dead in his hotel room from a cardiac arrest aged just thirty-one. 'I know, so sad', I said. The coach nodded his head. His eyes showed more the disappointment of missing out on the match. They had come all the way to Europe to watch Dukla Prague against Vysočina Jihlava on a Friday evening. It put my own travels into some perspective.

Urblik, Jihlava's outstanding midfielder, scored a fine goal to make it 3–0 with twenty minutes left. Dukla belatedly rallied, substitute Đuranović missed two opportunities and some surreptitious Jihlava fans behind me laughed happily. They had traded in the hardly febrile atmosphere of the away cage for our cinema-style seating. Dukla finally forced a consolation when Holenda flicked in a left-wing cross. It was a sprightly 3–1 win by the visitors.

Graham and I retired for some beer and dumplings in a local tavern. There was no respite for me. I needed to keep my energy levels high before my match in Austria the following day and in Slovakia on Sunday. This would be the second time, after my road trip around Belgium, Germany and the Netherlands, that I would watch three matches in as many countries over a long weekend. This time the train would take the strain.

It was a remarkably close relegation run-in with four points covering eight places. Jihlava lost their crucial final match against Karviná and were relegated. Dukla finished two points and four places better off in eleventh.

45 Austria

My last train to Vienna, back in 2010, was an unintentional one. The Icelandic ash cloud had led to my flight home from Romania being cancelled, and my friends and I considered hiring a car or travelling up the Danube in a boat. We ended up inter-railing home from Bucharest, via Budapest, Vienna, Cologne, Brussels, Antwerp and Calais. There was something necessarily spontaneous and refreshing about the entire experience. It was even eye-opening to pay the English coach driver a £5 bung to be dropped off in Lewisham rather than in central London. I didn't see much of Vienna then. This time I would see only the scrappy streets around the main station.

I was in quite a mellow mood. My Stobart Air flight to Prague two days earlier had been delayed by over three hours. I received 250 euros under the EU compensation scheme, a useful cash injection for visits to Austria, less expensive Slovakia and money-melting Switzerland and Liechtenstein. I was also pleased to have contacts in all five countries in Central Europe, especially as my time was seriously pressed.

Hans, an Admira Wacker fan, had found out about my travels after researching my French hosts Montpellier for a betting website. It was another bizarre link. I had never properly met an Austrian and expected a restrained German type. Hans, with his whitening stubble, thinning dark hair and quiet voice, met my stereotype. His first Admira match had, like some of my own experiences, been more memorable for the journey. Hans had taken the train for two hours, alighted at the wrong station and walked thirty minutes to watch 'a nil–nil draw'. I liked that he knew this term despite his stuttering English, which was admittedly far superior to the handful of German words I had learned from Munich stag weekends. Hans was hooked. His wife wasn't. She sent him photos of lamps for their home. 'I don't want a wife or girlfriend who is in the stadium', said Hans. This was his time.

Hans took me onto the VIP balcony overlooking the Südstadt pitch. He explained that Admira, a club from the north of Vienna, had merged with Wacker, from the south-west, in 1971 and moved to Mödling, a commuter town on the southern outskirts. A third team, Mödling, merged with Admira Wacker to form Admira Wacker Mödling in 1997 before Mödling left and restarted again in the lower leagues. Football identity in the likes of Austria, the Czech Republic and Romania was much more complicated than in England, where MK Dons, founded in 2004, remained the bastion of controversy.

Admira struggled to attract supporters to their matches. Mödling was a pleasant town with nice houses, good schools and small mountains that were 'not very high by Austrian standards'. I could tell Hans was frustrated by the paucity of fans. Maybe they thought, like me, that scarves were too expensive in the club shop: 15 euros for a strip of cheap polyester. The atmosphere was certainly muted, not helped by the Admira hardcore being located in the opposite corner to an energetic troupe of travelling Sturm Graz fans, the stands behind each goal having been deemed too steep to be safely used.

Hans was happy that Admira were playing good football with a young team. But even lowly Championship teams in England had more pulling power than the fourth-placed team in the Austrian Bundesliga – Admira having recently sold Christoph Knasmüllner, their best player and top scorer, to Barnsley. Hans, an unlikely fan of Sheffield United and traditional real ale since the 1990s, thought Knasmüllner would struggle in South Yorkshire, citing how Austrian football was more technical than the depths of the Championship.

There was a minute's silence for the Admira superfan Gertrude 'Trude' Poschalko, who stood with the hardcore and, in her later years, sat amongst them on a chair given to her by young Admira fans. She had recently passed away, aged ninety-one, and 'RIP Trude' was displayed on a flag. The Sturm fans had their own banner that read, 'If you forbid pyrotechnics in the stadium this is a big risk', and predictably greeted kick-off with a flurry of fireworks. The smoke drifted atmospherically across the pitch. The ever-diplomatic Hans said that Sturm had the best fans in Austria. Sturm had flares, Admira had a trumpet.

Admira took the lead after eleven minutes from a Kalajdzic header. Sturm were level minutes later after Edomwonyi finished off a fine passing move, reminiscent of Arsenal in their pomp. Schmidt soon slotted home a left-footed finish to make it 2–1 to Admira. Sturm looked to control, taking more touches in midfield, the sign of a more experienced team. Admira, brimming with the optimism of youth, mixed lateral midfield passes with longer balls to feet. It was an excellent tactical clash.

There was tempered dissent from the VIP balcony as a Sturm midfielder was adjudged to have been tripped in the penalty area. 'Definite contact', I imagined Alan Shearer uttering. The left-footed Žulj stepped up. My intuition is not to trust left-footed penalty takers. And, ever the statistician, I later found some supporting evidence from both international tournaments and the Champions League, where 78 per cent of right-footed penalties were scored between 2007 and 2014 compared to 63 per cent of left-footed efforts. Leitner, the Admira goalkeeper, read the telegraphed spot kick. A celebratory announcement across the PA system sought to charge the Admira fans. However, Sturm midfielder Žulj moved to the left wing, and not long after, played the ball inside to rampaging left back Potzmann, whose right-footed slash was hammered past Leitner. It was a highly entertaining 2–2 at half-time.

We took seats in the main stand for the second half. Hans was desperate for an Admira win. 'The team come over to the hardcore fans and sing a special song with them.' A special song didn't look likely when Edomwonyi fired a half-volley into the roof of the net. Sturm had a 3–2 lead and their fans launched into yet another rendition of 'Rivers of Babylon'. An Admira banner complained about the pyro ban. 'Pyrotechnics are not a crime', sang the Sturm fans in solidarity.

Admira were not getting very close. 'One goal. I only want one goal', pleaded Hans, forgetting that he really wanted two. He shrieked, uncharacteristically for such a quiet man, at a mislaid pass. 'Come on Admira, fight and win', sang the hardcore. 'Clap your hands and follow our team', announced the PA system. But it was not to be, as the Sturm substitute Alar curled in a fourth with the last kick, and Sturm Graz celebrated a fine 4–2 away win in front of their ecstatic fans.

Hans and I reflected on a surprisingly eventful match with schnitzel and goulash in the VIP enclave. I met Philip Thonhauser, the Admira president who looked dapper in a blue jacket and jeans. 'Do all Austrians ski?' I asked Hans. 'Most', he replied. Hans skied and didn't look an athlete. Philip looked like he skied before breakfast every day, with his rosy cheeks, blond hair and careful figure. He was guarded, yet rich territory for a quote. 'Forty points and then we refocus', he said, with more charm than Tony Pulis. 'We are the most efficient team in Austria if you divide budget by number of points' sounded highly Germanic.

Philip was also honest. He said that it was difficult for Admira to attract supporters when the largest shopping centre in Austria was nearby. Philip remarked that Mödling is a wealthy neighbourhood. 'A lot of golf is played.' Around 3,000 attended this match but many, even in the main stand, supported Sturm. 'The difference between the Bundesliga II in Germany and the Austrian league is infrastructure', said Philip. 'Some of the football in that league is horrible. But it's about perceptions. People think it's a good game because they see the packed stands on television.'

I later visited Salzburg for mountain air, a peerless castle and charmless mass tourism. Salzburg were playing Borussia Dortmund in the last sixteen of the Europa League, and I popped along hopeful of a last-minute ticket to the sold-out second leg. The touts, unused to such an occasion, longed for 100 euros even after the match had started. Along with the Skënderbeu match played behind closed doors in Albania, it was one of only two occasions when I didn't get into a match. But I felt that the fans, many wearing suspiciously fresh replica shirts, weren't the same as in Admira. Attendances in Salzburg, despite their serial titles, were lower than at Rapid Vienna and Sturm. And there was a strong rumour that their stadium, built for Euro 2008 and one of the largest in Austria, would be reduced in capacity.

Sturm Graz went on to win the Austrian Cup. I would catch their 3–2 semi-final win against Rapid Vienna on television in Slovenia. It was another high-quality match in a crackling atmosphere. I may have unknowingly sampled the peaks of Austrian football, but the domestic game was far better than I had expected, even though its profile loitered in the shadows of the Alps and the football limelight.

Sturm Graz finished second and qualified for the Champions League. Admira finished fifth and qualified for the Europa League thanks to Sturm's Cup triumph. Knasmüllner played three matches for relegated Barnsley and was transferred to Rapid Vienna.

Crowds and fans

English football fans can get very obsessed over attendances. 'You can't compare England and Armenia. There is a culture of going to the stadium in England', said Hayk from the Armenian Football Federation. And the population of Greater London, at nine million roughly the same as Austria, is exceeded by only twenty UEFA nations. My mean attendance of 5,500 per match was heavily influenced by large crowds in Germany, Portugal and Spain. The ten largest gates accounted for 60 per cent of the total, explaining why the median, the midpoint, crowd was just over 1,000.

The fans may be smaller in number than in England, but were often more active. A few giant flags at Selhurst Park is generally the limit of fan displays in the Premier League. 'English football is like going to a concert', said Vadim in Israel. It was different across much of Europe. There were protest signs against television in Norway and a ban on pyrotechnics in Austria. I marched with ADO fans in the Netherlands and Vardar ultras in Macedonia as they celebrated notable anniversaries.

There were impressive crowd displays at Brøndby in Denmark and Hapoel Be'er Sheva in Israel, and the smell of blue gunpowder accompanied my match at Porto. The committed away support of Hammarby in Sweden and Sturm Graz in Austria would have been worth watching even without the diversion of a football match.

It did sometimes feel that it was just me. It nearly would be in San Marino. The group of twenty-two teammates, family members and cameraman Giuseppe would be supplemented by two bored-looking paramedics slumped in a cabin on the halfway line. Around one-third of my matches had an attendance of 300 or fewer, and the lowest outside the micro-states was the eighty at the Mika Stadium in Armenia, a crowd erroneously recorded as 300 on football websites. (I knew it was incorrect because I counted the fans.)

'Happiness is the most important human emotion. Football gives us the opportunity of happiness', said a philosophical David Silva in Portugal. I met true devotees like Gert of Brann Bergen, Erik from the Häcken supporters' club and Yury, the Section 8 fan leader in Belarus. Their club was a vivid representation of their own identity, rather than a mere pastime. In other countries, domestic football was mostly ignored, something to be joked at, a disorganised symbol of their nations' woes. The worst atmosphere was certainly in Albania, not only at the crowdless match in Vlorë, but with the listless feel of a league so riddled with problems that even locals barely talked about it.

I expected to see some trouble somewhere. And it came mainly in the east: the Kosovan stoning, Macedonian flare throwing and Polish firework frenzy overshadowed strong home support. I was often amongst friendly fans and shielded from confrontations elsewhere. A Vardar fan was attacked by rival fans from a fellow Skopje club, Shkupi, after my

Macedonian match in November. Another died in a similar incident in June 2018. One of the Brann Bergen boys I met was lucky to survive after falling in front of an Oslo subway train when pyrotechnics caused platform chaos before an away match at Vålerenga in August 2018.

I was only involved in one minor spat, in Greece, but I played in a charity tournament for Gabriel Statistuta, my five-a-side team in London, two months after my travels, sliding in for a tackle, late yet without malice. ('A classic Walker tackle', said a Statistuta teammate.) My opponent leapt up and swung a punch. My reactions must have been honed in Corfu. I ducked.

OFF THE RAILS

46 Slovakia

It was a Sunday, the day after Admira in Austria. I was feeling jaded as I crossed the dark waters of the mighty Danube into Slovakia, for my third league of the weekend. Slovakia had been a very late call. The Slovak First Football League split into championship and relegation rounds in March. The regular season had ended the previous weekend and fixtures were scheduled just days before my visit. It was easy enough to decide. MŠK Žilina were the only team who played on a Sunday. Spartak Trnava would also play a midweek Slovak Cup match, giving me the opportunity to compare the champions and the surprise leaders.

I changed trains in Bratislava and journeyed towards Žilina, a hundred miles north-east of the Slovakian capital. 'We wish you a pleasant day and look forward to welcoming you on our trains soon', said an eerie Australian accent that felt as out of place as me. Three countries in three days was getting confusing. I travelled through a wide valley, past a ruined castle and half-melted lakes where perched birds looked bemused by their new fishing opportunity. It was all gently scenic.

Žilina, Slovakia's fourth largest city of some 80,000 people in the north-west of the country, is an unassuming place where factories spit out cars, paper and packaged food. Slovakia is really quite an unassuming country. But whilst I had been travelling between Andorra and Gibraltar, the nation had been rocked by the alleged political killing of investigative journalist Ján Kuciak and his fiancée. When I was ambling around Prague, tens of thousands had protested against the Slovak government in Bratislava. This was the largest demonstration there since the Velvet Revolution that toppled communism and Czechoslovakia in 1989. There were clusters of candles lit in front of black and white photographs of the murdered couple in Žilina, Bratislava and Trnava. 'Sloboda', said one homemade cardboard sign. Freedom.

It doesn't take long to wander around Žilina and its two squares. The lower one was populated with old men downing cans of lager, the upper one a more attractive courtyard of arcades and burgher houses. I walked towards the Štadión pod Dubňom, a mishmash of corrugated iron stands complete with matching television gantry. The east stand had a row of green arches, seven of which housed photographs of title-winning squads. There was space for several more championship teams. Žilina were only fourth. Their title defence was not going well ahead of taking on third-placed Slovan Bratislava in the championship round.

Žilina were proud of their academy: centre back Milan Škriniar was sold to Sampdoria in 2016 and now played for Inter, left back Robert Mazan had recently transferred to Celta Vigo and Martin Dúbravka, the Slovakian international goalkeeper who made an impressive start to his

Newcastle United career, began at Žilina. The home team started nine Slovakians whilst Sulla, the goalkeeper, was the only domestic player fielded by visitors Slovan. I watched Hancko, Žilina's vaunted Slovakia Under-21 international, in action. The centre back, tall and poised, looked comfortable on the ball and made a great saving challenge.

I was struggling to engage with a slow first half until Žilina hit a long goal kick straight down the middle and their forward Mráz scored from close range after two teammates had fluffed chances. Žilina then scored the crucial second on the hour. Slovan's Nigerian midfielder Rabiu, who played sixteen minutes for Celtic in 2012, picked up a loose ball in his own penalty area and played a suicidal dinked pass. It fell straight to Škvarka, who fired low into the corner. The female announcer, something of a rarity, screamed in encouragement. Celebrations were muted from supporters more used to silverware than a scrap for the Europa League. It finished 2–0 to Žilina.

I visited Bratislava the following day. It is a capital without the glamour of Prague, yet with some interesting architectural oddities. The brown Slovak Radio building, an inverted pyramid completed in 1983, is a must for fans of Jonathan Wilson's book. The baby blue art nouveau church of St Elizabeth stands out in a workaday part of the city. But best of all was the UFO Bridge over the Danube, so called for the flying-saucer-shaped structure, now an observation deck, that sits atop the bridge's lone pylon. I admired the view of the compact old town to the north and the modern apartment block clusters to the south, nudging the border with Austria.

I day-tripped to Trnava, a pleasant place known as 'little Rome' for its many churches. The town is a short train ride away from Bratislava, making it, like Mödling in Austria, popular amongst commuters. I met Marián Černý, the affable marketing manager for Spartak Trnava, before their Cup quarter-final against DAC 1904 Dunajská Streda. 'People say there are two passions in Trnava: churches and football', said Marián.

The churches might be fuller than the football stadium, though. I was getting used to the continued struggle to attract fans in most Eastern European countries. This was no exception in Žilina and Trnava. Both teams had suffered boycotts. Žilina fans had been enraged by the 300 euro cost of some tickets for their Champions League match against Chelsea in 2010. The Trnava hardcore were boycotting because of a conflict with the club's owner. I was beginning to think that ultras didn't actually like watching live football.

Trnava were a successful team in the Czechoslovakian era but had not won a title since 1973. They were top and nine points clear when the league split the previous weekend. Marián said that everybody at the club was surprised by this season and nobody expected them to be in the running for the championship. 'Maybe we're doing well because we're not under pressure. Maybe it's a similar thing to Leicester City because nobody takes us seriously.'

Or maybe it was the manager. Nestor El Maestro, a British citizen born in Serbia as Nestor Jevtić, had previously been an assistant manager in the German and Austrian Bundesligas. There was something, probably quite deliberately, of the Pep Guardiola about him on the touchline: the shaven head, velvet jacket, skinny jeans and brown loafers. Marián said that El Maestro had brought a lot of new ideas to Trnava, presumably referring not only to the influx of velour. El Maestro had recently turned down a mid-season offer from an Austrian club to focus on securing a surprise title for Trnava.

Marián spoke with a noticeable lilt to his English from two years as a Scottish goalkeeper after Billy Reid, the Clyde manager, had approached him in the mid-2000s. 'Scottish people are crazy. I couldn't understand nothing until I improved my English.' He noticed some cultural differences. 'Every morning I met the kitman in front of the changing rooms and said, "How are you?" The kitman responded, "Fine, bye". I think that I must not be speaking very good English because he doesn't care about my answer. In Slovakia, if you meet somebody and say, "How are you?" you automatically continue and explain how you are feeling. In Scotland, you just say, "How are you?" and you can go away. After a couple of days, I stopped him and wanted to explain how I was feeling but he didn't care.'

Marián gave me a press pass that said 'BBC' on it – well, I was British, broadcasting, to an extent, and co-operative – and I took my seat in the modern Štadión Antona Malatinského, regularly used by the Slovakian national team. Trnava looked more assured and my attention was drawn to Davis, the left-sided Panama international playing for DAC, who looked like a man who had won a competition to play a football match. He gave the ball away instantly on the rare occasions he got involved. I decided that Kyle Walker need not worry about playing against Davis in the forthcoming World Cup.

'Catastrophic football', said the DAC fan behind me. A promising match for spells of the first half was disrupted by injuries, substitutes and shocking balls in the second. A terrible defensive header fell perfectly for substitute Egho, Trnava's leading striker, who lashed home from close range. The cheery goal celebration music was appropriate given we were only ten minutes away from extra time no one wanted. DAC were out of the Slovak Cup when Egho swept in a second.

I went for a quick beer in the Spartak bar and was surprised when El Maestro sat with his assistant and right-sided Trnava attacker Ofuso on a neighbouring table. It was clear from my earwigging that Ofuso fancied himself as an outright striker. 'You need to be strong to play that position', said the assistant. I introduced myself. Ofuso, born in Hamburg, was friendly and said the right things. Trnava was 'a small place with everything you need'. He had a six-month contract and would 'take every game one at a time'. El Maestro's English tellingly gave way to German and eventually Serbo-Croat. I clearly wasn't part of his masterplan for the evening, and retreated back to my table.

I wandered into Trnava and bumped into a man named Andrei, who had something vaguely reminiscent of Lenin about his gnomic beard and battered work suit. He was smoking outside the Imperia, a Russian restaurant run by a Kazakh. I ate shashlik with Andrei and his Slovakian friend Matúš, who had never seen an English person before. 'He wants you to keep speaking. He likes your accent', said Andrei. They had both been drinking vodka.

Andrei was nostalgic for the Soviet Union, or at least was pretending to be, and showed me his Russian passport. I mentioned I had visited Gori. He looked misty-eyed. 'Stalin, our leader.' He asked what I thought about the Stalin museum. 'Unusual' was not the answer he expected. Andrei accompanied me back to a Russian memorial, not the first of my travels, for those who liberated Trnava. 'And now, as a Russian officer, I'm going to shoot you', said Andrei, before he wobbled back to the Imperia.

I had been confused when I arrived in Slovakia. After meeting a Slovak Scot, a German Nigerian, a British Serb and a Soviet Russian in quick succession I was no less bemused in Trnava. I needed a country I could understand. I needed to go to Switzerland.

Trnava won the title although allegations of match fixing, denied by the club, tarnished their achievement. El Maestro took up a new challenge at CSKA Sofia. Slovan Bratislava were second. Žilina finished a disappointing fourth, missing out on Europe altogether after losing a play-off, but sold Hancko to Fiorentina for around £3 million.

47 Switzerland

St Gallen, the oldest club in continental Europe still in existence, was formed in 1879 by English schoolboys studying at Swiss high schools. Fulham, the oldest professional club still playing in London, was founded in the same year. I was clearly destined to visit St Gallen, even though my choice of Swiss match was mainly dictated by proximity to Austria, and Liechtenstein, my next destination.

I wasn't really looking forward to Switzerland that much. My only previous visit had been on a family trip to watch Fulham's thrilling 3–2 win against Basel. Snowflakes peppered the dark December skies and Roy Hodgson wandered cheerily around the Christmas market. But my memories of Fulham's qualification for the knockout stages of the 2009–10 Europa League were subdued by retrospect: it would be the last Fulham match my mother attended before passing away just over a year later.

I laughed at the town names, Hard and Horn, as my train from Salzburg to St Gallen followed the southern shore of Lake Constance. The journey was pleasant enough. But wasn't that Switzerland's problem? It was just *too* nice, *too* clinical. I even had a calculator in my guesthouse bedroom in St Gallen. Three months later, I would meet Ruben, a Swiss journalist, in Haringey Borough's car park at the 2018 CONIFA World Football Cup. It was more industrial park than quaint, and Ruben, looking around at the decaying buildings, remarked, 'We call a district run down in Switzerland if there is one piece of litter'.

I looked for the unusual even in conventional countries. St Gallen was previously famous for cloth manufacturing, and its nineteenth-century wealth had been invested in individualistic ornate balconies, many depicting exotic fruits and animals. The city was now a centre for sedate banking and known for its business school, but was, perhaps, a little edgier than is often perceived. St Gallen had, after all, allowed the installation of a distinctive red carpet which gave otherwise undistinguished city-centre streets an interesting glow.

I visited the fabulous medieval library, part of the Abbey of St Gall. Photography was strictly prohibited. There were rules in Switzerland and I liked this one. Visitors absorbed the warm wooden interior without taking bad photographs on their phones. The Abbey is a UNESCO World Heritage site that includes a five-a-side pitch where monks can play one-twos off the cathedral walls. The door from the cloisters was ajar so I had a quick kickaround with a flat football. I had seen spectacular small-scale pitches in the Old City of Jerusalem and the mountains of Andorra, but this was the most unlikely.

St Gallen is also famous for Olma Bratwurst, a special sausage made from veal, pork and milk, and Klosterbräu, the smooth local beer made by Schützengarten, founded in 1779 and the oldest brewery in Switzerland. I drank a couple with Beat, an administrator for a Zurich sports agency and token St Gallen shareholder. 'The value now is symbolic', he laughed. I enjoyed hearing how football fans like Hans and Beat had found out about my travels. Beat's friend had attended a cycling conference in Belgium and read my interview with *La Dernière Heure*, the Belgian newspaper, who neatly listed all of my past and future matches. Beat's friend noticed St Gallen on my schedule; Beat, a burly middle-aged man with a fervent love for football, was a contributor to St Gallen's notelet-style programme. And he was a terrific host, though I couldn't stop the Ramones lyric 'Beat on the brat with a baseball bat' racing through my head.

Switzerland has four official languages; around two-thirds of its population speak German, a quarter French, and 8 per cent Italian, whilst Romansch is the mother tongue for less than 1 per cent. Beat said that for many decades there had been considerable discord between football in the German and French regions, making it difficult to forge a successful international team. Roy Hodgson, who managed Switzerland to their first major tournament in nearly thirty years when they qualified for the 1994 World Cup, believed that his neutrality was an advantage, as players could not claim he was biased towards those from a German- or French-speaking background.

English was Beat's third strongest language, after German and French, but he still had a great turn of phrase. Beat explained that the style of football was heavily linked to the dominant culture, with German-speaking teams pragmatic in their pursuit of victories whilst French-speaking clubs were more concerned with playing 'the beautiful game'. He grew up fascinated by the French influence and watched Servette, the Geneva-based side who had 'a wonderful team' in the late 1970s.

The proportion of French speakers in Switzerland had increased since Beat's childhood, but clubs in the western French and southern Italian areas of the country struggled to attract sponsorship as they were still minority languages. The ten-team Super League featured teams from nine cities, but only Lausanne, Sion and Lugano represented the French- and Italian-speaking parts, with Servette now playing in the second-tier Challenge League. Interestingly, Beat claimed that of the main sports, only basketball was more popular in French and Italian-speaking areas than amongst the German majority.

Beat's football allegiance had changed, from Servette to St Gallen, a real rarity in football fans. He started watching St Gallen in 1993 when they played in the Challenge League as it seemed a good opportunity to watch other teams and visit new stadiums. St Gallen gradually became his team. 'I still love Servette but I support St Gallen now.'

The difference between fans and ultras is sometimes blurred, but Beat was a St Gallen fan, not a frustrated ultra. Beat talked about a match when St Gallen were 3–0 down against Basel in 2010 and then trailed 3–1 with ten minutes remaining, with a fighting chance of completing a notable comeback. St Gallen's ultras did not respond to the on-field action and still chanted the same song as when their team were three goals behind. After the match, Beat complained to one of the ultras that they were not following the game. 'It is impossible to have such fans in England', said Beat. He was right: everyone concentrated on the match in England. And I agreed with him. It was great to have noisy, atmospheric fans, but it was a meaningless drone if there was no connection to the game.

St Gallen play in green and white. Beat also supported an English team that play in the same colours, Plymouth Argyle, and visited for the first time in 2015. Football is a drug and Plymouth had been hard to kick. Beat had been welcomed by Tony, a pub landlord and Plymouth fan. 'My friends and I stayed late in his pub. He was so happy and said, "You see there are people coming from Switzerland to our pub" to locals who were leaving.' Beat would visit London the weekend after my Swiss game to watch Plymouth play at Charlton Athletic. I would be at home for a few days and we met at a Deptford beer festival to try some new brews. It was a rare treat to meet someone more than once during my travels.

St Gallen's success, rather like Fulham's, was modest compared to their history. They had won two Swiss championships, in 1904 and 2000, possibly the longest-separated titles in Europe, and had been in the Swiss second flight as recently as 2012. St Gallen aspired to be in the top five clubs in Switzerland – alongside Zurich, Grasshoppers, Young Boys and Basel. And things were beginning to change. St Gallen were third after twenty-five matches, and Matthias Hüppi, a famous sports presenter known for his skiing commentary, had recently taken over as club president. Alain Sutter, the former Bayern Munich player who starred for Hodgson's Switzerland team, had joined him as sports director. This was big news in a small city.

Sutter was famous for being different. The charismatic midfielder had protested against French atom bomb testing and logging in the Amazon basin, and was vegetarian long before it was fashionable. He had also brought new ideas to St Gallen: his aspiration was for home matches to be entertaining days out for the fans, regardless of the result. Beat also said that it was more important for him to watch exciting matches, even if they ended in defeat, than to finish in a particular position. I suspected that Beat's and Sutter's liberal attitude arose partly from the fact it was quite difficult to be relegated from the Swiss Super League, as only the team that finished tenth was demoted to the Challenge League.

I was treated to an Appenzeller Alpenbitter, a warming green spirit made of natural ingredients that promised to fend off ailments, before we entered the Kybunpark, St Gallen's 20,000-capacity home since 2008. This wasn't going to be my warmest football experience. St Gallen, one of the highest cities in Switzerland, with an altitude of some 700 metres above sea level, was known as a 'snowhole', and it had been –7°C at the last home match. I felt lucky to be in a more clement 3°C.

'This is not normal', said Beat. I could tell. There was general impatience from the home crowd. Smoke from flares had delayed kick-off by ten minutes. Everything worked in Switzerland apart from my match between St Gallen and Grasshoppers. When the match finally kicked off, both teams looked suitably organised with three at the back. There was an early flurry of action, but the next flurries were waves of snow. Thankfully, a special hybrid grass and undersoil heating kept the surface slick and the snow from settling. Sigurjónsson, playing in front of the St Gallen defence, began to take my eye. He relished the conditions, worked hard to win the ball back and spread it wide. He was on loan from opponents Grasshoppers. I couldn't see why. Everyone needs an Icelandic midfielder these days.

Grasshoppers shaded an unadventurous first half. 'Sometimes there is an entertainment', said Beat, looking at the empty pitch at half-time. He could have been commenting on the match. The relentless snow, if anything heavier than before, was prettier than any midfield movement.

The second half started with an Icelandic eruption. There seemed little danger when Sigurjónsson collected the ball thirty yards out but he connected perfectly with a shot that blasted past the Grasshoppers goalkeeper. Sigurjónsson had made his point against his erstwhile employers with one of the best strikes of my entire trip. Moments later it was 1–1. Grasshopppers were getting plenty of corner practice, and centre back Rhyner glanced one in at the near post.

This seemed to inspire St Gallen, who injected more pace into their play. 'Shit St Gallen', chanted the Grasshoppers fans, who ignored the harrowing cold with some synchronised shirtless jumping. 'You are taking photos of naked boys', said a wit behind me. 'They're men, definitely men', I replied. Young, and cold, men.

St Gallen were on top and home midfielder Toko headed straight at the Grasshoppers goalkeeper from ten yards. A fit Andy Carroll would have buried the chance. St Gallen were the only side who looked likely to score and soon regained the lead. Sigurjónsson cleverly switched play to the right, where striker Ben Khalifa controlled and finished emphatically in the far corner. It finished 2–1 to St Gallen.

The hermitage that became the Abbey of St Gall was founded in the seventh century by Gallus, an Irish monk who, legend has it, befriended a bear in the Swiss woods. Gallus the bear was the St Gallen mascot, and he celebrated by sitting down with the team in front of the standing hardcore fans. Gallus then started playfully kicking the home players. It was an amusing end to St Gallen's fifth consecutive home win over Grasshoppers. 'Every Grasshopper is a son of a bitch' was a new chant for Beat as we celebrated with more beer and special sausage.

I had easily beaten my low Swiss expectations. There were some big-screen irritations – a yellow card accompanied by an advertisement for a cooling drink, the latest league table distractingly flashing up during the match – but it had been another good game. I had experienced an energetic second half, a stunning goal, a decent crowd of 14,000 and Beat's hospitality. I left feeling an affinity. St Gallen were now my Swiss team. But I doubted that my fine Alpine run of matches would continue in Liechtenstein.

St Gallen lost nine of their last ten matches, 'a horrible end of season' said Beat, and finished fifth, but still qualified for the Europa League. 'Not a good sign for the league that we are in Europe', said Beat. Charlton beat Plymouth and pipped the Pilgrims to a League One play-off place. Grasshoppers were ninth.

48 Liechtenstein

Liechtenstein was my inspiration. I read about this defiantly independent slice of the Alps in *Stamping Grounds*, Charlie Connelly's story of Liechtenstein's doomed attempt to qualify for the 2002 World Cup, and it pushed thoughts towards my own travels. I loved the simple idea. The book was based around seven matches over a year. It featured strong characters and developed my knowledge, both football and historical, about the country. Writing it had required motivation, a strong sense of observation and some balls, but Connelly was hardly rafting down the Amazon with a blindfold on. I could also somehow see a little of me in Connelly – his frustration about normal life and the over-exposure of sporting giants.

This was its turn. Liechtenstein remains a peculiarity, the third smallest UEFA member after Gibraltar and San Marino, and the only one without its own league. FC Vaduz, the leading team, play in the Swiss football system but were relegated from the Super League to the Challenge League in 2017. FC Vaduz were playing Schaffhausen this

afternoon. Coincidentally the two teams had been managed the previous season by current St Gallen and Grasshoppers managers Contini
and Yakin. The match was inconsequential: neither team was close
enough to challenge leaders Neuchâtel Xamax for the only promotion
spot, and both were safe from last place and relegation. Nevertheless
this was an important fixture for my challenge, and one that had been
lodged in my schedule for months.

I took the train from St Gallen to the frontier town of Buchs
and the bus across the Rhine, the border between Liechtenstein and
Switzerland, to Vaduz. There wasn't much to my eyes that made the
Liechtenstein capital distinctive: a postal museum, mentioned in Connelly's book, wasn't really my thing, and I wasn't paying £12 to visit
an art gallery that would hardly rival the Louvre. The buildings were
a mess of architectural styles, the soft colours of the classical town hall
jarring with modern sculptures and the mountains to the east.

I walked alongside the Rhine to the greeting of 'Hoi' from occasional
locals. The grey river and cloud-fringed scenery looked unappealing,
and the Rheinpark Stadium lurked on the horizon. I entered the
warming north-stand restaurant, bought a beer and looked for a man
who had been called 'the greatest football journalist in the world'.
Ernst Hasler had worked for *Vaterland*, the Liechtenstein newspaper,
for over three decades. And Charlie Connelly had kindly put me in
touch with Ernst, who had helped him nearly twenty years ago. I had
an old photograph of Ernst and was anxious not to miss my opportunity. Was that him by the window? A man clearly on his own, talking
to a middle-aged couple, gulping tea like a true hack. 'Are you Ernst?'
I asked. 'No, I'm the driver for Schaffhausen', he replied.

I chatted to Tomas, a local Vaduz fan. He knew Ernst and pointed him out when he bustled in with a team sheet and a laptop. As in my photo from years ago, he still looked like a physics teacher, with his whitened hair and friendly moustache. Ernst was busy working out the FC Vaduz formation for the minute-by-minute updates on the *Vaterland* website. I liked this, a man looking forward.

It was hard to impress someone who had been to every World Cup final since 1982 and every European Championship final since 1988. But you can notice things. Vaduz qualified for Europe nearly every season by winning the Liechtenstein Football Cup. I remarked that their last twelve European fixtures had been against teams from twelve different countries: Norway and Bala Town from Wales this season, Denmark, Macedonia, Switzerland, Estonia, San Marino, Poland, Gibraltar, Georgia, Israel and Serbia previously. 'That's very special', said Ernst. 'I didn't notice that.'

Vaduz had won nineteen of the last twenty Liechtenstein Football Cup finals, the previous four of them conclusively (6–0, 5–0, 11–0 and 5–1). But in 2012 Vaduz lost the final to fourth-tier USV Eschen/Mauren on penalties after being two goals and a man up. 'It was a big shock', said Ernst. USV's lone European tie against Icelandic powerhouse FH ended in a respectable 3–1 aggregate defeat. Ernst, who was born in the northern town of Eschen, missed the away fixture as he was almost solely responsible for writing the annual Liechtenstein football special for *Vaterland* every summer. The 2017 edition was an impressive booklet for such a small country. The gleaming body of Yanik Frick, son of the legendary Mario, the first Liechtensteiner to play in Serie A, adorned the cover. A map showed how the UEFA Cup and Europa League have given Vaduz – and, for one season, USV – the opportunity to play in many of the countries that I had visited.

Ernst believed that Vaduz's near annual participation in Europe was positive, but that some managers had not treated it that seriously, preferring to use European matches to prepare for the new league season. 'When you only take it as preparation you don't win matches', said Ernst. Vaduz pay the Swiss Football Association over £500,000 each year to play in their system, an amount that would increase, should FC Vaduz progress in European competition. 'That's unbelievable, I've written about that', said Ernst, who spoke with care and pride, frustrated when he couldn't find the word he needed in English, and routinely using 'we' to refer to both Vaduz and Liechtenstein.

Ernst was a proud advocate for Liechtenstein football and still irritated by a 2002 UEFA Cup match in Scotland. FC Vaduz seemed to have put Livingston out with a goal in the dying moments of the second leg, only for the referee to blow his whistle moments before. I expected Ernst, as a respected journalist, to be neutral towards other countries, but it was clear he didn't like the arrogance of German supporters. I asked him why. 'They just nod their heads and say, "We won because we're the best". They are not interested in how they got to the result.' Ernst eagerly informed me that he had a good record of seeing Germany lose, including many finals and their group match against Croatia in Klagenfurt at Euro 2008.

Ernst recalled a favourite memory from the build-up to the 1986 World Cup final in Mexico. He had played a friendly outside the Azteca Stadium with some other journalists against a Mexican team that included three former internationals. Ernst's team won 6–2. 'The Mexicans started arguing, punching one another. They had never lost a game before and didn't know what to do. It was unbelievable.' The referee stopped the match.

Ernst had become mildly famous at another World Cup after being featured in *Stamping Grounds*. 'I met English supporters on the train in Japan who were reading the book. I had to give autographs. It was unbelievable for me.' Ernst added that he didn't know if many readers visited Liechtenstein, but that the book, and a 2008 German-language documentary called *The Mouse that Scored*, raised the country's profile in the footballing world.

I was a little saddened when Vaduz were relegated from the Super League the previous season. I had to stretch my definition of the top flight to incorporate Liechtenstein. But it did mean that I would watch football in fifty-five leagues, not fifty-four leagues and the Swiss Super League twice. Ernst's disappointment about the relegation was tangible. He lamented how Lausanne were a weaker team and that Vaduz had suffered from poor refereeing decisions in matches against Young Boys and Basel. St Gallen fans were, at least, happy about Vaduz playing in the Challenge League – their team had a horrid record against Vaduz – and Ernst thought the Swiss Football Association shed few tears.

Vaduz played an unusual lopsided 3-5-2 against Schaffhausen to a backdrop of strangely half-frosted mountains and advertisements for banks and Radio Liechtenstein. The Swiss defender Von Nieder-häusern dropped back from right wing back into an orthodox 4-4-2 when Vaduz lost possession. And it was his attacking play that led to the opening goal, with former Bournemouth striker Coulibaly meeting his cross and the Schaffhausen goalkeeper unable to react. 'Shit Schaff-hausen', chanted the youthful Vaduz ultras near me, one of whom was wearing sunglasses for stylish effect.

Vaduz were very comfortable at 1–0. The boring passing between their defenders reminded me of Montpellier, and my attention turned to Peter Jehle, the bearded goalkeeper who had been a bright young thing at Grasshoppers in *Stamping Grounds* and had returned to Liechtenstein in 2009 to play for FC Vaduz. He stretched without the athleticism of youth and hacked away a long ball with the experience of someone who knew he couldn't take chances against faster opponents.

There was amusement and bemusement as the crowd of 1,534 was announced, a figure considerably inflated by absent season ticket holders. I had sympathy. It was a dead game on a dead winter day. I was beginning to clock-watch as the chilled wind picked up in the second half and fans huddled underneath a multicoloured array of blankets. The plastic seats were getting very cold. There were no velvet seats like at Dukla in the Czech Republic.

A ripple of applause greeted the substitute appearance of the legendary Burgmeier, who along with Jehle and Frick, was part of the 'golden generation' who each accrued more than 100 caps for Liechtenstein. Four minutes later, the only outfield Liechtensteiner I would see play scored. Schaffhausen gave the ball away, the ball was played in from the right and a clever flick from Muntwiler left Burgmeier with a simple side-foot. 'Burgi, Burgi', chanted the Vaduz ultras at the former Darlington player.

Ernst was greeted like a hero when he returned to the restaurant. The Dutch bar girl brought him a cup of tea and a lamb skewer. The Vaduz players, who dined on a communal table, found time for him. He knew everyone. 'When are you leaving?' asked Ernst. I explained that I had a late flight from Zurich the next day. 'Come around to my house, I have some guests over.' I didn't have any dinner plans in Vaduz.

We drove up the snowy mountains to Ernst's house in Triesenberg, an upland area with a population of 2,600 and a pretty antidote to the hard angles of Vaduz. A range of family members was clustered around a wide wooden table. 'They're here for some special occasion', muttered Ernst. It took me a few seconds. 'What's the occasion?' I asked Nicole, Ernst's niece. 'It's Ernst's birthday', she said. Everyone knew apart from me.

Ernst and his family chatted in Walser German, a soft dialect distinct from other forms of Swiss German. 'Can you understand us?' asked Nicole. 'Not a word', I replied. I couldn't even pick out any of the few German words I knew. 'The Germans don't understand us', said Nicole. And sometimes even Swiss people don't know where Liechtenstein is. 'They confuse us with Luxembourg', said Nicole, recounting tales of bemused border officials who had never seen a Liechtenstein passport before. And letters, using the country code for Liechtenstein which is 'FL', sometimes arrive in the post via Finland, where the code is 'FI'.

We celebrated Ernst's sixty-third birthday with laughter and local wine, cake and football chat. There didn't seem to be any gifts for Ernst until he revealed that Burgmeier had said, 'That goal was your birthday present' in the post-match interview. And, although Burgi retired at the end of this season, Ernst still had many years of reporting on FC Vaduz and Liechtenstein ahead.

Vaduz finished fourth in the Swiss Challenge League, won the Liechtenstein Football Cup again and played Bulgarians Levski Sofia and Lithuanians Žalgiris in the 2018–19 Europa League qualifiers, the thirteenth and fourteenth different countries in a row. Schaffhausen finished second. Ernst reported from eleven matches at the 2018 World Cup, including both semi-finals and the final.

ALTERED MICRO-STATES

49 San Marino

Björn, the wicked barman back in Finland, was cutting. 'San Marino is like the Åland Islands having their own league. You only need two barely functional legs and to be aged eighteen to forty.' I was now forty-one, but San Marino was surely my best chance of playing a match on my travels.

San Marino was the lowest-ranked league in Europe based on club results in European competition over the previous five seasons. Only Kosovo, unable to accrue ranking points until they became a member of UEFA in 2016, had a lower coefficient. My chances of playing action were improved further by watching the final round of matches in the regular league season. And I even chose a dead match, Murata against Virtus, involving the worst team in top-division European football. Murata had drawn one and lost eighteen of their league matches and had a goal difference of minus fifty.

I spoke to Matteo, an Italian follower of my travels who compiles San Marino statistics – appearances, goals and subjective attributes such as player values – for the computer game *Football Manager*. 'That's quite impossible', said Matteo when I asked about getting a game. Understandable, I guessed, this being a UEFA league and not suitable for a washed-out amateur. But it wasn't my lack of talent. 'San Marino has a foreigners limit of seven, so it is unlikely the teams will leave a blank spot for you.' Even Italians were classified as foreigners unless they lived in the country. I left my boots at home for my second visit to San Marino, having visited a friend in the nearby Italian town of Imola, where the San Marino Grand Prix was held, in 2005.

I had gazed down the list of UEFA nations during my pre-trip planning months before, and San Marino was the only country where I thought, 'Really, I've got to go back?' Knowing the answer to that question, I flew from Stansted to Rimini, the nearest Italian city, and took a packed bus from the airport to the centre. A man with slicked-back hair parked his car in the middle of the road, blocking the path of the bus. 'This is public transport', shouted the bus driver. The man shrugged his shoulders, a reminder I was in Italy, not more orderly Switzerland or Liechtenstein. I then took the hour-long international bus service from Rimini to San Marino, the world's oldest republic given its foundation as an independent monastic community in the fourth century. The country is dominated by the 739-metre peak of Mount Titano and the three towers silhouetted on its crest.

'It's not enough to imagine it. Come and live it', proclaimed the tourist brochure. I lived San Marino for two days in the spring sunshine. The views were astounding from the city walls: the Adriatic to the east, a snowy rut of mountains to the west. I walked through St Francis's Gate, where a policeman was needlessly directing the limited traffic, and spotted some young English cyclists. They were wearing the instantly recognisable purple of Durham University, where I was president of the Football Supporters' Society for one glorious year. I mentioned I was once a Durham student. 'In the 90s!' exclaimed one lycra. 'Were you sporty?' asked another. It was implicit that I no longer was. 'I used to play for the football team.' I didn't add it was Collingwood College's fourth team. And that I couldn't get a game in San Marino.

I met Luca from the San Marino Football Federation by the Palazzo Pubblico and gave a short interview for San Marino TV. Luca explained that notional home and away teams were randomly allocated to stadiums in San Marino. The league format was the most curious in Europe, with fifteen teams split into two leagues – one of eight, another of seven – and the top three from each playing off for the title and European places over a further six rounds. It was complex. San Marinese football could easily be improved with an additional team, and they already had one willing player.

San Marino had the craziest league with the latest kick-off times. My match started at 9.15 p.m. As in Andorra and Gibraltar, most of the players had been working during the day. Luca explained that San Marinese footballers tried to gain experience in amateur, semi-professional or professional leagues in Italy. Although, for some, they played in San Marino because it was easier to manage the three essentials: work, family and football.

I asked about Davide Gualtieri. The bored-looking cameraman who spoke no English suddenly laughed. England needed to beat San Marino and pray to qualify for the 1994 World Cup. I vividly remember Stuart Pearce, one of my favourite players from the 1990s, playing the under-hit back pass that Gualtieri converted in the ninth second.

'He's running an IT business now and he's the supplier for the San Marino Football Federation. Everybody from abroad who talks about San Marino football says "Gualtieri, nine seconds".' His fame had even spread to Scotland, where his holidaying brother had been bought drinks and a meal by jubilant Scots. Unfortunately for Gualtieri, his was no longer the fastest international goal on record, Christian Benteke having scored after 8.1 seconds for Belgium against Gibraltar in 2015.

Murata against Virtus was being played at the Fiorentino ground, three miles downhill from the historic centre. Luca estimated thirty minutes' walk, but I'm always sceptical about walking times quoted by people who drive everywhere. And San Marino is the king of cars. In 2014 the World Bank listed San Marino as having the highest number of cars per capita (1,263 per 1,000 people) of any country. 'I didn't know this statistic, maybe it's some Italians with licence plates registered here', laughed Luca.

I stopped at Piccolo, a local eatery, on the way, and ate fabulous ravioli stuffed with shrimps, my second superb meal in San Marino. The restaurant gave me a free glass of prosecco that helped my fears about finding the Fiorentino ground in the rolling hills fade away. I soon found out that the biggest danger was the cars. The road clearly wasn't designed for the few pedestrians in San Marino, and I had to sidestep every time a car passed to make sure the vehicle didn't clip me in the darkness. Black thoughts started racing through my mind. I really didn't want to die in San Marino, of all places, as I still had to get to Luxembourg the following day. After an hour's walk, I was relieved to be greeted by the incessant barking of a white dog outside the ground. I sat down in the small stand and tried to ignore the irony that my longest walk to a stadium was in one of the world's smallest countries.

A bushy tabby cat dashed the full length of the pitch, clearly frisky because of the small gathering of spectators on its territory. I introduced myself to Giuseppe Canine, 'Joseph Dogs' he laughed, an Italian cameraman who had been living in San Marino for eight years and was filming tonight's match for a television highlights package. I was surprised by Giuseppe's English. He had never been to England and had visited the United States only once. 'I learnt it from John Denver songs, I translated them into Italian.' He certainly spoke with a country twang.

Giuseppe recounted that an Italian journalist had visited a few years earlier and asked people whether they felt San Marinese or Italian. Everyone answered 'San Marinese'. Giuseppe said that Italians would always think about themselves first and their country second. But not in patriotic San Marino. There certainly weren't many cultural differences, but Luca had explained that some Italians still felt a rivalry with the micro-state. 'San Marino has been seen as an offshore paradise when salaries were higher than in Italy for the same job. Even if the situation changes, the mentality doesn't change.'

This match had a retrospective feel. Both teams lined up in shirts numbered one to eleven in their normal positions; there were no seventy-sevens or ninety-nines. I was backing Murata, the ultimate underdog, who were title winners three times in the mid-2000s but had struggled with finances and failed to attract better-quality players this season. This was their last chance to win a league match. Murata used to have a famous former player; Aldair, the AS Roma and Brazil defender, had made ten appearances for them at the prime age of forty-one. The club had even attempted to lure Formula One superstar Michael Schumacher to play in their 2008 Champions League campaign. Luca thought Murata had a good chance to break their duck because Virtus might be focused on their upcoming Titano Cup quarter-final.

Murata looked nervous from the start, and Virtus immediately showed superior control, opening the scoring after just five minutes from livewire left winger Tedesco. This already felt like it could be a real thrashing, and it was 2–0 when Tedesco crossed for Bozzetto to tap in. It was simple yet effective football. An artful Bozzetto shot soon made it 3–0. Ura added a fourth with what would turn out to be the last of twenty-three top-flight penalties on my travels (only four were missed, a highly respectable 83 per cent conversion rate.)

Murata had half-chances they never looked like converting. Cavalli, their striker, reminded me of an overweight schoolboy, not a top-flight footballer, with a heavy touch to match his build. But Murata surprised everyone by scoring the eleventh and last goal of their awful season when Giardi buried a shot past startled Broccoli in the Virtus goal. Virtus responded with a fifth when Bozzetto bundled in another Tedesco cross for his first-half hat-trick. And it was 6–1 when, roles reversed, Tedesco converted Bozzetto's right-wing cross.

'Are you going?' asked Giuseppe as I picked up my bag with purpose at half-time. 'No, I'm in San Marino. What else am I going to do? Stare at my hotel wall all night?' Giuseppe laughed. 'It's raining cats and goals', he said, a clever reference to the earlier feline and a bulldog that had growled its way through the first half.

The second half began with some silly play-acting from the Virtus striker Ura, who went down too easily for the Murata goalkeeper's liking. It was strange seeing an argument at 6–1 in a meaningless match. 'These guys have been at work all day and they want to have some fun', said Giuseppe. It was pure pride. Ura was hacked down moments later by a Murata defender in retaliation for the dive.

The scoring inevitably slowed, but Tedesco secured his own hat-trick with the best goal of the night, a left-footed volley that zipped off the artificial pitch into the corner. Zannoni, a latter-day Andrea Pirlo, flicked a pass with the outside of his right boot – 'pass bellissimo', purred a voice behind me – for Ura to make it 8–1. The giant Cavalli moved to left back and tried a shot from forty yards, inevitably off target. 'That's why you're going down', would be the chant in England. But there was no relegation in San Marino. Only twenty-two people, one dog and a passing cat watched this 8–1 thrashing, the lowest attendance and joint highest-scoring match of my travels. There was a ripple of excitement from the colleague in London who drew San Marino in the sweepstake: nine goals would be hard to beat with only five nations remaining.

Giuseppe secured his precious camera memory cards in a jar. 'I always use one card for the first half, another for the second, a third for extra time, a fourth for penalties.' Giuseppe then backed them up at San Marino television centre, which I had spotted near the historic centre. I asked for a lift and saved my legs from a lengthy trek up the mountain. 'You will be okay in Luxembourg', said Giuseppe. 'At least it's flat for walking.'

Murata finished bottom of the seven-team Group B and accrued the lowest points tally of any top-division team in Europe. Virtus were fifth in Group B.

50 Luxembourg

Esch-sur-Alzette is the second largest city in Luxembourg. And no, I had never heard of it. I discovered that Esch shares the mantle of European Capital of Culture with Kaunas of Lithuania in 2022, and, if readers are contemplating which to visit, it's something of a no-brainer to choose more attractive Kaunas. Esch might not be an instantly appealing place but it was a hidden footballing power, with three top-division football clubs: Fola, Jeunesse and upstarts US. My first match in Luxembourg was the lesser Esch derby between Fola and US.

I treated Luxembourg like a grenade: hot and dangerous. I was initially supposed to visit between Belgium and the Netherlands but no Saturday match was scheduled in November, and so I had watched Borussia Mönchengladbach in Germany instead. Thomas, the ground-hopping German and a Luxembourg league regular, then sent me a message shortly before my November trip, saying there was a Saturday match after all. I already had a ticket for Mönchengladbach. Luxembourg could wait.

Four months later, the National Division fixtures were released a week before my visit. But it was still necessary to regularly refresh football websites as kick-off times in Luxembourg were forever changing. Christelle, an Esch sports journalist, looked fairly irritated as she recounted that they could move up to four times in the week leading up to the match. And it was not because of television coverage. Christelle said that the fixtures were sometimes altered so that a small group of between twenty and thirty Luxembourger football fans could attend more matches as it was only around ten miles from one pitch to another. I had heard of the groundhopper influence on English non-league schedules. But this was top-division football. Albeit in Luxembourg.

Luxembourg didn't feel like a hotbed of football when I crossed the border on a Belgian motorway. I wondered if anyone else, apart from football clubs in European competition, had tried to travel between San Marino and Luxembourg in one day. It had been a long twelve-hour trawl. I rode the international bus service from San Marino back to Rimini, then the ninety-minute train to Bologna and a packed bus to the airport. My Ryanair flight to Charleroi in Belgium was strangely serene after the Easter chaos of Bologna airport. I then ate some tasty *frites* in Charleroi's airport car park before the near three-hour bus journey to Luxembourg City.

I love new places. But I was hungry, knackered and very unexcited when I arrived in Luxembourg City. I couldn't remember the last time I felt like this. Maybe Andorra. A takeaway from Mr Wok, a Chinese restaurant next to my apartment, sent me into a deep sleep. I woke up refreshed, if lacking motivation to explore another historic city centre. Luxembourg City was different though. The old town was set in a picturesque gorge, the Alzette River gurgling through it. I even tried to ignore the echoing sounds of drilling, pretending they were the cheers of excited football fans.

I followed the Alzette River to Esch, a tangle of confused architecture on a suitably grey day. I retreated from the rain-soaked, cigarette-butt-studded streets into the Pitcher, the best-looking option in a town thick with bland bars. I happened upon Sascha, a local journalist at *Tageblatt,* who explained that most bars were dominated by one nationality or another, and the Pitcher was the only pub where anyone can drink. Esch was, according to its own website, a perfect example of 'un melting pot', with more than 100 nationalities amongst its 35,000 inhabitants.

The big derby in Esch was not my match, but the clash between Jeunesse and Fola, the workers against the elite. According to Sascha, rival fans regularly used to scrap. A referee had also been attacked by US Bous players during a third-division match and the championship suspended in 2007. It was hard to envisage fiery football in Luxembourg. The people were laid-back and as cosmopolitan as its language – Luxembourgish, the native language closest to German or Dutch, reflected the country's location, with many French words and even odd English words such as 'ham' and 'bin' thrown into the linguistic mix.

I walked over the railway tracks on a bridge that looked like an alien's face, possibly the most distinctive structure in Esch, to the Émile Mayrisch Stadium. I had received a message from Mauro, Fola's president, inviting me to the match. He welcomed me into the VIP bar, where the plastic tables and lounge music gave it a feel somewhere between an office canteen and a mid-range hotel. (The half-time canapés would feel very like a wedding.) Mauro, of Italian heritage, was a Juventus fan who seemed surprised at my Italian choice of Crotone. I had walked between two Italian bars in Esch, and I heard it got a little lively outside the Juventus-supporting Café Italia and San Siro bar when Juventus played AC Milan.

Mauro invited me to watch the game with him. I had viewed several matches with club representatives since my journey began, but never with the president. I felt I couldn't be too critical or probing. Fola were in patchy form and fifth. But the pressure was alleviated somewhat with a match against relegation certainties US, who were struggling with only four points from seventeen matches following successive promotions.

A thrashing always looked more likely than a shock. Leading the line for Fola was Samir Hadji, son of the current Morocco assistant coach and former Coventry City midfielder, Mustapha Hadji, who had also played for Fola at the end of his career. A perfect long pass from impressive left back Kirch – 'probably the best left back in the division', said Mauro – was nudged by Hadji past Lopes in the US goal. Soon after, Hadji slotted the ball into the far corner to make it 2–0 after eighteen minutes. 'Game over', I said. Mauro wasn't so sure. Fola had only beaten US 1–0 in the reverse fixture.

Mauro said that Hadji was talented, but that there had been some-thing missing that prevented him making more of his career. This explained why Hadji was playing for a team in Luxembourg. Mauro clarified that only some of his players were full-time. 'The biggest difference is combining working and training with family time. The full-time players have it easier and sometimes part-time players get more tired during games.'

Mauro mentioned that Enes Mahmutovic, a young centre back, had left Fola for Middlesbrough in 2017. I asked if Fola received any money for him. 'Some', said Mauro. He didn't give much away. You don't become a successful businessman by discussing secrets with a random Englishman. The match was drifting at 2–0. 'One of the limitations of the team is that we score and get happy', said Mauro. Klapp must have been listening to his president. He charged down the right and crossed for Muharemović to head in a third. US midfielder Kwani, always a liability in possession, then gave the ball away, Koçur nipping in and finishing straight down the middle. It was 4–0 to Fola at half-time.

I was introduced to Jeff Strasser, arguably Luxembourg's greatest ever player with nearly 100 caps and a stellar Bundesliga career at Kaiserslautern and Borussia Mönchengladbach. 'It's a good project', said Strasser, a tall, no-nonsense defender, about my travels. Strasser had been Fola's manager until the previous summer when he joined Kaiserslautern, but he was back watching football at Fola after giving up his managerial post in Germany due to poor health. A match between Kaiserslautern and Darmstadt in January 2018 was abandoned at half-time when Strasser experienced heart problems. 'Strasser, Strasser', the Kaiserslautern fans had chanted as he departed in an ambulance.

Strasser, thankfully, was looking healthier now. And so were Fola. This was my second successive goal fest. Martin-Suarez scored an easy fifth and Klapp, who I heard had paid for the stadium scoreboard out of his own pocket, tapped in a sixth that his energetic performance merited. I had never seen a team score double digits and this might have been my chance had the US goalkeeper not made a fine treble save after another mistake by Kwani. Hadji fired in a free kick to make it 7–0, substitute Saiti curled a left-footed eighth and Hadji scored his fourth from a narrow angle. The match finished 9–0, matching my record scoreline from 2001, and only a later opening goal prevented Luxembourg from eclipsing San Marino in the office sweepstake. I had seen three hat-tricks and eighteen goals in two matches.

The VIP bar was abuzz with relief. Fola needed that win, the biggest in the league all season. The players shook everyone's hands, lingered and laughed, several drinking small beers at the bar. Hadji wore a winning smile. I spoke to Stéphane, Fola's stadium announcer. His great-grandfather had been taught by Jean Roeder, the English-language teacher who formed Fola, the country's oldest club, in 1906, taking the first two letters from 'football' and 'lawn tennis club' after a visit to England. I had noticed that top-division clubs were clustered in the south of Luxembourg. 'People are more committed in the south', said Stéphane. 'Immigrants stay here and are more interested in football.'

I could see a mishmash of influences in Luxembourg: the capital was a bit Belgian in places, like a medium-sized French city in others, whilst the infrastructure felt quite Germanic. I asked Stéphane what he was most proud of about Luxembourg. 'Steel', was his deadpan answer. Luxembourg was once one of the largest steel producers in the world. The nearby city of Differdange had provided much of the heavy metal for the original and new World Trade Centers in New York.

It was a good atmosphere at Fola. Mauro drove off in a large, blacked-out car and I followed with Stéphane in a more modest vehicle. We circled the outside of the athletics track, returned to the town centre and Stéphane retreated to the Pitcher. I vainly looked for something to eat around town before settling on leftover tortilla chips and a hotel chocolate. I may have been hosted by the charming Mauro and seen nine goals, but this was the reality of the fast football road.

I was in Niederkorn, just five miles north-west of Esch, the following day for Progrès Nièderkorn against F91 Dudelange, yellow playing turquoise, second versus the champions and leaders. 'This is the biggest crowd I've seen in Luxembourg', said Thomas, the German groundhopper, as 2,000 fans thronged the Stade Jos Haupert, possibly referring to any gathering and not just football matches. A steward surreptitiously swigged beer and smoked a cigarette passed to him by a fan. A false start to the kick-off was another reminder that this was a big game in a not very big league.

Lincoln Red Imps, one of the six teams I had watched in Gibraltar, were famous for their victory over Celtic. Progrès had won more recent fame for their aggregate victory over Rangers in this season's Europa League. A clock in the bar featured Progrès's fabulously evil bee club badge next to Rangers' familiar icon. '2–0', the second-leg score, was scrawled in white. Christelle, the Esch journalist, recalled Gary Lineker's tweet. 'Rangers lost to a club in Luxembourg. Not the best team in Luxembourg, the 4th best in Luxembourg.'

Play ebbed and flowed like a football match should. F91 were 2–1 up in the second half when a long clearance fell to the Progrès goalkeeper Flauss outside his area. Flauss had time to consider whether to launch the ball into safety or try a flying header for the Monday highlights package. Instead he attempted a big chest, a bit of the Manuel Neuer. Flauss wasn't, and never will be, Neuer. The chest trap went horribly wrong and the ball bounced innocently into the F91 striker Turpel's path. I grabbed my camera for the easiest photograph of a goal I will ever take. A Progrès fan in a cap called it 'un cadeau'. It could have been a title-deciding present.

F91 players sang loudly in the showers as Thomas and I left the stadium. The Progrès showers were silent. The injured Progrès defender

Mario Mutsch, a Luxembourg international with nearly a hundred caps, strolled out the stadium gates in front of us. This was Luxembourg. The players and the place didn't shout about themselves. But I had watched thirteen goals in very congenial settings. I had not been overly excited about visiting. But the football might draw me back one day.

F91 won the Luxembourg title ahead of Progrès Niederkorn and Fola Esch. US Esch gained only four points – the second worst record, after San Marino's Murata, in top-division European football this season.

Goal of the season

I watched 227 goals in my 79 top-division matches, an average of 2.87 goals per match. That's higher than the 2.61 reported from 31 top European leagues in 2017 and the 2.64 seen at the 2018 World Cup. But what were my very best nine goals and worst miss? I separated them into categories like a true analyst: long-range blaster, placement over power, finest free kick, best passing move, last-minute drama, biggest surprise, a crazy mistake, a truly unusual goal and most ludicrous own goal. I am as cruel as I am representative.

There is no debate over the finest long-distance welly. Sigurjónsson smashed a thirty-yarder into the top corner for Switzerland's St Gallen against his parent club Grasshoppers. It nearly broke the net with its intent. Efrem, a Cypriot substitute in a match full of foreigners, also made a statement with his delicious lob from the halfway line for APOEL against AEK. Surprisingly few free kicks were scored, just nine, but my favourite was by Pedro Santos for Santa Coloma in Andorra, possibly because I was sitting next to his family. I can be sentimental.

The best Arsenal-lite impression was Meijers' stunning strike for ADO against Dutch champions Feyenoord, which brought back memories of Jack Wilshere's goal of the season against Norwich City in 2013. I also love a last-minute goal, of which there was no better example than Mitrović's delicate injury-time chip against Red Star Belgrade for Napredak, his hometown club. It sent the press boxes and supporters into raptures.

The fastest goal I had previously seen live was Bobby Zamora's strike after twenty-one seconds of Fulham's Europa League quarter-final against Wolfsburg in 2010. It was the only goal in a fine away performance and one that many travelling Fulham fans missed as they were still walking to the stadium from the pub. Ben Basat eclipsed Bobby with his surprise effort after seven seconds for Hapoel Haifa. The home Hapoel Be'er Sheva support all seemed to be in their seats. There were clearly fewer beer options in southern Israel.

The craziest mistake is the most recent of these goals. Progrès Niederkorn's goalkeeper Flauss in Luxembourg gets enormous credit for shrugging off that title-deciding assist to F91 striker Turpel with a knowing smile. The most unusual goal was undoubtedly in Belarus where Kostyukevich's punt in Vitebsk is proving a YouTube sensation, although few know the full story behind the Krumkachy goalkeeper. And only one of these goals can't be found on YouTube at all. Tartu Tammeka defender Anderson will be pleased that no camera phones predicted his lob over his own goalkeeper in my Estonian match in July.

My miss of the season was in Andorra when a cross-shot was parried by the Engordany goalkeeper and fell perfectly to Gómez. The Lusitanos midfielder eyed the unguarded goal and blazed his shot over from ten yards. But there can only be one goal of the season. I chose my top three goals (Efrem's lob, Meijers' left-footed finish and Kostyukevich's long-range punt) and opened this up to votes on my website. Meijers, one of only six left backs playing in a flat back four to score, was the deserved winner for the final flourish he added to some slick passing. Tiki-taka in Den Haag!

BEAUTY AND THE BEAST

51 Slovenia

'I had some Slovenian wine this morning, really nice whites, very refreshing. I ate a speciality pork sandwich with horseradish. That was delicious.' I was interviewed by POP TV and, entertainingly, my musings on the local food and drink made the final cut. Although maybe it was quite apt. Slovenia was really quite lovely. A friendly, beautiful country, with seemingly few flaws, was exactly what I needed after charging around the Andorran mountains and through grey towns in Luxembourg.

Slovenians wanted to meet me. I gave interviews to the television station and newspaper *Ekipa 24* and was enthusiastically greeted by all three of my host clubs: Krško, Maribor and Domžale. Krško were the most curious. The team are based in a sleepy town near the Croatian border, better known for its viticulture, Speedway track and nuclear power station, the only one in the former Yugoslavia. Zoran Omerzu, the Krško president, welcomed me onto the VIP balcony for their match against leaders Olimpija Ljubljana.

Zoran explained that Krško, who played in the fourth tier as recently as 1999, were a solid Second League team until a remarkable final day to the 2014–15 season. Krško were in second place and had to beat leaders Aluminij – who needed and played for a draw – to secure promotion. The goalless match entered additional time and the Aluminij substitutes bench changed into 'Champions' T-shirts. But Krško scored an injury-time winner and stole promotion to the top flight with a team full of local players.

It was a stirring story and, from the VIP balcony, I had an equally inspiring view of the lush playing surface, the surrounding mountains and three giant factories: pharmaceuticals, paper and nuclear. Krško's fan group are called the Nuclear Power Boys and have a Megadeth-influenced badge based on the radiation hazard sign. However, it seemed that terrace anthems took more inspiration from the scenic location than the power station. 'By the river Sava, under the Sremič hill, where the wine is flowing and we're cheering with our hearts' was almost poetic.

The wine was flowing, as the song predicted, with Zoran in the downstairs VIP room after a goalless first half. It was difficult to keep track of time as I sampled five reds and whites from the surrounding Posavje region. There was a cheer. 'Is it a goal?' I asked. 'There is no goal' said a Krško official. But by the time we entered the main stand several minutes had passed. And there had been a goal. Olimpija had scored. It was the only goal I would miss on my travels, but it was worth it for the wine.

I absorbed the rest of the second half next to four Danish anthropology students watching their first ever live football match. They casually observed that the ball didn't go very close to the goal very often. They were right. Olimpija's manager Igor Bišćan, once of Liverpool, kept his arms firmly folded in a fetching midnight blue tracksuit as his team strode around the pitch confidently. Olimpija killed the match and won 1–0.

I tasted more grape varieties in Maribor, Slovenia's second city, wrapped by mountains and agreeably located alongside the river Drava. A riverside building, the Old Vine House, supports a tangle of vines that have been bearing fruit for over 400 years, the oldest in the world, and is home to what the tourist literature calls 'a temple of wine tradition and culture'. Another friendly Slovenian explained the produce from the three main vine-growing areas and the importance of the Wine Queen of Slovenia, who is elected annually to promote the country's burgeoning wine industry.

Wine aside, I was always looking forward to visiting Maribor. And it seemed that NK Maribor, Slovenia's dominant football power with thirteen of the last twenty titles, were really looking forward to my visit. I met with Miha, the enthusiastic club photographer, who in an earlier incarnation was a Maribor ultra with a loudspeaker, several times before and after their match against mid-table Celje. He explained how the club was founded in 1960 and decided to play in colours inspired by Fiorentina. It was impossible to buy purple shirts then, so Maribor coloured the jerseys themselves with dye and players ended up with purple on their skin.

Miha took me to the club shop, overflowing with purple gear, for a haircut. This was something unique I needed to experience, and to test my belief that the price of a haircut is a decent proxy for the relative expensiveness of a country. My trim was 8 euros, a little more than half my normal London cut, which seemed roughly in line with respective costs of living. Miha introduced me to Maribor's president

Drago Cotar, who was having a haircut with his dog and, a few hours later at the Ljudski Vrt Stadium, to manager Darko Milanič, previously in charge of Leeds United for just six matches in 2014.

Miha had noticed a problem. I had made the unwise decision to wear a green T-shirt, the home colours of rivals Olimpija. This was impossible in Maribor, where even the club's award for the most passionate player was called the 'Purple Warrior'. Miha dashed into a cupboard and came out with half the club shop: Maribor pennant, wristband, cap, pin badge, keyring, sunglasses and, of course, a purple T-shirt.

It was hard not to get swept away by the passion for Maribor, especially in the company of someone so fanatical. 'We don't have the biggest budget but we have the biggest heart', said Miha when I asked about the club's sparkling record in European competition (three group-stage appearances in both the Europa League and Champions League). They also had remarkably rich British football experience from encounters with Birmingham City, Wigan Athletic, Liverpool, Chelsea, Tottenham Hotspur, Celtic, Rangers, Aberdeen and Hibernian. Miha had been to all the Scottish games. 'I had haggis at least ten times', he reminisced.

Maribor had knocked Celtic out of the Champions League in 2014 and Rangers out of the Europa League in 2011. 'Rangers was a very special game, I was out of control. I couldn't speak English I was so excited. The fans shouted "Fuck off gypsy" at me. I was running around in front of the fans but I didn't care. I was shouting. I was insane. It was the same against Celtic. It was 8°C in August and so fucking cold. And I was wearing my lucky flip-flops and shorts.' Miha showed me pictures of him collapsed on the Celtic Park pitch. He explained that he didn't wear his lucky flip-flops in the group stage of European competition because they had already woven their magic by getting Maribor there.

This season, Maribor's Champions League adventures – where they took a credible three points in group matches against eventual finalists Liverpool, Sevilla and Spartak Moscow – had affected domestic form. They were ten points behind leaders Olimpija and had not won at home for five matches. And there was trouble on the sidelines as Maribor's director of football Zlatko Zahovič, the legendary Porto and Benfica midfielder who scored thirty-five times for Slovenia, had been suspended by the Slovenian Football Association following a spat with a journalist. His son, striker Luka Zahovič, was having a miserable time in front of goal, scoring only twice in the league, yet still played every match. 'Zahovič is sometimes unstoppable but there is pressure to play him', said one reporter.

Zlatko wasn't watching his son at this match. Perhaps the lack of paternal pressure helped Luka, as Maribor opened the scoring when Hotić, the impressive right-sided attacker, played a cute left-footed pass through to Zahovič. The Maribor striker sidestepped the Celje goalkeeper and gently passed the ball into the empty net. There was the strange phenomenon of a goal being celebrated before it had even crossed the line.

The busy Celje midfielder Požeg Vancaš equalised before Maribor went 2–1 up when Zahovič converted from close range early in the second half. Zahovič, quick and alert in the inside right channel, then struck the ball through the goalkeeper's legs for his hat-trick. Lupeta's late effort dribbled into the corner to make it 3–2 and a nervy last few minutes for Maribor. Miha was visibly relieved after the much-needed home win and gave me Zahovič's shirt to add to my growing collection of purple goods. It was tiny. I would later give it to Eliza, my seven-year-old niece.

I left Maribor and, with my cheap rental car, visited the pretty riverside town of Ptuj and coastal Piran, loaded with medieval and Venetian architecture respectively, before my final Slovenian match in Domžale, a Ljubljana commuter town. Domžale might be most famous for its straw hat museum, but it was another congenial setting, with white peaks of the gorgeously snowy Alps backing the town centre stadium. And I had yet another very amiable host. Alen, Domžale's head of communications, took me through an elongated players' tunnel that passed under a main road – apparently the Marakana, home to Red Star Belgrade, is one of the few other stadiums where the changing rooms are located outside the ground.

I walked through the darkness and into the bright spring light. It was such an obvious metaphor. I had travelled hard and fast through the tail end of the winter, watching football in around one-third of my fifty-five UEFA nations since the New Year. Now I had very little to organise and only a handful of countries left to visit in ever improving weather. I could sit back and really savour the final few weeks of my travels.

A powerful header from Nicholson, Domžale's big Jamaican striker, decided their match against Celje, the only team I would see play away twice. The players left the field to a tasty double header of 'We Are the Champions' and 'Simply the Best'. Domžale were not going to be champions, but Slovenia had been the most enjoyable of countries, possibly the best of my entire trip. If the whole world was made up of friendly, over-achieving Slovenians, it would surely be a better place.

I saw the top three in Slovenia. Maribor narrowed the gap to Olimpija and only lost out on head-to-head record. Luka Zahovič was the league's top scorer with eighteen goals and was called up to the full Slovenia squad for a friendly against Montenegro in May 2018. Domžale finished third, Celje fifth and Krško seventh.

52 Hungary

Tall trees surrounded the still, geothermal waters of Lake Hévíz. I paddled around the lily pads, hoping the minerals would soak away my strains. Hévíz, near Lake Balaton in the west of Hungary, was a brief stop between Slovenia and my Hungarian match. It refreshed me and my memories of the Reykjavik baths of Laugardalslaug last summer. Back then I was looking forward. Now I was looking back.

I drove on from Hévíz through the small rural villages of southwestern Hungary. I passed long queues of people waiting at bus stops that connected them to life. This was not a wealthy part of Europe. The roads, some of the worst in the European Union, were lined with never-ending signs warning of deer, of which I saw not a single one, leaping onto the tarmac.

The fine Ottoman city of Pécs offered some respite from the road, and I was glad to experience the idiosyncrasies of the Hungarian hinterland before driving on an empty highway to Budapest, two hours to the north. The joys of the irresistible Hungarian language and chunky forint coins, the national currency, can be found in metropolitan Buda and Pest. But provincial Hungary offered an unexpected treat when I passed a man mowing his front lawn in his swimming trunks.

I didn't really love Budapest when I first visited on a solo trip in 2005. Maybe I was too young, possibly Budapest was too old. But I knew I was going to like Peterjon Cresswell when we met in Buda. Peterjon is more punk and indie. I'm more metal and rock. We met in a prog rock bar with Genesis, Yes and Jethro Tull paraphernalia on the walls and epic noodling distracting the ears. This didn't really match either of our tastes, making it easier to focus on our mutual interests of football and travel.

Peterjon knew a lot about European football and Hungary. 'I realised from the earliest age that the only two things that were ever going to save me in this life would be music and football.' The 1970 World Cup was his punk rock. 'It just picked me up and threw me against the wall and said, "Look, this is just totally amazing". It was incredibly exotic to realise that there was more to life than Gillingham against Plymouth on a rainy Saturday afternoon.'

Peterjon studied languages alongside European football and, during his student days, watched Igor Belanov, Oleksandr Zavarov and Oleh Blokhin play for Dynamo Kiev and a Racing Club side with the sparkling talents of Enzo Francescoli and Pierre Littbarski. 'I found the international experience far more fascinating, the spotted ball, the klaxons, but can totally appreciate the guy who goes to see Rochdale every Saturday.' It seemed natural that Peterjon would write *The Rough Guide to European Football* with Simon Evans in the early 1990s, a pioneering book that included the main clubs and cities in about twenty-five countries.

His voice was still lifted by the heady experiences. 'In those days press passes were dead easy. You could be anyone. I went to the San Siro. Naples was amazing, Marseille was fantastic, Seville was great.' It was my travels without the crazy timeline but with a similarly tight budget. 'I could survive on a bread roll so I had money to spend in bars', said Peterjon. He travelled mainly by train with a secret pocket sewn into the calf of his jeans to hide credit cards and banknotes. 'Taking my notepads would have been literally over my dead body.' Peterjon had had to complete two runs from Amsterdam to transport his precious notes home.

I would only require four visas for this trip to fifty-five footballing lands: Russia (who asked for my university's telephone number, forcing me to resist the temptation to insert the number of my favourite Durham curry house), Belarus (who required me to have pre-paid accommodation), Azerbaijan and Turkey. The latter two were easily completed online. Peterjon had been caught up in the sort of visa trouble I had fortunately averted. He wanted to travel from Greece to Bulgaria and then fly from Sofia to Budapest. And you needed a visa to visit Bulgaria in the 1990s.

'I was in Salonica, which is a really amazing city but totally Balkan', said Peterjon. 'The Bulgarian embassy, instead of being in the diplomatic quarter in this gorgeous, ornate villa with greenery and a gravel drive up to the door, was a hut with a real big trail of piss leading from down to the pavement.' The Bulgarian official threw Peterjon's passport back at him and said, 'Type out your visa requirement and we'll let you know in six months. Your country has put our country on a blacklist.' Peterjon asked the British consulate for their help. 'Good God, are they still doing this? Damn Bulgars. Do you play cricket, Cresswell?' said the British official. 'It was like something out of the 1930s. He wrote this rude letter and, of course, I got into Bulgaria, but it still felt very old school.'

Peterjon had some great stories. The evening went on for a long time. I got the feeling that quite a lot of Peterjon's evenings went on for quite a long time. My closest league ground is Millwall. And Peterjon used to watch Ferencváros, Hungary's leading club side. I knew the connection. Ferencváros and Millwall had played each other in the 2004–05 UEFA Cup. Peterjon called Millwall after the draw was made and nabbed some work as translator. 'We're at the New Den talking about gate money. There was this big Ferencváros bouncer, a classic Eastern European with tattoos who the Millwall officials called "Mr Muscles", with a briefcase full of money. He put it on the table whilst they're all negotiating, opened the briefcase and at the same time someone opened the window. It was a really windy day and these dollars were flying around. It was phenomenal.' It sounded like a scene out of *Lock, Stock and Two Smoking Barrels*.

Peterjon went to both legs, supporting Ferencváros whilst working for Millwall. The Hungarians had booked a hotel near Loftus Road, some distance from the New Den, and were whingeing to Peterjon about the traffic and the food. 'I was in a limousine with Theo Paphitis – the former Millwall owner and *Dragons' Den* panellist – a really good guy. I said, "The Hungarians are moaning like crazy." Paphitis immediately picked up on this potential weakness and said, "Listen to him. We've got an advantage here. Tell us all."'

Peterjon sat with Millwall officials during the first leg in London and said, 'This is a goal' when Ferencváros midfielder Lipcsei lined up a free kick. 'I had seen millions of Lipcsei free kicks before. And, of course, it went straight in. They all looked at me in my Millwall club tie.' Ferencváros won the tie 4–2 on aggregate and there was inevitable trouble in Budapest between rival fans.

Peterjon recommended that I visit the '6–3 bar', which commemorated Hungary's famous 1953 victory against England with an annual showing of the match. 'They think I'm American there, I just go along with it.' I popped along. It was a barren wooden affair, once owned by Nándor Hidegkuti, the forward from that legendary side, with black and white photos, cheap beer and bread and dripping that may have been there since the Puskás era. An immense mural of the match also overlooked a car park behind the synagogue. This was the high point of Hungarian football. 'The country is now happy if Zoltán Gera plays at Fulham or West Brom or one of their players scores a few goals in the Bundesliga', said Peterjon. There was an immense disconnect between Hungary's rich footballing past and messy present. And this was epitomised in Felcsút, the controversial host of my Hungarian match against Honvéd.

Felcsút is a nothing place twenty-five miles west of the capital. But it was the childhood home of Viktor Orbán, the recently re-elected football-loving president. Orbán's government had embarked on an ambitious programme of stadium building with money that many thought would be better spent on schools and hospitals. Peterjon believed that the national team was only going to be improved by developing academies and grassroots football, not by building white elephant stadiums. Top division Haladás were built a new stadium and, rather like Darlington and the infamous Reynolds Arena, they couldn't afford the maintenance when it opened in 2017. Hungarian clubs received very little income from television, advertising or transfers.

The remarkable Pancho Aréna in Felcsút was one of the results of the stadium frenzy. It was home to Puskás Akadémia, the club founded in 2007 and controversially named after Hungary's greatest ever player. The 3,800 capacity is twice the town's population. The Pancho Aréna, with its pointy slate roof, looked like a cross between a Shinto shrine and Center Parcs. The detail was incredible. Modernist grey drainpipes were seamlessly integrated on the outside, a web of wood-lined roof girders spectacular from the inside. I felt like I was watching a summer concert in a forest clearing.

I was desperate to take my camera into this beautifully designed stadium and, after considerable advance negotiation, procured a press pass. I took unwelcomed photographs of Orbán's parking space before security ushered me into the media centre. I always thought these places would be a hive of experts discussing football, formations and predictions. But they often seemed full of people who looked like they would rather be at home. László, who wore a three lions England shirt and was collecting possession statistics for a betting company, was a rare exception. He explained that Orbán, a regular at Puskás, was more likely to be at Videoton, his favourite club and title challengers. László warned me not to take any photographs of Orbán should he turn up. Journalists had been thrown out of the Pancho Aréna for taking surreptitious shots of the premier. This was not the time for my journey to get political.

Puskás played a hard running 5-2-3 and opened the scoring from a corner. Centre back Hegedűs rose higher than his marker, headed into the ground and pleasingly over a Honvéd player on the line. There was a murmur from the home fans. Or at least those sitting in the home areas. There was no sign of Orbán.

Honvéd were reliant on mostly awful set pieces and slow build-up play. Their loud and proud fans waved flags that clearly demonstrated they felt the Puskás name had been stolen from their club, where Ferenc played his football in Hungary. They chanted 'cocksucker' – László laughed as he translated – at a corner taker and were promptly warned for abusive language by the PA system. The Honvéd fans ended the first half with a song about Puskás, titled 'You Can't Buy a Legend'.

The wooden girders looked like sweet honeycomb in the evening sun, the soft colours reminding me of the pink-hued Republican Stadium in Yerevan. It was, like my first Armenian fixture, a beautiful setting for a fairly crude match. Puskás sat back in the second half and nearly scored a second on the break. But Honvéd squeezed an equaliser when the Brazilian nomad Danilo headed in at the far post to make it 1–1. Danilo – who had played in Switzerland, Ukraine, Russia, Kazakhstan, Thailand and the United Arab Emirates since an earlier spell at Honvéd – celebrated in front of ecstatic travelling fans, who jumped up and down in their carefully slanted concrete corner.

It had been a strange experience, but one I would love to repeat for an evening game, when I imagined the stadium would be even more ethereal, like lanterns strung around a wooded glade. I drove along a bumpy gravel track outside the Pancho Aréna onto a sleepy side road. A car rounded the bend at high speed and swerved onto the other side to avoid me and an untimely crash. Football traffic was not common in Felcsút.

Puskás Akadémia finished in sixth, their highest ever position. Honvéd were fourth and qualified for the Europa League. Orbán rounded off a good personal season when Videoton won the title.

Best stadiums

I like things to be different. I understand how contemporary football arenas need to cater for modern football fans. But it doesn't necessarily make them interesting. I picked my favourite stadiums for an article in *Gib Footie* magazine and cheekily included Craven Cottage. But, club bias aside, these were the five stadiums, in no particular order, I enjoyed for being old and quirky or new and cleverly designed.

My first selection is the Oval, the historic home of Glentoran in Northern Ireland, a wonderfully old-school ensemble with its wooden seats, glass murals and dilapidated terracing. There won't be many grounds like this soon. My second is the Hibernians Stadium in Malta for the stunning panorama of Valletta harbour. The view from the Victoria Stadium in Gibraltar was certainly unique – the Rock to the right, the airport to the left – but an artificial pitch was circled by a running track, two things that I am never enamoured to see at a football stadium.

Fifteen of my top-division fixtures were played on artificial pitches, including three at the Victoria Stadium and two in Andorra. But at least all matches are played on synthetic grass in these nations. Juraj, marketing manager at Žilina, one of only two Slovakian clubs with an artificial pitch, admitted his club had an advantage. 'When you train every day on this pitch, you can play faster and improve your skills.' I felt a synthetic surface made matches more defensive and less entertaining. Goalkeeper Kostyukevich's goal in Belarus would certainly not have bounced in without the aid of skiddy turf.

Vitebsk in Belarus was one of the Soviet-era stadiums where views were marred by a wide athletics track. But it wasn't the most dilapidated. Kerkyra's stadium, called 'the worst in the Super League', wobbled in the almighty storm, and Greek football reporters will be glad that they were relegated in April 2018. The run-down Mika Stadium in Armenia was a sad symbol of neglect, whilst the clock at the timeless Makario, formerly the main sports venue in Cyprus, remains stuck firmly at 6.27.

My third and fourth choices are in Bucharest and Porto, both stadiums at their most atmospheric during evening matches. The National Arena in Romania was beautifully lit, with astounding views and a booming sound system. Its German architects were also responsible for three stadiums at the 2014 World Cup: Brasilia, Manaus and Belo Horizonte, where hosts Brazil crashed out 7–1 to eventual winners Germany in the semi-final. The Estádio do Dragão is another powerful stadium, where the acoustics were so good I could hear separate chants from three sets of fans. Porto's supporters celebrated their victory against Sporting with a nerve-tingling display of mobile phone lights.

The most extraordinary arena was in eastern Georgia, where the Kvareli football pitch is entirely enclosed by an eighteenth-century fortress. But I can't include a stadium where I didn't see a match so my final choice is my most recent. The Pancho Aréna in Hungary is an architectural masterpiece, unorthodox, challenging yet aesthetically pleasing. Morally, it's perhaps more dubious given it was built in President Orbán's back garden. But it gives groundhoppers and design students a brilliant reason to visit Felcsút. It is worth coming to Hungary just to see it.

THE FINAL COUNTDOWN

53 Croatia

Croatia is a land of Adriatic islands and dreamy vistas in many people's minds. And these were my own memories from a family holiday in 1984, when Yugoslavia, a country that no longer exists, became the first I visited outside my own. But it was the grittier coastal city of Pula, part of the Roman empire from the first century BC, that had long been lodged in my schedule for the conveniently midweek Istrian derby between Istra 1961 and champions Rijeka. It transpired that this would actually be the second of two matches I would watch in Croatia.

My drive from Budapest to Pula took me through the unexciting Croatian capital of Zagreb, where Lokomotiva Zagreb were conveniently playing against Slaven Belupo. I parked in a prime parking spot outside my Zagreb apartment and met with Ivan, the giant Lokomotiva PR man, at the crumbling Kranjčevićeva Stadium. He was enormous, several inches taller than me. It was the first time on this trip I had been dwarfed.

'The story of Croatian football is poor infrastructure and good players', said Ivan, who liked a soundbite and a statistic. Lokomotiva shared the Kranjčevićeva, just south of Zagreb's centre, with Rudeš, another top-division club, and now third-tier NK Zagreb, the fallen 2002 champions. 'Our stadium is like a training camp', lamented Ivan. He was proud to talk about high-calibre players – Milan Badelj (Fiorentina), Marcelo Brozović (Inter), Andrej Kramarić (Hoffenheim), Marko Pjaca (Juventus, on loan to Schalke) and Šime Vrsaljko (Atlético Madrid) – who had played for Lokomotiva and the Croatian national team. Ivan explained that around 90 per cent of Croatian clubs' income is from selling three or four players every season.

Lokomotiva were often criticised in the Croatian press for being the 'farm club' or 'younger sister' of Dinamo Zagreb. Ivan was quick to defend, explaining that when Lokomotiva were in the lower leagues Dinamo would send many of their young players to Lokomotiva on loan. Lokomotiva were promoted to the First League in 2009 and became formally separated from Dinamo, although they continued to benefit from Dinamo loans. Lokomotiva had, after twenty-seven consecutive failed attempts, finally beaten Dinamo in the league with a 4–1 away win in March 2018. It was a shock to the media, who claimed that Lokomotiva did not try against Dinamo. Ivan said that the criticism was unfair as other clubs also had a bad record against Dinamo, champions for eleven years in a row until Rijeka's title in 2017.

Ivan introduced me to a wonderful Croatian phrase. 'Football is the most important not so important thing in life.' His most memorable match – Croatia's 3–2 victory at Wembley in 2007 – was a painful one for England fans and Steve McClaren. Croatia had already qualified for Euro 2008, 'but the players were really hyped because the English media said, "England will win, they are just small Croatia."'

Ivan enthusiastically recalled the near 10,000-strong Croatian support who swarmed around central London before the match and sang with the celebrating players long after England fans had dispersed into the lashing rain. Ivan's hands were trembling as he spoke, and I can only imagine what they were like when Croatia reached the World Cup final later that summer.

The rocky Lokomotiva anthem reminded me I was back in the Balkans. I approached an ageing Albanian vendor selling Zoocorn – popcorn in cartons pictured with cats, dogs, Nemo fish and ducks – and bought one of the better football snacks I had seen in recent months. The crowd of around 400 for this match against fellow mid-table side Slaven Belupo was pitiful for top-division football in a European capital. Ivan said Lokomotiva would attract bigger crowds if they played at their base in the south of Zagreb, not at the dilapidated Kranjčevićeva. But most Croatians associated Lokomotiva with their lack of fans. And those who did arrive were quite late. A man in a Ramones T-shirt who sat behind me was one of a number who piled in after the match had started.

The late arrivals did not miss much. I wasn't expecting a classic – there had been three or fewer goals in every away game Slaven had played this season – but there was a good story to come from it. Tomislav Ivković, the current Slaven and former Lokomotiva coach, was reportedly the only goalkeeper to have saved two Diego Maradona penalties in one year: for Sporting against Napoli in the UEFA Cup and for Yugoslavia against Argentina in the quarter-final of the 1990 World Cup.

'Sunday league football', said Ivan, to the man in the Ramones shirt. It was not that bad, especially when I was fresh from Felcsút. Ivan was watching with his girlfriend, the sister of the Slaven left back Goda.

'He's one of the great hopes of Croatian football, write that down', he said, looking at my notepad scribbles. 'You can send him to Chelsea', he added, as Goda gave the ball away.

I was content to be watching a not particularly diverting match surrounded by friendly youngsters. And then it all happened. Lokomotiva's captain Šunjić, on loan from Dinamo, slotted the ball past the Slaven goalkeeper. 'Do the Locomotion' by Kylie Minogue was played in celebration. It was 2–0 to Lokomotiva moments later when Krstanović, the bulky veteran of numerous Croatian league campaigns, swept in at the near post. Ivan's expectations were raised as Ivanovski, Slaven's chunky Macedonian striker, looped in a header from a left-wing Goda cross to make it 2–1. 'Assist for Goda!' he said. No Kylie though. And it was 2–2 at half-time when Ivanovski headed in a free kick. I had seen four goals in eleven minutes.

Ivan spotted a familiar figure in the padded VIP seats, looking very much the faded rock star with his longish dark locks and a beige jacket. 'Hey, that's Boško Balaban, the worst player in the history of the Premier League.' I showed security my crumpled press pass and tried to look as professional as one can when holding a carton of cartoon popcorn. 'Nice project, which countries left?' Boško asked. Balaban, who played thirty-five times for Croatia, did not start a single Premiership match in two seasons after joining Aston Villa for a hefty £5.8 million in 2001. 'I was very young, it was good.' He could hardly say anything else. I asked him what he thought of the match. 'The pitch, it's awful.' It wasn't very good. Boško was working as a football agent, and predicted more goals.

The frantic start to the second half suggested Balaban's forecast would come true. Lokomotiva regained the lead through midfielder

Burić, before striker Radonjić volleyed in a fourth and half-volleyed another to make it 5–2. Kylie was aired for the fifth and final time. It had been an unexpectedly distracting match and I left with a spring in my stride. I decided to walk several miles across Zagreb to check out a famed punk bar, recommended by Peterjon in Hungary, only to find the music was Sunday reggae. I drank one beer and left.

I drove to Pula the following day. My grey car was decorated with sticky yellow flowers, as I finally realised why the opportune parking space outside my apartment had been vacant. A policeman stopped me for a routine check, took one look at my windscreen and suggested I cleaned a slightly bigger window in the petals. My car was looking battered, and so was Pula: by war, the sun and the sea. But it was a friendly place and, like Maribor, the perfect football town, with one special sight, the majestic Roman arena. I circled the inside twice and the outside once. I had seen quite a few Roman remains, in Plovdiv, Sicily and Spain, and this was the very finest.

Istra 1961 is a clunky moniker that in 2007 became the club's fifth name in as many years following previous incarnations as Istra, Istra 1856, Pula Staro Češko and Pula. I really wanted to buy an offbeat Istra shirt, especially as the club's vivid yellow and green logo incorporates a football ringed by the Roman arena, but Pula shops reflect visitors' preference for the famous red and white checks of the Croatian national team. I started horse-trading for a fake children's kit for my younger niece: 200 kuna, 150. 'I know who you are', said the salesman. He had read the article about my travels in *24sata*, Croatia's best-selling tabloid. The price came down to 100, and I bought a Croatia shirt with Mandžukić on the back. My niece Clara didn't wear it much after the World Cup.

The shirt salesman was a Dinamo fan and had a thought. 'You know, England players are over-rated.' I nodded with agreement. 'There has only ever been one good England player.' England have yet to find a Luka Modrić or Robert Prosinečki, but only one good player? Ever? 'Wayne Rooney.' The player who struggled to recapture early tournament highs after a storming match against, coincidentally, Croatia at Euro 2004. 'Maybe I'll get in your book', said the salesman, as I walked out of the shop.

The Aldo Drosina Stadium looked glorious in the evening sun. A purple mist floated on the hilly horizon. I grabbed a cheap beer from the bar built into the north stand and spoke to a group of seasoned Istra fans. Rade said that he and his friends had met at the stadium twenty years ago and that tradition was the only thing that kept them attending. It certainly wasn't Istra's fine form or prospects: the club had lost their last three matches, were in serious financial trouble and their players had not been paid for six months. 'They are volunteers, player volunteers in the top division in Croatia', said Rade. The Croatian media had reported that Dinamo Zagreb players had collected money to give to their colleagues at Istra for the Christmas holiday season.

Rade described, tongue firmly in cheek, Michael Glover, Istra's absent American owner, as the best businessman in the world. Glover had purchased the club in 2015, promised investment and disappeared without delivering on his promises. Rade asked me if I knew someone who might be interested in buying Istra. 'I have 15 euros. Is that enough?' Rade laughed. A blackened sense of humour was needed when your club had changed twenty-five players in the middle of the season. 'Where is a good place to sit?' I asked. 'Nowhere', said Rade.

Istra's hardcore fans call themselves 'demoni' after Jure Grando, a seventeenth-century resident of the Istrian town of Kringa, who died in 1656 due to illness but, according to legend, returned from the grave at night as a vampire until his decapitation in 1672. Three demoni flags flew in the sky above a banner that questioned 'Club vision?' Several hundred demoni jumped up and down to a drumbeat. They didn't look overly demonic but, according to the fan next to me, 'every team that has a supporters' group have had problems with the police'. I showed my driving licence when I bought my ticket, a requisite to prove I was not banned. And there was concern about my camera. Fortunately Pula is friendly towards visitors, who are a mainstay of the local economy. I played the tourist card and the bulky policeman waved me through.

Istra's 'player volunteers' battled hard in the first half but champions Rijeka's quality decided the match when substitute Kvržić scrambled home a second-half rebound. Three fans near me immediately walked out. There was not much hope of a comeback. Rade and his friends looked resigned but politely wished me well before disappearing into the darkness. I liked the salty charm of Pula and, although it seemed unlikely, hoped that the future of its club was as bright as their yellow and green shirts.

Istra finished second from bottom and escaped relegation after winning a play-off. Rijeka were second behind Dinamo Zagreb. Lokomotiva and Slaven Belupo were mid-table in fifth and sixth.

54 Bosnia-Herzegovina

I couldn't face another crushing bus journey. After my enjoyable circuit around Slovenia, Hungary and Croatia, I flew to Sarajevo and took a short bus ride to Zenica, the fourth largest city in Bosnia-Herzegovina. Zenica was not as badly affected by the Bosnian war as Sarajevo or Mostar. Čelik, the local club named after the city's steel industry, were beneficiaries, and won three successive titles in the mid-1990s. The steelworks, which employed over 20,000 people in 1991, had declined to less than a tenth of that number. And the team had also failed to recapture its heyday. Čelik were eleventh in the twelve-team Premier League and desperate for a win against eighth-placed Borac Banja Luka to try to avoid their first relegation since Bosnian independence in 1992.

I tried to find some 'convicts'. The Čelik ultras are called Robijaši, a reference to Zenica's famous prison, the largest and most notorious in the former Yugoslavia, which opened in 1886 when Bosnia was part of the Austro-Hungarian empire. I ambled around in the pleasant sunshine, bought a scarf and enjoyed being a foreigner in a city that doesn't see many tourists. Most overseas visitors come to Zenica to watch international football. Bosnia-Herzegovina beat Greece in Bilino Polje, Čelik's much-loved 'lucky' stadium, on their way to their first World Cup finals appearance in 2014.

I spotted some distinctive red and black T-shirts piled up outside a bar called Club 072. The Robijaši were celebrating their thirtieth anniversary with special shirts that looked like something from a *Beano* comic. The ultras gave me a T-shirt. 'Everyone loves Čelik in Zenica', said Kenan, a twenty-seven-year-old convict who had been shot in a fight between ultra groups. 'Every other club in Bosnia is forbidden here. We don't want other ultra groups representing themselves.' Kenan said most ultras were well protected, but fans from Sarajevo, only fifty miles to the south, sometimes got drunk and walked around Zenica. 'They think they've come to Disneyland and then they're going to go to hospital. Imagine a Liverpool fan going to Manchester five hours before the match. They would bash him up.' I wasn't sure about this.

Bosnia is a complex place, politically a mess, with three presidents and more than 180 ministers representing a little under four million ethnic Bosniaks, Croats and Serbs. Slovenia felt very European Union. Bosnia felt anarchic. The Robijaši had a rule that every Čelik match must be attended, if only by one fan, but Kenan explained how difficult it was to travel away. Bosnian bus agencies have strong political links that needed to be exploited to guarantee transport. Promises were often broken and bus drivers went missing on matchday. Kenan recalled a match in Zvornik, near the Serbian border in eastern Bosnia, when organised transport was banned; the police had thought that hundreds of Čelik fans would travel, and were surprised when only ten spilled out of a minivan.

Kenan was good company. He mixed passion and politics with humour and compassion. 'I am at my happiest when we have a ninety-minute song at an away match. I see one of my friends and his mouth is dry and his eyes are popping out.' Čelik lost 7–2 at Široki Brijeg three seasons ago after taking the lead. 'We kept singing until 7–2 and then we decided everyone would lie down on the ground like we were sunbathing because our players were acting like that.'

Kenan talked about their deliberately provocative songs that attacked Serbs, Croats and Bosniaks alike. He was a Muslim, but would insult fellow Muslims if it also irritated FK Sarajevo fans. Čelik Zenica was the only religion that mattered to the Robijaši. Ultra groups, almost by definition, have a hard exterior – but they care about their own. The Robijaši sing about their late friend 'Mirsad Fiesta' who drove to every away match in his Ford until he died from leukaemia. 'The day started with you, the day ended with you. We sing eternally, I love eternally, my love will be reserved for you. Mirsad Fiesta will ride again. He will never stop.' The Robijaši had a Ford Fiesta logo on one of their banners. I could feel Kenan's emotion as our conversation stuttered.

Robijaši kept popping into the bar to buy anniversary T-shirts in a strangely covert way. The ultras had a fractious relationship with the club management and attendances fluctuated. Čelik had a new Turkish investor, Olgun Aydın Peker, and results had improved, with eleven points from their last five matches. Olgun had made admission free, and the main stand was nearly full as the teams lined up to local rock music. The crowd of around 8,000 was my largest since St Gallen, seven countries earlier. Kick-off was delayed after Robijaši covered the Borac goal with toilet paper stolen from their cells. 'Čelik' chants sounded, and red, white and black flags, strangely reminiscent of Iraq flags, were waved in the south stand.

Visitors Borac controlled possession but Čelik fashioned a good chance when holding midfielder Okoli, a John Obi Mikel clone on loan from Bursaspor, headed over from five yards, the Robijaši celebrating the near goal with more streamers over the Borac goal. The referee motioned that Borac's custodian Vukliš should take the resultant goal kick with greater urgency. The goalkeeper remonstrated that he had a handful of streamers. There was more unlikely entertainment when a Borac defender wildly miskicked and dust flew into the air.

Čelik midfielder Šišić then tried an audacious Beckham-style lob from just inside the Borac half. Vukliš arched his back and tipped over. 'It's not the first time he's scored from way out', said Munib, the fan next to me. 'Did you come all this way from England just to see this game?' he asked. I hadn't, but it was good. I loved a tense match.

The second half started with a pretty pink bloom of smoke from the Robijaši, beautifully illuminated by the low sun setting behind the west stand. And then disaster struck. A Borac striker hit a low bobbler that Dujković should turn around for a corner. Instead, the Čelik goalkeeper parried into the path of Kunić, who duly converted. Borac led 1–0, and Čelik's survival was hanging by a thread.

There was a resigned feel amongst the Čelik crowd. But Čelik midfielder Anđušić, always the most likely creator, drove in a cracking left-wing cross for Nikolić to head into the near corner. It was 1–1 and the crowd were visibly lifted. But football is, and this match was, cruel. Delight was eroded by despair when, fifty-five seconds later, according to the highly accurate scoreboard – that, coincidentally, also denoted the number of UEFA nations I would visit – Salčinović was sent off for a loose elbow. The Čelik midfielder protested while his victim was stretchered off and immediately replaced.

Čelik now needed to win with ten men. 'Čelik, Čelik', chanted the crowd. A Borac defender was booked for a crude and calculated challenge on Anđušić, who limped on, Čelik having used all three substitutes. The atmosphere was vital. Borac were pressured into mistakes as the Čelik midfield took it in turns to hustle. A right-wing cross fell through the exit sign at the back of the north stand. Munib held his head in his hands as a man scampered to retrieve the ball. He muttered the words to the Čelik songs in hope. Borac missed several good chances to score a second.

Čelik were breaking quickly with their nine and a half men. Nikolić couldn't quite toe in a right-wing cross. There were seconds left. The battered Anđušić was fouled on the edge of the area. Čelik, the on-loan Dutch substitute who shared his name with his club, had the final chance to seal the match and headline puns. He smashed the free kick into the north stand. Čelik players collapsed on the floor. They had given everything in a thrilling encounter. But it was all over. Thirteen crows perched on the stadium roof like a haunting omen. Relegation was a near certainty after this 1–1 draw.

After the match, I travelled back to Sarajevo, nicknamed 'the European Jerusalem' for its centuries-old multiculturality. The Bosnian capital was one of my favourite cities in the Balkans, with a relaxed ambience, compact Ottoman centre and a shot of the bizarre. I strolled down the bullet-pocked and graffiti-strewn bobsleigh run from the 1984 Winter Olympics, now an abandoned symbol of tragic recent history on Trebević, a mountain that saw heavy fighting during the war. The now reconstructed Zetra Olympic Hall, where Torvill and

Dean won their famous figure-skating gold medal, was shelled, and its original wooden seats had been used as coffin boards. The nearby concrete bowl of the Koševo Stadium, where the Olympic opening ceremony was held, was the rented home of FK Sarajevo.

FK Sarajevo were not welcoming. I arrived for the match against Široki Brijeg on my own, a throwback to early matches when clubs ignored my messages. A drunk wailed 'Sarajevo' outside the locked gates of the east stand. I rounded the stadium and photographed graffiti by the ultras who, again, were boycotting matches. The atmosphere outside was listless. I bought nuts and cartons of drink from elderly vendors, stationed in the same spots for decades, now turning up out of routine to make a few Bosnian marks.

The Koševo Stadium, built into the side of a hill with gently sloping stands, was in a typically picturesque Sarajevo setting. This was my penultimate match and reminded me of my very first one at the Mikheil Meskhi Stadium in Tbilisi. The Koševo was a similarly vast arena with rows of empty seats, this time all green, rather than the multicoloured geometric patterns I had seen in Georgia. Inside the stadium, fans took care to wipe the filthy seats with paper. I was passed betting sheets with hundreds of international matches listed. True Bosnian hospitality that covered their twin loves: gambling and keeping their trousers clean.

I watched a solid 2–0 FK Sarajevo win with a group of holidaying South London boys wearing shorts and beards. We went for a beer after the match at an adjacent bar. 'No away fans and no one goes for a drink after the match.' This certainly wasn't Crystal Palace. The only fans clad in Sarajevo red were Kemal and Sunil, boycotting ultras who had watched the match on television in the bar. I asked what they didn't like about the club management. 'Everything.' They were blamed for financial mismanagement, the solitary title since 2007 and eight managerial changes since 2015. Nor did FK Sarajevo fans seem that well-disposed to Vincent Tan, who controversially changed Cardiff City's colours from blue to red and who has a financial interest in the club. 'If Vincent Tan changes our colours someone will shoot him, we have snipers', said my FK Sarajevo-supporting hotel owner.

There were no Široki fans at the match. 'They fear us', said Kemal. Vedran Puljić, an FK Sarajevo ultra, was killed in 2009 after a fight with home fans in Široki. The death caused controversy after newspapers reported that a local Široki man had shot Puljić. 'I was there', said Kemal. 'He was killed by a policeman with a Croatian passport who has gone to Croatia to escape judgement. He shot him because we are from Sarajevo. Our goalkeeper heard something and went from the stadium to help Vedran but it was too late.' Kemal showed me a photograph of a policeman with a gun and Vedran on the floor. It was a harrowing reminder that conflict was not over in Bosnia.

The FK Sarajevo team bus drove past. The South London boys and I gave them a round of applause to general bemusement from the players. It must be strange playing in empty stadiums; but Bosnian football seemed to be evolving as slowly as the country.

FK Sarajevo and Široki finished third and fourth and qualified for Europe. Čelik finished eleventh and would have been relegated but, in a turn of events quite typical in Bosnia, ninth-placed Borac were relegated in their place for financial irregularities.

55 Montenegro

My last country was an appropriate one. I had never visited Montenegro before, and the Montenegrin First League was ranked one of the
lowest in Europe. This was a journey of new experiences, especially
unheralded football teams and competitions. Montenegro also promised balmy weather. Miloš, a local journalist who had followed my
story since it appeared on the Serbian website Mondo the previous
October, said there was a '99 per cent chance of good weather at the
end of April', a level of confidence that satisfied a statistician like me.
And, most importantly, Montenegro offered a direct route home, with
an Easyjet flight from coastal Tivat, my last of a hectic year.

I heard a story in Bosnia. The president of Montenegro visited
China and the Chinese president asked, 'Where is Montenegro?' 'In
Europe.' The Chinese president needed more clues. 'Near Bosnia and
Serbia', said the Montenegrin leader. 'In the Balkans' seemed to seal it.
'How big is Montenegro?' asked the Chinese president. 'About 500,000
people.' 'The second time you visit China you can bring your people

with you.' This was probably a rogue Balkan tale. But there was no denying I had chosen a diminutive country as my last.

I took the six-hour bus from Mostar, famous for its reconstructed bridge, in Bosnia, to Kotor on the stunning Montenegrin coastline. We drove up hills, through forests and past streams filled with lily pads. Sheep blocked the road and lonely cattle grazed in virtually uninhabited landscapes. The bus got stuck in Trebinje, the last major Bosnian town before Montenegro. The bus company had sold more tickets than there were seats and everyone had turned up. Four Chinese tourists were bemused that the company would not give them a full refund and staged a protest. A heated hour was spent resolving who got the remaining seats and negotiating the safe passage of the Chinese to Kotor in a taxi. I was rather glad that this would be my last journey by public transport.

A dozen friends from home joined me in Kotor, a pretty medieval town with peaceful stone courtyards full of sleepy cats, their naps disrupted only when cruise passengers charged through. We took taxis for my final leg of some fifty miles on twisty, scenic roads to Podgorica, the capital set on a flat plain in this mountainous country. Miloš, the journalist, was bemused why I had chosen Kom against Mladost rather than the reigning champions Budućnost's match in the central Podgorica City Stadium. But Sutjeska, a football club from the second city of Nikšić, had already won the title. They were the fourth different winner in the last four seasons, and Budućnost were safe in the European spots. Their match was a dead rubber. And I liked my football to mean something. Kom were battling against relegation, whilst Mladost were pushing for the Europa League.

I nevertheless visited Budućnost with Nikola, their club secretary, bundling into the changing rooms and having my photograph taken with the team before they played out a goalless draw. Nikola presented me with a natty Budućnost shirt with 'Montenegro' and the number 55 on the back. Miloš also gave me two Montenegro national team shirts with 'Football Nations' above the number 55. They were great mementos, but I still had to watch my final match in Zlatica, an unglamorous northern suburb of Podgorica that houses people from other parts of Montenegro when they move to the capital.

I thought about my road to Podgorica. My challenge had not been as tricky as it could have been. The travel had been predictably fast, but I had had time to breathe between sprints. And fortune seemed to have been on my side several times: I only made my Faroes flight by minutes, my Scottish visit might have been rescheduled owing to runway snow, and I managed to gain entry to that torrid Albanian match, played, quite rightfully, behind closed doors. My hatred of cold weather helped. I hid around the Mediterranean over the winter months and was soaked in Spain and Portugal when the same storm postponed matches further north.

It was a blazing afternoon for my last fixture. Only my Alashkert and Ararat matches in Armenia had been hotter. I had travelled in a climatic circle, from summer heat in the ex-Soviet states, through the chill of Denmark and Poland and back to the balmy Balkans. My actual movements were more of a contorted spiral, completing the outer reaches of European football before finishing nearer the geographic heart.

Only five of my friends stuck it out for the entire match. There was no shade in the only stand, nor were there drinks on sale. A Kom official helpfully explained that no drinks were permitted in the stadium, to prevent people from throwing precious liquid on the pitch.

It was quite appropriate for me to encounter some ridiculous football bureaucracy before my last game. At least my camera made it in. I photographed the first half from a tiny triangle of shade by the corner flag. Mladost, the away side from Podgorica, seemed more confident; maybe it was having names plastered on the back of their red shirts. Kom only had numbers. There were twenty-one Montenegrins in the starting line-ups, every surname bar one ending in 'ić', giving the team announcements a pleasingly rhythmic feel.

The contest was only eight minutes old when Mladost midfielder Petrović muscled past some weak Kom defending and poked the ball in. I was relieved that my last match would not be goalless. Kom, low-budget and reliant on last season's Second League-winning squad, were short on goals. The most entertaining passage of play was when Kom right back Milić made a great tackle, fell and headed the ball away from his stricken position on the pitch. Milić then ran the length of the right wing before eventually receiving treatment. There was applause at this commitment from the temporary stand, where overheated locals were downing water straight from hosepipes.

The setting was quite beautiful for my final match. A paraglider floated serenely over lumpy mountains bisected by a blue sky dotted with fluffy white clouds. Goals in other First League matches were announced through the speaker behind me during the match. I jumped, but not too often. Montenegrin matches are renowned for being low scoring as few coaches played open, attacking football. Miloš explained that teams have a results-orientated philosophy, and are concerned only with trying to qualify for Europe to earn money from which they can survive for the next couple of seasons. 'Maybe that's why there is no audience', added Miloš, looking at the 250-strong crowd.

The burning sun dipped behind clouds to make my second half in the stands more bearable. There was excitement from several Japanese men around me when Otani, their compatriot, appeared as a substitute. Kom now resorted to long diagonal passes, aiming for Otani on the left and Milić, stationed further up the right wing.

A man in green fatigues and a matching hat, with the look of a delirious Vietnam war veteran, leapt up and down on a half-built structure on the far side. Miloš later introduced me to Savo Barac, the General Director of Kom. 'Ref, please don't do this', shouted Barac as a decision went against Kom. Barac lived every moment. He paced the semi-building like a lion and waved his arms to encourage Popović to shoot when the midfielder delayed in a good position. 'He was like this as a player', said Miloš. 'Everything for the win.'

Mladost missed opportunities to kill the game. 'Play strong with the heart', shouted Barac. Kom were clinging on. It would be a great story if Otani equalised for Kom, a rogue Japanese college player pushing unfashionable Kom closer to safety. But this book is based on reality, not fiction. Otani cut effortlessly onto his right foot in the penalty area, unleashed a cracking shot, but struck it straight at the Mladost goalkeeper, who tipped over. My final match ended 1–0 to Mladost, the twentieth away win in my seventy-nine top division league matches.

'This is football, huh', said Barac after the match. 'I am like English, I never sit down.' Barac told me about his short-term goals to stay in the First League, build a new stadium in Zlatica and produce 'young players who will be a star for the national team'. Kom, who helped develop the skills of the former Real Madrid forward Predrag Mijatović, were a small club. 'Annual budget of Kom is maybe one week's salary for a Premier League player', said Barac. 'Maybe one weekend.' It was not a glamorous finale, but was somehow appropriate.

I will never know whether my travels would have been as enjoyable had I visited Bayern Munich or Juventus. I was certainly glad to have framed my challenge around top-division games, with the exception of FC Vaduz in Liechtenstein, and to have experienced an incredible diversity of football, from household names like Griezmann and Rooney to part-time players who play with the passion of professionals.

I gave the tenth television appearance of my travels for Televizija Crna Gore wearing one of my '55 Football Nations' shirts. I celebrated with a Lebanese meal and Montenegrin rakia in Podgorica. My friends and I returned to spectacular Kotor, where we hired a speedboat. I soaked up the sun and, for the first time on my travels, the sea. I felt refreshed and a little relieved. I flew home still basking in the afterglow of having completed my challenge. The five-degree drizzle was an immediate jolt to my serenity when I returned to London. I couldn't face dragging my bags back from the station, ordered an Uber and tried to get in the driver's door. 'You've been away for too long', said the driver. Perhaps I had.

It was a sticky climax to the season for Kom, who finished eighth, enough to survive in most ten-team leagues, but were relegated after losing a play-off to Second League Lovćen. Mladost finished third, qualified for Europe and changed their name to Titograd: the name of Podgorica during the Yugoslav era.

Europe United

It was a tough task picking my best eleven players from the fifty-five UEFA nations. It's hard to judge a footballer based on ninety minutes, although that has never deterred some fans from voicing their discontent during a player's debut. My dream team would line up in a 4-2-3-1 formation, the most popular across Europe and fielded by nearly half the teams that I watched.

Ufa goalkeeper Belenov would start between the sticks after a solid clean sheet against Russian champions Spartak Moscow. It was a performance that might have looked more impressive than it was after some decidedly iffy goalkeeping in summer matches across Kazakhstan, Russia and Belarus. Norwegian right back Nouri was on fire for Brann Bergen in their 5–0 demolition of Stabæk, attacking with verve and scoring only his second ever league goal. My centre backs are Lindgren of Häcken, the experienced Swede formerly with Ajax, and Hancko, the young Slovakian who defended stoutly for Žilina. And rampaging

440

from left back would be Kirch of Fola Esch, a key player in the biggest thrashing of them all, my 9–0 in Luxembourg.

My defensive midfield duo combines a creator and a water carrier. Ivan Šunjić, the young Lokomotiva player now back with Dinamo Zagreb, looked very much a mini Modrić, scoring and dictating play in a 5–2 win. I expect he will not stay in Croatia for many more years. The Morocco captain El Ahmadi, nicknamed 'the gladiator', drove forward his Feyenoord team against ADO. The midfielder traded the docks of Rotterdam for the port of Jeddah when he joined the Saudi Arabian club Al-Ittihad in July 2018.

The right side of my attacking trident goes to Xhevdet Shabani. The Kosovan charmer showed tremendous skill, scored an awe-inspiring chip and crossed for two Drita goals. Playing centrally in my trio is Griezmann. The Frenchman had a quiet start to his Atlético match against Sevilla, then promptly scored a hat-trick and assisted in another goal. Few players shredded their opponents as effectively as Kozlov, the Russian left-winger at Latvian champions Spartaks Jūrmala, who had a hand in both goals against FC Riga. Kozlov would then move to Belarusian runners-up Shakhtyor Soligorsk in the summer of 2018.

There were several contenders to play the lone striking role. Gnohéré, 'the bison', scored three with his left foot for FCSB in Romania, and Hadji netted four for Fola in Luxembourg. But apart from Vágner Love in Turkey, only Zahovič of Maribor scored a hat-trick in a tight match. And my niece now has his tiny shirt.

My best eleven has a wealth of experience at the back, a mixture of precision and power in central midfield and an attacking quartet that combines direct pace, supreme guile and finishing ability. It did, after all, contribute ten goals during my matches. It does lack a midfield chunk, a Dickson Etuhu, and the nine different nationalities might, like the author, struggle with communication at times. Nevertheless, football is a universal language, and I would expect my dream team to comfortably dispatch most of the teams I saw in top-flight action.

Europe United: Belenov (Ufa); Nouri (Brann Bergen), Lindgren (Häcken), Hancko (Žilina), Kirch (Fola Esch); Šunjić (Lokomotiva Zagreb), El Ahmadi (Feyenoord); Shabani (Drita), Griezmann (Atlético), Kozlov (Spartaks Jūrmala); Zahovič (Maribor)

Watching lots of football

'You can't write a book, you're a statistician', said a colleague who didn't know me very well. Others assumed I would be compiling a coffee-table book of football photographs. I never set out to prove anything, but my life had previously been, perhaps, a touch comfortable. I had even won my office Fantasy Premier League two years in succession (despite not selecting Chelsea players, quite tricky when they were champions in 2017). I had definitely needed a challenge. The more I travelled watching football, the more I felt this was a perfect fit, an adrenalin-fuelled adventure with a fine balance of randomness and structure. I asked Peterjon in Hungary why no one had ever undertaken my mission before. 'It was waiting for you.'

There were still four weeks of the Montenegrin season remaining when I watched Kom slip to defeat against Mladost. I had been helped by finding out in advance about unexpected changes to my plans: the cancellation in Latvia after the Babīte match fixing scandal, the postponements at Jonava in Lithuania and Sabail in Azerbaijan due to opponents' European commitments, and the PAOK match in Greece being played behind closed doors. My route barely strayed from what I anticipated. Lithuania and Latvia were a month later than originally planned, and Luxembourg was squeezed in after San Marino. My matches in Scotland, England and Wales, pencilled in for the summer, were moved to coincide with my Christmas break. Serbia and Hungary, countries bordered by many others, were switched around in my schedule without much difficulty.

I loved the unpredictability of the football. The spectacular fluke from Kostyukevich in Belarus and the almighty lob from Efrem in Cyprus, the see-saw 4–3 matches in Turkey and Kosovo, the 9–0, 8–1 and 7–0 thumpings in Luxembourg, San Marino and Romania, and even my personal 322-minute goal drought in Malta and Italy. The atmospheres varied, from the crackling to the moribund, the crowds from 53,000 to 22. But that reflected the rich tapestry of football, a game that always provoked a reaction whenever I asked anyone anything about it.

I visited a wealth of beautiful and distinctive places, including forty-four UNESCO World Heritage sites across thirty-one countries, but it was harder to motivate myself in cities, such as Ghent and Porto, that I had visited in the years leading up to my challenge. I also found that, as my enthusiasm for cathedrals and old towns waned, the days between matches became increasingly difficult to enjoy. My travel tastes were sharpened. I needed places to have an angle to interest me. I relished unusual sites, like the medieval library in St Gallen, and historic gems, such as the vast Roman amphitheatre in Syracuse and the stunning Mezquita in Córdoba, which were delightfully quiet in February.

I noticed the changes when I revisited cities. The grungy Bucharest nightclub that throbbed in a ruined building in 2010 was being developed into a boutique hotel; the Budapest waterfront sparkled with optimism that had been missing a dozen years before; and Istanbul, an inspirational city, becomes more clogged with cars each time I visit.

I loved the spontaneity. My travels took me to offbeat places that would never be conventional city breaks. I enjoyed the Islamic architecture of Edirne in European Turkey, the deeply forested mountains around Çamlıhemşin in Anatolia and the relaxed vibe of Maribor in Slovenia. It was impossible to over-research everything. Maybe, nearly twenty years on, this was something of a throwback to my backpacking days, when I relied on an out-of-date guidebook and word of mouth. I bumbled into restaurants that were sometimes astounding, on other occasions revolting. I stumbled upon a heavy metal craft beer bar in Plovdiv, my nirvana, and a fantastic Sicilian seafood restaurant, where I couldn't buy a glass of white wine. They only sold wine by the five-euro bottle.

The dark months were hard on the diet. Bad burgers and poor pizza have bred across Europe. There were culinary highlights – the delicious food in San Marino, Andalusian delicacies, majestic Middle Eastern fare in Israel – but a lot of rubbish. I felt sorry for the Hungarian policeman who breathalysed me after a double bacon burger and a kebab. The gorgeous fresh salads of Georgia and Turkey seemed like distant dreams after I had dined on multiple brown meals in Central and Eastern Europe. I was looking forward to not eating alone. Or in restaurants. When some people asked what I had gained from my experiences, they weren't expecting to hear the answer 'about half a stone'.

I certainly gained a greater understanding of how reliant clubs in many countries were on European qualification for income. There was little money from sponsorship or television. UEFA reduced the number of Champions League group places available for teams progressing through the qualifying rounds from ten to six in 2018, making it harder for leading clubs from non-elite leagues, such as Maribor, to compete. 'I think the big clubs would like to play against other big clubs', said Miha in Slovenia. 'But I think the name of the competition is the Champions League, which means you have champions from fifty-four countries competing for that title.'

The big leagues were thriving, and even smaller countries like Sweden, the Netherlands and Switzerland saw healthy attendances. But the future of some looked bleak. 'I fear for the future of European club football east of Vienna', said Peterjon. 'Hungary has a fantastic history and is almost, but not quite, the West. And I don't know how the domestic game in Hungary survives. I'm not sure how it survives in Bulgaria or Romania without some sugar-daddy, egomaniac guy trying to launder money by pouring it into clubs.'

I wondered what would happen when these owners and die-hard fans, mostly of a certain age, disappeared. Future generations may be content watching digital streams of big-name teams on their laptops and phones with little hope of ever watching their virtual heroes live. But perhaps, like vinyl, we may see a renewal of interest in something that was important in the past – a movement of fans wanting to ditch technology for something more vital, something happening in their own country at this very moment. And you can better understand an offside decision at the time it's given. Normally.

There may be hope from the most unlikely of sources. The Nations League, another UEFA brainchild, gives almost every international team a chance of qualifying for the European Championships. It's just possible that an unlikely burst into a major tournament might promote domestic football somewhere. The gap between very rich clubs and the rest may grow in the Champions League. But F91 Dudelange from Luxembourg qualifying for the Europa League group phases in 2018 showed that some hope remains for aspirant teams in the second-tier tournament.

My journey had not changed me, at least not according to journalists, who rehashed old articles and wrote about the 'forty-year-old Fulham fan' many months after my next birthday. But whilst I always had an eye on the story, this trip was never about the individual matches or the media storm that accompanied me and then suddenly ended, leaving me feeling rather like a faded pop star. It was about striking out on my own and doing something different. And, just maybe, it will inspire a few more football fans to watch a random game, grab a beer in a stadium bar and gain a better sense of place than from increasingly homogenised city centres. Somebody may even stay in the bleach-fumed rooms of the Hotel Demi in Kosovo, cheer on Drita in their ramshackle stadium and, if he's still around, watch the charismatic Xhevdet Shabani play.

I can hardly stop watching football in unusual places. After writing a short piece about an Indonesian second-division match in September 2018, I received an unexpected message from Gary, a Malaysia-based Brit who had started his own project, a South-east Asian view on Premier League football, partly inspired by my own. 'I liked your single-minded determination and spirit of adventure', said Gary, nicely encapsulating two things I tried to embrace. Along with watching lots of football.

World Cup epilogue

There were some things I knew I would miss this season. I said in an interview with talkSPORT radio, live from Kazakhstan, that I was convinced Fulham would mount a serious promotion challenge. I had already sacrificed watching a Kevin Keegan-inspired promotion from the third tier to go backpacking in 1999. But this time I still managed to squeeze in fourteen Fulham matches. I was fairly certain we wouldn't get promoted after watching a 3–1 defeat at Brentford in early December that left us in fifteenth. But the Championship is a very long season, even longer than the Belgian top flight, and a stunning twenty-three-match unbeaten run nearly led to automatic promotion.

Maybe it was meant to be. My last Fulham match of the season, against Aston Villa in the Championship play-off final, was my first ever at the revamped Wembley. I watched with my father, who had seen us lose 2–0 to West Ham in the 1975 FA Cup final, our only previous Wembley appearance. It was a hot, sunny day, and I wore a green St Gallen cap with '1879' emblazoned on the front, the branding bridging the gap between my travels and my club. And it was a beautiful moment when Ryan Sessegnon, the prodigy, and Tom Cairney, the creator, combined for the only goal of the game. Fulham had won at Wembley and were promoted to the Premier League.

I went to a packed pub afterwards to celebrate. I stood to watch Loris Karius's nightmare for Liverpool against Real Madrid in the Champions League final. A Fulham fan pissed on my bare leg and the threadbare carpet. I didn't really care. It was somehow a fitting end to an unforgettable season of club football.

I washed my leg, flew to Lithuania and took the train to Kaliningrad and the World Cup. Kaliningrad, the curious enclave bordered by Lithuania and Poland, had a mainly Soviet feel with traces from its Germanic existence as Königsberg, most notably the ring of nineteenth-century fortifications that outlasted most of what they were designed to protect.

I watched Serbia against Switzerland in Kaliningrad and roared as Aleksandar Mitrović, Fulham's promotion talisman, boomed home an early header to please the predominantly Serbia-supporting crowd. The German neutrals around me barely registered the goal as they nipped out to the toilet or to buy more branded beer. This was a modern day out: anthemic and selfie-friendly, the arena concert of the football world. Granit Xhaka equalised, and Xherdan Shaqiri scored a last-minute winner for Switzerland. Both celebrated with an Albanian eagle, a nod towards my Kosovan travels to Gjilan, Shaqiri's birthplace, the previous autumn.

It rained a lot in Kaliningrad. The atmosphere was muted, frustrated even, as Spain and Morocco fans longed to hang out in squares, not gaze at grey skies from inside pubs. I had a comically bad seat for their match, three rows from the front behind the goal. Morocco were already out of the tournament, after unfortunate defeats to Iran and Portugal. But this match meant a lot to many. I displayed my massive Morocco flag, a £3 eBay purchase. The couple from Casablanca next to me were impressed, fished in their bag and pulled out a spare Morocco shirt. 'This is for you.' I wore it proudly during a 2–2 draw full of spirit and drama.

I flew to a sunnier St Petersburg, looking its most beautiful in the summer light, for the crucial group match between Argentina and Nigeria. I paraded my Super Eagles shirt, a China fake of the original like Thorgan Hazard, around the city. 'Be kind to us', said a passing Argentinian in the street. The spaceship-style stadium was a slice of Buenos Aires, spiritual stripes of light blue and white that became a crackling wave of relief when Marcos Rojo scored a late winner. I was quite irritated that a deeply flawed Argentina side had scraped through, but this was an amazing atmosphere for my 112th match, in all competitions, since my travels began in Tbilisi the previous June.

I visited the St Petersburg Fan Park expecting to watch Germany steamroller South Korea on the big screen. Instead, my last experience in Russia was watching South Korea pull off a shock 2–0 win in one of the most remarkable matches of the World Cup. Brazilians danced, as they would now play Mexico, not Germany, their nemesis from 2014. Mexicans were relieved that they were still in the tournament whilst, back home in Mexico City, fans swarmed around the South Korean embassy, encouraging the Korean ambassador to drink tequila in celebration. A small group of Koreans posed for photographs with everyone in the Fan Park. 'You won't need to buy a drink tonight', said an English football fan to them.

The 2018 World Cup, the most entertaining of the modern era, featured forty-nine players I had seen play top-division football across Europe, including two, Griezmann and Nzonzi, who won the entire tournament. I felt slightly out of place in Russia. It was better organised and cheaper than the previous World Cup in Brazil, but it wasn't my challenge. Or even my club. The World Cup is experienced by billions. My travels were my own, independently crafted football challenge. It might not be remembered as fondly or by as many. But it was the best experience of my life.

I returned to work at the Ministry of Justice in January 2019 and Fulham were relegated from the Premier League three months later. I am considering my next foreign football adventure.

Acknowledgements

Football

I salute the football people who provided the colour behind *Europe United*: the stories and songs, the titbits and tickets. It's impossible to list you all, or even your surnames, but thanks to (football clubs and media represented are in italics):

Georgia – Nika, Giorgi; Iceland – Victor (*Stjarnan*); Norway – Thomas, Jørgen; Sweden – Malin (*Häcken*), Erik; Finland – Peter (*Mariehamn*), Toni (*Ilves*); Kazakhstan – Eric; Russia – Nikita; Republic of Ireland – Darragh; Northern Ireland – Norman (*Glentoran*), Stephen (*Cliftonville*); Azerbaijan – Orkhan (*Sabail*); Turkey – Doruk, Laz, Ergin; Bulgaria – Teodor (*Meridian Match*); Serbia – Valentina (*Napredak*), Jovan (*Mondo*); Ukraine – Nikolay (*Chornomorets*); Moldova – Anastasia; Belgium – Vincent (*Le Soir*); Netherlands – Jacco, Albert; Germany – Thomas; Macedonia – Dusan; Denmark – Erling, Peter; Poland – Paweł (*Canal+*);

Scotland – Steven (*BT Sport*); England – Matt, Conor, Simon, Erik; Wales – Grant (*Llandudno Town*); Israel – Yaad, Yossi (*Babagol*), Doron, Gad and Vadim (*Kaduregel Shefel*); Cyprus – Stephen; Malta – Tom; Italy – Marco, Giovanni (*Rai 2*); France – Byllel, Alex; Portugal – Miguel; Czech Republic – Graham; Austria – Hans; Slovakia – Juraj (*Žilina*), Marian (*Spartak Trnava*), Alexander; Switzerland – Beat; Liechtenstein – Ernst (*Vaterland*); San Marino – Matteo; Luxembourg – Mauro (*Fola Esch*); Slovenia – Miha (*Maribor*); Hungary – Peterjon (*Libero*); Croatia – Ivan (*Lokomotiva Zagreb*); Montenegro – Miloš (*Dnevne Novine*).

Friends

Many thanks to those who gave up their money, time and sanity to join me for a game or two (or just the Montenegrin rakia): Allan Cox, Emma Crowhurst, Mark Dickson, Nicola Dobson, Amy Fulwood, Martin Hill, Mischa Gulseven, Will Gulseven, Stuart Lock, Doug McCarthy, Ross MacFarlane, Cinzia Molendini, Daniel Murdolo, Sophia Reid, Jon Souppouris, Linda Vardy, Kevin Wrake.

Justice

Europe United may not even have been possible were it not for Steve Ellerd-Elliott, John Marais and Osama Rahman, the Ministry of Justice analysts who supported the idea from the very beginning.

Special thanks

Richard Arcus at Quercus was the perfect editor. His love for football and travel helped shape my experiences into something unique. And hats off to Ed Wilson, the seasoned literary agent at Johnson & Alcock who spotted the potential of the story and my writing.

Very special mentions to: Mark Stuart, my cousin, for hosting 55footballnations.com and offering techie support; Matthew Knight, my brother-in-law, for legal advice; and Mischa for helping with the hotel bookings and commenting on drafts.